IN THE
PLEX

How Google Thinks, Works, and Shapes Our Lives

STEVEN LEVY

SIMON & SCHUSTER

New York   London   Toronto   Sydney

Simon & Schuster
1230 Avenue of the Americas
New York, NY 10020

First Simon & Schuster hardcover edition April 2011

SIMON & SCHUSTER and colophon are registered trademarks
of Simon & Schuster, Inc.

For information about special discounts for bulk purchases,
please contact Simon & Schuster Special Sales at
1-866-506-1949 or business@simonandschuster.com

The Simon & Schuster Speakers Bureau can bring authors to your live event.
For more information or to book an event contact the Simon & Schuster Speakers
Bureau at 1-866-248-3049 or visit our website at www.simonspeakers.com.

Designed by Ruth Lee Mui

Manufactured in the United States of America

10

Library of Congress Cataloging-in-Publication Data

Levy, Steven.
    In the plex : how Google thinks, works, and shapes our lives / Steven Levy.
—1st Simon & Schuster hbk. ed.
        p.   cm.
Includes bibliographical references and index.
1. Google (Firm).   2. Google.   3. Internet industry—United States.   I. Title.
    HD9696.8.U64G6657 2011
        338.7'6102504—dc22   2010049964

ISBN 978-1-4165-9658-5
ISBN 978-1-4165-9671-4 (ebook)

CONTENTS

In memory of Philip Klass (1920–2010)

SEARCHING FOR GOOGLE

"Have you heard of Google?"

It was a blazing hot July day in 2007, in the rural Indian village of Ragihalli, located thirty miles outside Bangalore. Twenty-two people from a company based in Mountain View, California, had driven in SUVs and vans up an unpaved road to this enclave of seventy threadbare huts with cement floors, surrounded by fields occasionally trampled by unwelcome elephants. Though electricity had come to Ragihalli some years earlier, there was not a single personal computer in the community. The visit had begun awkwardly, as the outsiders piled out of the cars and faced the entire population of the village, about two hundred people, who had turned out to welcome them. It was as if these well-dressed Westerners had dropped in from another planet, which in a sense they had. Young schoolchildren were pushed forward, and they performed a song. The visitors, in turn, gave the children notebooks and candy. There was an uncomfortable silence, broken when Marissa Mayer, the delegation's leader, a woman of thirty-two, said, "Let's interact with them." The group fanned out and began to engage the villagers in awkward conversation.

That is how Alex Vogenthaler came to ask a spindly young man with a wide smile whether he had heard of Google, Vogenthaler's employer. It was a question that he would never have had to ask in his home country: virtually everyone in the United States and everywhere in the wired-up world knew Google. Its uncannily effective Internet search product had changed the way people accessed information, changed the way they *thought* about information. Its 2004 IPO had established it as an economic giant. And its founders themselves were the perfect examples of the superbrainy engineering mentality that represented the future of business in the Internet age.

The villager admitted that, no, he had never heard of this Google. "What is it?" he asked. Vogenthaler tried to explain in the simplest terms that Google was a company that operated on the Internet. People used it to search for information. You would ask it a question, and it would immediately give you the answer from huge repositories of information it had gathered on the World Wide Web.

The man listened patiently but clearly was more familiar with rice fields than search fields.

Then the villager held up a cell phone. "Is this you what mean?" he seemed to ask.

The little connectivity meter on the phone display had four bars. There are significant swaths of the United States of America where one can barely pull in a signal—or gets no bars at all. But here in rural India, the signal was strong.

Google, it turns out, was on the verge of a multimillion-dollar mobile effort to make smart phones into information prostheses, adjuncts to the human brain that would allow people to get information to a vast swath of all the world's knowledge instantly. This man might not know Google yet, but the company would soon be in Ragihalli. And then he *would* know Google.

I witnessed this exchange in 2007 as an observer on the annual trip of Google associate product managers, a select group pegged as the company's future leaders. We began our journey in San Francisco and touched down in Tokyo, Beijing, Bangalore, and Tel Aviv before returning home sixteen days later.

My participation on the trip had been a consequence of a long relationship with Google. In late 1998, I'd heard buzz about a smarter search engine and tried it out. Google was miles better than anything I'd used before. When I heard a bit about the site's method of extracting such good results—it relied on sort of a web-based democracy—I became even more intrigued. This is how I put it in the February 22, 1999, issue of *Newsweek:* "Google, the Net's hottest search engine, draws on feedback from the web itself to deliver more relevant results to customer queries."

Later that year, I arranged with Google's newly hired director of corporate communications, Cindy McCaffrey, to visit its Mountain View headquarters. One day in October I drove to 2400 Bayshore Parkway, where Google had just moved from its previous location above a Palo Alto bicycle shop. I'd visited a lot of start-ups and wasn't really surprised by the genial chaos—a vast room, with cubicles yet unfilled and a cluster of exercise balls. However, I hadn't expected that instead of being attired in traditional T-shirts and jeans, the employees were decked out in costumes. I had come on Halloween.

"Steven, meet Larry Page and Sergey Brin," said Cindy, introducing me to the two young men who had founded the company as Stanford graduate students. Larry was dressed as a Viking, with a long-haired fur vest and a hat with long antlers protruding. Sergey was in a cow suit. On his chest was a rubber slab from which protruded huge, wart-specked teats. They greeted me cheerfully and we all retreated to a conference room where the Viking and the cow explained the miraculous powers of Google's PageRank technology.

That was the first of many interviews I would conduct at Google. Over the next few years, the company became a focus of my technology reporting at *Newsweek*. Google grew from the small start-up I had visited to a behemoth of more than 20,000 employees. Every day, billions of people used its search engine, and Google's remarkable ability to deliver relevant results in milliseconds changed the way the world got its information. The people who clicked on its ads made Google wildly profitable and turned its founders into billionaires—and triggered an outcry among traditional beneficiaries of ad dollars.

Google also became known for its irreverent culture and its data-driven approach to business decision making; management experts rhapsodized about its unconventional methods. As the years went by, Google began to interpret its mission—to gather and make accessible and useful the world's information—in the broadest possible sense. The company created a series of web-based applications. It announced its intention to scan all the world's books. It became involved in satellite imagery, mobile phones, energy generation, photo storage. Clearly, Google was one of the most important contributors to the revolution of computers and technology that marked a turning point in civilization. I knew I wanted to write a book about the company but wasn't sure how.

Then in early July 2007, I was asked to join the associate product managers on their trip. It was an unprecedented invitation from a company that usually limits contact between journalists and its employees. The APM program, I learned, was a highly valued initiative. To quote the pitch one of the participants made in 2006 to recent and upcoming college graduates: "We invest more into our APMs than any other company has ever invested into young employees. . . . We envision a world where everyone is awed by the fact that Google's executives, the best CEOs in the Silicon Valley, and the most respected leaders of global non-profits all came through the Google APM program." Eric Schmidt, Google's CEO, told me, "One of these people will probably be our CEO one day—we just don't know which one."

The eighteen APMs on the trip worked all over Google: in search, advertising, applications, and even stealth projects such as Google's attempt to capture the rights to include magazines in its index. Mayer's team, along with the APMs themselves, had designed the agenda of the trip. Every activity had an underlying purpose to increase the participants' understanding of a technology or business issue, or make them more (in the parlance of the company) "Googley." In Tokyo, for instance, they engaged in a scavenger hunt in the city's legendary Akihabara electronics district. Teams of APMs were each given $50 to buy the weirdest gadgets they could find. Ducking into backstreets with stalls full of electronic parts and gizmos, they wound up with a cornucopia: USB-powered ashtrays shaped like football helmets that suck up smoke; a plate-sized disk that simulated the phases of the moon; a breathalyzer you could install in your car; and a stubby wand that, when waved back and forth, spelled out words in LED lights. In Bangalore, there was a different shopping hunt—an excursion to the market area where the winner of the competition would be the one who haggled best. (Good training for making bulk purchases of computers or even buying an Internet start-up.) Another Tokyo high point was the 5 A.M. trip to the Tsukiji fish market. It wasn't the fresh sushi that fascinated the APMs but the mechanics of the fish auction, in some ways similar to the way Google works its AdWords program.

In China, Google's top executive there, Kai-Fu Lee, talked of balancing Google's freewheeling style with government rules—and censorship. But during interviews with Chinese consumers, the APMs were discouraged to hear the perception of the company among locals: "Baidu [Google's local competitor] knows more [about China] than Google," said one young man to his APM interlocutors.

At every office the APMs visited, they attended meetings with local Googlers, first learning about projects under way and then explaining to the residents what was going on at Mountain View headquarters. I began to get an insider's sense of Google's product processes—and how serving its users was akin to a crusade. An interesting moment occurred in Bangalore when Mayer was taking questions from local engineers after presenting an overview of upcoming products. One of them asked, "We've heard the road map for products, what's the road map for revenues?" She almost bit his head off. "That's *not* the way to think," she said. "We are focused on our *users*. If we make them happy, we will have revenues."

The most fascinating part of the trip was the time spent with the young Googlers. They were generally from elite colleges, with SAT scores approaching or achieving perfection. Carefully culled from thousands of people who would have killed for the job, their personalities and abilities were a reflection of Google's own character. During a bus ride to the Great Wall of China, one of the APMs charted the group demographics and found that almost all had parents who were professionals and more than half had parents who taught at a university—which put them in the company of Google's founders. They all grew up with the Internet and considered its principles to be as natural as the laws of gravity. They were among the brightest and most ambitious of a generation that was better equipped to handle the disruptive technology wave than their elders were. Their minds hummed like tuning forks in resonance with the company's values of speed, flexibility, and a deep respect for data.

Yet even while immersed in an optimism bubble with these young people, I could see the strains that came with Google's abrupt growth from a feisty start-up to a market-dominating giant with more than 20,000 employees. The APMs had spent a year navigating the folkways of a complicated corporation, albeit a determinedly different one—and now they were almost senior employees. What's more, I was stunned when a poll of my fellow travelers revealed that not a single one of them saw him- or herself working for Google in five years. Marissa Mayer took this news calmly, claiming that such ambition was why they had been hired in the first place. "This is the gene that Larry and Sergey look for," she told me. "Even if they leave, it's still good for us. They're going to take the Google DNA with them."

After covering the company for almost a decade, I thought I knew it pretty well, but the rare view of the company I got in those two weeks made me see it in a different, wider light. Still, there were considerable mysteries. Google was a company built on the values of its founders, who harbored ambitions to build a powerful corporation that would impact the entire world, at the same time loathing the bureaucracy and commitments that running such a company would entail. Google professed a sense of moral purity—as exemplified by its informal motto, "Don't be evil"—but it seemed to have a blind spot regarding the consequences of its own technology on privacy and property rights. A bedrock principle of Google was serving its users—but a goal was building a giant artificial intelligence learning machine that would bring uncertain consequences to the way all of us live. From the very beginning, its founders said that they wanted to change the world. But who were they, and what did they envision this new world order to be?

After the trip I realized that the best way to answer these questions was to report as much as possible from inside Google. Just as I'd had a rare glimpse into its inner workings during that summer of 2007, I would try to immerse myself more deeply into its engineering, its corporate life, and its culture, to report how it really operated, how it developed its products, and how it was managing its growth and public exposure. I would be an outsider with an insider's view.

To do this, of course, I'd need cooperation. Fortunately, based on our long relationship, Google's executives, including "LSE"—Larry Page, Sergey Brin, and Eric Schmidt—agreed to let me in. During the next two years—a critical time when Google's halo lost some of its glow even as the company grew more powerful—I interviewed hundreds of current and former Googlers and attended a variety of meetings in the company. These included product development meetings, "interface reviews," search launch meetings, privacy council sessions, weekly TGIF all-hands gatherings, and the gatherings of the high command known as Google Product Strategy (GPS) meetings, where projects and initiatives are approved or rejected. I also ate a lot of meals at Andale, the burrito joint in Google's Building 43.

What I discovered was a company exulting in creative disorganization, even if the creativity was not always as substantial as hoped for. Google had massive goals, and the entire company channeled its values from the founders. Its mission was collecting and organizing all the world's information—and that's only the beginning. From the very start, its founders saw Google as a vehicle to realize the dream of artificial intelligence in augmenting humanity. To realize their dreams, Page and Brin had to build a huge company. At the same time, they attempted to maintain as much as possible the nimble, irreverent, answer-to-no-one freedom of a small start-up. In the two years I researched this book, the clash between those goals reached a peak, as David had become a Goliath.

My inside perspective also provided me the keys to unlock more of the secrets of Google's two "black boxes"—its search engine and its advertising model—than had previously been disclosed. Google search is part of our lives, and its ad system is the most important commercial product of the Internet age. In this book, for the first time, readers can learn the full story of their development, evolution, and inner workings. Understanding those groundbreaking products helps us understand Google and its employees because their operation embodies both the company's values and its technological philosophy. More important, understanding them helps us understand our own world—and tomorrow's.

The science fiction writer William Gibson once said that the future is already here—just not evenly distributed. At Google, the future is already under way. To understand this pioneering company and its people is to grasp our technological destiny. And so here is Google: how it works, what it thinks, why it's changing, how it will continue to change us. And how it hopes to maintain its soul.

PART ONE

THE WORLD ACCORDING TO GOOGLE
Biography of a Search Engine

1

"It was science fiction more than computer science."

On February 18, 2010, Judge Denny Chin of the New York Southern District federal court took stock of the packed gallery in Courtroom 23B. It was going to be a long day. He was presiding over a hearing that would provide only a gloss to hundreds of submissions he had already received on this case. "There is just too much to digest," he said. He shook his head, preparing himself to hear the arguments of twenty-seven representatives of various interest groups or corporations, as well as presentations by some of the lawyers for various parties, lawyers who filled every place in two long tables before him.

The case was *The Authors Guild, Inc., Association of American Publishers, et al. v. Google Inc.* It was a lawsuit tentatively resolved by a class settlement agreement in which an authors' group and a publishers' association set conditions for a technology company to scan and sell books. Judge Chin's decision would involve important issues affecting the future of digital works, and some of the speakers before the court engaged on those issues. But many of the objectors—and most who addressed the court were objectors to the settlement—focused on a young company headquartered on a sprawling campus in Mountain View, California. That company was Google. The speakers seemed to distrust it, fear it, even despise it.

> "A major threat to . . . freedom of expression and participation in cultural
>   diversity"
> "An unjustified monopoly"
> "Eviscerates privacy protections"
> "Concealment and misdirection"
> "Price fixing . . . a massive market distortion . . . preying on the desperate"
> "May well be a per se violation of the antitrust laws"

(That last statement held special weight, as it came from the U.S. deputy assistant attorney general.)

But the federal government was only one of Google's surprising opponents. Some of the others were supporters of the public interest, monitoring the privacy rights and pocketbooks of citizens. Others were advocates of free speech. There was even an objector representing the folksinger Arlo Guthrie.

The irony was that Google itself explicitly embraced the lofty values and high moral standards that it was being attacked for flouting. Its founders had consistently stated that their goal was to make the world better, specifically by enabling humanity's access to information. Google had created an astonishing tool that took advantage of the interconnected nature of the burgeoning World Wide Web, a tool that empowered people to locate even obscure information within seconds. This search engine transformed the way people worked, entertained themselves, and learned. Google made historic profits from that product by creating a new form of advertising—nonintrusive and even useful. It hired the sharpest minds in the world and encouraged them to take on challenges that pushed the boundaries of innovation. Its focus on engineering talent to accomplish difficult goals was a national inspiration. It even warned its shareholders that the company would sometimes pursue business practices that serve humanity even at the expense of lower profits. It accomplished all those achievements with a puckish irreverence that captivated the public and made heroes of its employees.

But that didn't matter to the objectors in Judge Chin's courtroom. Those people were Google's natural allies, and they thought that Google was no longer . . . good. The mistrust and fear in the courtroom were reflected globally by governments upset by Google's privacy policies and businesses worried that Google's disruptive practices would target them next. Everywhere Google's executives turned, they were faced with protests and lawsuits.

The course of events was baffling to Google's two founders, Larry Page and Sergey Brin. Of all Google's projects, the one at issue in the hearing—Google's Book Search project—was perhaps the most idealistic. It was an audacious attempt to digitize every book every printed, so that anyone in the world could locate the information within. Google would not give away the full contents of the books, so when users discovered them, they would have reason to buy them. Authors would have new markets; readers would have instant access to knowledge. After being sued by publishers and authors, Google made a deal with them that would make it even easier to access the books and to buy them on the spot. Every library would get a free terminal to connect to the entire corpus of the world's books. To Google, it was a boon to civilization.

Didn't people understand?

By all metrics, the company was still thriving. Google still retained its hundreds of millions of users, hosted billions of searches every day, and had growing businesses in video and wireless devices. Its employees were still idealistic and ambitious in the best sense. But a shadow now darkened Google's image. To many outsiders, the corporate motto that Google had taken seriously—"Don't be evil"—had become a joke, a bludgeon to be used against it.

What had happened?

Doing good was Larry Page's plan from the very beginning. Even as a child, he wanted to be an inventor, not simply because his mind aligned perfectly with the nexus of logic and technology (which it did) but because, he says, "I really wanted to change the world."

Page grew up in Lansing, Michigan, where his father taught computer science at Michigan State. His parents divorced when he was eight, but he was close with both his father and mother—who had her own computer science degree. Naturally, he spoke computers as a primary language. As he later told an interviewer, "I think I was the first kid in my elementary school to turn in a word-processed document."

Page was not a social animal—people who talked to him often wondered if there were a jigger of Asperger's in the mix—and could unnerve people by simply not talking. But when he did speak, more often than not he would come out with ideas that bordered on the fantastic. Attending a summer program in leadership (motto: "A healthy disregard for the impossible") helped move him to action. At the University of Michigan, he became obsessed with transportation and drew up plans for an elaborate monorail system in Ann Arbor, replacing the mundane bus system with a "futuristic" commute between the dorms and the classrooms. It seemed to come as a surprise to him that a fanciful multimillion-dollar transit fantasy from an undergraduate would not be quickly embraced and implemented. (Fifteen years after he graduated, Page would bring up the issue again in a meeting with the university's president.)

His intelligence and imagination were clear. But when you got to know him, what stood out was his ambition. It expressed itself not as a personal drive (though there was that, too) but as a general principle that everyone should think big and then make big things happen. He believed that the only true failure was not attempting the audacious. "Even if you fail at your ambitious thing, it's very hard to fail completely," he says. "That's the thing that people don't get." Page *always* thought about that. When people proposed a short-term solution, Page's instinct was to think long term. There would eventually be a joke among Googlers that Page "went to the future and came back to tell us about it."

Page earned a degree in computer science like his father did. But his destiny was in California, specifically in the Silicon Valley. In a way, Page's arrival at Stanford was a homecoming. He'd lived there briefly in 1979 when his dad had spent a sabbatical at Stanford; some faculty members still remembered him as an insatiably curious seven-year-old. In 1995, Stanford was not only the best place to pursue cutting-edge computer science but, because of the Internet boom, was also the world capital of ambition. Fortunately, Page's visions extended to the commercial: "Probably from when I was twelve, I knew I was going to start a company eventually," he'd later say. Page's brother, nine years older, was already in Silicon Valley, working for an Internet start-up.

Page chose to work in the department's Human-Computer Interaction Group. The subject would stand Page in good stead in the future with respect to product development, even though it was not in the HCI domain to figure out a new model of information retrieval. On his desk and permeating his conversations was Apple interface guru Donald Norman's classic tome *The Psychology of Everyday Things*, the bible of a religion whose first, and arguably only, commandment is "The user is always right." (Other Norman disciples, such as Jeff Bezos at Amazon.com, were adopting this creed on the web.) Another influential book was a biography of Nikola Tesla, the brilliant Serb scientist; though Tesla's contributions arguably matched Thomas Edison's—and his ambitions were grand enough to impress even Page—he died in obscurity. "I felt like he was a great inventor and it was a sad story," says Page. "I feel like he could've accomplished much more had he had more resources. And he had trouble commercializing the stuff he did. Probably more trouble than he should've had. I think that was a good lesson. I didn't want to just invent things, I also wanted to make the world better, and in order to do that, you need to do more than just invent things."

The summer before entering Stanford, Page attended a program for accepted candidates that included a tour of San Francisco. The guide was a grad student Page's age who'd been at Stanford for two years. "I thought he was pretty obnoxious," Page later said of the guide, Sergey Brin. The content of the encounter is now relegated to legend, but their argumentative banter was almost certainly good-natured. Despite the contrast in personalities, in some ways they were twins. Both felt most comfortable in the meritocracy of academia, where brains trumped everything else. Both had an innate understanding of how the ultraconnected world that they enjoyed as computer science (CS) students was about to spread throughout society. Both shared a core belief in the primacy of data. And both were rock stubborn when it came to pursuing their beliefs. When Page settled in that September, he became close friends with Brin, to the point where people thought of them as a set: LarryAndSergey.

Born in Russia, Brin was four when his family immigrated to the United States. His English still maintained a Cyrillic flavor, and his speech was dotted with anachronistic Old World touches such as the use of "whatnot" when peers would say "stuff like that." He had arrived at Stanford at nineteen after whizzing through the University of Maryland, where his father taught, in three years; he was one of the youngest students ever to start the Stanford PhD program. "He skipped a million years," says Craig Silverstein, who arrived at Stanford a year later, and would eventually become Google's first employee. Sergey was a quirky kid who would zip through Stanford's hallways on omnipresent Rollerblades. He also had an interest in trapeze. But the professors understood that behind the goofiness was a formidable mathematical mind. Soon after arriving at Stanford, he knocked off all the required tests for a doctorate and was free to sample the courses until he found a suitable entree for a thesis. He supplemented his academics with swimming, gymnastics, and sailing. (When his father asked him in frustration whether he planned to take advanced courses, he said that he might take advanced swimming.) Donald Knuth, a Stanford professor whose magisterial series of books on the art of computer programming made him the Proust of computer code, recalls driving down the Pacific coast to a conference with Sergey one afternoon and being impressed at his grasp of complicated issues. His adviser, Hector Garcia-Molina, had seen a lot of bright kids go through Stanford, but Brin stood out. "He was brilliant," Garcia-Molina says.

One task that Brin took on was a numbering scheme for the new Gates Computer Science Building, which was to be the home of the department. (His system used mathematical flourishes.) The structure was named after William Henry Gates III, better known as Bill, the cofounder of Microsoft. Though Gates had spent a couple of years at Harvard and endowed a building named after his mother there, he went on a small splurge of funding palatial new homes for computer science departments at top technical institutions that he *didn't* attend, including MIT and Carnegie Mellon—along with Stanford, the trifecta of top CS programs. Even as they sneered at Windows, the next generation of wizards would study in buildings named after Bill Gates.

Did Gates ever imagine that one of those buildings would incubate a rival that might destroy Microsoft?

The graduate computer science program at Stanford was built around close relationships between students and faculty members. They would team up to work on big, real-world problems; the fresh perspective of the young people maintains the vitality of the professor's interests. "You always follow the students," says Terry Winograd, who was Page's adviser. (Page would often remind him that they had met during his dad's Stanford sabbatical.) Over the years Winograd had become an expert at figuring out where students stood on the spectrum of brainiacs who found their way into the department. Some were kids whose undergrad record was straight A pluses, GRE scores scraping perfection, who would come in and say, "What thesis should I work on?" On the other end of the spectrum were kids like Larry Page, who would come in and say, "Here's what I think I can do." And his proposals were *crazy*. He'd come into the office and talk about doing something with space tethers or solar kites. "It was science fiction more than computer science," recalls Winograd. But an outlandish mind was a valuable asset, and there was definitely a place in the current science to channel wild creativity.

In 1995, that place was the World Wide Web. It had sprung from the restless brain of a (then)-obscure British engineer named Tim Berners-Lee, who was working as a technician at the CERN physics research lab in Switzerland. Berners-Lee could sum up his vision in a sentence: "Suppose all the information stored on computers everywhere were linked . . . there would be a single global information space."

The web's pedigree could be traced back to a 1945 paper by the American scientist Vannevar Bush. Entitled "As We May Think," it outlined a vast storage system called a "memex," where documents would be connected, and could be recalled, by information breadcrumbs called "trails of association." The timeline continued to the work of Douglas Engelbart, whose team at the Stanford Research Institute devised a linked document system that lived behind a dazzling interface that introduced the metaphors of windows and files to the digital desktop. Then came a detour to the brilliant but erratic work of an autodidact named Ted Nelson, whose ambitious Xanadu Project (though never completed) was a vision of disparate information linked by "hypertext" connections. Nelson's work inspired Bill Atkinson, a software engineer who had been part of the original Macintosh team; in 1987 he came up with a link-based system called HyperCard, which he sold to Apple for $100,000 on the condition that the company give it away to all its users. But to really fulfill Vannevar Bush's vision, you needed a huge system where people could freely post and link their documents.

By the time Berners-Lee had his epiphany, that system was in place: the Internet. While the earliest websites were just ways to distribute academic papers more efficiently, soon people began writing sites with information of all sorts, and others created sites just for fun. By the mid-1990s, people were starting to use the web for profit, and a new word, "e-commerce," found its way into the lexicon. Amazon.com and eBay became Internet giants. Other sites positioned themselves as gateways, or portals, to the wonders of the Internet.

As the web grew, its linking structure accumulated a mind-boggling value. It treated the aggregate of all its contents as a huge compost of ideas, any one of which could be reached by the act of connecting one document to another. When you looked at a page you could see, usually highlighted in blue, the pointers to other sites that the webmaster had coded on the page—that was the hypertext idea that galvanized Bush, Nelson, and Atkinson. But for the first time, as Berners-Lee had intended, the web was coaxing a critical mass of these linked sites and documents into a single network. In effect, the web was an infinite database, a sort of crazily expanding universe of human knowledge that, in theory, could hold every insight, thought, image, and product for sale. And all of it had an intricate lattice of cross-connections created by the independent linking activity of anyone who had built a page and coded in a link to something elsewhere on the web.

In retrospect, the web was to the digital world what the Louisiana Purchase was to the young United States: the opportunity of a century.

Berners-Lee's creation was so new that when Stanford got funding from the National Science Foundation in the early 1990s to start a program called the Digital Library Project, the web wasn't mentioned in the proposal. "The theme of that project was interoperability—how can we make all these resources work together?" recalls Hector Garcia-Molina, who cofounded the project. By 1995 though, Garcia-Molina knew that the World Wide Web would inevitably be part of the projects concocted by the students who worked with the program, including Page and Brin.

Brin already had a National Science Foundation fellowship and didn't need funding, but he was trying to figure out a dissertation topic. His loose focus was data mining, and with Rajeev Motwani, a young professor he became close with, he helped start a research group called MIDAS, which stood for Mining Data at Stanford. In a résumé he posted on the Stanford site in 1995, he talked about "a new project" to generate personalized movie ratings. "The way it works is as follows," he wrote. "You rate the movies you have seen. Then the system finds other users with similar tastes to extrapolate how much you like other movies." Another project he worked on with Garcia-Molina and another student was a system that detected copyright violations by automating searches for duplicates of documents. "He came up with some good algorithms for detecting copies," says Garcia-Molina. "Now you use Google."

Page was also seeking a dissertation topic. One idea he presented to Winograd, a collaboration with Brin, seemed more promising than the others: creating a system where people could make annotations and comments on websites. But the more Page thought about annotation, the messier it got. For big sites, there would probably be a lot of people who wanted to mark up a page. How would you figure out who gets to comment or whose comment would be the one you'd see first? For that, he says, "We needed a rating system."

Having a human being determine the ratings was out of the question. First, it was inherently impractical. Further, humans were unreliable. Only algorithms—well drawn, efficiently executed, and based on sound data—could deliver unbiased results. So the problem became finding the right data to determine whose comments were more trustworthy, or interesting, than others. Page realized that such data already existed and no one else was really using it. He asked Brin, "Why don't we use the links on the web to do that?"

Page, a child of academia, understood that web links were like citations in a scholarly article. It was widely recognized that you could identify which papers were really important without reading them—simply tally up how many other papers cited them in notes and bibliographies. Page believed that this principle could also work with web pages. But getting the right data would be difficult. Web pages made their outgoing links transparent: built into the code were easily identifiable markers for the destinations you could travel to with a mouse click from that page. But it wasn't obvious at all what linked *to* a page. To find that out, you'd have to somehow collect a database of links that connected to some other page. Then you'd go *backward*.

That's why Page called his system BackRub. "The early versions of hypertext had a tragic flaw: you couldn't follow links in the other direction," Page once told a reporter. "BackRub was about reversing that."

Winograd thought this was a great idea for a project, but not an easy one. To do it right, he told Page, you'd really have to capture a significant chunk of the World Wide Web's link structure. Page said, sure, he'd go and download the web and get the structure. He figured it would take a week or something. "And of course," he later recalled, "it took, like, years." But Page and Brin attacked it. Every other week Page would come to Garcia-Molina's office asking for disks and equipment. "That's fine," Garcia-Molina would say. "This is a great project, but you need to give me a budget." He asked Page to pick a number, to say how much of the web he needed to crawl, and to estimate how many disks that would take. "I want to crawl the *whole* web," Page said.

Page indulged in a little vanity in naming the part of the system that rated websites by the incoming links: he called it PageRank. But it was a sly vanity; many people assumed the name referred to web pages, not a surname.

Since Page wasn't a world-class programmer, he asked a friend to help out. Scott Hassan was a full-time research assistant at Stanford, working for the Digital Library Project program while doing part-time grad work. Hassan was also good friends with Brin, whom he'd met at an Ultimate Frisbee game during his first week at Stanford. Page's program "had so many bugs in it, it wasn't funny," says Hassan. Part of the problem was that Page was using the relatively new computer language Java for his ambitious project, and Java kept crashing. "I went and tried to fix some of the bugs in Java itself, and after doing this ten times, I decided it was a waste of time," says Hassan. "I decided to take his stuff and just rewrite it into the language I knew much better that didn't have any bugs."

He wrote a program in Python—a more flexible language that was becoming popular for web-based programs—that would act as a "spider," so called because it would crawl the web for data. The program would visit a web page, find all the links, and put them into a queue. Then it would check to see if it had visited those link pages previously. If it hadn't, it would put the link on a queue of future destinations to visit and repeat the process. Since Page wasn't familiar with Python, Hassan became a member of the team. He and another student, Alan Steremberg, became paid assistants to the project.

Brin, the math prodigy, took on the huge task of crunching the mathematics that would make sense of the mess of links uncovered by their monster survey of the growing web.

Even though the small team was going somewhere, they weren't quite sure of their destination. "Larry didn't have a plan," says Hassan. "In research you explore something and see what sticks."

By March 1996, they began a test, starting at a single page, the Stanford computer science department home page. The spider located the links on the page and fanned out to all the sites that linked to Stanford, then to the sites that linked to *those* websites. "That first one just used the titles of documents because collecting the documents themselves required a lot of data and work," says Page. After they snared about 15 million of those titles, they tested the program to see which websites it deemed more authoritative.

"Even the first set of results was very convincing," Hector Garcia-Molina says. "It was pretty clear to everyone who saw this demo that this was a very good, very powerful way to order things."

"We realized it worked really, really well," says Page. "And I said, 'Wow, the big problem here is not annotation. We should now use it not just for ranking annotations, but for ranking *searches.*'" It seemed the obvious application for an invention that gave a ranking to every page on the web. "It was pretty clear to me and the rest of the group," he says, "that if you have a way of ranking things based not just on the page itself but based on what the world thought of that page, that would be a really valuable thing for search."

▼ ▼ ▼

The leader in web search at that time was a program called AltaVista that came out of Digital Equipment Corporation's Western Research Laboratory. A key designer was Louis Monier, a droll Frenchman and idealistic geek who had come to America with a doctorate in 1980. DEC had been built on the minicomputer, a once innovative category now rendered a dinosaur by the personal computer revolution. "DEC was very much living in the past," says Monier. "But they had small groups of people who were very forward-thinking, experimenting with lots of toys." One of those toys was the web. Monier himself was no expert in information retrieval but a big fan of data in the abstract. "To me, that was the secret—data," he says. What the data was telling him was that if you had the right tools, it was possible to treat everything in the open web like a single document.

Even at that early date, the basic building blocks of web search had been already set in stone. Search was a four-step process. First came a sweeping scan of all the world's web pages, via a spider. Second was indexing the information drawn from the spider's crawl and storing the data on racks of computers known as servers. The third step, triggered by a user's request, identified the pages that seemed best suited to answer that query. That result was known as search quality. The final step involved formatting and delivering the results to the user.

Monier was most concerned with the second step, the time-consuming process of crawling through millions of documents and scooping up the data. "Crawling at that time was slow, because the other side would take on average four seconds to respond," says Monier. One day, lying by a swimming pool, he realized that you could get everything in a timely fashion by parallelizing the process, covering more than one page at a time. The right number, he concluded, was a thousand pages at once. Monier figured out how to build a crawler working on that scale. "On a single machine I had one thousand threads, independent processes asking things and not stepping on each other's toes."

By late 1995, people in DEC's Western Research Lab were using Monier's search engine. He had a tough time convincing his bosses to open up the engine to the public. They argued that there was no way to make money from a search engine but relented when Monier sold them on the public relations aspect. (The system would be a testament to DEC's powerful new Alpha processing chip.) On launch day, AltaVista had 16 million documents in its indexes, easily besting anything else on the net. "The big ones then had maybe a million pages," says Monier. That was the power of

AltaVista: its breadth. When DEC opened it to outsiders on December 15, 1995, nearly 300,000 people tried it out. They were dazzled.

AltaVista's actual search quality techniques—what determined the ranking of results—were based on traditional information retrieval (IR) algorithms. Many of those algorithms arose from the work of one man, a refugee from Nazi Germany named Gerard Salton, who had come to America, got a PhD at Harvard, and moved to Cornell University, where he cofounded its computer science department. Searching through databases using the same commands you'd use with a human—"natural language" became the term of art—was Salton's specialty.

During the 1960s, Salton developed a system that was to become a model for information retrieval. It was called SMART, supposedly an acronym for "Salton's Magical Retriever of Text." The system established many conventions that still persist in search, including indexing and relevance algorithms. When Salton died in 1995, his techniques still ruled the field. "For thirty years," wrote one academic in tribute a year later, "Gerry Salton *was* information retrieval."

The World Wide Web was about to change that, but the academics didn't know it—and neither did AltaVista. While its creators had the insight to gather all of the web, they missed the opportunity to take advantage of the link structure. "The innovation was that I was not afraid to fetch as much of the web as I could, store it in one place, and have a really fast response time. *That* was the novelty," says Monier. Meanwhile, AltaVista analyzed what was on each individual page—using metrics like how many times each word appeared—to see if a page was a relevant match to a given keyword in a query.

Even though there was no clear way to make money from search, AltaVista had a number of competitors. By 1996, when I wrote about search for *Newsweek*, executives from several companies were all boasting the most useful service. When pressed, all of them would admit that in the race between the omnivorous web and their burgeoning technology, the web was winning. "Academic IR had thirty years to get to where it is—we're breaking new ground, but it's difficult," complained Graham Spencer, the engineer behind the search engine created by a start-up called Excite. AltaVista's director of engineering, Barry Rubinson, said that the best approach was to throw massive amounts of silicon toward the problem and then hope for the best. "The first problem is that relevance is in the eye of the beholder," he said. The second problem, he continued, is making sense of the infuriatingly brief and cryptic queries typed into the AltaVista search field. He implied that the task was akin to voodoo. "It's all wizardry and witchcraft," he told me. "Anyone who tells you it's scientific is just pulling your leg."

No one at the web search companies mentioned using links.

The links were the reason that a research project running on a computer in a Stanford dorm room had become the top performer. Larry Page's PageRank was powerful because it cleverly analyzed those links and assigned a number to them, a metric on a scale of 1 to 10, that allowed you to see the page's prominence in comparison to every other page on the web. One of the early versions of BackRub had simply counted the incoming links, but Page and Brin quickly realized that it wasn't merely the number of links that made things relevant. Just as important was who was doing the linking. PageRank reflected that information. The more prominent the status of the page that made the link, the more valuable the link was and the higher it would rise when calculating the ultimate Page-Rank number of the web page itself. "The idea behind PageRank was that you can estimate the importance of a web page by the web pages that link to it," Brin would say. "We actually developed a lot of math to solve that problem. Important pages tended to link to important pages. We convert the entire web into a big equation with several hundred million variables, which are the PageRanks of all the web pages, and billions of terms, which are all the links." It was Brin's mathematic calculations on those possible 500 million variables that identified the important pages. It was like looking at a map of airline routes: the hub cities would stand out because of all the lines representing flights that originated and terminated there. Cities that got the most traffic from other important hubs were clearly the major centers of population. The same applied to websites. "It's all recursive," Page later said. "In a way, how good you are is determined by who links to you and who you link to determines how good you are. It's all a big circle. But mathematics is great. You can solve this."

The PageRank score would be combined with a number of more traditional information retrieval techniques, such as comparing the keyword to text on the page and determining relevance by examining factors such as frequency, font size, capitalization, and position of the keyword. (Those factors help determine the importance of a keyword on a given page—if a term is prominently featured, the page is more likely to satisfy a query.) Such factors are known as *signals*, and they are critical to search quality. There are a few crucial milliseconds in the process of a web search during which the engine interprets the keyword and then accesses the vast index, where all the text on billions of pages is stored and ordered just like an index of a book. At that point the engine needs some help to figure out how to rank those pages. So it looks for signals—traits that can help the engine figure out which pages will satisfy the query. A signal says to the search engine, "Hey, consider me for your results!" PageRank itself is a signal. A web page with a high PageRank number sends a message to the search engine that it's a more reputable source than those with lower numbers.

Though PageRank was BackRub's magic wand, it was the combination of that algorithm with other signals that created the mind-blowing results. If the keyword matched the title of the web page or the domain name, that page would go higher in the rankings. For queries consisting of multiple words, documents containing all of the search query terms in close proximity would typically get the nod over those in which the phrase match was "not even close." Another powerful signal was the "anchor text" of links that led to the page. For instance, if a web page used the words "Bill Clinton" to link to the White House, "Bill Clinton" would be the anchor text. Because of the high values assigned to anchor text, a BackRub query for "Bill Clinton" would lead to www.whitehouse.gov as the top result because numerous web pages with high PageRanks used the president's name to link the White House site. "When you did a search, the right page would come up, even if the page didn't include the actual words you were searching for," says Scott Hassan. "That was pretty cool." It was also something other search engines failed to do. Even though www.whitehouse.gov was the ideal response to the Clinton "navigation query," other commercial engines didn't include it in their results. (In April 1997, Page and Brin found that a competitor's top hit was "Bill Clinton Joke of the Day.")

PageRank had one other powerful advantage. To search engines that relied on the traditional IR approach of analyzing content, the web presented a terrible challenge. There were millions and millions of pages, and as more and more were added, the performance of those systems inevitably degraded. For those sites, the rapid expansion of the web was a problem, a drain on their resources. But because of PageRank, BackRub got *better* as the web grew. New sites meant more links. This additional information allowed BackRub to identify even more accurately the pages that might be relevant to a query. And the more recent links would improve the freshness of the site. "PageRank has the benefit of learning from the whole of the World Wide Web," Brin would explain.

Of course, Brin and Page had the logistical problem of capturing the whole web. The Stanford team did not have the resources of DEC. For a while, BackRub could access only the bandwidth available to the Gates Building—10 megabits of traffic per second. But the entire university ran on a giant T3 line that could operate at 45 megabits per second. The Back-Rub team discovered that by retoggling an incorrectly set switch in the basement, it could get full access to the T3 line. "As soon as they toggled that, we were all the way up to the maximum of the entire Stanford network," says Hassan. "We were using all the bandwidth of the network. And this was from a single machine doing this, on a desktop in my dorm room."

In those days, people who ran websites—many of them with minimal technical savvy—were not used to their sites being crawled. Some of them would look at their logs, and see frequent visits from www.stanford.edu, and suspect that the university was somehow stealing their information. One woman from Wyoming contacted Page directly to demand that he stop, but Google's "bot" kept visiting. She discovered that Hector Garcia-Molina was the project's adviser and called him, charging that the Stanford computer was doing terrible things to her computer. He tried to explain to her that being crawled is a harmless, nondestructive procedure, but she'd have none of it. She called the department chair and the Stanford security office. In theory, complainants could block crawlers by putting a little piece of code on their sites called /robots.txt, but the angry webmasters weren't receptive to the concept. "Larry and Sergey got annoyed that people couldn't figure out /robots.txt," says Winograd, "but in the end, they actually built an exclusion list, which they didn't want to." Even then, Page and Brin believed in a self-service system that worked in scale, serving vast populations. Handcrafting exclusions was anathema.

Brin and Page fell into a pattern of rapid iterating and launching. If the pages for a given query were not quite in the proper order, they'd go back to the algorithm and see what had gone wrong. It was a tricky balancing act to assign the proper weights to the various signals. "You do the ranking initially, and then you look at the list and say, 'Are they in the right order?' If they're not, we adjust the ranking, and then you're like, 'Oh this looks really good,'" says Page. Page used the ranking for the keyword of "university" as a litmus test. He paid particular attention to the relative ranking of his alma mater, Michigan, and his current school, Stanford. Brin and Page assumed that Stanford would be ranked higher, but Michigan topped it. Was that a flaw in the algorithm? No. "We decided that Michigan had more stuff on the web, and that was reasonable," says Page.

This listing showed the power of PageRank. It made BackRub much more useful than the results you'd get from the commercial search engines.

Their list of institutions for the "university" query seemed totally random. The number one result for that generic term in AltaVista would give you the Oregon Center for Optics. Page recalls a conversation back then with an AltaVista engineer who told him that with the way pages were scored, a query for "university" was likely to get a page where that word appeared twice in the headline. "That doesn't make any sense," Page said, noting that such a search was more likely to get a minor university with redundancy in its title.

"If you want major universities, you should type 'major universities,'" said the engineer. Page was appalled. "I'm like, well, they teach you in human computer interaction, which is my branch, that the user is never wrong. The person in the system is never wrong."

Until that moment, the task of compiling a list of universities and ranking them in significance had been complicated, intellectually challenging, and labor-intensive. Some magazines employed large teams working for months to do just that. If you were to try to teach a computer to do that, your instinct would be to feed it data about SAT scores, graduation rates, prizewinners among faculty, and a thousand other factors. Then you'd have to figure out how to weigh them. The odds were low that a machine would crank out a rating that squared with the gut feeling of a well-educated citizen. But BackRub knew nothing about those statistics. It just knew how to take advantage of the fact that links created by the web community had implicitly produced a ranking that was better than any group of magazine editors or knowledge curators could come up with. Larry Page and Sergey Brin had figured out how to mine that knowledge before the information retrieval establishment and commercial search engines even realized that it existed.

"The whole field had suffered blinders," says the computer scientist Amit Singhal, then a Bell Labs researcher who had been a protégé of Jerry Salton. "In some sense, search really did need two people who were never tainted by people like me to come up with that shake-up."

Larry Page was not the only person in 1996 who realized that exploiting the link structure of the web would lead to a dramatically more powerful way to find information. In the summer of that year, a young computer scientist named Jon Kleinberg arrived in California to spend a yearlong postdoctoral fellowship at IBM's research center in Almaden, on the southern edge of San Jose. With a new PhD from MIT, he had already accepted a tenure-track job in the CS department at Cornell University.

Kleinberg decided to look at web search. The commercial operations didn't seem effective enough and were further hobbled by spam. AltaVista's results in particular were becoming less useful because websites had gamed it by "word stuffing"—inserting multiple repetitions of desirable keywords, often in invisible text at the bottom of the web page. "The recurring refrain," says Kleinberg, "was that search doesn't work." But he had an intuition of a more effective approach. "One thing that was not being used at all was the fact that the web was a network," he says. "You could find people saying in the academic papers that links ought to be taken advantage of, but by 1996 it still hadn't been."

Kleinberg began to play around with ways to analyze links. Since he didn't have the assistance, the resources, the time, or the inclination, he didn't attempt to index the entire web for his link analysis. Instead he did a kind of prewash. He typed a query into AltaVista, took the first two hundred results, and then used that subset for his own search.

Interestingly, the best results for the query were often not included in those AltaVista solutions. For instance, if you typed in "newspaper," AltaVista would not give you links for *The New York Times* or *The Washington Post*. "That's not surprising, because AltaVista is about matching strings, and unless *The New York Times* happened to say, 'I'm a newspaper!' AltaVista is not going to find it," Kleinberg explains. But, he suspected, he'd have more luck if he checked out what those 200 sites pointed to. "Among those 200 people who were saying 'newspapers,' someone was going to point to *The New York Times*," he says. "In fact, a *bunch* of people were going to point to *The New York Times*, because among those 200 pages were some people who really liked to collect links for newspapers on the web. If you pulled in those links, and got a set of 5,000 to 10,000 of them, in a sense, you'd have a vote. The winner would be the one with the most in-links from the group." It was the same lightbulb that had brightened over Larry Page's head.

Sometime in December 1996, Kleinberg got the balance right. One of his favorite queries was "Olympics." The summer games had been held in Atlanta that year, and there were thousands of sites that in some way dealt with the athletic contests, the politics, the bomb that a domestic terrorist had planted. The AltaVista results for that keyword were riddled with spam and were generally useless. But Kleinberg's top result was the official Olympics site.

Kleinberg began showing his breakthrough around IBM. His managers quickly put him in touch with the patent lawyers. Most people took a look at what Kleinberg had set up and wanted him to find stuff for them. Even the patent attorney wanted Kleinberg to help him find sources for his hobby, medieval siege devices. By February 1997, he says, "all sorts of IBM vice presidents were trooping through Almaden to look at demos of this thing and trying to think about what they could do with it." Ultimately, the answer was . . . not much. IBM was a $70 billion business, and it was hard to see how a research project about links on this World Wide Web could make a difference. Kleinberg shrugged it off. He was going to teach computer science at Cornell.

Through mutual friends at Stanford, Kleinberg heard about Larry Page's project, and in July 1997 they met at Page's office in the Gates Building. Kleinberg was impressed with BackRub. "In academia, when there's a hard problem everyone wants to solve, you're always implicitly competing with the other people who are working on it," says Kleinberg. But neither mentioned that issue. Kleinberg encouraged Page to publish his findings, but Page wasn't receptive. "Larry was worried about writing a paper," says Kleinberg. "He was wary because he wanted to see how far he could get with it while he refined it."

Kleinberg could see that his goals were different from Page's. "They wanted to crawl the whole web and get it on racks of servers that they would accumulate," Kleinberg says. "My view was 'How can I solve this problem without having to sink three months into indexing the web?' We had the same core idea, but how we went about it was almost diametrically opposite." Kleinberg was trying to understand network behavior. Page and Brin were *building* something. "Kleinberg had this notion of authority, where your page can become good just by linking to the right pages," says Page. "Whereas what I was doing was more of a traffic simulation, which is actually how people might search the web."

Kleinberg kept up with Google. He turned down job feelers in 1999 and again in 2000. He was happy at Cornell. He'd win teaching awards and a MacArthur fellowship. He led the life in academia he'd set out to lead, and not becoming a billionaire didn't seem to bother him.

There was yet a third person with the idea, a Chinese engineer named Yanhong (Robin) Li. In 1987, he began his studies at Beijing University, an institution that claimed prominence in the country by way of a metric: The Science Citation Index, which ranked scientific papers by the number of other papers that cited them. The index was used in China to rank universities. "Beijing University, measured by the number of citations its professors got from their papers, was ranked number one," said Li.

Li came to the United States in 1991 to get a master's degree at SUNY Buffalo, and in 1994 took a job at IDD Information Services in Scotch Plains, New Jersey, a division of Dow Jones. Part of his job was improving information retrieval processes. He tried the search engines at the time—AltaVista, Excite, Lycos—and found them ineffectual and spam-ridden. One day in April 1996 he was at an academic conference. Bored by the presentation, he began to ponder how search engines could be improved. He realized that the Science Citation Index phenomenon could be applied to the Internet. The hypertext link could be regarded as a citation! "When I returned home, I started to write this down and realized it was revolutionary," he says. He devised a search approach that calculated relevance from both the frequency of links and the content of anchor text. He called his system RankDex.

When he described his scheme to his boss at Dow Jones, urging the company to apply for a patent, he was at first encouraged, then disappointed when nothing happened. "So a couple of months later, I decided to write the application by myself." He bought a self-help book on patent applications and filed his in June 1996. But when he told his boss, Dow Jones reasserted itself and hired a lawyer to review the patent, which it refiled in February 1997. (Stanford University would not file its patent for Larry Page's PageRank system until January 1998.) Nonetheless, Dow Jones did nothing with Li's system. "I tried to convince them it was important, but their business had nothing to do with Internet search, so they didn't care," he says.

Robin Li quit and joined the West Coast search company called Infoseek. In 1999, Disney bought the company and soon thereafter Li returned to China. It was there in Beijing that he would later meet—and compete with—Larry Page and Sergey Brin.

Page and Brin had launched their project as a stepping-stone to possible dissertations. But it was inevitable that they began to eye their creation as something that could make them money. The Stanford CS program was as much a corporate incubator as an academic institution. David Cheriton, one of the professors, once put it this way: "The unfair advantage that Stanford has over any other place in the known universe is that we're surrounded by Silicon Valley." It was not uncommon for its professors to straddle both worlds, maintaining posts in the department while playing in the high-tech scrum of start-ups striving for the big score. There was even a joke that faculty members couldn't get tenure until they started a company.

Cheriton himself was a prime example of how the Stanford network launched companies and enriched the founders. One of the earlier gold strikes from Stanford was the founding of Sun Microsystems by a group that included Andy Bechtolsheim, Vinod Khosla, and Bill Joy. Cheriton was close to Bechtolsheim, so in 1995, when the latter decided to start Granite Systems, a networking start-up, the two collaborated. Eighteen months later, Cisco bought the company for $220 million.

Sergey Brin, Rollerblading his way around the corridors of Gates Hall, took notice. Though Brin and Page didn't have classes with Cheriton, they headed to his office for some advice. They specifically wanted to know how they might interest a company into using PageRank in its own search technology. Cheriton told them that it would be difficult—Sun Microsystems, he reminded them, had been started out of frustration when companies had spurned Bechtolsheim's attempts to sell his workstation technology.

Yet Brin and Page were reluctant at that point to strike out on their own. They had both headed to Stanford intending to become PhDs like their dads.

But licensing their search engine wasn't easy. Though Brin and Page had a good meeting with Yahoo founders Jerry Yang and David Filo, former Stanford students, Yahoo didn't see the need to buy search engine technology. They also met with an AltaVista designer, who seemed interested in BackRub. But the wise men back in DEC headquarters in Maynard, Massachusetts, nixed the idea. Not Invented Here.

Maybe the closest Page and Brin came to a deal was with Excite, a search-based company that had begun—just like Yahoo—with a bunch of sharp Stanford kids whose company was called Architext before the venture capitalists (VCs) got their hands on it and degeekified the name. Terry Winograd, Sergey's adviser, accompanied them to a meeting with Vinod Khosla, the venture capitalist who had funded Excite.

That led to a meeting with Excite's founders, Joe Kraus and Graham Spencer, at Fuki Sushi, a Palo Alto restaurant. Larry insisted that the whole BackRub team come along. "He always likes to have more people on his side than the opposite side, to get the upper hand," says Scott Hassan, who attended along with Page, Brin, and Alan Steremberg. "They sent two people, so we had four." The Excite people began comparison tests with BackRub, plugging in search queries such as "Bob Marley." The results were a lot better than Excite's.

Larry Page laid out an elaborate plan, which he described in detail in emails to Khosla in January 1997. Excite would buy BackRub, and then Larry alone would go to work there. Excite's adoption of BackRub technology, he claimed, would boost its traffic by 10 percent. Extrapolating that in terms of increased ad revenue, Excite would take in $130,000 more every day, for a total of $47 million in a year. Page envisioned his tenure at Excite lasting for seven months, long enough to help the company implement the search engine. Then he would leave, in time for the fall 1997 Stanford semester, resuming his progress toward a doctorate. Excite's total outlay would be $1.6 million, including $300,000 to Stanford for the license, a $200,000 salary, a $400,000 bonus for implementing it within three months, and $700,000 in Excite stock. (Since Page and Brin were working for Stanford while developing their work, the school owned the PageRank patent. Stanford would commonly make financial arrangements so that such inventors could hold exclusive licenses to the intellectual property they created. Eventually Stanford did so with Google, in exchange for 1.8 million shares.) "With my help," wrote the not-quite-twenty-four-year-old student, "this technology will give Excite a substantial advantage and will propel it to a market leadership position."

Khosla made a tentative counteroffer of $750,000 total. But the deal never happened. Hassan recalls a key meeting that might have sunk it. Though Excite had been started by a group of Stanford geeks very much like Larry and Sergey, its venture capital funders had demanded they hire "adult supervision," the condescending term used when brainy geeks are pushed aside as top executives and replaced by someone more experienced and mature, someone who could wear a suit without looking as though he were attending his Bar Mitzvah. The new CEO was George Bell, a former Times Mirror magazine executive. Years later, Hassan would still laugh when he described the meeting between the BackRub team and Bell. When the team got to Bell's office, it fired up BackRub in one window and Excite in the other for a bake-off.

The first query they tested was "Internet." According to Hassan, Excite's first results were Chinese web pages where the English word "Internet" stood out among a jumble of Chinese characters. Then the team typed

"Internet" into BackRub. The first two results delivered pages that told you how to use browsers. It was exactly the kind of helpful result that would most likely satisfy someone who made the query.

Bell was visibly upset. The Stanford product was *too* good. If Excite were to host a search engine that instantly gave people information they sought, he explained, the users would leave the site instantly. Since his ad revenue came from people *staying* on the site—"stickiness" was the most desired metric in websites at the time—using BackRub's technology would be counterproductive. "He told us he wanted Excite's search engine to be 80 percent as good as the other search engines," says Hassan. And we were like, "Wow, these guys don't know what they're talking about."

Hassan says that he urged Larry and Sergey right then, in early 1997, to leave Stanford and start a company. "Everybody else was doing it," he says. "I saw Hotmail and Netscape doing really well. Money was flowing into the Valley. So I said to them, 'The search engine is the idea. We *should do this.*' They didn't think so. Larry and Sergey were both very adamant that they could build this search engine at Stanford."

"We weren't . . . in an entrepreneurial frame of mind back then," Sergey later said.

Hassan quit the project. He got a job with a new company called Alexa and worked part-time on a start-up called eGroups. In fact, Larry and Sergey—this was before they had gotten a dollar in funding for Google—pitched in $5,000 each to help him buy computers for eGroups. (The investment paid off less than three years later when Yahoo bought eGroups for an estimated $413 million.)

But for the next year and a half, all the companies they approached turned them down. "We couldn't get anyone interested," says Page. "We did get offers, but they weren't for much money. So we said, 'Whatever,' and went back to Stanford to work on it some more. It wasn't like we wanted a lot of money, but we wanted the stuff to get really used. And they would want us to work there and we'd ask, 'Do we really want to work for this company?' These companies weren't going to focus on search—they were becoming portals. They didn't understand search, and they weren't technology people."

In September 1997, Page and Brin renamed BackRub to something they hoped would be suitable for a business. They gave serious consideration to "The Whatbox," until they realized that it sounded too much like "wetbox," which wasn't family-friendly. Then Page's dorm roommate suggested they call it "googol." The word was a mathematical term referring to the number 1 followed by 100 zeros. Sometimes the word "googolplex" was used generically to refer to an insanely large number. "The name reflected the scale of what we were doing," Brin explained a few years later. "It actually became a better choice of name later on, because now we have billions of pages and images and groups and documents, and hundreds of millions of searches a day." Page misspelled the word, which was just as well since the Internet address for the correct spelling was already taken. "Google" was available. "It was easy to type and memorable," says Page.

One night, using a new open-source graphics program called GIMP, Sergey designed the home page, spelling the new company name in different colors, making a logo that resembled something made from children's blocks. It conveyed a sense of amiable whimsy. He put an exclamation point after the name, just like Yahoo, another Internet company founded by two Stanford PhD dropouts. "He wanted it to be playful and young," says Page. Unlike a lot of other web pages, the Google home page was so sparse it looked unfinished. The page had a box to type in requests and two buttons underneath, one for search and another labeled I'm Feeling Lucky, a startling bid of confidence that implied that, unlike the competition, Google was capable of nailing your request on the first try. (There was another reason for the button. "The point of I'm Feeling Lucky was to replace the domain name system for navigation," Page said in 2002. Both Page and Brin hoped that instead of guessing what was the address of their web destination, they'd just "go to Google.") The next day Brin ran around the CS department at Stanford, showing off his GIMP creation. "He was asking everybody whether it made any sense to put other stuff on the page," says Dennis Allison, a Stanford CS lecturer. "And everybody said no." That was fine with Page and Brin. The more stuff on the page, the slower it would run, and both of them, especially Page, believed that speed was of the essence when it came to pleasing users. Page later found it humorous that people praised the design for its Zen-like use of white space. "The minimalism is that we didn't have a webmaster and had to do it ourselves," he says.

Meanwhile, BackRub-turned-Google was growing to the point where it was difficult to run using Stanford's facilities. It was becoming less a research project than an Internet start-up run from a private university. Page and Brin's reluctance to write a paper about their work had become notorious in the department. "People were saying, 'Why is this so secret? This is an academic project, we should be able to know how it worked,'" says Terry Winograd.

Page, it seemed, had a conflict about information. On one hand, he subscribed heartily to the hacker philosophy of shared knowledge. That was part of what his project was all about: making human knowledge accessible, making the world a better place. But he also had a strong sense of protecting his hard-won proprietary information. He remembered Nikola Tesla, who had died in poverty even as his inventions enriched others. Later, there would be speculation whether Page, a private person to begin with, had pulled back a little more after his father's death in June 1996. Scott Hassan recalls that the team conveyed its condolences to Page that month, but Hassan didn't speak much about the loss with Page. "Mostly we talked about technical stuff," he would recall. Mike Moritz, one of the venture capitalists who would fund Google, later surmised that "a large part" of Page's later wariness could be associated with that loss. "He felt that the world was pulled out from underneath him," Moritz said. "It makes it hard to trust anything again."

But it wasn't just the secrecy that stalled Brin and Page. Writing a paper wasn't as interesting to them as building something. "Inherently, Larry and Sergey aren't paper-oriented—they're product-oriented," says Winograd. "If they have another ten minutes, they want to make something better. They don't want to take ten minutes to tell you something they did." But finally Winograd convinced them to explain PageRank in a public forum. They presented a paper called "The Anatomy of a Large-Scale Hypertextual Web Search Engine" at a conference in Australia in May 1998.

Arthur Clarke once remarked that the best technology was indistinguishable from magic. The geeks of Silicon Valley, assuming he was talking about them, have never forgotten that and have invoked the quote in countless press releases about their creations. But Google search really did feel like magic. At Stanford, Larry's and Sergey's professors and friends were using the search engine to answer questions and telling their friends about it. Google was handling as many as 10,000 queries a day. At times it was consuming half of Stanford's Internet capacity. Its appetite for equipment and bandwidth was voracious. "We just begged and borrowed," says Page. "There were tons of computers around, and we managed to get some." Page's dorm room was essentially Google's operations center, with a motley assortment of computers from various manufacturers stuffed into a homemade version of a server rack—a storage cabinet made of Legos. Larry and Sergey would hang around the loading dock to see who on campus was getting computers—companies like Intel and Sun gave lots of free machines to Stanford to curry favor with employees of the future—

and then the pair would ask the recipients if they could share some of the bounty.

That still wasn't enough. To store the millions of pages they had crawled, the pair had to buy their own high-capacity disk drives. Page, who had a talent for squeezing the most out of a buck, found a place that sold refurbished disks at prices so low—a tenth of the original cost—that something was clearly wrong with them. "I did the research and figured out that they were okay as long as you replaced the [disk] operating system," he says. "We got 120 drives, about nine gigs each. So it was about a terabyte of space." It was an approach that Google would later adopt in building infrastructure at low cost.

Larry and Sergey would be sitting by the monitor, watching the queries—at peak times, there would be a new one every second—and it would be clear that they'd need even more equipment. *What next?* they'd ask themselves. *Maybe this is real.*

Stanford wasn't kicking them out—the complications of running the nascent Google were outweighed by pride that something interesting was brewing in the department. "It wasn't like our lights were dimming when they would run the crawler," says Garcia-Molina, who was still hoping that Larry and Sergey would develop their work academically. "I think it would have made a great thesis," he says. "I think their families were behind them to get PhDs, too. But doing a company became too much of an attraction."

There was no alternative; no one would pay enough for Google. And the happy visitors they were attracting gave them confidence that their efforts could make a difference. After years of dreaming how his ideas could change the world, Larry Page realized that he'd done something that might do just that. "If the company failed, too bad," says Page. "We were really going to be able to do something that *mattered.*"

They went back to Dave Cheriton, who encouraged them to just get going. "Money shouldn't be a problem," he said. Cheriton suggested that they meet with Andy Bechtolsheim. Brin dashed off an email to Bechtolsheim that evening around midnight and got an immediate reply asking if the two students could show up at eight the next morning at Cheriton's house, which was on the route Bechtolsheim used to go to work each day. At that ungodly hour Page and Brin demoed their search engine for Bechtolsheim on Cheriton's porch, which had an ethernet connection. Bechtolsheim, impressed but eager to get to the office, cut the meeting short by offering to write the duo a $100,000 check.

"We don't have a bank account yet," said Brin.

"Deposit it when you get one," said Bechtolsheim, who raced off in his Porsche. With as little fanfare as if he were grabbing a latte on the way to work, he had just invested in an enterprise that would change the way the world accessed information. Brin and Page celebrated with a Burger King breakfast. The check remained in Page's dorm room for a month.

Soon afterward, Bechtolsheim was joined by other angel investors, including Dave Cheriton. One was a Silicon Valley entrepreneur named Ram Shriram, whose own company had recently been purchased by Amazon.com. Shriram had met Brin and Page in February 1998; although he had been skeptical about a business model for search engines, he was so impressed with Google that he had been advising them. After the Bechtolsheim meeting, Shriram invited them to his house to meet his boss Jeff Bezos, who was enthralled with their passion and "healthy stubbornness," as they explained why they would never put display ads on their home page. Bezos joined Bechtolsheim, Cheriton, and Shriram as investors, making for a total of a million dollars of angel money.

On September 4, 1998, Page and Brin filed for incorporation and finally moved off campus. Sergey's girlfriend at the time was friendly with a manager at Intel named Susan Wojcicki, who had just purchased a house on Santa Margarita Street in Menlo Park with her husband for $615,000. To help meet the mortgage, the couple charged Google $1,700 a month to rent the garage and several rooms in the house. At that point they'd taken on their first employee, fellow Stanford student Craig Silverstein. He'd originally connected with them by offering to show them a way to compress all the crawled links so they could be stored in memory and run faster. ("It was basically to get my foot in the door," he says.) They also hired an office manager. But almost as if they were still hedging on their PhDs, they maintained a presence at Stanford that fall, coteaching a course, CS 349, "Data Mining, Search, and the World Wide Web," which met twice a week that semester. Brin and Page announced it as a "project class" in which the students would work with the repository of 25 million web pages that they had captured as part of what was now a private company. They even had a research assistant. The first assigned reading was their own paper, but later in the semester a class was devoted to a comparison of PageRank and Kleinberg's work.

In December, after the final projects were due, Page emailed the students a party invitation that also marked a milestone: "The Stanford Research Project is now Google.com: The Next Generation Internet Search Company."

"Dress is Tiki Lounge wear," the invitation read, "and bring something for the hot tub."

2

"We want Google to be as smart as you."

Larry Page did not want to be Tesla'd. Google had quickly become a darling of everyone who used it to search the net. But at first so had AltaVista, and that search engine had failed to improve. How was Google, led by two talented but inexperienced youngsters, going to tackle the devilishly difficult problems of improving its service?

"If we aren't a lot better next year, we will already be forgotten," Page said to one of the first reporters visiting the company.

The web was growing like digital kudzu. People were coming to Google in droves. Google's plan was to get even more traffic. "When we started the company, we had two computers," says Craig Silverstein. "One was the web service, and one was doing everything else—the page rank, the searches. And there was a giant chain of disks that went off the back of the computer that stored twenty-five million web pages. Obviously that was not going to scale very well." Getting more computers was no problem. Google needed brainpower, especially since Brin and Page had reached the limits of what they could do in writing the software that would enable the search engine to grow and improve. "Coding is not where their interests are," says Silverstein.

The founders also knew that Google had to be a lot smarter to keep satisfying users—and to fulfill the world-changing ambitions of its founders. "We don't always produce what people want," Page explained in Google's early days. "It's really difficult. To do that you have to be smart—you have to understand everything in the world. In computer science, we call that artificial intelligence."

Brin chimed in. "We want Google to be as smart as you—you should be getting an answer the minute you think of it."

"The ultimate search engine," said Page. "We're a long way from that."

Page and Brin both held a core belief that the success of their company would hinge on having world-class engineers and scientists committed to their ambitious vision. Page believed that technology companies can thrive only by "an understanding of engineering at the highest level." Somehow Page and Brin had to identify such a group and impress them enough to have them sign on to a small start-up. Oh, and they had a policy that limited the field: no creeps. They were already thinking of the culture of their company and making sure that their hires would show traits of hard-core wizardry, user focus, and starry-eyed idealism.

"We just hired people like us," says Page.

Some of Google's early hires were simply brainy recent grads, people like Marissa Mayer, a hard-driving math whiz and ballet dancer in her high school in Wausau, Wisconsin, who had become an artificial intelligence star at Stanford. (During her interview with Silverstein, she was asked for three things Google could do better; ten years later, she was still kicking herself that she listed only two.) But Page and Brin also went after people with résumés more often seen in the recruitment offices of Microsoft Research or Carnegie Mellon's CS department. One of their first coups was a professor at the University of California at Santa Barbara named Urs Hölzle. He'd played with the earlier crop of search engines such as AltaVista and Inktomi and concluded that, as a computer scientist familiar with Boolean syntax and other techniques, he could use those techniques to find what he wanted on the Internet. But he assumed that search would never be something his mother would use. Google instantly changed his mind about that: you just typed in what you wanted, and, bang, the first thing was right. Mom would like that! "They definitely seemed to know what they were doing," he says of Larry and Sergey.

More important to him, when he visited the new company in early 1999, he understood that though he had no background in information retrieval, the problems Brin and Page were working on had a lot in common with his own work in big computer systems. This little search engine was butting up against issues in performance and scalability that only huge projects had previously grappled with. That was Google's secret weapon to lure world-class computer scientists: in a world where corporate research labs were shutting down, this small start-up offered an opportunity to break ground in computer science.

Hölzle, still wary, accepted the offer but kept his position at UCSB by taking a yearlong leave. He would never return. In April he arrived at Google with Yoshka, a big floppy Leonberger dog, in tow, and dived right in to help shore up Google's overwhelmed infrastructure. (By then Google had moved from Wojcicki's Menlo Park house to a second-floor office over a bicycle shop in downtown Palo Alto.) Though Google had a hundred computers at that point—it was buying them as quickly as it could—it could not handle the load of queries. Hundreds of thousands of queries a day were coming in.

The average search at that time, Hölzle recalls, took three and a half seconds. Considering that speed was one of the core values of Page and Brin—it was like motherhood, and scale was apple pie—this was a source of distress for the founders. "Basically during the middle of the day we were maxed out," says Hölzle. "Nothing was happening for some users, because it would just never get a page basically back. It was all about scalability, performance improvements." Part of the problem was that Page and Brin had written the system in what Hölzle calls "university code," a nice way of saying amateurish. "The web server couldn't handle more than ten requests or so a second because it was written in Python, which is a great idea for a research system, but it's not a high-performance solution," he says. He immediately set about rewriting the code.

Hölzle was joined by other computer scientists who were more daring in taking the leap to permanent Google employment. This included a minimigration of engineers from DEC's research division. Established legend in Silicon Valley cited Xerox's Palo Alto Research Center (PARC) as the canonical lab brimming with breakthrough innovation that had been misunderstood, buried, or otherwise fumbled by the clueless parent company. (Its inventions included the modern computer interface with windows and file folders.) But when it came to missed opportunities, PARC had nothing on DEC's Western Research Laboratory, which was handed over to Compaq when that personal computer company bought Digital Equipment Corporation in 1998. (In 2002, Hewlett-Packard would acquire Compaq.) In 1998, two years before Apple even began work on the iPod, DEC engineers were developing a digital music player that could store a whole music collection and fit in your pocket. In addition, DEC had some of the founding fathers of the Internet, as well as scientists writing pioneering papers on network theory. But DEC never used its engineers' ideas to help AltaVista become Google. ("From the moment I left DEC, I never used AltaVista," says Louis Monier, who split in 1998. "It was just pathetic. It was completely obvious that Google was better.") So it was little wonder that some of them went to Google. "The number [of former DEC scientists at Google] is really kind of staggering," says Bill Weihl, a DEC refugee who came to the company in 2004.

One of the DEC engineers had already independently discovered the power of web links in search. Jeffrey Dean suspected that it would be helpful to web users if a software program could point them to pages that were related to the ones they liked. In his vision, you would be reading an article in *The New York Times* and his program would pop up, asking if you'd like to see ten other interesting pages related to the one you were reading.

Dean had never been much interested in information retrieval. Now that he suspected a revolution was afoot, he was. But his attempts to join up with the AltaVista crew ended ignominiously. "The AltaVista team had grown really fast," he says, "and hired a bunch of people who I think were not as technically good as they could have been." In other words—*get me away from here.* In February 1999, Dean bailed from DEC to join a start-up called mySimon.

Within a few months, though, he was bored. Then he heard that Urs Hölzle, whom he'd known through his grad school adviser, had joined up with the guys who did PageRank. "I figured Google would be better because I knew more of the people there, and they seemed like they were more technically savvy," he says. He was so excited about working there that even though his official starting date wasn't until August 1999, in July he began coming to Google after his workday at mySimon ended.

Dean's hiring got the attention of another DEC researcher, Krishna Bharat. He had also been thinking of ways to get web search results from links. Bharat was working on something called the Hilltop algorithm, which algorithmically identified "expert sites" and used those to point to the most relevant results. It was something like Jon Kleinberg's hub approach, but instead of using AltaVista as a prewash to get top search results and then figure out who the expert sites were, Bharat went straight to a representation of the web—links and some bits from the pages—stored in computer memory. Bharat's algorithms would roam around the "neighborhood of the query" to find the key sites.

The India-born computer scientist had already been on Google's radar: when he ate lunch at a joint called World Wraps in Palo Alto, he'd run into Sergey Brin, who would invariably hand him a business card and urge him to apply to Google. Bharat was impressed with Google—he'd actually presented his Hilltop algorithm in the same session at the conference in Australia when Brin and Page showed off Google to a bowled-over audience of IR people. He also liked Sergey. Their mutual friend Rajeev Mowani once hosted a seminar where Brin had arrived on Rollerblades and began rhapsodizing about PageRank without missing a beat. Bharat thought that was incredibly cool. But Google was so *small.* It was hard for

Bharat to imagine leaving the creature comforts of a big company for an operation with a single-digit workforce located over a bicycle shop and decorated in a style that mixed high-tech Dumpster with nursery school. Plus he cherished the ability to pursue research, something he doubted was possible at a tiny start-up.

Then Google hired Jeff Dean, and Bharat was stunned. It was like some basketball team playing in an obscure minor league grabbing a player who was first-round NBA material. Those guys were *serious*. Soon after, Bharat heard that this just-born start-up, which could barely respond to its query traffic, was starting a research group! It sounded improbable, but he climbed the flight of stairs in the Palo Alto office for an interview. Bharat said straight out that he was skeptical of Google's research ambitions. From what he could see, there were a lot of people running around with pagers and flicking at their keyboards to keep the system going. "Larry, why do you say you want to do research?" he said to Page. "You are such a tiny group!" Page's answer was surprising and impressive. Looking at things from a different perspective could lead to unexpected solutions, he said. Sometimes in engineering you look at things with tunnel vision and need a broader perspective. He told Bharat a story about Kodak that involved some seemingly intractable practical problem that was solved by an unexpected intervention from someone in the research division. Page wanted that kind of thing to happen at Google.

That interaction sold Bharat. Here was a guy who was young, inexperienced, and probably half nuts—but technically adept and infectiously confident. "I could respect Larry in a way that I couldn't respect people running other start-ups," says Bharat. "I knew the technical content of his work." What's more, Bharat could feel the pull of Page's crusade to make the world better by cracking hard problems at the intersection of computer science and metaphysics. Bharat had thought a lot about search and was enthralled with its mysteries. On the face of things, it seemed so tantalizingly easy. But people had grasped only the slightest fraction of what was possible. To make progress, even appreciate this space, you would have to live in the data, breathe them in like a fish passing water through its gills. Here was his invitation. Bharat would wind up working an evolution of his Hilltop algorithm, called web connectivity analysis, into Google's search engine. It would be the company's first patent.

The same almost mystical attraction of Google's ambitions led to another impressive hire in early 2000: Anurag Acharya, a Santa Barbara professor who was a colleague of Hölzle. Acharya, who'd gotten his PhD at Carnegie Mellon, had spent his entire life in academia but at age thirty-six had been questioning his existence there. He had tired of a routine where people took on a problem of limited scope, solved it, published the results, and then went on to the next. He remembered when he'd been a student and had sat with his adviser, a deep thinker who spent his entire life grappling with a single giant mystery: *what is the nature of mind?* More and more, Acharya thought that there was beauty in grappling with a classically hard problem that would survive after you leave the earth. Talking to Hölzle during an interview for this little company, he realized that search was that kind of problem. "I had no background in search but was looking for a problem of that kind," he says. "It appeared that, yes, that could be it." Adding to Google's appeal was his own background—like several of his new colleagues, he was from provincial India. (And like many at Google, including the founders, his parents were academics.) He often thought of the people in his home country, who were not just poor but information-impoverished as well. "If you were successful at Google, people from everywhere would have the ability to find information," he says. "I come from a place where those boundaries are very, very apparent. They are in your face. To be able to make a dent in that is a very attractive proposition."

Bharat recommended another friend named Ben Gomes, who worked at Sun. The two had studied for exams together as high school friends in Bangalore, India. Gomes joined Google the same week Bharat did. And Bharat had another friend who was among the best catches of all: Amit Singhal.

Born in the Indian state of Uttar Pradesh, in the foothills of the Himalayas, Singhal had arrived in the United States in 1992 to pursue a master's degree in computer science at the University of Minnesota. He'd become fascinated with the field then known as information retrieval and was desperate to study with its pioneering innovator, Gerard Salton. "I only applied to one grad school, and it was Cornell," he says. "And I wrote in my statement of purpose that if I was ever going to get a PhD, it's with Gerry Salton. Otherwise, I didn't think a PhD was worth it." He became Salton's assistant, got his PhD at Cornell, and eventually wound up at AT&T Labs.

In 1999, Singhal ran into Bharat at a conference in Berkeley. Bharat told him he was leaving DEC for an exciting start-up that wanted to take on the biggest problems in search. It had a funny name, Google. Singhal should work there, too. Singhal thought the idea was ridiculous. Maybe it was all right for Bharat, who was a couple of years younger and unmarried.

But Singhal had a wife and daughter and a second child on the way. "These little companies are all going to die," he said. "I work for *AT&T*—the big ship that always sails. I can't go to Google-schmoogle because I have a family to support."

Not too long afterward, the big ship AT&T began to take on water. "In 2000, I was here," says Singhal.

In barely a year since Brin and Page had formed their company, they had gathered a group of top scientists totally committed to the vision of their young founders. These early employees would be part of team efforts that led to innovation after innovation that would broaden Google's lead over its competitors and establish it as synonymous with search. But those breakthroughs were in the future. In 2000, those big brains were crammed into a single conference room working on an emergency infrastructure fix. Google had taken ill.

The problem was the index storing the contents of the web in Google's servers. For a couple of months in early 2000, it wasn't updating at all. Millions of documents created during that period weren't being collected. As far as the Google search engine was concerned, they didn't exist.

The problem was a built-in flaw in the crawling and indexing process. If one of the machines devoted to crawling broke down before the process was completed, indexing had to begin from scratch. It was like a role-playing computer game in which you would spend hundreds of hours building a character and then lose all that effort if your character got killed by a stray beast or a well-armed foe. The game world had learned to deal with the problem—dead avatars could be resurrected after a brief pause or an annoying dislocation. But Google hadn't.

The flaw hadn't been so bad in the earlier days of Google, when only five or so machines were required to crawl and index the web. It was at least a ten-day process with one of Google's first crawl engineers, Harry Cheung (everyone called him Spider-Man), at his machines, monitoring progress of spiders as they spread out through the net and then, after the crawl, breaking down the web pages for the index and calculating the page rank, using Sergey's complicated system of variables with a mathematical process using something called eigenvectors, while everybody waited for the two processes to converge. ("Math professors love us because Google has made eigenvectors relevant to every matrix algebra student in America," says Marissa Mayer.) Sometimes, because of quirks in the way the web addresses were numbered, the system crawled the same pages and showed no movement, and then you'd have to figure out whether you were actually done or had hit a black hole. This problem, though, had been generally manageable.

But as the web kept growing, Google added more machines—by the end of 1999, there were eighty machines involved in the crawl (out of a total of almost three thousand Google computers at that time)—and the likelihood that something would break increased dramatically. Especially since Google made a point of buying what its engineers referred to as "el cheapo" equipment. Instead of commercial units that carefully processed and checked information, Google would buy discounted consumer models without built-in processes to protect the integrity of data.

As a stopgap measure, the engineers had implemented a scheme where the indexing data was stored on different hard drives. If a machine went bad, everyone's pager would start buzzing, even if it was the middle of the night, and they'd barrel into the office immediately to stop the crawl, copy the data, and change the configuration files. "This happened every few days, and it basically stopped everything and was very painful," says Sanjay Ghemawat, one of the DEC research wizards who had joined Google.

"The whole thing needed rethinking," says Jeff Dean.

Actually, it needed redoing, since by 2000 the factors impeding the crawl were so onerous that after several attempts it looked as though Google would *never* build its next index. The web was growing at an amazing pace, with billions of more documents each year. The presence of a search engine like Google actually accelerated the pace, offering an incentive to people as they discovered that even the quirkiest piece of information could be accessed by the small number of people who would appreciate it. Google was trying to contain this tsunami with more machines—cheap ones, thus increasing the chance of a breakdown. The updates would work for a while, then fail. And now, weeks were passing before the indexes were updated.

It's hard to overestimate the seriousness of this problem. One of the key elements of good search was freshness—making sure that the indexes have recent results. Imagine if this problem had happened a year later, after the September 11, 2001, terrorist attacks. Doing a Google search for "World Trade Center" that November or December, you would have found no links to the event. Instead, you'd have results that suggested a fine-dining experience at Windows on the World, on the 107th floor of the now-nonexistent North Tower.

A half-dozen engineers moved their computers into a conference room. Thus Google created its first war room. (By then—less than a year after moving from the house in Menlo Park to the downtown Palo Alto office—Google had moved once again, to a roomier office-park facility on Bayshore Road in nearby Mountain View. Employees dubbed it the Googleplex, a pun on the mathematical term googolplex, meaning an unthinkably large number.) When people came to work, they'd go to the war room instead of the office. And they'd stay late. Dean was in there with Craig Silverstein, Sanjay Ghemawat, and some others.

They built a system that implemented "checkpointing," a way for the index to hold its place if a calamity befell a server or hard disk. But the new system went further—it used a different way to handle a cluster of disks, more akin to the parallel-processing style of computing (where a computational task would be split among multiple computers or processers) than the "sharding" technique Google had used, which was to split up the web and assign regions of it to individual computers. (Those familiar with computer terms may know this technique as "partitioning," but, as Dean says, "everyone at Google calls it sharding because it sounds cooler." Among Google's infrastructure wizards, it's key jargon.)

The experience led to an ambitious revamp of the way the entire Google infrastructure dealt with files. "I always had wanted to build a file system, and it was pretty clear that this was something we were going to have to do," says Ghemawat, who led the team. Though there had previously been systems that handled information distributed over multiple files, Google's could handle bigger data loads and was more nimble at running full speed in the face of disk crashes—which it had to be because, with Google's philosophy of buying supercheap components, failure was the norm. "The main idea was that we wanted the file system to automate dealing with failures, and to do that, the file system would keep multiple copies and it would make new copies when some copy failed," says Ghemawat.

Another innovation that came a bit later was called the in-RAM system. This involved putting as much of the index as possible in actual computer memory as opposed to the pokier, less reliable hard disk drives. It sped things up considerably, allowed more flexibility, and saved money. "The in-memory index was, like, a factor of two or three cheaper, because it could just handle many, many more queries per machine per second," says Dean.

The system embodied Google's approach to computer science. At one point, the cost of fixed memory (in chips as opposed to spinning hard disks) would have been so expensive that using it to store the Internet would have been a daffy concept. But Google's engineers knew that the pace of technology would drive prices down, and they designed accordingly. Likewise, Google—as its very name implies—is geared to handling the historic expansion of data that the digital revolution has triggered. Competitors, especially those who were successful in a previous age, were slow to wrap their minds around this phenomenon, while Google considered it as common as air. "The unit of thinking around here is a terabyte," said Google engineering head Wayne Rosing in 2003. (A terabyte is equal to around 10 trillion bits of data.) A thirty-year Silicon Valley veteran whose résumé boasted important posts at DEC, Apple, and Sun, Rosing had joined Google in 2001 in part because he saw that it had the potential to realize the vision of Vannevar Bush's famous memex paper, which he had read in high school. "It doesn't even get interesting until there's more than many terabytes involved in problems. So that drives you into thinking of hundreds of thousands of computers as the generic way to solve problems." When you have that much power to solve problems, you have the ability to do much more than solve them faster. You can tackle problems that haven't even been considered. You can build your own paradigms.

Implementing the Google File System was a step toward that new paradigm. It was also a timely development, because the demands on Google's system were about to increase dramatically. Google had struck a deal to handle all the search traffic of Yahoo, one of the biggest portals on the web.

The deal—announced on June 26, 2000—was a frustrating development to the head of Yahoo's search team, Udi Manber. He had been arguing that Yahoo should develop its own search product (at the time, it was licensing technology from Inktomi), but his bosses weren't interested. Yahoo's executives, led by a VC-approved CEO named Timothy Koogle (described in a *BusinessWeek* cover story as "The Grown-up Voice of Reason at Yahoo"), instead were devoting their attention to branding—marketing gimmicks such as putting the purple corporate logo on the Zamboni machine that swept the ice between periods of San Jose Sharks hockey games. "I had six people working on my search team," Manber said. "I couldn't get the seventh. This was a company that had thousands of people. I could not get the seventh." Since Yahoo wasn't going to develop its own search, Manber had the task of finding the best one to license.

After testing Google and visiting Larry Page several times, Manber recommended that Yahoo use its technology. One concession that Yahoo gave Google turned out to be fateful: on the results page for a Yahoo search, the user would see a message noting that Google was powering the search. The page even had the Google logo. Thus Yahoo's millions of users discovered a search destination that would become part of their lives.

As part of the deal, Google agreed to update its index on a monthly basis, something possible after the experience in the war room. Google now had the most current data in the industry. It also boasted the biggest index; on the day it announced the Yahoo deal, Google reported that its servers now held more than a billion web pages. This system remained state of the art until the summer of 2003, when Google launched a revamp of its entire indexing system to enable it to refresh the index from day to day, crawling popular sites more often. The code name for the 2003 update was BART. The title implied that Google's system would match the aspirations (if not the accomplishments) of the local mass transit system: "always on time, always fast, always on schedule." But the code name's actual origin was an engineer named Bart.

Even though Google never announced when it refreshed its index, there would invariably be a slight rise in queries around the world soon after the change was implemented. It was as if the global subconscious realized that there were fresher results available.

The response of Yahoo's users to the Google technology, though, was probably more conscious. They noticed that search was better and used it more. "It increased traffic by, like, 50 percent in two months," Manber recalls of the switch to Google. But the only comment he got from Yahoo executives was complaints that people were searching too much and they would have to pay higher fees to Google.

But the money Google received for providing search was not the biggest benefit. Even more valuable was that it now had access to many more users and much more data. It would be data that took Google search to the next level. The search behavior of users, captured and encapsulated in the logs that could be analyzed and mined, would make Google the ultimate learning machine.

Amit Patel first realized the value of Google's logs. Patel was one of Google's very first hires, arriving in early 1999 as a part-timer still working on his Stanford CS PhD. Patel was studying programming language theory but realized he didn't like the subject too much. (Unlike his bosses, though, he would complete his degree.) Google seemed more fun, and fun was important for Patel, a cherub-faced lover of games and distractions whose business card reads "Troublemaker." One of his first projects at Google turned out to be more significant than anyone expected. "Go find out how many people are using Google, who's using it, and what they're doing with it," he was told.

The task appealed to Patel, who was only beginning to learn about search engines and data analysis. He realized that Google could be a broad sensor of human behavior. For instance, he noticed that homework questions spiked on weekends. "People would wait until Sunday night to do their homework, and then they'd look up things on Google," he says. Also, by tracking what queries Google saw the most, you could get a glimpse in real time of what the world was interested in. (A few years later, Patel would be instrumental in constructing the Google Zeitgeist, an annual summation of the most popular search subjects that Google would release to the public at the end of the year.)

But the information that users provided to Google went far beyond the subject matter of their queries. Google had the capacity to capture everything people did on the site on its logs, a digital trail of activities whose retention could provide a key to future innovations. Every aspect of user behavior had a value. How many queries were there, how long were they, what were the top words used in queries, how did users punctuate, how often did they click on the first result, who had referred them to Google, where they were geographically. "Just basic knowledge," he recalls.

Those logs told stories. Not only when or how people used Google but what kind of people the users were and how they thought. Patel came to realize that the logs could make Google smarter, and he shared log information with search engineers such as Jeff Dean and Krishna Bharat, who were keenly interested in improving search quality.

To that point, Google had not been methodical about storing the information that told it who its users were and what they were doing. "In those days the data was stored on disks which were failing very often, and those machines were often repurposed for something else," says Patel. One day, to Patel's horror, one of the engineers pointed to three machines and announced that he needed them for his project and was going to reformat the disks, which at that point contained thousands of query logs. Patel began working on systems that would transfer these data to a safe place. As Google began to evolve a distribution of labor, eventually it mandated that at least one person be working on the web server, one on the index, and one on the logs.

Some years earlier, an artificial intelligence researcher named Douglas Lenat had begun Cyc, an incredibly ambitious effort to teach computers all the commonsense knowledge understood by every human. Lenat hired students to painstakingly type in an endless stream of even the most mundane truisms: a house is a building . . . people live in houses . . . houses have front doors . . . houses have back doors . . . houses have bedrooms and a kitchen . . . if you light a fire in a house, it could burn down—millions of pieces of information that a computer could draw upon so that when it came time to analyze a statement that mentioned a house, the computer could make proper inferences. The project never did produce a computer that could process information as well as a four-year-old child.

But the information Google began gathering was far more voluminous, and the company received it for free. Google came to see that instant feedback as the basis of an artificial intelligence learning mechanism. "Doug Lenat did his thing by hiring these people and training them to write things down in a certain way," says Peter Norvig, who joined Google as director of machine learning in 2001. "We did it by saying 'Let's take things that people are doing naturally.' "

On the most basic level, Google could see how satisfied users were. To paraphrase Tolstoy, happy users were all the same. The best sign of their happiness was the "long click"—this occurred when someone went to a search result, ideally the top one, and did not return. That meant Google had successfully fulfilled the query. But unhappy users were unhappy in their own ways. Most telling were the "short clicks" where a user followed a link and immediately returned to try again. "If people type something and then go and change their query, you could tell they aren't happy," says Patel. "If they go to the next page of results, it's a sign they're not happy. You can use those signs that someone's not happy with what we gave them to go back and study those cases and find places to improve search."

Those logs were tutorials on human knowledge. Google's search engine slowly built up enough knowledge that the engineers could confidently allow it to choose when to swap out one word for another. What helped make this possible was Google's earlier improvement in infrastructure, including the techniques that Jeff Dean and Sanjay Ghemawat had developed to compress data so that Google could put its index into computer memory instead of on hard disks. That was a case where a technical engineering project meant to speed up search queries enabled a totally different kind of innovation. "One of the big deals about the in-memory index is that it made it much more feasible to take a three-word query and say, 'I want to look at the data for fifteen synonymous words, because they're all kind of related,'" says Dean. "You could never afford to do that on a disk-based system, because you'd have to do fifteen disk seeks instead of three, and it would blow up your serving costs tremendously. An in-memory index made for much more aggressive exploration of synonyms and those kinds of things."

"We discovered a very early nifty thing," says search engineer Amit Singhal, who worked hard on synonyms. "People change words in their queries. So someone would say, 'Pictures of dogs,' and then they'll say 'Pictures of puppies.' That said that maybe dogs and puppies were interchangeable. We also learned that when you boil water, it's hot water. We were learning semantics from humans, and that was a great advance."

Similarly, by analyzing how people retracked their steps after a misspelling, Google devised its own spell checker. It built that knowledge into the system; if you typed a word inaccurately, Google would give you the right results anyway.

But there were obstacles. Google's synonym system came to understand that a dog was similar to a puppy and that boiling water was hot. But its engineers also discovered that the search engine considered that a hot dog was the same as a boiling puppy. The problem was fixed, Singhal says, by a breakthrough late in 2002 that utilized Ludwig Wittgenstein's theories on how words are defined by context. As Google crawled and archived billions of documents and web pages, it analyzed which words were close to each other. "Hot dog" would be found in searches that also contained "bread" and "mustard" and "baseball games"—not "puppies with roasting fur." Eventually the knowledge base of Google understood what to do with a query involving hot dogs—and millions of other words. "Today, if you type 'Gandhi bio,' we know that 'bio' means 'biography,'" says Singhal. "And if you type 'bio warfare,' it means 'biological.'"

Over the years, Google would make the data in its logs the key to evolving its search engine. It would also use those data on virtually every other product the company would develop. It would not only take note of user behavior in its released products but measure such behavior in countless experiments to test out new ideas and various improvements. The more Google's system learned, the more new signals could be built into the search engine to better determine relevance.

Sergey Brin had written the original part of the Google search engine that dealt with relevance. At that point it was largely based on PageRank, but as early as 2000 Amit Singhal realized that as time went on, more and more interpretive signals would be added, making PageRank a diminishing factor in determining results. (Indeed, by 2009, Google would say it made use of more than two hundred signals—though the real number was almost certainly much more—including synonyms, geographic signals, freshness signals, and even a signal for websites selling pizzas.) The code badly needed a rewrite; Singhal couldn't even stand to read the code that Brin had produced. "I just wrote new," he says.

Singhal completed a version of the new code in two months and by January 2001 was testing it. Over the next few months, Google exposed it to a percentage of its users and liked the results. They were happier. Sometime that summer, Google flipped the switch and became a different, more accurate service. In accordance with the company's fanatical secrecy on such matters, it made no announcement. Five years later, Singhal was acknowledged by being named a Google Fellow, awarded an undisclosed prize that was almost certainly in the millions of dollars. There was a press release announcing that Singhal had received the award, but it did not specify the reason.

Google's search engines would thereafter undergo major transformations every two or three years, with similar stealth. "It's like changing the engines on a plane flying a thousand kilometers an hour, thirty thousand feet above the earth," says Singhal. "You have to do it so the passengers don't feel that something just happened. And in my time, we have replaced our propellers with turboprops and our turboprops with jet engines. The passengers don't notice, but the ride is more comfortable and the people get there faster."

In between the major rewrites, Google's search quality teams constantly produced incremental improvements. "We're looking at queries all the time and we find failures and say, 'Why, why, why?'" says Singhal, who himself became involved in a perpetual quest to locate poor results that might have indicated bigger problems in the algorithm. He got into the habit of sampling the logs kept by Google on its users' behavior and extracting random queries. When testing a new version of the search engine, his experimentation intensified. He would compile a list of tens of thousands of queries, simultaneously running them on the current version of Google search and the proposed revision. The secondary benefit of such a test was that it often detected a pattern of failure in certain queries.

As best as he could remember, that was how the vexing query of Audrey Fino came into Amit Singhal's life.

It seemed so simple: someone had typed "Audrey Fino" into Google and was unhappy with the result. It was easy for Singhal to see why. The results for that query were dominated by pages in Italian gushing about the charms of the Belgian-born actress Audrey Hepburn. This did not seem to be what the user was looking for. "We realized that this was a person's name," says Singhal. "There's a person somewhere named Audrey Fino, and we didn't have the smarts in the system to know this." What's more, he realized that it was a symptom of a larger failure that required algorithmic therapy. As good as Google was, the search engine stumbled with names.

This spurred a multiyear effort by Singhal and his team to produce a name detection system within the search engine. Names were important. Only 8 percent of Google's queries were names—and half of those celebrities—but the more obscure name queries were cases where users had specific, important needs (including "vanity searches" where people Googled themselves, a ridiculously common practice). So how would you devise new signals to more skillfully identify names from queries and dig them out of the web corpus? Singhal and his colleagues began where they almost always did: with data. To improve search, Google often integrated external databases, and in this case Google licensed the White Pages, allowing it to use all the information contained in hundreds of thick newsprint-based tomes where the content consisted of nothing but names (and addresses and phone numbers). Google's search engine sucked up the names and analyzed them until it had an understanding of what a name was and how to recognize it in the system.

But the solution was trickier than that. One had to take context into effect. Consider the query "houston baker." Was the user looking for a person who baked bread in Texas? Probably. But if you were making that query very far from the Lone Star State, it's more likely that you were seeking someone named after the famous Texan. Google had to teach its search engine to tell the difference. And a lot of the instruction was done by the users, clicking millions of times to direct their responses to the happy zone of short clicks.

"This is all just learning," says Singhal. "We had a computer learning algorithm on which we built our name classifier."

Within a few months Singhal's team built the system to make use of that information and properly parse name queries. One day not long after that, Singhal typed in the troublesome query once more. This time, rising above the pages gushing about the gamine who starred in *Roman Holiday*, there was a link providing information about an attorney who was, at least for a time, based in Malta: Ms. Audrey Fino.

"So now we can recognize names and do the right thing when one comes up," says Singhal five years after the quest. "And our name recognition system is now far better than when I invented it, and is better than anything else out there, no matter what anyone says."

One day in 2009, he showed a visitor how well it worked, also illuminating other secrets of the search engine. He opened his laptop and typed in a query: "mike siwek lawyer mi."

He jabbed at the ENTER key. In a time span best measured in beats of a hummingbird's wing, ten results appeared. There were the familiar "ten blue links" of Google search. (The text consisting of the actual links to the pages cited as results was highlighted in blue.) Early in Google's history Page and Brin had decided that ten links was the proper number to show on a page, and numerous tests over the years had reinforced the conviction that ten was the number that users preferred to see. In this case, the top result was a link to the home page of an attorney named Michael Siwek in Grand Rapids, Michigan. This success came as a result of the efforts put into motion by the Audrey Fino problem. The key to understanding a query like this, Singhal said, was the black art of "bigram breakage": that is, how should a search engine parse a series of words entered into the query field, making the kind of distinctions that a smart human being would make?

For instance, "New York" represents two words that go together (in other words, a bigram). But so do the three words in "New York Times," which clearly indicate a different kind of search. And everything changes when the query is "New York Times Square," in which case the breakage would come . . . well, *you* know where.

"Deconstruct this [Siwek] query from an engineer's point of view," says Singhal. "Most search engines I have known in my academic life will go 'one word, two words, three words, four words, done.' We at Google say, 'Aha! We can break this here!' We figure that 'lawyer' is not a last name and 'Siwek' is not a middle name," he says. "And by the way, lawyer is *not* a town in Michigan. A lawyer is an attorney."

This was the hard-won view from inside the Google search engine: a rock is a rock. It's also a stone, and it could be a boulder. Spell it *rokc*, and it's still a rock. But put "little" in front of "rock," and it's the capital of Arkansas. Which, is not an "ark." Unless "Noah" is around.

All this helped to explain how Google could find someone whose name may have never appeared in a search before. (One-third of all search queries are virgin requests.) "Mike Siwek is some person with almost no Internet presence," says Singhal. "Finding that needle in that haystack, it just happened."

Amit Singhal turned forty in 2008. The search team celebrated with a party in his honor. As one might expect, it was a joyous celebration. Certainly there was much to celebrate besides a birthday. Consider that these were geeky mathematicians who in an earlier era would have written obscure papers and be scraping by financially on an academic's salary. Now their work directly benefited hundreds of millions of people, and they had in some way changed the world. Plus, many of them owned stock options that had made them very wealthy.

Just before the dinner was to commence, Singhal's boss handed a phone to him. "Someone wants to talk to you," he said.

A female voice that Singhal did not recognize congratulated him on his milestone. "I'm sorry," he said. "Do I know you? Did we overlap academically?"

"Oh, I'm an academic," she said. "But we didn't overlap."

"Did I influence your work, or did you influence my work?"

"Well," the woman said, "I think I influenced your work."

Singhal was at a loss.

"I'm Audrey Fino," she said.

Actually, she was *not* Audrey Fino. Singhal's boss had hired an actress to portray the woman. The Google search engine had been able to locate the digital trail of Audrey Fino, but could not produce the actual person. That sort of magic would have to wait until later.

The secret history of Google was punctuated by similar advances, a legacy of breaking ground in computer science and keeping its corporate mouth shut. The heroes of Google search were heroes at Google but nowhere else. In every one of the four aspects of search—crawling, indexing, relevance, and speedy delivery of results—Google made advances. Search quality specialists such as Amit Singhal were like the quarterbacks and wide receivers on a football team: the eye-popping results of their ranking efforts got the lion's share of attention. But those results relied on collecting as much information as possible. Google called this "comprehensiveness" and had a team of around three hundred engineers making sure that the indexes captured everything. "Ideally what we want to have is sort of a true mirror of the web," says a Google engineering VP. "We want to have a copy of every document that's out there or as many as we can possibly get, we want our copy to be as close to that original as possible both in time and in terms of representation, and then we want to organize that in such a way that it's easy and efficient to serve, and ultimately to rank."

Google did all it could to access those pages. If a web page required users to fill out a form to see certain content, Google had probably taught its spiders how to fill out the form. Sometimes content was locked inside programs that ran when users visit a page—applications running in the JavaScript language or a media program like Adobe's Flash. Google knew how to look inside those programs and suck out the content for its indexes. Google even used optical character recognition to figure out if an image on the website had text on it.

The accumulation of all those improvements lengthened Google's lead over its competitors, and the circle of early adopters who first discovered Google was eventually joined by the masses, building a dominant market share. Even Google's toughest competitors had to admit that Brin and Page had built something special. "In the search engine business, Google blew away the early innovators, just blew them away," says Bill Gates. "And the remains of those people will be long forgotten."

One of PageRank's glories (and its original advantage over AltaVista) was its resistance to spam. (The term in this sense meant not unwanted email but links in its results page that secured undeservedly high rankings by somehow tricking the system.) But as Google became the first place that millions of people looked for information on shopping, medical concerns, their friends, and themselves, the stakes were raised.

The engineer who found himself at the center of the company's spam efforts was an inveterately social twenty-eight-year-old Kentuckian named Matt Cutts. In the summer of 1999, he was pursuing a doctorate at the University of North Carolina when he got stuck with his thesis and on a whim called Google asking what it paid engineers. He got a response saying that it didn't reveal such information until it was actually negotiating with job candidates. Cutts went back to his thesis, but a couple of days later, he got another message: "Would you *like* to be in active negotiation?" Clearly, he'd been Googled. After some phone screeners, he flew out to California, getting a taste for the company's frugality when Google put him up in one of the funky clapboard motels on El Camino Real. Visiting the Google headquarters, he was taken aback by the scene: people working at haphazardly placed sawhorse desks and the director of engineering, Urs Hölzle, playing a high-tech game of fetch with his huge dog, making the floppy beast chase the beam of a laser pointer. In the whirl of interviews, Cutts would remember one question: "How's your UNIX kung fu?" (UNIX being a popular operating system used in many of Google's operations.) "My UNIX kung fu is strong," Cutts replied, deadpan.

He got the job, though his fiancée wouldn't move to California unless they married immediately. After a courthouse wedding and a Caribbean honeymoon, bride and groom drove across the country to Cutts's new job in January 2000, where he sat in a cubicle outside Larry and Sergey's office. Eventually he found himself in an office with Amit Singhal, Ben Gomes, and Krishna Bharat. It was like entering the high temple of search.

Cutts's first job was helping to create a product called SafeSearch, which would allow people to block pornography from search results. Getting rid of unwanted porn was always a priority for Google. Its first attempt was to construct a list of five hundred or so nasty words. But in 2000, Google got a contract to provide search to a provider that wanted to offer a family-safe version of search to its customers. It needed to step up its game. Brin and Page asked Cutts how he felt about porn. He'd have to see a lot of it to produce a system to filter it out of Google.

Cutts asked his colleagues to help him locate adult websites so he could extract signals to better identify and block them, but everyone was too busy. "No one will help me look for porn!" he complained to his wife one night. She volunteered to bake chocolate chip cookies for Cutts to award to Googlers who found porn sites that slipped through Cutts's blockade. At the time, Google was updating the index once a month, and before the new version was released, Cutts would host a Look for Porn Day, bringing in his spouse's confections. "She's still known as the porn cookie lady at Google," he says.

The major porn sites were fine with the process; they knew it was bad for them when searchers unintentionally stumbled upon their warehouses of sin, making them a target for muckrakers and publicity-seeking legislators. But not all such sites were good citizens. Cutts noticed that one nasty site used some clever methods to game Google's blocking system and score high in search results. "It was an eye-opening moment," says Cutts. "PageRank and link analysis may be spam-resistant, but nothing is spam-proof."

The problem went far beyond porn. Google had won its audience in part because it had been effective in eliminating search spam. But now that Google was the dominant means of finding things on the Internet, a high ranking for a given keyword could drive millions of dollars of business to a site. Sites were now spending time, energy, and technical wizardry to deconstruct Google's processes and artificially boost page rank. The practice was called search engine optimization, or SEO. You could see their handiwork when you typed in the name of a hotel. The website of the actual hotel would not appear on the first page. Instead, the top results would be dominated by companies specializing in hotel bookings. This made Google less useful. Cutts went to Wayne Rosing and told him that the company really needed to work on stopping spam. Rosing told him to go ahead and try.

A delicate balance was required. Legitimate businesses as well as shady ones partook in the sport. Highly paid consultants tried to reverse-engineer PageRank and other Google techniques. Even amateurs could partake in the hunt for "Google juice," buying books like *Search Engine Optimization for Dummies*. The conjurers of this field would gather several times a year at conferences, with hotel ballrooms packed to the gills with webmasters and consultants.

Google maintained that certain SEO methods—such as making sure that the subject matter of the page was reflected in the title and convincing webmasters of popular websites to put links to your site when relevant—were good for the web in general. This begged the question: if a website had to hire outside help to improve its rankings, wasn't that a failure of Google, whose job it is to find the best results for its users, no matter how the information is formatted or who links to it?

"Ideally, no one would need to learn SEO at all," Cutts says. "But the fact is that it exists and people will be trying to promote themselves, so you want to be a part of the conversation and say, 'Here are some good ethical things to do. Here are some things that are very high risk. Stay away from them.'" Cutts would admit that because not everyone has SEO expertise, sometimes Google underranks worthy sites. One example was famous: the query "Eika Kerzen." That was not a name but a German candle manufacturer (*kerzen* is the German word for "candles"), whose presence was shamelessly low in rankings for keywords that should have unearthed its excellent products. This matter was dumped on Amit Singhal, who launched an algorithmic revamp of the threshold by which Google translated part of a query into another language, a solution that resolved a whole category of such troublesome results.

A perpetual arms race was waged between Google's search quality algorithms and companies attacking the system for gain. For several years,

Google implemented spam-fighting changes in its monthly index update. It generally aligned those updates to the lunar cycle. "Whenever the full moon was about to appear, people would start jonesing for a Google update," says Cutts. The SEO community would nervously await changes that could potentially knock its links down the relevance chain. As soon as the new values were reflected in the scores, the SEO crowd would try to divine the logic behind the new algorithms and devise responses so the downgraded links could reclaim their previous rankings. This interaction was dubbed "the Google dance." (Things got more complicated after the BART project switched index updates from batch-processed to incremental.)

Often the changes in ranking were slight and there were measures available to restore a link to former glory. But other times Google would identify behavior that it judged an attempt to exploit vulnerabilities in its ranking system and would adjust the system to shore up those weaknesses—relegating those using that method to the bottom of the results pile. Generally, the places that got such treatment had no business showing up in the upper reaches of results for popular keywords: they sneakily worked their way up by creating Potemkin villages full of "link farms" designed to pump up a PageRank. Nonetheless, companies whose sites were downgraded in that matter were often outraged. "It's not like we've put all our eggs in one basket," said the president of an SEO company called WebGuerrilla to CNET in October 2002, "it's just that there's no other basket." That was the month that a company called SearchKing sued Google after a bad night at the Google dance lowered its PageRank score from 8 to 4 and its business tanked. (In May 2003, a judge dismissed the suit, on the grounds that PageRank is essentially an opinion about a website—albeit an opinion expressed by algorithms—and thus was constitutionally protected.)

Cutts understood that the obscurity of the process could sour people on the company and took it upon himself to be the company's conduit to the SEO world. Using the pseudonym "Google Guy," Cutts would answer questions and try as best he could to dispel various conspiracy theories, many of them centered around the suspicion that a sure way to rise in search rankings was to buy ads from Google. But there was only so much he could tell. In large part because of the threat from spammers—as well as fear that the knowledge could benefit competitors—Google treated its search algorithms with utmost confidentiality. Over the years Cutts's spam team grew considerably (as was typical for Google, Cutts wouldn't specify the number). "I'm proud to say that web spam is much lower than it was a few years ago," he says.

But Google's approach had its cost. As the company gained a dominant market share in search—more than 70 percent in the United States, higher in some other countries—critics would be increasingly uncomfortable with the idea that they had to take Google's word that it wasn't manipulating its algorithm for business or competitive purposes. To defend itself, Google would characteristically invoke logic: any variance from the best possible results for its searchers would make the product less useful and drive people away, it argued. But it withheld the data that would prove that it was playing fair. Google was ultimately betting on maintaining the public trust. If you didn't trust Google, how could you trust the world it presented in its results?

3

"If you've Googled it, you've researched it, and otherwise you haven't."

To get a sense of how far Google search advanced in the first six or seven years of the company, one could look through the eyes of Udi Manber.

Manber had watched it all happen, from the outside. He was born in the town of Kiryat Haim, north of Haifa in Israel. He spent so much time in the small library there that he knew nearly every volume in the collection. Manber loved telling visitors to the library which books they might enjoy and which ones might answer their questions. He studied information retrieval and eventually wound up at Yahoo where he brokered the Google deal, until he quit in disgust in 2002. His next job was as the leader of A9, a search start-up funded by Jeff Bezos. In February 2006, he accepted an offer from Google to become the czar of search engineering. It was like someone who worked on space science all his life finally arriving at NASA. "Suddenly I'm in charge of everybody asking questions in the whole world," he says. "I thought I had a reasonable idea of the main problems facing search—what was minor and major. When I got here, I saw they solved many of the minor problems and made more headway on the major problems than I thought possible. Google hadn't just said, 'Here's the state of the art, here's what the textbooks say, let's do it,' they developed things from scratch and did it better."

He was also amazed at how pampered employees were. Every search engineer had exclusive use of a set of servers that stored an index of the entire web—it was the digital equivalent of giving a physicist her own particle accelerator.

One of the first things that happened on Manber's watch was something called Universal Search. In its first few years, Google had developed a number of specialized forms of search, known as verticals, for various corpuses—such as video, images, shopping catalogs, and locations (maps). Krishna Bharat had created one of those verticals called Google News, a virtual wire service with a front page determined not by editors but algorithms. Another vertical product, called Google Scholar, accessed academic journals. But to access those verticals, users had to choose the vertical. Page and Brin were pushing for a system where one search would find *everything*.

The key engineer in this project was David Bailey, who had worked with Manber at A9. Bailey was a Berkeley computer science PhD who had once worried that by following his interests—artificial intelligence and the way computers dealt with natural language—he was locking himself in a field with few practical applications. "I figured that no one is ever going to employ someone who's got a PhD in those things because everybody knows that no computer application worth its salt would deal with plain English text." That was before Google, which he joined in 2004.

At Google, he had the luxury to figure out what he wanted to do. He found himself in an office with Amit Singhal, Matt Cutts, and Ben Gomes (who'd been his buddy in grad school)—"definitely the cool kids' office," he says—and was bowled over by the rich conversations. He needed all the expertise he could find when he was assigned the task of augmenting Google search so that the results page included not only web results but hits from pictures, books, videos, and other sources. If Google really cared about "organizing and making accessible the world's information," as it continually boasted (to the point of arrogance, it seemed), it really had to expand its ten blue links beyond web pages. But the challenges were considerable, and several attempts at executing that vision had flopped. "It had become the project of death," says Bailey.

Nonetheless, Bailey took on the task. He gathered together a team that included a bright product manager named Johanna Wright. Even though Universal Search was something that Larry Page had been urging for years, there was a lot of resistance. "There was definitely a momentum-gathering phase," says Wright, "and finally there was a point where everyone wanted to work on the project, and it all came together."

A big challenge in Universal Search was how to determine the relative value of information when it came from different places. Google had gotten pretty good at figuring out how to rank websites for a given query, and it had also learned a lot about ordering the corpus of pictures or video results to satisfy search requests. Every corpus had a different mix of signals. (Everything on the web, of course, had the benefit of linking information, but things such as videos did not have an equivalent.)

For Universal Search, though, Google had to figure out the relative weight to assign to different sets of signals. It became known as the apples-and-oranges problem. The answer, as with many things in Google, lay in determining context from the data in its logs—specifically in analyzing the long clicks in the past. "We have a lot of signals that tell us the intent of the queries," says Wright. "There could be information in the query that tells us a news result is really relevant and extremely important, and then we'd put it on top of the page." But clearly the solution involved decoding the intent of a query. In some cases, it turned out that Google's signals in a given area weren't effective enough. "It became an opportunity for us to revisit the rankings on those," says Bailey. Eventually, they got to the point where Google, he says, "transformed the ranking problem to be apples to apples."

A knottier problem turned out to be how to show these results on the page. Although Google could figure out that certain results—a video clip, a book, a picture, or a scholarly article—might be relevant to a request, the fact was that users mainly expected web links to dominate the results page.

When the Universal Search team showed a prototype to Google's top executives, everyone realized that taking on the project of death had been worth it. The results in that early attempt were all in the wrong order, but the reaction was visceral—you typed in a word, and all this *stuff* came out. It had just never happened before. "It definitely was one of the riskier things," says Bailey. "It was hard, because it's not just science—there are some judgment calls involved here. We are to some degree using our gut. I still get up in the morning and am astonished that this whole thing even works."

Google's search now wasn't just searching the web. It was searching everything.

In his 1991 book, *Mirror Worlds*, Yale computer scientist David Gelernter sketched out a future where humans would interact, and transact, with modeled digital representations of the real world. Gelernter described these doppelgänger realities as "a true-to-life mirror image trapped inside a computer." He made it a point to distinguish his vision from the trendy sci-fi sensation of the moment, virtual reality—fantasy simulations inside the computer as opposed to a digital companion of the physical world. "The whole point of a mirror world is that it's wired in real time and place—it's supposed to mirror reality rather than being a parallel reality or cyberworld," he once said. But though Gelernter looked on the overall prospect of mirror worlds with enthusiasm, he worried as well. "I definitely feel ambivalent about mirror worlds. There are obvious risks of surveillance, but I think it poses deeper risks," he said. His main concern was that mirror worlds would be steered by the geeky corporations who built them, as opposed to the public. "These risks should be confronted by society at large, not by techno-nerds," he said. "I don't trust them. They are not broad-minded and don't know enough. They don't know enough history, they don't have enough of a feel for the nature of society. I think that's a recipe for disaster."

But like it or not, Google, the ultimate techno-nerd corporation, was building a mirror world. For many practical purposes, information not stored in the vast Google indexes, which contained, among other things, all the pages of the publicly available web, may as well not have existed. "I'd like to get it to a state that people think of it as 'If you've Googled it, you've researched it, and otherwise you haven't, and that's it,'" says Sergey Brin.

While working on its big revisions like Universal Search, Google kept trying to improve its search in general. Dozens of engineers plugged away at failed queries, trying to determine if, as with the case of Audrey Fino, they pointed to deeper algorithmic shortcomings.

The wrong way to fix things was to patch the algorithm to address a specific failed query. That was an approach that didn't scale; it clashed with the idea that Google's giant search algorithm could find the most relevant material by its own logic alone. A legendary story at Google illustrated this principle. Around 2002, a team was testing a subset of search limited to products, called Froogle. But one problem was so glaring that the team wasn't comfortable releasing Froogle: when the query "running shoes" was typed in, the top result was a garden gnome sculpture that happened to be wearing sneakers. Every day engineers would try to tweak the algorithm so that it would be able to distinguish between lawn art and footwear, but the gnome kept its top position. One day, seemingly miraculously, the gnome disappeared from the results. At a meeting, no one on the team claimed credit. Then an engineer arrived late, holding an elf with running shoes. He had bought the one-of-a kind product from the vendor, and since it was no longer for sale, it was no longer in the index. "The algorithm was now returning the right results," says a Google engineer. "We didn't cheat, we didn't change anything, and we launched."

Over the years, Google evolved a set process for search engine tweaks. After an engineer identified a flaw, he or she would be assigned a "search analyst" to manage the next several weeks, during which the improvement would be implemented. The engineer would determine the problem and recode the relevant part of the search algorithm. Maybe it would require adjusting the importance of a signal. Or perhaps altering the interpretation of multiword "bigrams." Or even integrating a new signal. Then the counselor would submit it to testing.

Part of that testing involves hundreds of people around the world who sit at their home computers and judge results for various queries, marking whether the new tweaks return better or worse results than the previous versions. "We cover over a hundred locales," says engineering director Scott Huffman, who is in charge of the testing process. "We have Swiss-French evaluators and Swiss-German evaluators and so on." But Google also employs a much bigger army of testers—its millions of users, virtually all of whom are unwitting lab rats for Google's constant quality experiments.

The mainstay of this system was the "A/B test," where a fraction of users—typically 1 percent—would be exposed to the suggested change. The results and the subsequent behavior of those users would be compared with those of the general population. Google gauged every alteration to its products that way, from the hue of its interface colors to the number of search results delivered on a page. There were so many changes to measure that Google discarded the traditional scientific nostrum that only one experiment should be conducted at a time, with all variables except the one tested being exactly the same in the control group and the experimental group. "We want to run so many experiments, we can't afford to put you in any one group, or we'd run out of people," says a search quality manager. "On most Google queries, you're actually in multiple control or experimental groups simultaneously. Essentially *all* the queries are involved in some test."

In search tweaks, the culmination of the process would come in the weekly Search Quality Launch Meeting. In a typical session in 2009, fifty engineers, mostly in their twenties and early thirties, participated. One test query was "Terry Smith KS," a search that appeared on a screen and had been launched from Springfield, Missouri. The baseline, or unaltered result, assumed that the user wants a link to a town called Smith, in Kansas. A tweaked version of the search included a link to a Terry Smith who lives in Kansas. That was considered a win by the engineers. On the other hand, when a tester in Sykesville, Maryland, tried the query "weather.com Philadelphia," the new version gave a high ranking to a map showing the location of the long-defunct main office of Bell Telephone of Pennsylvania. That was strange and a big loss. This result spurred a vigorous discussion. Someone figured it out: probably, in some earlier period of technology when Bell Telephone was a sort of search engine, that office was the source of the dial-up phone service that told you the weather. Buried on the web somewhere was that factoid, and the alteration to the algorithm had somehow routed it out of its obscurity. In 2009, Google search engineers made more than six hundred changes to improve search quality.

It was no coincidence that the man who eventually headed Google's research division was the coauthor of *Artificial Intelligence: A Modern Approach*, the standard textbook in the field. Peter Norvig had been in charge of the Computational Science Division at NASA's facility in Ames, not far from Google. At the end of 2000, it was clear to Norvig that turmoil in the agency had put his programs in jeopardy, so he figured it was a good time to move. He had seen Larry Page speak some months before and sensed that Google's obsession with data might present an opportunity for him. He sent an email to Page and got a quick reply—Norvig's AI book had been assigned reading for one of Page's courses. After arriving at Google, Norvig hired about a half-dozen people fairly quickly and put them to work on projects. He felt it would be ludicrous to have a separate division at Google that specialized in things like machine learning—instead, artificial intelligence should be spread everywhere in the company.

One of the things high on Google's to-do list was translation, rendering the billions of words appearing online into the native language of any user in the world. By 2001, Google.com was already available in twenty-six languages. Page and Brin believed that artificial barriers such as language should not stand in the way of people's access to information. Their thoughts were along the lines of the pioneer of machine translation, Warren Weaver, who said, "When I look at an article in Russian, I say, 'This is really written in English, but it has been coded in some strange symbols. I will now proceed to decode.'" Google, in their minds, would decode every language on the planet.

There had been previous attempts at online translation, notably a service dubbed Babel Fish that first appeared in 1995. Google's own project, begun in 2001, had at its core a translation system licensed from another company—basically the same system that Yahoo and other competitors used. But the system was often so inaccurate that it seemed as though the translated words had been selected by throwing darts at a dictionary. Sergey Brin highlighted the problems at a 2004 meeting when he provided Google's translation of a South Korean email from an enthusiastic fan of the company's search technology. It read, "The sliced raw fish shoes it wishes. Google green onion thing!"

By the time Brin expressed his frustration with the email, Google had already identified a hiring target who would lead the company's translations efforts—in a manner that solidified the artificial intelligence focus that Norvig saw early on at Google. Franz Och had focused on machine translations while earning his doctorate in computer science from the RWTH Aachen University in his native Germany and was continuing his work at the University of Southern California. After he gave a talk at Google in 2003, the company made him an offer. Och's biggest worry was that Google was primarily a search company and its interest in machine translation was merely a flirtation. A conversation with Larry Page dissolved those worries. Google, Page told him, was committed to organizing all the information in the world, and translation was a necessary component. Och wasn't sure how far you could push the system—could you really build for twenty language pairs? (In other words, if your system had twenty languages, could it translate any of those to any other?) That would be unprecedented. Page assured him that Google intended to invest heavily. "I said okay," says Och, who joined Google in April 2004. "Now we have 506 language pairs, so it turned out it was worthwhile."

Earlier efforts at machine translation usually began with human experts who knew both languages that would be involved in the transformation. They would incorporate the rules and structure of each language so they could break down the original input and know how to recast it in the second tongue. "That's very time-consuming and very hard, because natural language is so complex and diverse and there are so many nuances to it," says Och. But in the late 1980s some IBM computer scientists devised a new approach, called statistical machine translation, which Och embraced. "The basic idea is to learn from data," he explains. "Provide the computer with large amounts of monolingual text, and the computer should figure out himself what those structures are." The idea is to feed the computer massive amounts of data and let him (to adopt Och's anthropomorphic pronoun) do the thinking. Essentially Google's system created a "language model" for each tongue Och's team examined. The next step was to work with texts in different languages that had already been translated and let the machines figure out the implicit algorithms that dictate how one language converts to another. "There are specific algorithms that learn how words and sentences correspond, that detect nuances in text and produce translation. The key thing is that the more data you have, the better the quality of the system," says Och.

The most important data were pairs of documents that were skillfully translated from one language to another. Before the Internet, the main source material for these translations had been corpuses such as UN documents that had been translated into multiple languages. But the web had produced an unbelievable treasure trove—and Google's indexes made it easy for its engineers to mine billions of documents, unearthing even the most obscure efforts at translating one document or blog post from one language to another. Even an amateurish translation could provide some degree of knowledge, but Google's algorithms could figure out which translations were the best by using the same principles that Google used to identify important websites. "At Google," says Och, with dry understatement, "we have large amounts of data and the corresponding computation of resources we need to build very, very, very good systems."

Och began with a small team that used the latter part of 2004 and early 2005 to build its systems and craft the algorithms. For the next few years, in fact, Google launched a minicrusade to sweep up the best minds in machine learning, essentially bolstering what was becoming an AI stronghold in the company. Och's official role was as a scientist in Google's research group, but it is indicative of Google's view of research that no step was required to move beyond study into actual product implementation.

Because Och and his colleagues knew they would have access to an unprecedented amount of data, they worked from the ground up to create a new translation system. "One of the things we did was to build very, very, very large language models, much larger than anyone has ever built in the history of mankind." Then they began to train the system. To measure progress, they used a statistical model that, given a series of words, would predict the word that came next. Each time they doubled the amount of training data, they got a .5 percent boost in the metrics that measured success in the results. "So we just doubled it a bunch of times." In order to get a reasonable translation, Och would say, you might feed something like a billion words to the model. But Google didn't stop at a billion.

By mid-2005, Google's team was ready to participate in the annual machine translation contest sponsored by the National Institute of Standards and Technology. At the beginning of the event, each competing team was given a series of texts and then had a couple of days for its computers to do the translation while government computers ran evaluations and scored the results. For some reason, NIST didn't characterize the contest as one in which a participant is crowned champion, so Och was careful not to declare Google the winner. Instead, he says, "Our scores were better than the scores of everyone else." One of the language pairs it was tested on involved Arabic. "We didn't have an Arabic speaker on the team but did the very best machine translation."

By not requiring native speakers, Google was free to provide translations to the most obscure language pairs. "You can always translate French to English or English to Spanish, but where else can you translate Hindi to Danish or Finnish or Norwegian?"

A long-term problem in computer science had been speech recognition—the ability of computers to hear and understand natural language. Google applied Och's techniques to teaching its vast clusters of computers how to make sense of the things humans said. It set up a telephone number, 1-800-GOOG-411, and offered a free version of what the phone companies used to call directory assistance. You would say the name and city of the business you wanted to call, and Google would give the result and ask if you wanted to be connected. But it was not a one-way exchange. In return for giving you the number, Google learned how people spoke, and since it could tell if its guess was successful, it had feedback that told it where it went wrong. Just as with its search engine, Google was letting its users teach it about the world.

"What convinced me to join Google was its ability to process large-scale information, particularly the feedback we get from users," says Alfred Spector, who joined in 2008 to head Google's research division. "That kind of machine learning has just not happened like it's happened at Google."

Over the years Google has evolved what it calls "a practical large scale machine learning system" that it has dubbed "Seti." The name comes from the Search for Extra Terrestrial Intelligence, which scans the universe for evidence of life outside Earth; Google's system also works on the scale of the universe as it searches for signals in its mirror world. Google's indexes almost absurdly dwarf the biggest data sets formerly used in machine learning experiments. The most ambitious machine learning effort in the UCI KDD Archive of Large Data Sets for Data Mining Research and Experimentation is a set of 4 million instances used to detect fraud and intrusion detection. Google's Seti learning system uses data sets with a mean training set size of *100 billion* instances.

Google's researchers would acknowledge that working with a learning system of this size put them into uncharted territory. The steady improvement of its learning system flirted with the consequences postulated by scientist and philosopher Raymond Kurzweil, who speculated about an impending "singularity" that would come when a massive computer system evolves its way to intelligence. Larry Page was an enthusiastic follower of Kurzweil and a key supporter of Kurzweil-inspired Singularity University, an educational enterprise that anticipates a day when humans will pass the consciousness baton to our inorganic progeny.

What does it mean to say that Google "knows" something? Does Google's Seti system tell us that in the search for nonhuman intelligence we should not look to the skies but to the million-plus servers in Google's data centers?

"That's a very deep question," says Spector. "Humans, really, are big bags of mostly water walking around with a lot of tubes and some neurons and all. But we're knowledgeable. So now look at the Google cluster computing system. It's a set of many heuristics, so it knows 'vehicle' is a synonym for 'automobile,' and it knows that in French it's *voiture*, and it knows it in German and every language. It knows these things. And it knows many more things that it's learned from what people type." He cited other things that Google knows: for example, Google had just introduced a new heuristic where it determined from your searches whether you might be contemplating suicide, in which case it would provide you with information on sources of aid. In this case, Google's engine gleans predictive clues from its observations of human behavior. They are formulated in Google's virtual brain just as neurons are formed in our own wetware. Spector promised that Google would learn much, much more in coming years.

"Do these things rise to the level of knowledge?" he asks rhetorically. "My ten-year-olds believe it. They think Google knows a lot. If you asked anyone in their grade school class, I think the kids would say yes."

What did Spector, a scientist, think?

"I'm afraid that it's not a question that is amenable to a scientific answer," he says. "I do think, however, loosely speaking, Google is knowledgeable. The question is, will we build a general-purpose intelligence which just sits there, looks around, then develops all those skills unto itself, no matter what they are, whether it's medical diagnosis or . . ." Spector pauses. "That's a long way off," he says. "That will probably not be done within my career at Google." (Spector was fifty-five at the time of the conversation in early 2010.)

"I think Larry would very much like to see that happen," he adds.

In fact, Page had been thinking about such things for some time. Back in 2004, I asked Page and Brin what they saw as the future of Google search. "It will be included in people's brains," said Page. "When you think about something and don't really know much about it, you will automatically get information."

"That's true," said Brin. "Ultimately I view Google as a way to augment your brain with the knowledge of the world. Right now you go into your computer and type a phrase, but you can imagine that it could be easier in the future, that you can have just devices you talk into, or you can have computers that pay attention to what's going on around them and suggest useful information."

"Somebody introduces themselves to you, and your watch goes to your web page," said Page. "Or if you met this person two years ago, this is what they said to you." Later in the conversation Page said, "Eventually you'll have the implant, where if you think about a fact, it will just tell you the answer."

It was a fantastic vision, straight out of science fiction. But Page was making remarkable progress—except for the implant. When asked in early 2010 what will come next for search, he said that Google will know about your preferences and find you things that you don't know about but *want* to know about. So even if you don't know what you're looking for, Google will tell you.

What Page didn't mention was how far along Google was on that path. Ben Gomes, one of the original search rock stars, showed a visitor something he was working on called "Search-as-You-Type." Other internal names for it were "psychic" and "Miss Cleo," in tribute to a television fortune-teller. As the more prosaic name implied, this feature enables search to start delivering results even before you finish typing the query. He started typing "finger shoes"—the term that people often use to describe the kind of footwear Sergey Brin often sports, rubberized slippers with individual sleeves that fit toes the way gloves fit your fingers. Of course, Google search, with all the synonyms and knowledge fed to it by billions of searchers who clicked long and those who clicked short, knew what he was talking about. Gomes hadn't finished typing the second word before the page filled with links—and ads!—confidently assuming that he wanted information, and maybe a buying opportunity, involving "Vibram Five Fingers, the barefoot alternative." "It's a weird connection between your brain and the results," Gomes said. (In September 2010, Google introduced this product as "Google Instant.")

"Search is going to get more and more magical," says search engineer Johanna Wright. "We're going to get so much better at it that we'll do things that people can't even imagine." She mentioned one example of a demo being passed around. "Say you type in 'hamburger.' Right now, Google will show you hamburger recipes. But we're going to show you menus and reviews of where you can get a hamburger near you, which is great for anyone living in a place where there are restaurants. I call this project Blueberry Pancakes because if I want to check those out, it'll tell me about the pancake house in Los Altos, and I'll go there. It's just another example of where we're going—Google's just going to really understand you better and solve many, many, many more of your needs."

That would put Google in the driver's seat on many decisions, large and small, that people make in the course of a day and their lives. Remember, more than 70 percent of searches in the United States are Google searches, and in some countries the percentage is higher. That represents a lot of power for the company founded by two graduate students just over a decade ago. "In some sense we're responsible for people finding what they need," says Udi Manber. "Whenever they don't find it, it's our fault. It's a huge responsibility. It's like we're doctors who are responsible for life."

Maybe, it was suggested to Manber, however well intentioned Google's brainiacs were, it was not necessarily a good thing for any single entity to have *the* answer, whether it was hardwired to your brain or not.

"It may surprise you," says Udi Manber, "but I completely agree with that. And it scares the hell out of me."

PART TWO

GOOGLENOMICS
Cracking the Code on Internet Profits

1

"What's a business plan?"

Google CEO Eric Schmidt called it "the hiding strategy." It was Google's biggest secret, maybe even better protected than the secrets behind search. Those who knew the secret—virtually everyone working at Google—were instructed quite firmly to keep their mouths shut about it. Outsiders who suspected the secret were given no winks of confirmation. What made this information easier to keep is that almost none of the experts tracking the business of the Internet believed that Google's secret was even possible.

What Google was hiding was how it had cracked the code to making money on the Internet. Google had invented one of the most successful products in corporate history, and the company was swimming in black ink.

David Krane, who joined Google in 2000 as one of its first press reps, was charged with maintaining the hide and thwarting the seek. Every company he'd ever worked for previously had been more than eager to emphasize the positive when it came to financial results. But at Google, his job was misdirecting journalists away from good news. "We'd cracked one of the unsolved puzzles on the Internet—making money at scale in a way that users embrace," says Krane. "The longer we could avoid other companies figuring that out, the better."

The secrecy dovetailed with Larry Page's hardwired secret-keeping in any case, but Schmidt, who'd joined Google in 2001, had made this covertness a top priority. The new CEO was worried about Microsoft. In the 1990s, at Sun Microsystems and then as leader of the networking company Novell, Schmidt had seen what happened when the 800-pound gorilla of high tech had awakened to a threat to its livelihood, the Internet. Now the scope of Google's success put search into that category; Microsoft just didn't know it yet. Sooner or later the beast would awake, but Schmidt preferred it to do so later.

The hiding ended on April 1, 2004. As a consequence of going public, the company was required to share its internal information with the bankers who would potentially handle the IPO. Google's finance people had gathered the bankers in its headquarters, then located in Mountain View. On the eve of the meeting, chief financial officer George Reyes and Lise Buyer, the director of business optimization, came up with a plan to reveal the secret Google style.

Opening the meeting, Reyes welcomed them. Since the bankers had taken a big gamble by signing on without seeing the bottom line, he said, he'd go straight to the numbers. Then he put up slides with some figures. "You could hear a pin drop," Buyer would later recall. The slides indicated that Google was indeed making pretty good profits. Not earthshaking but more than respectable, especially for an Internet business offering a free service supported only by ads. The bankers listened politely, but you could tell that they'd heard chatter that things had been, well, *better* than good, and they were apparently doing some mental recalculations.

Then Reyes told the bankers he was sorry, but he'd mistakenly put up the wrong slide. Could he display the real numbers? A balance sheet appeared with more than double the revenues and profits on the previous slide. It exceeded even the wildest expectations. April fool!

"George was flawless," says Buyer. "It was a beautiful moment."

As was typical with start-ups, Google was slow out of the gate in generating revenues, but sometime in 2001, net revenues jumped, finishing at $86 million, more than a 400 percent jump from 2000. Then the rocket ship blasted off. Google took in $347 million in 2002, just under a *billion* dollars in 2003, and 2004 was on track to nearly double that. Profits were equally impressive. The 2001 ledger was over $10 million in the black. By 2002 there was a profit of more than $185 million. From that point, profits fluctuated because of huge expenditures in hiring and infrastructure—basically, Google was building the scaffolding to become an Internet behemoth. And its dizzying revenues made it clear that it could afford to do so.

Everyone knew how amazing Google's search technology was. But if you were a banker in that room, you were thinking that the magical ability of Google to find obscure facts on the web was nothing compared to its much more fantastic achievement in building a money machine from the virtual smoke and mirrors of the Internet. In addition, by applying its algorithmic, datacentric approach to economics, Google had quietly begun a revolution that would transform and upheave the worlds of media and advertising.

What was really mind-boggling was that this came from a company that had begun with no idea how to make a buck.

When Salar Kamangar joined Google, his résumé was as threadbare as those of his just-out-of-grad-school bosses. Born in Tehran but raised in the United States, Kamangar was the son of a surgeon. He entered Stanford as a premed student, majoring in biology, but then he decided he didn't want to become a doctor or a scientist. Instead he took courses to get a second degree in economics. Drawing inspiration from his Silicon Valley surroundings, he wanted to start a company. His idea was to speed the transition in classified ads from newspapers to online by setting up Internet photo kiosks. He even pitched the idea to Yahoo cofounder Jerry Yang. Ultimately, he decided that before plunging into entrepreneurial waters, he should get some actual experience in the business world. He was twenty-one years old.

Kamangar more than compensated for his lack of experience with quiet determination. Though he appeared placid and self-contained—and loathed the spotlight—he had a steely, gnawing resolve. As a Stanford junior, he ran for president of the campus Persian Student Association. His campaign platform included boosting membership by combing old freshman picture books for Persian-sounding names; enhancing appreciation of Persian culture in the CIV (Cultures, Ideas, Values) survey courses the university required of all students; and establishing coursework in Farsi. "Stanford," he charged in a speech before the group, "is among the few schools with the shameful record of offering no Farsi classes." He also vowed to have more ski trips. He won the election.

Kamangar made a short list of companies he might like to work for—brand-new start-ups that might take a chance on someone like him—and because, like many Stanford students, he had been playing with an early version of Google, he put it on his list. One day in March 1999 he saw in the *Stanford Daily* that Google was recruiting. He went to the Tresidder student center and found Sergey Brin in a small booth. "Unlike everyone else I'd talked to, he wasn't using jargon. He had a very clear, very ambitious, grand—in some ways grandiose—vision for what Google could become," Kamangar would recall. But Brin was not interested in hiring him. Kamangar was a biology major, not an engineer. Even at that stage, the Google preference was for computer science majors.

Kamangar kept pressing. "He would walk in every day and say, 'I want to work for free,'" says investor Ram Shriram, who was taking a day off from Amazon every week to help protect his investment in Google. Brin finally agreed to take him on part-time to do things that engineers couldn't be bothered with, such as drawing up a business plan. "Neither founder had any interest in that," says Shriram, "They said, 'Yeah, we need money, but we're not really interested in spending too much time on that. What's a business plan?'"

Whatever it was, Google needed one. Its original million-dollar funding had been granted solely on the basis of Google's technology. But the company was already struggling to pay for equipment—its servers were overwhelmed by new users—and Brin and Page needed full coffers to finance their ambitious hiring plans. Venture capital could provide that. But they'd have to make a credible case that Google could one day be profitable.

Kamangar became the point man in one of the weirder VC rounds in Silicon Valley's history. Shriram helped him out, but Salar had a remarkable degree of responsibility. He wrote the slides for the presentations, crunched numbers for the valuation, and, of course, drew up the business plan. Though hired as a part-timer, he went full-time two weeks later, dropping his pursuit of a second degree at Stanford. "It was ten times more exciting than what I was doing at school," he says of Google.

Kamangar sometimes thought the team was in way over its head. He couldn't believe the way Brin and Page would behave. They would go into VC meetings and refuse to answer questions. Even a basic query such as how much traffic was on the site would be stonewalled. What's more, says Kamangar, "Larry and Sergey didn't have the language to say things nicely. They'd be kind of blunt and say, 'We can't tell you.' And the VCs would get very frustrated." One VC actually stormed out of the room. Salar would go to Page and Brin and say, "Did we really want to do that? These are major figures in the Valley, and they seem really pissed off at us. Isn't this bad?"

But Larry and Sergey had complete confidence. They'd tell Salar that the VCs didn't need to know the figures unless they were going to commit the money. Page was working the "hiding strategy" even before he had something to hide.

The elite of the elite venture capital firms in Silicon Valley was Kleiner Perkins Caufield & Byers. The head was John Doerr, a bony blond man with oversize spectacles who looked a bit like Sherman in the *Mr. Peabody* cartoons but loomed over Silicon Valley like Bill Russell in the Boston Celtics' glory years. Originally an engineer at Intel, he joined KPCB in 1980 and rose to the top of the VC heap during the Internet craze, funding Amazon.com and Netscape, among others. At industry conferences, Doerr would speak so rhapsodically of technology's potential to save the world that one might assume his work had been solely in nonprofits.

He was indeed a businessman, though, and his judgment of the brainy, shaggy-haired supplicants who filed into his conference room in the glass-walled buildings in Menlo Park's Sand Hill Road was astute. He'd seen plenty of smart nerds with good ideas, and was more than happy, on the recommendation of Andy Bechtolsheim, to see two more. Google's idea, presented with Kamangar's slides, was compelling. And its founders seemed straight out of the mold of previous winners from Stanford. The meeting was just ending when Doerr asked a final question: "How big do you think this can be?"

"Ten billion," said Larry Page.

Doerr just about fell off his chair. Surely, he replied to Page, you can't be expecting a market cap of $10 billion. Doerr had already made a silent calculation that Google's optimal market cap—the eventual value of the entire company—could go maybe as high as *one* billion dollars. "Oh, I'm very serious," said Page. "And I don't mean market cap. I mean revenues."

More than a decade after that meeting, Doerr would still marvel at the conversation. "I didn't think the guy could do it, but I was impressed," he says. "It had to do with the tone of voice. He wasn't saying this to impress me or himself. This is what he believed. This was Larry's ambition, in a very thoughtful, considered way."

Kleiner Perkins wasn't the only VC that made a connection with Google. Larry and Sergey had also made a big impression on Mike Moritz at Sequoia Capital. Moritz, a former journalist for *Time*, had made his VC bones by funding Yahoo. Like Doerr, he was inundated with pitches at the tail end of the Internet boom days. "It was 1999, so nobody had their feet on the ground," says Moritz. "Everybody was just reacting. The parking lots were always full. There were always queues of people waiting to see us."

But he was primed for this meeting. He believed that the companies that could excel in search had a great future. "That and the fact that these two people were really unusual and that their early version tasted far better than Pepsi," he says. Moritz liked Brin, who did most of the talking, but was equally impressed with Page. "There's always one guy who doesn't talk much, and it's easy to pay attention to the one that talks—invariably that's a big mistake," he says.

Brin and Page wanted to work with Moritz. But they also wanted to work with Doerr. According to Page, it was Andy Bechtolsheim who opined that there was a "zero percent possibility" that it would happen. That was the kind of statement that made Page want to make something happen. "We thought, 'That would be exciting, why don't we do that?'" Page later said. Having not one but two coequal lead funders was like a built-in insurance policy. They would have the combined connections of both firms but not be seen as too closely aligned with either. Also, Page said, an unprecedented combo like that "makes the company very notable." It was not a choice that either Doerr or Moritz would have preferred. But both VCs recognized Google as perhaps the last big score of the Internet boom, so they agreed to the unusual arrangement, splitting the $25 million of capital that the company required.

There were some caveats. Both Doerr and Moritz believed that at some point, Google would have to hire an experienced CEO to head the firm. "It was a very clear understanding," says Doerr. "It's not saying anything negative about them, but I thought we would do a much better job of building a world-class management team if they had a world-class CEO. They agreed, and we closed the financing." Doerr and Moritz would join the founders on the board of directors, along with Shriram. Brin was president and chairman of the board; Page was CEO.

If the founders of Google had difficulty dealing with the $100,000 check they had received from Andy Bechtolsheim, you can imagine how Salar Kamangar felt when he was charged with processing $25 million from the VCs. "This was my first wire transfer, and I wasn't really sure how to do it," he says. But he figured it out, and the $25 million was crucial in building the company.

At that point—spring 1999—Google had yet to formally announce itself to the public. Its product was still in beta. The geek world was already familiar with the search engine, and enthusiastic reviews had appeared in the press. But with news of the twin peaks of venture capital investing $25 million, Brin and Page scheduled their first press event.

Google's first press release was something of a battlefield. Larry and Sergey were both finicky about language. Meanwhile, the VC firms were both determined that no one would read the release and think that the other firm was the lead investor. After more back-and-forths than a long tennis volley, Sergey finally told them to stop. Page and Brin also insisted that the event be held at Stanford, at the Gates Building, where the company had begun. They sent out the map in ASCII characters, which looked cool but was of no help to those unfamiliar with the Stanford campus. The meeting had to start late because some of the reporters couldn't find the building.

Once under way, it went well—a half-dozen or so reporters in a classroom politely listening to Larry and Sergey, who were dressed in matching white polo shirts with the Google logo. Larry began by explaining Google's recently refined mission: "To organize the world's information, making it universally accessible and useful." He talked about Google using artificial intelligence and having a million computers someday. None of this was surprising to the reporters. Start-up founders talked like that all the time. How could the press know that this was the one time when the fantastic predictions would be realized? Sticking to script, the reporters asked how Google would make its money. Brin said it was working on a means to target ads to search. Still, he cautioned, Google's ad system, whatever it turned out to be, would respect its visitors. "Our goal is to maximize the user experience, not maximize the revenue per search," he said.

The meeting over, the young executives offered T-shirts to the reporters. They both looked hugely relieved.

Though Kamangar had done a good job with the business plan, Brin and Page knew that they needed an experienced hand to run Google's business operations, ideally someone with a reputation that would bring credibility to the company. From Kleiner Perkins came a recommendation for a thirty-five-year-old Iran-born executive named Omid Kordestani. He was working for Netscape, which had recently been purchased by AOL, and was looking for a new job. As the engine rooms of the tech boom hadn't yet begun taking water, Kordestani had plenty of choices. One of the most enticing was Apple, newly revitalized with the return of Steve Jobs. Kordestani took a breakfast meeting with Jobs, who gave him a dizzying, messianic pitch. But Kordestani preferred a start-up. He was sufficiently experienced in Silicon Valley ways to know that scruffy former grad students recommended by top VCs were more likely to deliver treasures than even the wizard of Cupertino.

So one evening after work—still wearing the jacket and tie he wore to work at Netscape—he dropped into Google's Palo Alto office over the bike shop. Sergey took Kordestani into the little conference room—and fell silent. Finally, he addressed Kordestani, who was patiently sitting across the Ping-Pong table, and admitted that he'd never tried to hire a business executive and didn't know what he was looking for. "Well, let me help you," said Kordestani, never at a loss in social situations, and he began to talk about what qualities they might consider in a vice president of business operations. Brin called in Urs Hölzle and everyone else still hanging around the office. They all went out for dinner at the Mandarin Gourmet in Palo Alto. Kordestani picked up the tab—not a bad investment, considering that the stake he was granted by accepting the job at Google would be worth $2 billion within a decade.

The VCs thought it would be a good idea for Google to do some marketing to increase traffic and brand recognition—its competitors were running TV ads—but Brin and Page resisted. "Marketing was always the poor stepchild at Google, because Larry and Sergey really thought you can build a company without it," says Cindy McCaffrey, who joined in 1999 to head communications.

Still, on the recommendation of one of its early investors, Google hired a temporary vice president of marketing in August 1999. Scott Epstein had early experience marketing products like Miller Beer, Gorton Fish Sticks, and Tropicana. Later at Excite, he built a multimillion-dollar campaign around the Jimi Hendrix song "Are You Experienced?" His time at Google was brief and rocky.

"They were contrarian," Epstein would later say of the Google founders. "They rejected everything that smacked of traditional marketing wisdom." Larry and Sergey had their own spin on spin. In 1999, at Burning Man (the posthippie festival in Death Valley that Page and Brin regularly attended), they'd been impressed that someone had projected a laser image onto a nearby hill. Wouldn't it be great, they asked Epstein, if we could laser GOOGLE onto the *moon*? More plausible was their suggestion that Google underwrite shows on NPR, and thus began a long history of public radio sponsorship.

To create his marketing plan, Epstein wanted to get a good sense of how consumers viewed Google. This would help him identify the traits to emphasize in his branding efforts. He set up focus groups in San Francisco, Chicago, and Atlanta. Page accompanied him for some of the sessions.

With his obsession on pleasing users, Page was interested in people's impressions about Google search. But Epstein remembers that Page was most engaged when they rented a Hertz car in Atlanta. It had a new NeverLost navigation system, and Page griped about how this feature or that was poorly executed. *He'd* do it better. (Eventually Google would create its own navigation system.)

After a few months, Epstein came up with an elaborate plan, including TV ads, and presented it to the board. The board rejected it.

"It really came down to this," McCaffrey later said. "We have a limited budget. Do we want to put that money into the technology, into the infrastructure, into hiring really great people? Or do we want to blow it on a marketing campaign that we can't measure?" Larry and Sergey told Epstein that his interim stint was over.

The fact was, the Google search engine marketed itself. As people discovered novel ways to use it, the company name became a verb, and the media seized on Google as a marker of a new form of behavior. Endless articles rhapsodized about how people would Google their blind dates to get an advance dossier or how they would type in ingredients on hand to Google a recipe or use a telephone number to Google a reverse lookup. Columnists shared their self-deprecating tales of Googling themselves. McCaffrey and her staff helped this name recognition process along with a list of "true story testimonials." They included the long-lost father discovered after thirty-four years, the job seeker hired after an employer found his résumé through a Google search, the fourth-grader who finally found the information on the plant genus Dinizia needed to finish her rain forest project. A contestant on the TV show *Who Wants to Be a Millionaire?* arranged with his brother to tap Google during the Phone-A-Friend lifeline, instantly discovering that the city founded on the Trinity River was Dallas, and winning $125,000. And a fifty-two-year-old man suffering chest pains Googled "heart attack symptoms" and confirmed that he was suffering a coronary thrombosis. "You saved my life! Had I putzed around waiting for another website to display interminable graphics and banner ads, I might not be here today," he wrote Google. It was the query that launched a thousand feature articles, marketing success that could not be bought—all to the good, because Google wasn't making money.

The post-VC business plan anticipated three streams of revenues: Google would license search technology to other websites; it would sell a hardware product that would allow companies to search their own operations very quickly, called "Google Quick Search Box"; and it would sell ads.

Brin and Page themselves had made the very first licensing deal, with a company called Red Hat, a software company that distributed a version of the free Linux operating system. It earned Google around $20,000. The first substantial web partnership was with Netscape. Kordestani still had good contacts there. It was an ambitious move for Google, because the company did not really have enough equipment to handle the sudden boost in traffic. On the first day of the deal, early arrivals at headquarters discovered that there weren't enough servers to run searches on both Google and the Netscape home page. So Google turned off its own home page—stranding its loyal home page users—until it could get more servers. "It showed we were a real business, doing the right thing and following through on our commitments," says one early Google employee, Susan Wojcicki. (After sharing her home with Google, she had joined the company.)

Google's first stab at selling advertising began in July 1999. When Jeff Dean arrived from DEC—a couple of months before he toiled in the war room to fix the indexing problem—Brin and Page told him that they needed an ad system. But they had no idea what a Google ad should be. Some at Google—including the director of technology, Craig Silverstein—thought that the whole effort was a distraction and that Google should outsource its ad system to some company more accustomed to waddling in the muck of Mammon. "I was like, 'We're not an advertising company, we're a search company—let someone else worry about the advertising,'" says Silverstein. "It was good they did not take my advice."

At the time the dominant forms of advertising on the web were intrusive, annoying, and sometimes insulting. The most common was the banner ad, a distracting color rectangle that would often flash like a burlesque marquee. Other ads hijacked your screen. Google wanted none of that. Brin and Page understood that because of the very nature of search—people are looking for things—Google could provide advertisers a terrific environment. The information in ads could even be as valuable to users as the results Google provided from search queries, they believed.

Dean worked with Marissa Mayer and another engineer to set up a system that could eventually be used for Google to sell such ads to big companies. Google ads would not offend eyeballs or sensibilities. They would be small blocks of text targeted to actual searches. The right keyword would trigger an appropriate ad. Google had an idea for its first test of the system—whenever it saw that a search query had relevance to a published book in print, Google would present a link that would connect to the page where you could buy the tome on the online bookstore Amazon.com. Even for a trial run, Google thought big. "We wanted a different ad for every book in the world," says Jeff Dean.

Dean and his team went through the Amazon.com site to get descriptions of the top 100,000 sellers and extracted relevant keywords. By the fall, the system was running. Google itself placed those ads, perching them on top of the search results with a notation that they were "sponsored links." Because Amazon paid an affiliate fee to anyone who sent a book buyer its way, Google's plan was not only to be the first advertiser on its own system but to make money as well.

"It didn't make much money," admits Dean. Google was not yet drawing enough traffic to amass significant numbers of buyers, and Amazon's affiliate fees—5 percent of the sale—weren't all that high to begin with. "I think we made enough to buy the beer for TGIF [Google's Friday-afternoon employee meeting] for a couple of weeks."

Susan Wojcicki later admitted the real problem: "No one clicked on the ads." But she felt that the experiment was a great success. "It was incredible that we were going to build an ad system at all. What, we didn't have enough to do with search? Now we're asking our engineers, 'Can you develop subsecond delivery times in every language in the world for every specific keyword?' It was impressive that they actually did it."

One contingent unimpressed at this point was Google's investors. By the time of the Amazon affiliate bust in January 2001, it was almost two years after the $25 million investment, and the company was yet to make any money from the 70 million daily searches on its site. One angel, David Cheriton, was joking to friends that all he'd gotten from his six-figure Google investment was a T-shirt—"the world's most expensive T-shirt." To the money people on Google's board, the problem was no joking matter. According to one account, there was a real possibility that some of the funders would be willing to pull out if other investors stepped in to replace their stakes. Page and Brin took steps to seek out those funders. Shriram was helping the effort even as he begged the VCs to stay patient.

But according to Doerr, Google's uncertain financial future wasn't his primary concern. To his horror, only a few months after taking the $25 million from Kleiner Perkins and Sequoia, Page and Brin were welshing on their commitment to hire a CEO. "They called me up one day and said, 'We've changed our mind. You know, we actually think we can run the company between the two of us,'" recalls Doerr.

Doerr's first instinct was to get rid of his shares immediately, but he held off. By then he understood Page and Brin well enough to realize that the way to get them to change their course was by data. The data he had in mind were the firsthand exposure to the most brilliant founder CEOs in the Valley, all of whom, of course, were close to Doerr. He offered Larry and Sergey a deal: They would meet with these leaders and report back, and "after that," he told them, "if you think we should do a search, we will. And if you don't want to, then I'll make a decision about that." Page and Brin agreed to Doerr's Magical Mystery Tour of high-tech royalty: Apple's Steve Jobs, Intel's Andy Grove, Intuit's Scott Cook, Amazon's Jeff Bezos, and others. Then they came back to Doerr. "This may surprise you," they told him, "but we agree with you." They were ready to hire a CEO.

One person, and one only, had met their standards: Steve Jobs.

This was ludicrous for a googolplex of reasons. Jobs was already the CEO of two public companies. In addition, he was *Steve Jobs*. You would sooner get the Dalai Lama to join an Internet start-up. Doerr and Mortiz kept pressing, and the founders reluctantly agreed to keep considering. An Intel executive came close but didn't win them over. Then Doerr fixated on Eric Schmidt.

Schmidt, then forty-six, had been the chief technology officer at Sun Microsystems and was the CEO of the big networking company Novell. He was familiar with boardrooms and bottom lines. But the big factor in his favor was that he was an excellent engineer, with a Berkeley computer science PhD and geek renown as the coauthor of lex, a coding tool that was beloved by hard-core UNIX programmers. "He really understood computer science," says Page. "We actually used lex at Google." What's more, Schmidt wasn't a stuffed shirt. At Sun, there were famous stories of his workers making him the good-natured butt of their annual April Fool's joke. In a video of the 1986 prank, you can see Schmidt, wearing glasses with lenses so huge that he looks sort of like a grown-up version of the nerd kid Steve Urkel in *Family Matters*, staring in stunned but admiring disbelief at the Volkswagen Beetle that his employees had fully disassembled and then reassembled in his office. To cap things off, Brin later said, "He was the only candidate who had been to Burning Man."

When Doerr put Schmidt together with Page and Brin in late 2000, all parties saw the advantages of having Schmidt at Google. Even though they had disagreements in the hours of conversation leading up to the job offer, the Google cofounders respected his acumen and saw that his experience—ranging from start-up to heading a public company—would be a virtue. "He has an amazing group of skills," says Page. For Schmidt's part, he clearly got a charge from the energy and precociousness of the two Stanford dropouts, who were nearly twenty years younger than he.

From the start, Schmidt adopted a public stance toward the founders of unfettered admiration, a position he carefully maintained thereafter. "I fairly quickly figured out these guys are good at what they do," he told me in early 2002. "Sergey is the soul and the conscience of the business. He's a showman who cares deeply about the culture, the one who talks more, with a bit of Johnny Carson. Larry is the brilliant inventor, the Edison. Every day I am thankful I accepted this job offer."

His anecdotes about disagreements with Sergey and Larry followed a consistent storyline: Schmidt expresses a tradition-bound preconception. The young men who, technically at least, report to him, reject the idea and demand that Google pursue an audacious, seemingly absurd alternative. The punch line? "And of course they were right," Schmidt would say. What had seemed crazy was actually a canny assessment of how things worked in the new Internet-based economy! During joint public appearances with Brin or Page, when one of the founders blurted out an outlandish or intemperate remark, Schmidt would place an avuncular hand on the younger man's shoulder and say, "What Larry really means is . . ." and offer a more measured interpretation.

"He kind of came in here like a visiting professor, not the classic CEO with command and control," says Omid Kordestani. That deference would prove a winning strategy, even though for a couple of years there were serious adjustment problems, because the founders clearly suspected that they would have done just fine on their own. Kordestani remembers that as Schmidt's arrival was impending, both founders expressed their anxiety to him. Ostensibly, the issue concerned the titles each of the founders would use to describe his respective role. On a deeper level Sergey was troubled, says Kordestani, because "he was hiring his own boss, in a way, knowing he wants to be the boss." Brin took the title president of technology. Larry was even more troubled. Kordestani had to assure Page that he was still essential and Google would fail without him. Kordestani also reminded Page that he would no longer have to perform tasks that he didn't enjoy, such as dealing with Wall Street and talking to customers. Page wound up describing himself as president of products.

As late as 2002, the founders still sounded bitter when explaining why

Schmidt was hired. "Basically, we needed adult supervision," said Brin, adding that their VC investors "feel more comfortable with us now—what do they think two hooligans are going to do with their millions?" The transition was rocky, but as the years went by, Page and Brin seemed to genuinely appreciate Schmidt's contribution. Page would come to describe the CEO's hiring as "brilliant."

The reaction to Schmidt at Google was instantly positive. His first exposure to the collected Googlers went well, as he smoothly answered questions for an hour at a TGIF. That day, search engineer Matt Cutts came home and told his wife (she of the porn cookies), "I think the value of our stock options just went up a lot." But Schmidt still had to prove that he had the requisite flexibility—and tolerance for flakiness—that would make him an appropriate fit for Google. A test arose almost immediately.

In 2001, Amit Patel, who had focused on the importance of Google's search logs, was in an office with four other people. He noticed that Schmidt was not sharing his relatively small office with anyone. So one day Patel ran into Schmidt and asked if he minded sharing his office.

It was a delicate query for Schmidt, because replying as a CEO at any other company in the world would reply—"No!"—would instantly mark him as "un-Googley." Schmidt's answer showed that he understood the implications of a refusal. "Sure," he said. Patel figured that Schmidt was humoring him and that the new CEO would probably go to Patel's boss, Wayne Rosing, and explain why such an arrangement wouldn't work. But Rosing took Patel's side.

The facilities people, fearing Schmidt's disapproval, wouldn't move Patel's stuff into the CEO's office. No problem. "The rule at Google is that you want to do something, you should do it yourself," Patel says. "I took a desk and moved it myself into Eric's office." Schmidt was on a trip at the time but was forewarned by his administrator that upon his return he would find a cherub-cheeked search scientist in his office. His reaction was indicative of the adaptability that would stand him in good stead at Google—he went with the flow. Then, after six months had passed, "he found a space for me that wasn't so crowded," says Patel.

What did Patel learn about being CEO? "Anything that's wrong sort of bubbles up, so you have to deal with all these problems that aren't the sort of problems I would want to solve," he says. "It's not a job I would want."

He had a better job, anyway. He was an engineer at Google.

▼ ▼ ▼

The fact was, 2001 was a tough time to be Google's CEO. Funds were getting so low that Schmidt instituted a tight-pocketbook policy that limited expenditures to one day a week: if an executive wanted to spend money, he or she would have to petition Schmidt for approval in his office at 10 A.M. on Friday. The VCs were screaming bloody murder. Tech's salad days were over, and it wasn't certain that Google would avoid becoming another crushed radish.

Then came a development that was sudden, transforming, decisive, and, for Google's investors and employees, glorious. Google launched the most successful scheme for making money on the Internet that the world had ever seen. More than a decade after its launch, it is nowhere near being matched by any competitor. It became the lifeblood of Google, funding every new idea and innovation the company conceived of thereafter. It was called AdWords, and soon after its appearance, Google's money problems were over. Google began making so much money that its biggest problem was hiding how much.

2

"When we became profitable, I felt like we had built a real business."

"I hate ads," says Eric Veach, the Google engineer who created the most successful ad system in history.

Veach hailed from Sarnia, a small city in Ontario, Canada. The son of a chemical engineer and a chemistry teacher, he'd been obsessed with math from an early age. He was on the national team in the Math Olympiad, won a contest for a scholarship at the University of Waterloo, and placed in the top twenty in the prestigious William Lowell Putnam Mathematics Competition. After earning a computer science degree at Stanford, he got a job at Pixar, working on the software that renders computer images into lifelike animation. (If you squint, you can see his name in the credits of *A Bug's Life*, *Toy Story 2*, and *Monsters, Inc.*) He liked the work but felt his group at Pixar was "screwed up politically"—he'd had two managers in two years—and began looking for a new gig. He was impressed at the technical chops of the people who interviewed him at Google, so he joined the company in 2000. He found himself working on ads. "At the time, it was a backwater of the company," he says. Seven people worked there.

Considering Veach's loathing of advertising, it was an interesting job switch. But contempt for traditional advertising permeated Google from the top down. In their original academic paper about Google, Page and Brin had devoted an appendix to the evils of conventional advertising. The founders weren't sure what their ads would be but were adamant that they somehow be different.

When Veach arrived, Google's search ads were plain blocks of text that were deemed relevant to the search query that a user typed into Google's search engine. The text blocks had highlighted links that led to a page on the advertiser's website known as a landing page. This had two advantages over traditional advertising: the ads were more effective because they related to what people were looking for at that very moment, and the clicks that registered interest by users could be tracked by Google in its logs. Nonetheless, the early Google ads worked like traditional ones in one key aspect: the advertiser was billed according to how many people viewed the ad. This CPM (cost per thousand) model was the basis of almost all ad markets.

Google ads were sold by actual salespeople. The head of the New York sales force was Tim Armstrong, a tall, engaging veteran of the brief dot-com boom who had majored in sociology and business at Connecticut College. He'd been captain of the lacrosse team. Armstrong had been impressed with Sergey Brin during a breakfast job interview when Sergey made a compelling argument that Google wanted its ads to be not fluff that imposed itself on users but important information that its users wanted. While Google expected to make most of its money from licensing, Armstrong was told, advertising might one day account for as much as 10 to 15 percent of its revenue. Not long after he took the job, a media director at an agency he'd worked with lectured him on the huge mistake he was making. "I don't know much about this place Google," the director said, "but I can tell you that whatever it is, it's not advertising—you should get out of there as quickly as possible." Nonetheless, Armstrong hung on.

Brin emphasized frugality—Eric Schmidt would often admiringly say, "he's cheap"—which Armstrong experienced firsthand when he began signing up customers. The standard way to confirm an ad buy in the business was faxing the insertion orders. But when Armstrong ordered a fax machine, he got a call from George Salah, Google's director of facilities. "Larry and Sergey want to know why you need a fax machine," Salah said. Armstrong explained about insertion orders. Then he got another call. This time, Larry and Sergey wanted to make sure there would be enough sales in the pipeline to justify the cost of the machine.

Google's name for the ads from big accounts that Armstrong visited was "premium sponsored links." They were positioned on top of the search results, against a background of yellow to distinguish them from the search results. Most of his team was in New York City, the hub of the advertising world. (His apartment on the Upper West Side was unofficially the first Google office in New York.) As salespeople had done for nearly a century, Armstrong's team took customers to dinner, explained what keywords meant, and told advertisers what it would cost to buy ads, which were priced according to the number of people who saw them.

But Google wanted something that would work on Internet scale. Since Google searches were often unique, with esoteric keywords, there was a possibility to sell ads for categories that otherwise never would have justified placement. On the Internet it was possible to make serious money by catering to the "long tail" of businesses that could not buy their way into mass media. (The long tail is the term used to refer to smaller, geographically disparate businesses and interests. The Internet—particularly with the help of a search engine like Google—made long-tail enterprises easy to reach.) If you made the system self-service, you could handle thousands of small advertisers, and the overhead would be so low that customers could buy ads very cheaply. So in October 2000 Google launched a product catering to smaller operations that had not previously contemplated an online buy. (Armstrong's team kept selling premium sponsored links to big advertisers.)

Google named the self-service system "AdWords." It was a do-it-yourself marketplace for keywords, purchased by credit card. When someone came to Google and searched using one of those keywords, a few words of text with a link to the advertiser's home page would appear. The ad would be very similar to a search result, only paid for. Those ads ran to the right of the search results, as suggested by an adviser to Google, the Israeli high-tech investor Yossi Vardi. If you drew a vertical line two-thirds of the way across the page and put text ads to the right, he told Brin one day, it would be clear which were the real algorithm-discovered search results—known as "organic" results—and which were paid links. Google also made sure to label the ads "sponsored links" to further distinguish them from the purity of its organic search results.

AdWords prices were fixed according to the position on the page an ad would occupy. If it was in the most desirable position, the top ad on the right, the client would pay $15 per thousand exposures. The second position cost $12, the third $10. There was one feature built in to try to ensure that the most useful ads would appear: advertisers couldn't pay their way to secure the best positions. Instead, the more successful ones—the ones that lured the most people to click on them and go to the advertiser's landing page—would get priority. The percentage of people exposed to ads who responded to them became known as the click-through rate.

This was Google's first stab at what became known as ad quality. It would become a vital component of the company's strategy, which viewed the ad system as a virtuous triangle with three happy parties: Google, the advertiser, and especially the user. Unwanted ads made unhappy customers, so Google made it a high priority to calibrate the system to drive out ads that were irrelevant or annoying.

One day in October 2000 the engineers who coded the system tested AdWords with a little text ad of their own that read, "Have a credit card and 5 minutes? Get your ad on Google today." It was shown to only a small number of users. Within minutes, someone had clicked on it and began filling out the form. And barely a half an hour after that, someone who typed in the words "Live Lobsters" on Google would see a "sponsored link" on the right side of the search results that read, "Live Mail Order Lobsters," placed by a small business called Lively Lobsters that had never previously placed an online ad.

Though the system quickly became popular, it was too easy to game. Advertisers had a huge incentive to click on their own ads to generate a high click-through rate and thus improve the position of the ads in subsequent searches.

As a consequence of the VC pressure on Google to make some real money, Page and Brin had instructed Salar Kamangar to look into ways to make more money with the ad system. In November 2000, Kamangar visited Veach, and as they spoke Veach realized that Google's desperate financial situation would give him an opportunity to use his mathematical expertise to improve the concept of advertising. Maybe, he thought, he could even make advertising itself less hateful. Veach believed that a well-placed search ad could be more useful than a search result. They began working together.

Every week or so, Brin or Page, sometimes both, would come by to toss ideas around and ask why the system wasn't done yet. Page was adamant that the system be simple and scalable. He thought that the system should be so easy for advertisers that all they would need to do was give their credit card number and point Google to their website. They shouldn't even get involved with choosing keywords—Google would choose them. That was an idea that made sense, though many advertisers always want a say in choosing keywords.

Some other suggestions from Page, though, were baffling. "Larry always has far-fetched ideas that may be very difficult to do, that he wants done now," says Veach. During one session, when discussing the fact that not all countries commonly use credit cards, Page proposed taking payments in barter appropriate to the home country. For instance, Page suggested, for transactions in Uzbekistan, Google could take its payment in goats. "Maybe we can get to that," Veach responded, "but first let's make sure we can take VISA and MasterCard."

One of the key breakthroughs came when Veach and Kamangar decided to use auctions to sell ads. It made perfect sense. In a dynamic marketplace, auctions allow you to find the sweet spot where buyers and sellers both win. The source of their idea was the business model of one of Google's competitors. GoTo was the brainchild of one of the most fecund minds of the Internet age, an energetic Caltech grad named Bill Gross. Gross's IQ and geek factor were both off the charts. He began to make a name for himself in the 1980s as an entrepreneur who came up with ideas that applied clever technological tricks, often ones that exploited tempting market niches.

During the late 1990s Internet boom, Gross created Idealab, a company that would incubate new companies. He envisioned creating several tech start-ups a year, rolling them out the way a movie studio launches films. During the next few years, several Idealab companies had smashingly successful IPOs—and even more spectacular crashes when the music stopped in 2000. But one Idealab company had emerged as a winner, its search company GoTo.

In a way, GoTo was a Bizarro-world version of Google. Whereas Google had skyrocketed to fame as a search engine with innovative technology and no discernable way to make money, GoTo got pans for its search strategy, specifically its mixing of paid and organic search results. But its revenue model was brilliant. Gross's basic model was Yellow Pages ads, in which businesses paid a premium to place their ads in the relevant category. The biggest impact was made by a full-page ad, and the equivalent of that in a search engine was a high place in search results. Gross's innovation was to have advertisers compete for those places: to get your ad in the search results under a given keyword, you had to outbid other advertisers in an auction. His colleagues didn't warm to it. "Everybody in the room had a look on their faces like, 'You've gone nuts.' But I kept pitching it, and they admitted that there might be something to it, but it would be controversial," he says.

As Idealab prototyped the idea, Gross had another one. Every month he would gather the CEOs from his fifteen or so companies and have them compare how much they paid to get traffic to their websites through the banner ads that were then the only form of Internet advertising. The most useful metric was arrived at when the cost of the ad was divided by how many times someone clicked on a banner and actually went to a site. Even though ads were paid for according to how many people saw them, it was the clicks that made them worthwhile. "So the thing hit me," says Gross. "Why don't we make a search engine where you just pay by the click?" That way, advertisers could know the values of ads from the start.

Gross announced GoTo at the TED conference, a high-profile industry conclave, in February 1998. His presentation introduced the hugely innovative pay per click and auction, but what stuck in people's minds was that GoTo's paid search results showed up in the sacred territory of organic results. Techno-pundits viewed the ethics of search engines like the ad/editorial separation in newspapers and magazines. There seemed something fishy, even venal, in selling results that would be intermingled with the best guesses of algorithms. (For its nonpaid results, GoTo licensed search engine technology from Inktomi.) The audience at TED, where even fairly tepid presentations often get standing ovations, actually *hissed* during Gross's demo. (Page and Brin considered GoTo's mixing of paid and organic links an abomination.) "It was very distasteful to people," says Gross. "But I didn't consider that the paid links were part of the organic results."

GoTo's search capabilities weren't strong enough to lure users to its site. Instead, Gross paid other Internet companies to use GoTo in the search engine they offered visitors, figuring he'd come out ahead when people clicked on the ads. His biggest and most successful arrangement was struck in late 2000: GoTo paid AOL $50 million to become its search engine. When AOL's users did a search, they would see Inktomi web results mixed with GoTo's ads. In 2000, GoTo reaped $100 million in revenue and as was customary in the dot-com world, it went public while still in the red. The IPO brought in a billion dollars.

In all the excitement, GoTo made a big mistake of omission. "We were ready to go public and were on fire, revenues going through the roof and all that, and were getting our IP [intellectual property] portfolio together for the bankers, and everybody was like, 'What patents do we have?' And we didn't have too many," says Gross. Worse, since patents had to be filed within one year of public exposure, GoTo had missed the window to patent ad sales with real-time auctions and pay per click. All GoTo could do, Gross says, "was patent everything else we could think of, a bunch of obscure things like the way we accepted bids. These were silly patents, but the real patents would have been worth billions."

In 2001, GoTo changed its name to Overture. The new moniker reflected the direction the company had taken. Very few people thought to "go to" Gross's company. Instead, like a musical introduction, Overture, embedded in various portals such as AOL, was a prelude to an ultimate destination. Gross himself felt that the approach was misguided. Originally, he had thought of GoTo as a consumer brand. That was gone. "We thought we could win more deals by only being a service provider and not having our own site. It was the beginning of the end for us, but Overture was still worth a fortune."

Google knew all about Overture, of course. At the TED conference in 2001, Gross had actually suggested to Page and Brin that the companies merge. The Googlers would have nothing to do with any system that mixed organic search results with ads. Still, they wondered whether taking over Overture's contracts would solve some of their revenue problems at the time, and there was talk of a partnership. Bill Gross even ginned up a demo called GOTOOGLE, with two columns of results, one of them the Google organic results and the other GoTo's paid result. But Salar Kamangar successfully argued against any kind of deal, saying that Google could do it alone. He was sure that he could build a better system, beating Overture at its own cost-per-click, auction-ized game.

Eric Veach particularly disliked one aspect of the Overture auction system: the fact that advertisers were bound to pay the amount they had bid, even if the next lowest bidder had offered significantly less. "That means that advertisers always have an incentive to lower their bids [in subsequent rounds]," he says. (This was known in the auction world as "bid shading.") As an example, he would cite the case where an advertiser bid 50 cents and the next highest bidder offered only 40 cents. Clearly the high bidder would be unhappy, because the optimal bid was 41 cents, and the winner was stuck with paying nine cents too much. A cottage industry of software vendors had provided programs to automate bid shading on Overture, so winners would keep submitting slightly lower bids, and losers would edge up. "I wanted to avoid that cat-and-mouse game," says Veach.

So Veach devised a different model: the winner of the auction wouldn't be charged for the amount of his victorious bid but instead would pay a penny more than the runner-up bid. (Example: If Joe bids 10 cents a click, Alice bids 6, and Sue bids 2, Joe wins the top slot and pays 7. Alice is in the next slot, paying 3.) It was incredibly liberating because it eliminated the fear of "winner's remorse," where the high bidder in an auction feels suckered by paying too much. In the Google model, no one would feel like an idiot for paying a dollar a click when the competitor below them bought a slot on the same page, positioned just a few pixels lower than their ad, for only 10 cents a click. In that case, a winner would get the prime position for 11 cents.

Veach knew in his heart this was the right way to go, but he had to do a lot of explaining. "Larry and Sergey kept asking me if it wasn't simpler to have an auction where we just have people pay what they bid," he says. "And I kept saying, 'No,' because then people have this incentive to keep lowering their bids."

To run its ad operation, Google had hired Sheryl Sandberg, former chief of staff to the secretary of the treasury in the Clinton administration. She'd gotten to know Eric Schmidt when he visited D.C. to argue against Internet taxes. Though she'd never been involved in high tech—besides her Treasury post, her résumé included McKinsey & Company and the World Bank—she'd spent the past few years observing what was happening in Silicon Valley. Part of her job at Google was explaining its innovative auction. She kept staring at the formula, wondering why it seemed so familiar. So she called her former boss, Treasury Secretary Larry Summers.

"Larry, we have this problem," she said. "I'm trying to explain how our auction works—it seems familiar to me." She described it to him.

"Oh yeah," said Summers. "That's a Vickery second-bid auction!" He explained that not only was this a technique used by the government to sell Federal Reserve bonds but the economist who had devised it had won a Nobel Prize.

Veach had reinvented it from scratch.

One fan of Veach's system was the top auction theorist, Stanford economist Paul Milgrom. "Overture's auctions were much less successful," says Milgrom. "In that world, you bid by the slot. If you wanted to be in third position, you put in a bid for third. If there's an obvious guy to win the first position, nobody would bid against him, and he'd get it cheap. If you wanted to be in every position, you had to make bids for each of them. But Google simplified the auction. Instead of making eight bids for the eight positions, you made one single bid. The competition for second position will automatically raise the price for the first position. So the simplification thickens the market. The effect is that it guarantees that there's competition for the top positions."

Veach and Kamangar's implementation was so impressive that it changed even Milgrom's way of thinking. "Once I saw this from Google, I began seeing it everywhere," he says, citing examples in spectrum auctions, diamond markets, and the competition between Kenyan and Rwandan coffee beans. "I've begun to realize that Google somehow or other introduced a level of simplification to ad auctions that was not included before." And it wasn't just a theoretical advance. "Google immediately started getting higher prices for advertising than Overture was getting," he notes.

That wasn't only because of the auction model; Veach and Kamangar had made other significant advances. One of the biggest was the adoption of the other Overture idea, pay per click. Google's improved version of the original AdWords, called AdWords Select, would no longer charge per impression, according to how many people saw an ad. Instead, the click-through rate would become the measure of online advertising. The bids advertisers submitted would specify how much they were willing to pay each time a user clicked on the ad and was sent to the landing page on the advertiser's website.

The longtime joke in the marketing world was that only half of advertising is worth the money—but no one can tell which half. Google was switching the game: using its system, you would pay for ads only when they worked.

That was not all. The ad model that Veach and Kamanger created had yet another major innovation, but this one was exclusively Google's. It would become the least understood, most controversial, and ultimately most powerful component of AdWords Select: a built-in function to regulate ad quality. The new system instituted financial incentives for *better* ads. It lowered the price for effective ads and meted out monetary punishment and even an online ad version of the death penalty for bad ads. It also opened Google to the charge that it had created a "black box" in which advertisers could never understand, or trust, the calculations that Google made to place their ads.

Here was the rub: The bids submitted by contenders for the ad slots were only half of what ultimately determined the winners of the auction. The other half was the quality score. This metric would assure that the ads Google showed on its results page were helpful to its users—a high quality score meant that the ad was relevant to the user's quest. Low quality scores were for ads that were irrelevant, misleading, or even spamlike. In the early version of AdWords, the sole determinant of the quality score was Google's guess at the percentage of times a user would click on an ad when it appeared on a results page—the click-through rate. Later Google used a more complicated formula to determine quality score by adding factors such as the relevance of the ad to the specific keyword and the quality of the landing page. But the biggest factor remained the predicted click-through rate.

Say that Alice, Juan, and Ted are all bidding for the keyword "hand lotion." Alice is selling an artisanal form of hand lotion popular in upscale spas. Juan owns a big drugstore that sells hand lotion, among many sundries. Ted has a travel site. He isn't selling hand lotion at all but wants to expose his ad to the kind of person who buys hand lotion. Alice bids ten cents per click. Juan bids fifteen cents. Ted bids fifty cents. If you think that Ted's high bid automatically puts him in the top position, you're wrong. It's quite possible that Alice, the low bidder, would get the favored spot. Google's calculations might determine that users who click on her site are more likely to find what they want and thus assign her a very high quality score. Juan's quality score would be downgraded—as would his effective bid—because users may go to his site and have difficulty finding hand lotion. He may be in position two, paying a little less than Alice. Ted would have an even lower quality score. People looking for hand lotion are unlikely to click on a travel ad. His bid would be downgraded even more. (He may even be required to pay a prohibitively high "minimum bid"—a practice that ultimately engendered a lot of grumbling among certain advertisers.)

The beauty of the ad quality formula, says Sheryl Sandberg, is that "it made the advertiser do the work to be relevant. You paid less if your ads were more relevant. So you had a reason to work on your keyword, your text, your landing page, and generally improve your campaign." There were some downsides, though. Chief among them was that the system was fairly complicated and risked befuddling an advertiser.

Veach would acknowledge this. "It's not so much that any of these ideas on their own are complicated," he says. "But when you put the three together, you can't easily explain it to advertisers." On the other hand, he adds, "It actually turns into a fun mathematical problem, which I loved."

From the start, Page and Brin had an idealistic view that Google would run ads only if users deemed them a useful feature. Using mathematical wizardry, Veach and Kamangar had come up with a mechanism to realize that fantastic aspiration. Google's original system asked advertisers to pay a fixed rate to expose their ads on a results page triggered by targeted keywords. The new system asked advertisers to participate in an auction that determined how much they would pay every time someone clicked on the targeted ad. What's more, by rewarding better ads the new system made users happier by increasing the odds that what appeared on the page was relevant to their queries. The system enforced Google's insistence that advertising shouldn't be a transaction between publisher and advertiser but a three-way relationship that also included the user.

But would it work? For one thing, executing the system was a huge technological challenge. Every AdWords Select ad would be the winner of a unique auction requiring the execution of a complicated formula. The auction would be conducted in stealth, generated the instant someone typed a keyword into the Google search box, with the result shown in a fraction of a second. "I don't know the number of auctions that we run per day, but for purposes of argument, use a billion or a hundred million," says Schmidt. "We run many more auctions than anyone else on the planet because we run them in real time, we run one auction per ad per page, and that's multiplied by the numbers of ads per page. It's a phenomenal number. Technologically, because of latency, you have to do this very, very quickly." Fortunately for Google, even in 2002, when the new system was completed, the company was fanatically focused on huge computational feats performed at dizzying speed on a platform of thousands of computers, so it was able to leap the technology hurdle.

The dicier challenge was getting skeptical customers of the original AdWords to leave a system they were happy with to try this complicated new one. On January 24, 2002, Google tested AdWords Select by offering it to selected advertisers. In order to lure them to the new program, Google stacked the deck: it placed ads bought under the new AdWords Select system in more favorable positions than the advertisers had actually paid for. "The old AdWords customers would say, 'How do we get to position one?' And we'd say, 'Oh, you sign up to this system over here.' They were signing up in droves, so it really simplified our lives," says Veach. Spurred by the initial returns from higher positions, advertisers began spending more money in the new system—and getting clearly better returns. Within a month, Google simply pulled the plug on the old CPM system and sent all its advertisers an email informing them of the change.

From that point on, revenue from the right-hand side of Google's search results page—which had previously constituted only 10 to 15 percent of Google's ad take, with the bulk coming from the direct sales of premium ads—began rising. That area of screen real estate, which had previousxly been regarded as the wrong side of the tracks in Googleland, had been transformed as suddenly and dramatically as South Beach after Madonna bought a condo there. It wasn't just little guys with credit cards buying AdWords Select. National corporations such as Procter & Gamble and Coca-Cola began bidding at figures that exceeded those coming from the corporations that had been occupying slots in the premium program. "There was definitely a bit of a conflict there, because now some of the internal salespeople had to deal with AdWords, almost against their will," says Veach.

In any case, Google was reaping rewards, and 2002 was its first profitable year. "That's really satisfying," Brin said at the time. "Honestly, when we were still in the dot-com boom days, I felt like a schmuck. I had an Internet start-up—so did everybody else. It was unprofitable, like everybody else's, and how hard is that? But when we became profitable, I felt like we had built a real business."

Best of all was that Google, against all odds, was making that profit without surrendering its ideals. "Do you know the most common feedback, honestly?" Brin asked. "It's 'What ads'? People either haven't done searches that bring them up or haven't noticed them. Or the third possibility is that they brought up the ads and they did notice them and they forgot about them, which I think is the most likely scenario." (This would track with an experiment that Google repeated regularly—the "no ads" test that compared users who saw ads with those served results pages free of sponsored links. Every time the test was run, the outcome was similar: dropping ads did not increase searching. More often than not, the users in the control group who continued to see ads searched *more* than those with ad-free pages. Google's relieved conclusion: its ads made people happy.)

From that point on, Brin and Page saw nothing but glory in the bottom line. Google was profitable, and its hiding strategy was successfully masking the extent of its success. Its name was synonymous with search. *The Wall Street Journal*'s famous tech critic Walt Mossberg called it "the most useful site on the World Wide Web." Everyone was asking the founders when they would have an IPO, but "it's not an issue for us," Page said in 2002. "Every month we make more money than the last one."

The only slight regret? They never got those PhDs.

"I've been meaning to," said Sergey.

"Maybe someday," said Larry.

"My mom keeps asking," said Sergey.

Larry frowned. "My mom doesn't ask me anymore."

Originally, Google's goal in providing its search engine results to portals such as Yahoo and Excite was to collect licensing fees in exchange for providing a higher quality of search. Now that Google search came bundled with ads that brought cash with every click, the business model changed. Google could offer a portal not only an effective search feature but a nice share of the revenue that came from those clicks. Google's business plan, with revenues split in thirds among syndication of search, customized search for businesses, and advertising, was delegated to the delete bin. Hereafter, ads would dominate.

Google's main competition for the portal deals was the company that had invented ad auctions, Overture. "For a long time they were ahead of us," says Susan Wojcicki, who began leading the ad team in 2002. "But now we had a more targeted ad system that could generate better results for our advertisers and more revenue for our publishers." Google's first breakthrough was a deal with the Internet service provider EarthLink. On the day the arrangement was announced, Overture's total stock value dropped by $800 million. But the big whale was AOL, the dominant portal on the Internet, with hundreds of millions of daily visitors. Its contract with Overture was due to expire in 2002. "It was one of the biggest profit centers at AOL, making them hundreds of millions," says Bill Gross. "We would put our paid results at the top of the list for AOL search queries. Once they got hooked on that heroin, there was no changing."

Nonetheless, AOL was eager to have Google and Overture compete for the new contract, and its huge audience allowed the online service to dictate onerous terms, including a huge guarantee, requiring the winner to pay AOL a giant nonrefundable advance on sales. Google's executives were split on whether to meet its demands. "There was real risk," says Wojcicki. "We could make $40 million on the deal, or we could lose $40 million. We only had $10 million in the bank. So it really mattered who was right."

Eric Schmidt, the CEO for only a year and not yet unconditionally trusted by Brin and Page, thought it too risky. "I was the conservative, everyone else was a liberal," he says. But the founders were gung ho. To make sure that not every minute of their interaction was spent arguing about AOL, Schmidt suggested that they limit the discussion to a daily bout at 4 P.M. "We would haul everybody in and just argue the numbers," he says. Ultimately, Schmidt would take his case to the board—and find that in this case the VCs were willing to back Brin and Page. "The board said that in the worst possible case, they would come up with the $50 million, so it wouldn't bankrupt the company," says Schmidt.

As negotiations progressed, Omid Kordestani became a familiar figure in Dulles airport, near AOL's Vienna, Virginia, headquarters, trying to convince AOL that this not-quite-ripe company would be able to satisfy all its requirements in a big ad deal. AOL wanted to know the difference between Google's auction and Overture's. One of those requirements was that the winning company have a broad sales force. "There was a perception that there weren't a lot of people working for Google," says former Google ad exec Jeff Levick. And, he admits, the perception was accurate. When AOL did an onsite visit to New York, "we had to physically marshal in people to make it look like we were a real company," he says.

Google was better positioned for the deal than Overture was. First, its search technology was better. Also, adding AOL users to its search traffic would increase the value of Google ads, even those served at www.google.com, because it would have a larger inventory for search ads, and more spirited bidding. As a result, Google could afford to give up a much higher share of the revenue from the ads clicked on by AOL users. At least that was Google's best judgment; later on, even Brin would acknowledge that if that assessment had been overly optimistic, the $50 million guarantee would have bankrupted Google.

Ultimately, AOL became convinced that Google could make it more money than Overture and so gave the Googlers the contract.

Now Google had to handle a deluge. The difficulties didn't come in the raw traffic; Google had been quietly building its infrastructure for years and was confident it could handle more users. But Google had assured AOL that no ad would appear on its service that violated AOL's standards. It was unprepared to implement that promise.

Google had already given some thought to the matter of ad approval. Originally, there had been a consensus that screening ads was a good idea. The lone dissenter was Larry Page, who believed that letting customers see their ads appear almost instantly would be intoxicating. Not to mention that skipping a labor-intensive step could pacify Google's god of scale. The AdWords business team, who had actual experience selling ads in traditional media, worried that if you didn't screen ads, users' screens would be plagued by neo-Nazi and sex ads. But Page argued that if something distasteful showed up, Google could address it afterward. Fixing the small percentage of bad ads after the fact was much more efficient than building a bureaucracy to prevent any from appearing in the first place.

But AOL wanted a system guaranteed to ensure that no objectionable phrases would appear for even a second. "The only way to meet the policy was manually reviewing the ads," says Sandberg. She was taken aback when Kordestani came by one day to say, "We're going live at midnight—how many approved ads do we have?" The answer was none.

Sandberg had to quickly assemble a human wave of screeners to zip through thousands of ads for instant review. She contacted a temp agency, which sent over fifty people. She also pulled people from other areas of Google on an emergency basis. Still, Google's software for approving ads and putting them into the approval bin wasn't built to handle such volume. Sandberg told everyone to stop and go home. "Over the weekend, our ads engineering team built us a new approval bin," she says.

The job was trickier than anyone thought—to do it right, the screeners actually needed deft judgment to quickly determine whether thumbs would be up or down on each ad. Two weeks later, only one of the fifty workers was deemed worth keeping. Sandberg found some better suppliers. One was a specialized temp agency that had done some hiring for Microsoft. Another was craigslist, which was just emerging. Both had access to unemployed victims of the recent tech bust. "We could hire all these graduates of the Ivy League and great state schools to be temps," says Sandberg.

Later, Google figured out how to scale the process by using better algorithms and data. "Google does a hundred thousand ads a day, and most of it's automated," Sandberg later said. "We had to get fast and good because we grew so quickly."

But the ad policy had more implications than just pleasing AOL—it turned out that Page and Brin had their own ideas about what was proper in an ad. When Alana Karen arrived at Google in late 2001 and volunteered to work on ad policy issues, she found only a rudimentary set of rules, such as a ban on pornography. But she learned that Page and Brin were concerned that Google ads uphold their "make the world better" standard. That presented tricky problems. Products such as tobacco were clearly out. Also, Google started to ban liquor ads. Then came the discovery that some advertisers were offering wine or other soft liquor in gift baskets. That didn't seem wrong. So the policy was amended to allow beer and wine. Later Google realized that it was appropriate to have different standards in different countries. For instance, in Japan hard-liquor advertising was more culturally acceptable in mass media. Eventually Google figured out a way to balance its corporate conscience with the concept of running ads that didn't meet a standard of healthy living. In 2003, Alana Karen took charge of a program called Google Grants, which gives free ads to nonprofit, socially beneficial organizations. "It's like carbon offsets," she explains.

Google came to see the AOL deal as a tipping point. Before AOL, it had a limited inventory of searches that would be relevant to a given keyword—if you were selling ski equipment in early 2002, your ads would run only in response to people who typed a keyword that involved winter sports. But after AOL the number of pages multiplied, so the inventory of popular terms almost always met the demand.

No one was sure how advertisers would respond when their opportunities were just about infinite; Google now could give them more customers for keywords than they could possibly budget for. Yet money spent for Google ads seemed well spent. "We didn't know how valuable increased inventory would be—what happens if you double it overnight?" says Wojcicki. "It turns out that advertisers will keep using it up."

In July 2003, Yahoo bought Overture for $1.63 billion, sending shockwaves through the Googleplex. Overture's ad technology would be linked to an effective search engine—and perched on the world's biggest portal. In addition, Overture had an active lawsuit going against Google. Even though Overture had failed to nail down the patent for the core of its ad system, it claimed that Google was infringing on the "obscure, silly patents" (in Bill Gross's words) it did own.

Google's biggest fear was that Yahoo would begin innovating with Overture and improve its system to Google's level. Yahoo had already decided to replace Google's search engine with its own system. Its then CEO, a former Hollywood executive named Terry Semel, recalls that after that announcement, Page and Brin came to his office and told him the two companies were now at war. Semel was amused. "Are you going to *bomb* us?" he asked. Semel knew that there were profits to be made even as a runner-up to Google. But Yahoo never figured out how to innovate with Overture.

"We used to benchmark ourselves against Overture," says David Fischer, a former Google ad executive who worked under Sheryl Sandberg. "But at some point Sergey just said, 'Why are we paying attention to them?' That's the Google way—we don't confine ourselves to catching other people."

Years later, Gary Flake, the chief science officer at Overture and leader of Yahoo's search efforts in the mid-2000s, would amuse audiences with a slide show that documented Overture's failures to respond to Google's advances. "How did I lose so badly?" he would ask, calling it a classic case of the innovator's dilemma, where the pioneer in a field—in this case, search advertising—found itself locked into the model that had initially brought it success. Google innovated circles around Overture, focusing on its core obsessions of speed and scale. Overture required its advertisers to pick specific keywords; Google would match an ad to many keywords, some of them with subtle connections discovered by analysis of the behavior of its millions of users. Overture concentrated on high-value accounts that it sold by hand. Google built a self-service system that allowed it to accommodate hundreds of thousands of advertisers. Overture did implement some of Google's innovations, such as the second-price auction. But by then AdWords had left Overture and Yahoo in the dust.

(Bill Gross would later shrug off the fact that his ideas involving pay per click and ad auctions had made billionaires at Google but not at Idealab. "I feel we won," he says. "There was the satisfaction of breaking the code. We originally invested $200,000 in GoTo, and when we sold Overture, we made $200 million. That was a pretty great return. And we learned our lessons about patent protection.")

AdWords Select rolled out in February 2002. The AOL deal went into effect in May. Suddenly, Google's financial crisis was over. Now Google had a cash cow that would fund the next decade's worth of projects, from brilliant to lunatic. In 2007, writing about the "spectacular commercial success" of the second-price auction model, economists at Stanford, Harvard, and the University of California at Berkeley described it as "the dominant transaction mechanism in a large and rapidly growing industry."

Before AdWords Select and the AOL deal, Eric Schmidt often passed by Sheryl Sandberg's cubicle and asked her how many advertisers Google had. "Not many," she would say. Later in the day, he'd ask her the same question. "Eric," she'd say, "not many more than we had three hours ago." In 2002, all that changed. AdWords Select was drawing new advertisers to the Internet, and the AOL partnership was pulling in ones that had resisted Google. "So we just started growing," says Sandberg. "It went unbelievably well. And nobody knew just how well until the IPO."

3

"When the money keeps rolling in, you don't ask how."

AdWords would soon get a sibling that would be a mighty companion in piling up revenues. It would expand Google's advertising power beyond search pages, establishing the company as a provider of ads to all sorts of online properties—and giving it a foothold to making all the world a platform for Google ads.

Typically, it began as an engineering obsession. Georges Harik, one of Google's first ten employees, had impressed Larry Page during his initial interview in 1999 when he described his longtime goal of using artificial intelligence to analyze data, winnowing down digital content to themes that human beings would recognize. If you did that, he told Page, you might use the information to target ads to web pages. Or, who knew, maybe something else. "It was one of ten ideas I brought up which were equally nonobvious," he says. And Larry Page said, "Why don't you work here?" (Harik actually had him at "artificial intelligence.") Harik, who had a doctorate in machine learning from the University of Michigan, was also impressed with Page. "He was the smartest guy I talked to in Silicon Valley, and I told my parents I just interviewed with a six-person company that in five or six years was going to be the biggest on the Internet," he says. So Harik left his job at Silicon Graphics and joined Google.

Harik began by helping Urs Hölzle create Google's infrastructure, but he kept thinking about data analysis and artificial intelligence. One day, while talking to Ben Gomes in the kitchen in the Googleplex at 2400 Bayshore Avenue, he described his concept of how compressing data was equivalent in many ways to understanding it. That concept, he argued, could be a key to algorithmically squeezing meaning from web pages. Gomes told him that another Googler, Noam Shazeer, had similar ideas. (While studying at Duke, Shazeer had worked on a computerized crossword puzzle solver.) From that point, Harik and Shazeer, two of Google's best engineers, stopped working on projects related to Google's overstressed operations and began an artificial intelligence project that would have seemed more appropriate in a research lab.

"A large number of people thought it was a really bad thing to spend our talents on," says Harik. But one of Google's star engineers, Sanjay Ghemawat, thought the project was really cool. So Harik would posit the following argument to doubters: Sanjay thought it was a good idea, and just about no one in the world was as smart as Sanjay. *So why should I accept your view that it's a bad idea?*

For the next year and a half, Harik and Shazeer studied probabilistic models of things such as why people often use clusters of words in the same phrases. "For instance," he says, "when people write the word 'gray,' what words are they willing to write afterwards, like 'elephant'?" The secret to compressing web pages into themes, they discovered, turned out to be prediction: if you can predict what will happen next, you can compress the page. The payoff is that as you get better at predicting a page, you get better at understanding it. Since Harik and Shazeer had the benefit of many terabytes of data documenting the web and the way Google's users interacted with it, they made good progress and developed ideas about identifying what clusters of words went together. Then, using machine learning, they trained the system to find more clusters and develop rules. "Google had about ten or fifteen thousand servers then, so we had about two thousand to play with," says Harik. They were using about 15 percent of Google's computers on their project.

They named the project Phil, because it sounded friendly. (For those who required an acronym, they had one handy: Probabilistic Hierarchical Inferential Learner.) That was bad news for a Google engineer named Phil who kept getting emails about the system. He begged Harik to change the name, but Phil it was.

In February 2003, spurred by the success of AdWords, Susan Wojcicki wondered whether it might make sense to apply the same auction-based, pay-per-click model to a system that involved publishers other than Google. "The advertisers kept demanding *more clicks, more clicks, more clicks!*" she says. "The idea of putting ads on nonsearch pages had been floating around here for a long time. If we did this, we could go to AOL and offer to put ads not just on the search pages but the content pages, too." AOL would be only a start. The potential exposure of Google ads on the web would go from the 5 percent or so they currently served to virtually all of the web. And it certainly was no coincidence that Google had bought the world's most popular blogging service—named, appropriately, Blogger—that same month. Though Google explained the purchase with only a cryptic statement about "many synergies and future opportunities between our two companies," this new project showed that buying Blogger could reap material benefit, and quickly. It put millions of blog pages, as yet bare of advertising, under Google's control—a perfect outlet to satisfy the demands of advertisers for more inventory.

And Google already had the crucial technology to anchor a system that matched ad keywords to web pages: Phil.

Sergey Brin thought this was a terrific idea and became Wojcicki's most powerful benefactor in pushing the program. It took only a week for Harik and Shazeer to make Phil into a system that would match keywords to web pages. (If a page was full of information about winter sports, for instance, Phil would extract keywords like "skis," "ice skates," and "hockey pucks.") Jeff Dean pitched in to merge Phil with the AdWords technology, while another team tried to build all of this into a complete self-service system for advertisers.

As it turned out, Harik and Shazeer were not the only Google engineers working on a project that analyzed content and extracted keywords that could be used for ads. Paul Buchheit, one of the first twenty-five hires at Google, was creating a web-based email system, and he had an idea for analyzing the text of emails so Google could run ads alongside them. By early 2003, he already had a pilot project working that served ads alongside email. Buchheit's technology wasn't used in the Google publisher project, but "it was a great proof of concept," says Wojcicki. (Buchheit's name appears on the patent, along with Harik's and Jeff Dean's.)

Brin wanted to launch a pilot version quickly and have the full program running by May. Google didn't even have a payment system in place to distribute the commissions to publishers. The only thing close to such an in-house scheme was the method used in a search backwater called Google Answers, an ill-fated experiment that let users bypass algorithms for tough queries and instead solicit answers from anonymous fellow users, who would be paid small sums for satisfactory responses. The new project used that payment system.

In March 2003, Google announced the pilot product, saddled with the awkward moniker Google content-targeted advertising. The blog post trumpeting the program didn't garner much attention in the general press, but some sharp industry observers grasped the implications. Danny Sullivan, the editor of the website Search Engine Watch, noted that Google—with more than 2 billion web pages in its index by then—had advantages in the field of contextual advertising that no one else had. "The potential exists for the entire web to be Google's ad canvas," he wrote. "Everything could become Google's indirect content." This was a sentiment that Google itself explicitly endorsed. "We could change the economics of the web," Susan Wojcicki said not long after the program launched. "You do the content and leave the selling of the ads to Google."

The idea of analyzing web pages and selling ads that matched with their information was not original to Google. One person who'd had that idea was Bill Gross of GoTo. His brainstorm had come in 1999. "Our product was called LinkAds," he says. "We did content analysis and then placed our ads on someone's site. The revenue took off like a rocket ship. But our

CEO said it was too complicated for advertisers, and we canceled the product. It kills me that I didn't fight harder for that."

In 2003, a Santa Monica–based start-up called Applied Semantics posed a threat to Google in contextual advertising. Founded by Caltech graduates Adam Weissman and Gil Elbaz, it had patented technology that, according to its own description, "understands, organizes, and extracts knowledge from websites and information repositories in a way that mimics human thought." It used its system in a product called AdSense (with the intentional pun on the "cents" that people would be paid for links) that analyzed web pages and tried to extract the key themes in order to place relevant ads on the page. It sounded awfully similar to what Google wanted to do—and its patent could have been a problem.

Google was in luck, though—Applied Semantics' exclusive contract with Overture was due to expire that year. Also, Elbaz was friendly with Brin. When Brin asked Elbaz what was happening with the contract, he said that Overture was dangling "a more strategic" arrangement, meaning an actual stake in the company. Brin asked Elbaz to bring his team to Mountain View to discuss whether Google should work with Applied Semantics.

The two teams met in a Mountain View conference room. Jason Liebman, an Applied Semantics executive, showed slides touting the company's business. Liebman concluded by claiming that AdSense was "a billion-dollar opportunity." It was basically the same presentation he had given to Overture the day before. In that meeting, Liebman's billion-dollar parting shot had been met with derision. "Maybe a hundred million," snorted an Overture exec. Brin's reaction was different. "We actually think it's a *two*-billion-dollar opportunity," he said. If you were negotiating a contract, maybe that wasn't the cagiest approach. But Brin, who had been obsessed with selling ads on other sites for months at that point, had something "more strategic" in mind. He shooed the Google engineers out of the room, and the Applied Semantics people were left with Brin and Google's business development team. Soon, Google had agreed to buy Applied Semantics. It was its biggest acquisition to that point. Google paid $42 million cash and 1 percent of its stock.

Google changed the name of its content-targeted advertising program to the catchier AdSense. But the product technology was still Google's, based on the Phil system. (Years later the confusion caused by adopting the name used by the acquired company would lead some to inaccurately accuse Google, and Wojcicki in particular, of claiming credit for Applied Semantics' achievement.)

Google identified its first AdSense customers as large publishers such as web portals and big newspapers and quickly did what it could to get those accounts. "Google felt that they had a window to be the only game in town," says Liebman, who came over from Applied Semantics. Just to show that the system could help advertisers and publishers, Google assumed all the costs while it proved its point. Normally, the process began when a publisher signed up for the program and assigned space on a page for relevant AdWords ads Google would find. Then, when visitors to the page clicked on the ads, Google would split the revenues with the publisher. But Google was so eager to get things rolling that it didn't wait for publishers to sign up and speculatively assign part of their pages to Google. It bought the ad space itself, paying the publishers retail rates. "We'd call them up and say, 'We'd like to buy some media,' and then we would run our ads," says Wojcicki. Google wouldn't charge the AdWords advertisers for the clicks either, so they were more than happy to have their ads show up on those nonsearch pages. Essentially, Google was paying the costs from both sides, just to launch AdSense.

Google used this approach to expose the system to some of its biggest potential customers, huge digital publishers such as *The New York Times.*

All this advertising involved a considerable outlay of cash. Eric Schmidt thought it excessive. That would ultimately lead to one of Schmidt's "and-it-turned-out-they-were-right" anecdotes: "Sergey walked in and said, 'I'm going to invent this business,' and I said, 'Fine.' Then he said, 'I need money because I'm going to preguarantee these deals.' And I said, 'That's bad business,' and we argued for a good half an hour, because Sergey wouldn't give up. Eventually, I said, 'Okay, take a million dollars.' Which was a lot of money for us then. Two months later, he comes back and they've spent a million and a half.

"Sergey, you couldn't just stick to the million, could you?" Schmidt asked. Brin just gave Schmidt a broad smile.

"We could do that because we had the money," says Liebman. "Google's mantra was 'Get this puppy launched.'" (In fact, the AdSense codename was "Puppy.") After a few months, Google announced that it was no longer going to buy the ad space outright. By then it had enough data to show that if publishers signed up for the official AdSense program and kept running the ads, the commissions they earned from advertiser-paid clicks would justify the commitment.

It was an easy sell, because publishers could use AdSense for only the spots on their pages that otherwise would go unsold. Advertisers loved it because it gave them a chance of getting their ads on prestigious sites, such as *The New York Times* or *Forbes.* (A later twist in the program let advertisers specify where the ads would run.) "Those were brand names that our people could sell," says Liebman.

The only hitch in the program was the risk that the ads Google placed on a website would be inappropriate or even offensive. When human beings created an ad for a publication, they took care to avoid situations where the combination of a certain ad with a certain type of article would produce a tasteless match that would appall readers and win no business for the advertisers. Google's algorithms weren't so sensitive. "The editors would get freaked out," says Liebman. Some of the unintentionally offensive matches became classics. Liebman would cite an ad that ran alongside a gory murder story in the *New York Post:* someone had chopped up a body and stuffed it in a garbage bag. Alongside this gruesome text was a Google ad for plastic bags.

"We didn't foresee that there were times when you don't want to target ads to the content," says Georges Harik. "We would analyze a page about a plane crash and happily place an ad for airline tickets. I think we rapidly discovered that this was a bad idea." Google engineers started working on ways to mitigate this problem, but it would never be totally eliminated. It was just too hard for an algorithm trained to discover matches between articles and ads to exercise human good taste. In 2008, a story about the Mumbai attacks headlined "Terrorists kill the man who gave them water" was accompanied by an ad that read "Terrorism: Pursue a certificate in terrorism 100% online. Enroll today. Ads by Google." An account of massive food poisoning at an Olive Garden restaurant in Los Angeles was accompanied by a coupon offering a "FREE Dinner for Two at Olive Garden."

As the program continued, Google opened up AdSense on June 21 to long-tail businesses such as blogs and small-business websites, using a self-service model. Sergey Brin joined the team to monitor its progress. They sat in rapt attention as one publisher after another signed up, pasted the line of JavaScript code in their HTML code that would enter them in the program, and began hosting ads on their websites and blogs. The team hung out at the offices until 3 A.M., transfixed by the response. A few months later, again at Brin's urging, they "localized" the product, making it available in ten languages. That doubled the business.

Even beyond the revenues, AdSense was important to Google because it showed that the company could make money outside of search. "You can think of the search engine as the crown jewel of Google," says Gokul Raja-ram, the AdSense product manager. "With a program like AdSense, Google was able to make money from its partners—it was kind of a moat that protects the king's castle."

One aspect of AdSense was reminiscent of the black box that determined the ad quality rating of AdWords. When someone clicked on an AdSense ad, the money paid by the advertiser was split between Google and the publisher whose site hosted the ad. According to Rajaram, the original thought was to split the money down the middle—Google would take half and the AdSense publisher would take the other half. But Brin thought that such a split gave too much to Google. The idea was to build the program for the long run, and if Google made it clear that it was taking half the money, a competitor might undercut the program by giving 80 or even 90 percent of the fee to the publisher. So Google decided to give the majority of the money to the publisher. Then Susan Wojcicki came up with an idea that some might find strange: What if we don't reveal the revenue share percentage with the publisher? That way Google wouldn't have to worry about a competitor boasting a better split.

Gokul Rajaram was startled by the idea. "What?" he said. "How can we not tell the publishers what percentage of the revenue they get?"

"The publishers shouldn't care about the revenue share," Wojcicki told him. "What they should care about is the bottom line."

On the face of it, the scheme flew in the face of Google's stated goal of transparency. But when Google decided that it was in its interest to keep something secret—as the "hiding strategy" showed—it reconsidered. The dichotomy of closed and open at Google might be traced to Larry Page's personal library. On one hand there was Don Norman's book, a polemic urging total fealty to the user, making everything clear to customers and visitors to a site. On the other hand, there was Nikola Tesla, exploited and dying alone in a New York City hotel. With regard to the revenue split in AdSense, Google wasn't going to be Tesla. Besides, why would publishers complain if Google made them more money than the competitors?

"It was one of the single biggest painful things for me," says Rajaram. "On every panel I went to for the first year, I would get questions about why isn't Google sharing the revenue split and why isn't Google being transparent. People said we were doing it because we weren't generous. But quite to the contrary, we *were* being generous. We just didn't want our competitors to tell publishers that they were offering a better revenue share."

(In May 2010, Google finally revealed the split. "In the spirit of greater transparency," Google reported that of the money received from advertisers on AdSense for content, 68 percent went to the publishers whose pages hosted the ads. Google kept the other 32 percent. That was close to the proportions that participants and analysts had long assumed. Google's belated announcement only raised more questions as to why it had been a secret in the first place.)

Google took a viral approach to luring small businesses and bloggers to run ads. For bloggers who didn't have many visitors to their sites, the money they would get from AdSense commissions was a piddling sum, arguably not enough to sully the pure relationship between an impassioned citizen-writer and engaged readers. On the other hand, it was free money. To help build the program, Sheryl Sandberg hired an old friend.

Kim Malone had, in Sandberg's view, "the perfect Google résumé," at least for a nonengineer. A Princeton grad (like Eric Schmidt), she had studied Russian literature, venturing into the mother country after graduation to write reports on converting military technology to private-sector uses. Then she started a diamond-cutting factory in Moscow. She returned to the United States to get a Harvard Business School MBA and emerged as a founder of high-tech companies. After Malone went through three start-ups—and two unpublished novels, because she believed that her true calling was fiction—Sandberg urged her to apply to Google. Twenty-five interviews later, she arrived in Mountain View to help sell AdSense to more small publishers.

Malone dubbed herself "the high priestess of the long tail" and came to view her job—the dubiously virtuous task of sticking ads on pages that otherwise would have been ad-free—as a mission to empower small publishers in the age of search. She considered the AdSense arrangement the best sales pitch in advertising history. "Here's the deal," she'd say. "You take ten seconds to put a little snippet of code on your website, and from that moment on, Google sends you a check every month." It became evangelical for her. "I'd tell people that AdSense funds creativity a nickel at a time," she says. "So if you have an idea, you can start making money on it with AdSense immediately without having to get it published or to raise money from venture capitalists."

One of the first things she did was become an AdSense customer herself. She formatted one of her unpublished novels as a blog and applied for the program. To her astonishment, Google's algorithms rejected her, citing excessive profanity. "It made me think that we should reevaluate our policies," she said, and she began to introduce different means to segment

AdSense customers. The idea was to make the program as inclusive as possible. If your site was profane (but not pornographic—there were still boundaries), Google would place ads only from customers who were okay with that.

Even though Malone's domain was limited to the small players on the Internet—if the page views of a site exceed a certain limit, it would be turned over to direct sales—she understood that her potential customer base was vast. By making it simple to sign up and collect money, Malone saw the number of AdSense publishers grow dramatically. In early 2004, she gave a progress report at a Google Product Strategy meeting. Eric Schmidt asked her how many publishers AdSense had signed up. He figured the number would be in the thousands. But she reported a number well up in the hundreds of thousands. "They almost fell off their chairs," she said. But not Brin. "That's pretty good," he said. Later people would explain to Malone that Brin's "pretty good" is the equivalent of a Nobel Prize.

As AdSense kept delivering more and more of Google's revenues, Malone thought of a song from the musical *Evita*:

> *When the money keeps rolling in, you don't ask how*
> *Think of all the people guaranteed a good time now*

Later in the year, AdSense achieved a milestone in its run rate—$1 million a day. Kim Malone wanted to have a party for her team, but Google had gone into an advanced mode of its "hiding strategy." By then its IPO had been announced, and though some of Google's numbers were public, its stealth had morphed into something more subtle. It was increasingly clear that beyond the minimum disclosures required by law, Google was going to keep the most important figures to itself—such as how much its individual products were making. (In contrast, Microsoft would break down the figures for each of its divisions.) So Malone had to negotiate the terms of her celebration with Google's lawyers. Only after some hardball dickering did Malone win a concession: she could bring in a cake to mark the milestone. But the lawyers were adamant that the actual milestone—the million-dollar number—could not appear on the cake.

It didn't really matter. The $1 million a day would soon be $2 million. And more.

And the $2 billion that Brin had brashly predicted to the Applied Semantics group would eventually produce *$10 billion* for Google—every year.

4

"The barometer of the world"

While AdSense was a great success, the bulk of Google's revenues came from AdWords. Eric Veach and Salar Kamangar's auction-based AdWords Select product had first been thought of as a supplement to the more traditional, impression-based ads in the premium program, which was now called AdWords Premium. But it was working so well that Google would sometimes allow its auction-based ads to break out of their side-of-the-page ghetto and leapfrog to the premium zone sitting on top of the search results. If Google felt that the outcome would raise more revenue, a select ad would "trump" a premium ad and knock it out of that coveted position. As more and more auction-based ads trumped the hand-sold premium ads, Kamangar argued that Google should entirely end the practice of selling premium ads by a sales force that set prices and charged by impression. He set up a project, code-named D4, to implement the idea. Most Googlers called the plan Premium Sunset.

Even as he argued for it, Kamangar had his concerns about the shift. Customers used to certain prerogatives might balk at a system determined totally by auction and algorithms. For instance, it was common for a big advertiser to insist that its ad be the first one to appear above the search results, so that its impact wasn't mitigated by a competitor's ad above it. Also, moving to auctions would introduce uncertainty. Clients and agencies were used to guarantees that if they budgeted a specific sum of money they'd get a specific number of ads in predictable positions. Finally, some advertisers didn't want to budge from impression-based ads. They would insist that their ads were intended to build up their brands and having a percentage of people clicking on their ads wasn't as important as having lots of people *see* the ads.

Eric Veach believed that the data showed that the auction-based, pay-per-click model was actually better for everybody. The key was the ad quality, which made sure that ads would appear before sympathetic eyeballs. He did a close analysis and concluded that ads bought through AdWords Select performed better. He also uncovered hard proof that some premium advertisers were paying way too little for some valuable keywords. Armed with a PowerPoint presentation full of this information, he went to an executive meeting and argued that there was no reason to cater to the statistically unsound assumptions of big advertisers. "We should just make our advertisers live with it," he said.

How did that go over? "Like a lead brick," he recalls. But the disagreement came from the business people at Google. The engineers, he noticed, were behind it a hundred percent. And considering that this was Google, such support made the adoption of Veach's solution inevitable. He had the data on his side.

Indeed, after months of wrangling, the ruling troika, nicknamed "LSE"—Larry, Sergey, Eric—signed off on the plan. Sales head Tim Armstrong thought that 99 out of 100 companies he was familiar with would have hemmed and hawed and decided to test some more and revisit the idea in six months. But Google was going for it.

Google had already used scale, power, and clever algorithms to change the way people accessed information. By turning over its sales process entirely to an auction-based system, it would similarly upend the entire world of advertising, removing guesswork-ridden human intervention. It would also provide a leveling function among its customers. "We would have everyone competing for the same ad position," says Schmidt. "So regardless of whether you were a large company or a small one, you had to bid, and you had to bid at market value."

Nonetheless, the move would be painful. It meant giving up campaigns that were selling for hundreds of thousands of dollars, all for the unproven possibility that the auction process would generate even bigger sums. "We were doing $300 million in CPM ads and now were going to turn this other model on and cannibalize that revenue," says Tim Armstrong.

The role of Google's advertising sales force had always been awkward. Its members had long suspected, not without foundation, that Larry Page wanted to do away with them entirely. At one point, Sheryl Sandberg made a major presentation to Larry, Sergey, and Eric, arguing that with the ad model's success her team needed reinforcements for things such as ad approval, organization, and management. She thought the presentation was going great. Then Page chimed in. "I have a question," he said. "Why do we need this team?"

Brin wasn't terribly engaged with salespeople, either. In December 2001, Google had run its first sales conference, at the Hilton Garden Inn in Mountain View, a mid-price hotel a few miles from the Googleplex. Jeff Levick, who had just been hired by the company, recalls Brin dropping into the tiny conference room where the team of maybe twenty people was huddled. Brin ignored the conversation and instead remained in the back of the room, where the controls of the audiovisual system were located. "Everyone is talking about what's going on with sales, and Sergey was paying no attention, just pushing buttons on the AV system and trying to unscrew a panel to understand it," says Levick. "And I remember thinking, this man does not give a rat's ass about this part of the business. He doesn't get what we do. He never will. That set the tone for me very early in terms of the two Googles—the engineering Google and this other Google, the sales and business side."

No matter how much you exceeded your sales quota, a salesperson wouldn't be coddled as much as a guy with a computer science degree who spent all day creating code. And some tried-and-true sales methods were verboten. For instance, golf outings. "Larry and Sergey hate golf," says Levick. "Google has never sponsored a golf event and never will." There would be days when Google salespeople would call agencies and discover that everybody was off on a golf retreat with Yahoo. But Tim Armstrong would tell his troops, "*They* have to take people on golf outings because they have nothing else."

The salespeople at Google did have something special, and they were terrified that a change would kill the golden goose. They had worked hard to overcome the reluctance of advertisers. "We spent a tremendous amount of time trying to figure out how to get people to believe in relevancy," says Armstrong. But AdWords Premium was working. Salespeople were assigned sectors of the economy and they would ring up contacts, if they had them, or just cold-call, and explain the concept of targeted keywords. One difficulty was that agencies were used to discrete ad campaigns where they ran something for a few months, shut down, and then ran something else. Google's idea was that you could have something running all the time, measure the results, and reinvest as long as the payoff is positive. It had data to prove it.

AdWords Premium even had a way to enforce ad quality, a daily email called the underperforming keyword list. Even though Google was charging by how many people saw the ad, it tracked very closely how many people actually clicked on the ads. If the rate was under 1 percent, Google would pull the ad. "That was four times the average success rate of current ads," says Armstrong. "So if you told anyone else in the Internet industry at that time to shut off ads with a 1 percent click rate they would have said, 'What are you doing?'" The businesses with the underperforming ads would often go ballistic when Google told them that they had to improve the ads or find different keywords. The traditionalists would rage:

Who the hell is Google to tell me the success of my ads? I've been in advertising for fifty years—I know what a bad ad is, and this isn't it! "We'd say yes they are, and here's the data," says Armstrong. "It was a major reason that some of our people flamed out, day after day of going to advertisers who told us we were wrong."

The policy reflected the different philosophy Google brought to advertising in general. Google ads were *answers*. They were solutions. "Ideally we wanted people to have a 50 to *100* percent click rate," says Armstrong.

Jeff Levick, whose job it was to gin up ads from companies servicing other businesses (B2B), would cold-call prospective advertisers. They would say, "What's Google?" He would tell them about the searches conducted in Google and what keywords were already performing for advertisers. One sector ripe for this pitch was the box business—boxes for shipping, boxes stuffed with Bubble Wrap. So he called a company called Uline, which, like Levick, was based in Chicago. "Do you know that in the last twenty-four hours 1,500 people typed the word 'boxes' into the Google search engine?" he said to the guy in purchasing whom he finally managed to reach. "Would you like those people to come to your website?" Levick wound up doing a lot of business in boxes.

With Premium Sunset the algorithm was displacing the handshake. The system itself would police ad quality by estimating the success of an ad and incorporating that into the bid price. And the sales force would have different kinds of interactions with clients. The old job was making a sale. Their new job would be . . . getting the big companies they dealt with to *place bids in an auction*? "We thought it was a little half cocked," says Jeff Levick. "If we let the auction set prices, we worried that we could actually lose a lot of money."

But the die was cast. Tim Armstrong, the executive in the New York office in charge of sales, gave his people an upbeat description of the system. Schmidt came to New York to assure them that it was the right move. "People were extremely upset, because this was a material change in the way they were doing business," Schmidt would later recall. Ultimately, since the engineers in Mountain View had made good on their promises so far, the salespeople trusted them on this one. They weren't going to be replaced. They were going to assume a new role as mediators between advertisers and algorithms.

"Our group's job was to build the largest bridge we could between Silicon Valley and Madison Avenue," says Armstrong. "It was really bringing science to the art of advertising and being able to scale the art of advertising through science."

For Jeff Levick the big test came in his favorite product category—the boxes. Box firms had become some of the biggest advertisers at Google, and he spent a lot of time on the road seeing them, one in Southern California, one in Boston, and one nearby in Chicago. All were seeing an excellent return in their investments in Premium. Now Levick would explain that Google was pulling the plug on Premium and they were now going to have to participate in a high-stakes version of eBay. "The guy in California literally almost threw us out of his office and told us to fuck ourselves. The guy in Chicago said, 'This is going to be the worst business move you guys ever made.' But the guy in Massachusetts said, 'I trust you.'"

It wasn't only trust that led the advertiser to stick. "The guy knew math," says Levick. When all the numbers were crunched—and Google worked hard to give advertisers all the crunching tools they would hope for—advertisers saw that the auction system paid off for them.

Even sectors that had once been deemed impossible proved winnable. The first time Tim Armstrong visited General Motors, in 2005, "they kicked us out of the building," says Levick. "They said, 'We're never going to buy anything from you, don't waste our time and don't come back.'" When Google salespeople visited BMW, they got a similar reaction: Google is a fad, said the auto exec. "Who does research on cars online? They just use *Consumer Reports*!"

But Google kept at it, slowly collecting people who weren't fossils, and eventually Jeff Levick was invited to represent Google at a GM global marketing event. His presentation underlined the fact that 80 percent of car buyers do research their purchase online, and almost all of them use Google to do it. In Mexico, for example, Google had 90 percent of the search market and millions of auto-related search queries—yet GM spent only 1 percent of its ad budget on online marketing. Even Rick Wagoner, the company's CEO, was sentient enough to see the absurdity of it.

Google had tools to help advertisers, but they were rudimentary. Salar Kamangar tapped a smart young associate product manager named Wesley Chan to improve the services. One of Google's better tools was called conversion tracking, which made rough estimates of how many users were lured by AdWords to the checkout page on a website, but "it was miserable," says Chan. It was hard to set up and not very accurate. A number of independent companies had sprung up to provide analytic services, but Chan found most of them cumbersome. "You pay $5,000 or $10,000 a month plus the consultant services, and it's still hard to read the reports."

Chan decided that Google needed a new product that would deliver a much higher level of service—something that would give a full reporting of all sorts of information about a website, including how many people visited it, which sites referred them, and of course whether the visitors from ad networks such as AdWords actually bought something. But he didn't have many engineers at his disposal. "So I decided, 'I'm going to buy something,' even though I'd never bought a company before in my life."

He quickly learned how. First, scan the marketplace until you found a match. In this case it was a small firm called Urchin Software, which offered a better quality of analytics and was run by guys who seemed Googley. Then propose a partnership, because any company worth buying really doesn't want to sell itself. Finally, switch the rules and ask the founders if they want to *join* Google. All along, you had to operate a second front—getting the Google brain trust to okay the purchase. In this case, Larry Page was skeptical, but Chan won him over. After months of negotiation, Google bought Urchin for about $20 million in late 2004.

Thus began a long process of making Urchin into what became known as Google Analytics. Chan's original idea was that Google would charge $500 a month to use the service, but offer discounts to AdWords customers. But Chan's team was undermanned and had no experience in building a billing system. Finally, he went to Page and suggested that Google offer the product for free. It would take another eighteen months to build a billing system, and wasn't it better to spend all that energy figuring out ways to make users happy? Page relented, and in November 2005, Google Analytics went live.

Chan had predicted that opening up this easy-to-use service that would provide for instant statistics on websites—free—could result in ten times the current activity in analytical products. So he "provisioned" the data centers to handle the volume. (This meant reserving the necessary clusters of servers to handle the estimated load of a service.) Nonetheless, within forty-eight hours, virtually all of Google's servers crashed, unable to process the tidal wave of data washing into the company's servers. Eric Schmidt would later call the meltdown Google's most successful disaster. For almost a year, Google had to limit access until finally opening the service up to all comers. Even though Google Analytics didn't require a client to be an AdWords customer, the data it provided revealed the value of the Google ad world, enticed new customers, and kept current ones assured that their investment in Google ads was a genius purchase. "Analytics generates about three billion dollars in extra revenue," says Chan. "Know more, spend more."

"Every advertising should be measurable," says Susan Wojcicki. "You should be able to adjust it, right? Then you should be able to tune it, track the right users, and target it to the right people."

Eric Schmidt saw this dynamic in action even before Analytics was rolled out, on the day that the sun set on AdWords Premium. Schmidt had come to New York to witness the historic switch. At around five o'clock he was sitting in a cubicle and couldn't help but overhear a conversation being conducted between a young woman in Google's sales force and a client on the other end of the phone. She seemed typical of the people there: dark-haired, cut-to-the-chase, loud in a way that shouted "New York." Maybe not so Googley. She was explaining the transition to a baffled client. It was clearly a difficult conversation. Afterward, Schmidt introduced himself and apologized for the trouble that the transition was causing her. She explained to him that the client's tension was rooted in the fact that Google ads were the way his company made all its money.

"You're kidding," said Schmidt. She wasn't.

Schmidt finally got it. He'd been viewing the transformation of the advertising business from thirty thousand feet, but now he saw firsthand that countless businesses had discarded the old handshake method of buying ads and had embraced Google's model. "Our system doesn't work that way," Schmidt says. "There's an auction, it sets the price, you win, it's a fair price, and then there's another auction." The role of Google's saleswoman was not to sell her client something he didn't want, but to provide data to help him sell more, using tools that Google provided not only to assess the ad but possibly to transform the way his company thought about itself. Not to mention the transformation of the ad industry, which could never again claim that its business was an unquantifiable mystery. The right algorithm would make partners of the woman and her client, make everything efficient and measurable, and turn on the money tap for both sides. And since Google had devised the best algorithms, it had emerged as the winner of the ad game. The next step was to leverage that advantage so that no one else could ever come close.

Premium Sunset was an apotheosis for Google. Google's business plans may have begun as a means to support the search business, where its founders' hearts lay. But by the mid-2000s, Google's business became much more. In most advertising-driven companies, the business side was regarded as less interesting and creative than the consumer-directed activities. But at Google, the ad effort became a more or less equal sibling to search. When Google recruited its alpha geeks, it was just as likely to ask them to get involved in some AdWords project as it was to ask them to focus on some effort in search or apps. The reason was that in order to succeed on a major scale, AdWords needed that kind of talent in mathematics, computer science, and statistics.

"Search has a luxury that ads don't have," says Jeff Huber, who came to Google to head engineering on the ad side in 2003. Previously, he'd been eBay's vice president of architecture and systems development. "Yes, search is a huge system, but it's stateless—you can easily serve it from ten different places in the world, and if this version is slightly different than that version, the user won't know, nobody will notice. But with advertising, the state is important, because advertisers are always updating their campaigns, and microtransactions are happening at ferocious rates per second, and all that has to be synchronized." Compared to Google's demands, the auction volume that Huber handled at eBay was like spitting in the ocean—and this complication of "state" meant technical challenges that would keep brilliant computer scientists up at night. "We needed to invest. The amount of data was doubling every quarter. Things were straining at the seams, and we would have ad outages or delays of stats reporting of a day or more. Every time we had an operational issue, it became national news. There were very explicit discussions about how we were going to survive Christmas in 2004."

That was just the operations end of it, where Huber had to hire (or lure from other areas of Google) engineers and computer scientists to scale the system and build new infrastructure. An even tougher part of the system was performing the complex calculations that kept the system vital. Serious math and statistics were required. In order to figure out the critical ad quality score, Google had to estimate in advance how many users would click on an ad. That involved building systems that could process an incredible amount of data and accurately predict a future event millions of times a day. Since the Google ad model depended on absolute mastery in predicting click-through, over the years the company would spend enormous amounts of effort and prodigious amounts of brainpower to get it right.

A new arrival at Google would act as a godfather to the advertising effort. His name was Hal Varian, and he would eventually hold the title of Google's chief economist. In 2001 newly hired CEO Eric Schmidt ran into

Varian at the Aspen Institute, Schmidt was with Larry Page, and Varian remembers thinking, Why did Eric bring his nephew from high school here? Nonetheless, Schmidt, whose father was an economist, suggested to Varian that he spend time at Google, maybe a day or two a week. On his first visit Varian asked Schmidt what he might do. "Why don't you take a look at the ad auction?" Schmidt told him. "It might make us a little money."

Varian was uniquely qualified to vet Google's approach to making money online. He'd been thinking like an economist ever since he was twelve, when he'd read Isaac Asimov's Foundation Trilogy and become enchanted with a character who constructed mathematical models to explain societal behavior. "When I went to college at MIT, I looked around for that subject," he says. "I thought it might have been psychology or sociology, but it was economics." He also learned to program computers at MIT. After getting his doctorate at Berkeley, he taught at MIT and then at the University of Michigan, where he began studying the topology of the Internet from an economic perspective. He became fascinated with what seemed to him "a lab experiment that got loose—it wasn't designed for commerce at all." But Varian understood that the net's unique attributes gave it an opportunity to redefine commerce, and he took that idea with him to Berkeley in the mid-1990s, when he became dean of the UC Berkeley School of Information Management. With Carl Shapiro, he wrote a popular book called *Information Rules: A Strategic Guide to the Network Economy*, and became the go-to economist on e-commerce.

After examining Google's system, Varian realized that it was the embodiment of the Silicon Valley ethic he'd been studying. Though the Internet was different from other media, most Internet companies were still selling ads the way Madison Avenue had always done it. Google saw the entire exchange differently. Advertising in Google was less comparable to television or print than it was to computer dating. Google was a yenta—the Yiddish term for the pesky, persistent matchmakers who linked brides and grooms in the shtetl. It matched advertisers with users. And since, as Varian says, "in economics there's no shortage of theories," there already was a body of work dealing with these things. One of the classic papers in the field was a 1983 study by the Harvard economist Herman Leonard that dealt with matching problems such as assigning students to dorm rooms. It was called a two-sided matching market. "Ironically, the mathematical structure of the Google auction is the same as one of those two-sided matching markets," says Varian.

During Varian's first summer at Google, when he was coming in a day or two a week, he tapped a recently hired computer scientist and mathematician from Stanford named Diane Tang to create Google's search-word advertising equivalent of the stock market, called the Keyword Pricing Index. "It's like a consumer price index," says Tang, who came to be known internally as the Queen of Clicks. "But instead of a basket of goods like diapers and beer and doughnuts, we have keywords." Different categories were ranked by the cost per click that advertisers generally have to pay and then separated into high-cap, midcap, and low-cap bundles. "The high caps were very competitive keywords like flowers and hotels," Tang says. (The very highest CPCs [cost-per-clicks] were for categories such as mesothelioma, used by litigation attorneys to troll for clients—winning bids could go for fifty dollars per click. Also, anything touching on insurance rates made for pricey keywords.) In the midcap realm were keywords that might vary seasonally—in the winter the price to place ads alongside results for "snowboarding" would skyrocket. Low-caps were the stuff of long tails. Meanwhile, Google had an equivalent to the Dow Jones Industrial Average: the average cost per click, which was calculated by summing up all the ad revenue and dividing by the total of paid clicks. "If you change the mix or get more low-cap ads, it can go down even though your pricing is going quite well," says Tang.

Tang's goal was to construct what she calls a "data warehouse" so that the simpler analyses could be turned over to the sales force or the customers themselves—to whom Google would supply all sorts of tools to figure out where their ads were and how they were working. Meanwhile, Google collected a phalanx of statisticians, physicists, and data miners to unearth every twist and turn in the Google economy.

"We have Hal Varian, and we have the physicists," says Eric Schmidt. "Hal's interaction with his group is like a professor and his students. His job is to get them to deeply understand an issue and then move it forward. And the physicists' job is to figure out the lifetime flow of a click."

Varian referred to his team as "econometricians." "Sort of a cross between statisticians and economists," he says. Of the early statisticians hired, Daryl Pregibon joined Google in 2004, after twenty-three years as a top scientist at Bell and AT&T labs. "We needed a class of mathematical types that had a rich tool set for looking for signals in noise," he says. "The rough rule of thumb here is one statistician for every hundred computer scientists," he says.

Pregibon says that in a certain sense, what Google did with advertising wasn't much different from what AT&T had done in the era of Ma

Bell. "Google makes its money in volume. It gets a quarter or fifty cents whenever someone clicks on an ad. AT&T did the same thing—it had hundreds of millions of phone calls a day, and it would make a dime, fifteen cents on every phone call." But though both businesses were driven by data, there was a monstrous difference in how they approached it. "AT&T was a hundred-year-old company, and it collected its billing data originally to send out bills! Later it realized that the data was useful for understanding the network, traffic, fraud detection, marketing, and other things. It backed into the importance of data underlying its basic business."

Google, on the other hand, had been diving for data from day one. Brin and Page *began* with data mining. That shaped Google's mind-set from the start. That's why Google populated not just its search business but its ad business with scientists like Pregibon. If one were to be cynical about his job, you'd say his mission is to get people to click on ads. But Pregibon believed that his role was doing science. He was tackling deep, interesting questions. "It wasn't presupposed that that is where I would have ended up, but that's kind of what happened," he says.

Eventually Google got so adept at understanding what Wojcicki refers to as "the physics of clicks" that it was able to predict not only how many clicks an ad would probably draw but how many sales those clicks would deliver to the advertiser. Google developed a product available to advertisers (like other tools to analyze the success of ads, it was free) called conversion optimizer that shared this information with customers.

To keep making consistently accurate predictions on click-through rates and conversions, Google needed to know *everything*. "We are trying to understand the mechanisms behind the metrics," says Qing Wu, a decision support analyst at Google. His specialty was forecasting. He could predict patterns of queries from season to season, in different parts of the day, and the climate. "We have the temperature data, we have the weather data, and we have the queries data so we can do correlation and statistical modeling." To make sure that his predictions were on track, Qing Wu and his colleagues made use of dozens of onscreen dashboards with information flowing through them, a Bloomberg of the Googlesphere. "With a dashboard you can monitor the queries, the amount of money you make, how many advertisers we have, how many keywords they're bidding on, what the ROI is for each advertiser." It's like the census data, he would say, only Google does much better analyzing its information than the government does with the census results. Google did predictions so well that anomalies shook him. "We wonder if there's something wrong with us. Are we losing market share?" One year, some weird results came from Belgium at Eastertime, and "we all kind of panicked." (Turns out it was *too* warm, and more people than usual stayed home and clicked on Google ads.)

Qing Wu calls Google "the barometer of the world." Indeed, analyzing the clicks of Google users was like sitting beside a window with a panorama on the world. You saw the changes of seasons—clicks gravitating toward skiing and heavy clothes in the winter, bikinis and sunscreens in the summer—and could track who was up and down in popular culture. Most of us remember news events from television or the newspapers; Googlers analyzing click-through rates recalled them as spikes in their graphs. "One of the big things a couple of years ago was the SARS epidemic," says Diane Tang. "There was a big spike during the 2008 election. A big spike with Janet Jackson after the Super Bowl." One Googler studied Google's data on the day of a massive blackout; there was almost a perfect correlation of Google use with the restoration of electricity.

Varian himself once even did a study that compared Google traffic in individual countries to the state of their respective economies. Not surprisingly, Varian says, high GDP tracks closely with how much people use Google. His paper was titled "International Googlenomics."

The piles of money that Google made from its golden geese of AdWords and AdSense enabled the company to fund a dizzying array of projects, initiatives, and creature comforts that make it a unique competitor and a most desirable company to work for. "Larry and Sergey think that engineering and computer science can make a big difference in the world," says CFO Patrick Pichette. "And to have the freedom to do it without having a gun to your head every quarter on financial matters is an immense luxury." Google's ad products were a gold-threaded safety net underneath every daring innovation. And Google's success was hiding in plain sight.

PART THREE

DON'T BE EVIL

How Google Built Its Culture

1

"Make sure it looks like a dorm room."

One day in 2005, Marissa Mayer was trying to explain why the looniness of Google was actually the crazy-like-a-fox variety and not the kind calling for straitjackets. Responding to the company's ventures beyond search, outsiders had been charging that Google was out of control, tossing balls into the air like a drunken juggler. And that was *before* Google decided to remake the energy industry, the medical information infrastructure, the book world, radio, television, and telecommunications. She conceded that to an outsider, Google's new-business process might indeed look strange. Google spun out projects like buckshot, blasting a spray and using tools and measurements to see what it hit. And sometimes it did try ideas that seemed ill suited or just plain odd. Finally she burst out with her version of the corporate Rosebud. "You can't understand Google," she said, "unless you know that both Larry and Sergey were Montessori kids."

"Montessori" refers to schools based on the educational philosophy of Maria Montessori, an Italian physician born in 1870 who believed that children should be allowed the freedom to pursue what interested them.

"It's really ingrained in their personalities," she said. "To ask their own questions, do their own things. To disrespect authority. Do something because it makes sense, not because some authority figure told you. In Montessori school you go paint because you have something to express or you just want to do it that afternoon, not because the teacher said so. This is really baked into how Larry and Sergey approach problems. They're always asking 'Why should it be like that?' It's the way their brains were programmed early on."

Both Brin and Page were certainly smart enough and sufficiently self-aware to understand the disrupting impact of unconventional behavior, but it's as if somewhere along the line—Montessori?—they made independent decisions to act on impulse—even if the results sometimes were, as Mayer says, "mildly socially mortifying."

Larry—do you realize you just questioned the physical constant to [famed inventor] Dean Kamen? Are you sure you're right about that?

Sergey—you just asked Colin Powell whether he made the right moves in Desert Storm. Seriously, you're talking to Colin Powell!

Then there was the time in St. James's Palace, when they were having dinner with the queen's husband, Prince Philip. The pomp was intense, a multicourse formal menu. The waiters brought out soufflés along with tiny glasses of passion fruit juice to adorn them, like a syrup. Mayer did what was expected—she mashed down her soufflé and poured the juice over it; otherwise it would have been too dry. She looked on in horror as Larry Page picked up the glass and downed it like a tequila shot. Sergey did the same. Prince Philip looked stunned. Later Marissa explained that the juice was to be regarded as a syrup to flavor the soufflé. She recalls their response with a mixture of awe and repulsion: "Who says?"

"Their attitude is just like, 'We're Montessori kids,'" said Mayer. "We've been trained and programmed to question authority."

Thus it wasn't surprising to see that attitude as the foundation of Google's culture. "Why aren't there dogs at work?" asked Marissa, parroting the never-ending Nerdish Inquisition conducted by her bosses. "Why aren't there *toys* at work? Why aren't snacks free? Why? Why? Why?"

"I think there's some truth to that," says Larry Page, who spent his preschool and first elementary school years at Okemos Montessori Radmoor School in Michigan. "I'm always asking questions, and Sergey and I both have this."

Brin wound up in Montessori almost by chance. When he was six, recently emigrated from the Soviet Union, the Paint Branch Montessori

School in Adelphi, Maryland, was the closest private school. "We wanted to place Sergey in a private school to ease up his adaptation to the new life, new language, new friends," wrote his mother, Eugenia Brin, in 2009. "We did not know much about the Montessori method, but it turned out to be rather crucial for Sergey's development. It provided a basis for independent thinking and a hands-on approach to life."

"Montessori really teaches you to do things kind of on your own at your own pace and schedule," says Brin. "It was a pretty fun, playful environment—as is this."

He was gesturing to his surroundings in an odd little loft in the Googleplex that is restricted to the founders. It was a combination of a rich child's bedroom and an exhibit hall in the National Air and Space Museum. The floor was covered with an AstroTurf-like carpet. There were sports equipment, game tables, and an astronaut's suit. A giant Apple display glowed on his desk. The aerie overlooked a savannah of cubicles with shelves lined with gizmos, yurtlike conference rooms, and countless microkitchens equipped with goodie-stuffed fridges and high-end espresso machines. Red physio balls were scattered here and there. The workplace was similar to those in more than a dozen buildings within scooter range here in Mountain View and in Google offices in New York, Kirkland, Moscow, and Zurich. Google offices appeared to be a geek never-never land for unspeakably brainy Lost Boys (and Girls). If you looked closely, though, there were endless bureaucratic structures—data-driven, logically drawn schemata—that kept a $23 billion business humming.

As an indication of this, Brin's elementary school reverie was interrupted by an unusual occurrence in the Googleplex—a brief power brownout that dimmed the lights. Brin bolted from his chair to his terminal, where he quickly accessed a software dashboard that monitored the building's electrical system and determined that it was an anomaly. "That's like the beginner of a Terminator movie!" he said, shrugging it off.

As a corporation, Google was determined to maintain its sense of play, even if it had to work to do it. The high holy day of Google culture is April 1, when imaginations already encouraged to run wild are channeled into elaborate pranks requiring months of work. The effort involves considerable organization, as ideas go through an elaborate approval process to find a place in the company's ever-increasing roster of seasonal spoofs. The need for some oversight became clear as early as 2000, when Brin sent employees an email announcing that Google had a new valuation (meaning the estimate of its market price had gone up) and would soon reprice its employee stock options—from 25 cents to $4.01. Some people didn't realize that $4.01 was a reference to the calendar and frantically tried to buy up all the shares that they were entitled to before the price went up. They dug into savings and borrowed from their families. Google eventually had to make people whole.

Google's external April Fool's joke that year was an announcement of "MentalPlex," a search engine that reads your mind, eliminating the need to type in queries. This started an odd succession of self-parodying jokes, where a seemingly outrageous April Fool's announcement, often involving a step in moving Google toward omniscience, omnipresence, or consciousness, reflected Brin and Page's actual dreams. (In 2009, there was a complicated announcement of a system called CADIE—Cognitive Autoheuristic Distributed-Intelligence Entity.) As the years went on, more Google divisions felt compelled to devise their own jokes, and by 2010 Wikipedia listed seventeen major April Fool's initiatives for that year alone.

If April Fool's was an indulgence of the founders, it must be said that indulgence is spread around at Google. Early in its history, Google instituted a "20 percent rule," stating that employees can devote one day a week, or the equivalent, to a project of their choosing, as opposed to something imposed by a manager or boss. The idea was Page's, inspired by similar programs at HP and 3M (supposedly, Post-it notes came from such a spare-time effort). In practice, the self-directed labors often came in addition to a full week's work. Thus the companywide joke that such endeavors were actually "120 percent projects." But people participated anyway, and some important products, including Google News, came from the program.

You could even see the company's work/play paradox in its bathrooms. In some of Google's loos, even the toilets were toys: high-tech Japanese units with heated seats, cleansing water jets, and a control panel that looked as though it could run a space shuttle. But on the side of the stall—and, for men, at an eye-level wall placement at the urinals—was the work side of Google, a sheet of paper with a small lesson in improved coding. A typical "Testing on the Toilet" instructional dealt with the intricacies of load testing or C++ microbenchmarking. Not a second was wasted in fulfilling Google's lofty—and work-intensive—mission.

It's almost as if Larry and Sergey were thinking of Maria Montessori's claim "Discipline must come through liberty. . . . We do not consider an individual disciplined only when he has been rendered as artificially silent as a mute and as immovable as a paralytic. He is an individual *annihilated*, not *disciplined*. We call an individual disciplined when he is master of himself."

Just as it was crucial to Montessori that nothing a teacher does destroy a child's creative innocence, Brin and Page felt that Google's leaders should not annihilate an engineer's impulse to change the world by coding up some kind of moon shot.

"We designed Google," Urs Hölzle says, "to be the kind of place where the kind of people we wanted to work here would work for free."

From the very beginning, Page and Brin had an idea of how Google would be different. "Even when we were three people, we had a culture," says Craig Silverstein, the first person hired by the founders. "Partly it's just our personalities, and partly it was the vision that we had for the company."

That culture took shape even as Page and Brin changed Google from a research project to a company and moved off the Stanford campus. Susan Wojcicki, who owned the house that hosted the company after it moved from Stanford, thought that Google's origins in a residential setting, with all the comforts of home, set a tone for the eventual bounty of amenities the company would offer its employees. "Because they were working out of a house, they realized that a lot of these conveniences are really important to have," she says. "For example, having a shower is really important. When you're attracting a really young group that's mostly come out of college, having these services is pretty important, like having the food around, having a washer and dryer."

The Google half of her house, separated from her kitchen by a flimsy door, consisted of a garage packed with equipment; two small rooms used as offices by factotum Heather Cairns and Harry "Spider-Man" Cheung; and a back room with several desks where Sergey, Larry, Craig Silverstein, and another engineer worked, with a view of the backyard and hot tub. Their desks were doors on sawhorses, a setup that would become a Google tradition. "Being a house, it didn't have a lot of core things you want from a business," Wojcicki says. "It didn't have a lot of parking, and you can't park on the street in Menlo Park at night. And also, they needed a cable modem to get Internet access. I thought it was great, because I got free cable out of it." (The servers were off-site.)

Wojcicki believes the fabled Google perk of free food began the day Sears delivered the refrigerator she ordered. Her intention was to stay around the house that day so she could instruct the deliveryman to install it in her kitchen; it was intended for her and her husband. But she was in the shower when the truck arrived. "Sergey and Larry answered the door and said, 'Oh, a new refrigerator! Install it here, in the garage!'" By the time

Wojcicki realized what had happened, she was the unintentional benefactor of the first Google snack station.

"We just had to be clear about the rules," says Wojcicki. When guests came to Google, they had to enter by the garage; using the front door would mean traipsing through her home. There was the occasional weird moment, like the meeting at Intel, where she worked. Her coworkers were talking about this hot new start-up called Google. "They work from my house," she said, drawing astonished stares. Generally, she loved being the landlady. She could have contractors come by even when she was at work. "I would say, 'The electrician's going to come, show him the light that needs to be fixed.'" Her husband traveled a lot, and when she got lonely, she would go to the other side of the house and talk to the Googlers. After a number of late-night sessions when she'd heard Larry and Sergey's dreams time and again, she quit Intel to join Google herself. Eventually Sergey began dating her sister. (Anne Wojcicki and Sergey would marry in 2007.)

In early 1999, Google moved to its new office space on University Place in Palo Alto, over the bicycle shop. The conference room had a Ping-Pong table, and, maintaining the tradition, the desks were doors on sawhorses. The kitchen was tiny, and food was yet to be catered. Larry and Sergey's fondness for physio balls was apparent, as the red and blue plastic spheres were scattered about.

There is a special magic in a start-up of barely a dozen people whose entire existence centers around the shared dream of building the next Apple or Microsoft, only better. At the end of the night, when people who had families and homes with furnishings and air conditioners would otherwise have gone home, Google's young engineers would engage in an iteration of the kind of rambling bull sessions they had experienced in college—only a year or two earlier. "We're all working, like, a hundred and thirty hours a week and sleeping under our desk and doing all this stuff," recalls Marissa Mayer. "But at two or three in the morning, the office would degenerate to us all sitting around on the couches and balls, chitchatting about what we'd do if there weren't only ten or twelve of us," says Mayer. Amping up the thrill was the fact that Google search was generating feedback and excitement far beyond the few cluttered rooms they occupied. Press notices were coming in. They were getting fan letters from librarians, scholars, schoolkids. This was real data indicating that Google actually could change the world. It was like some amazing logic drug.

Marissa Mayer would retain a strong memory of one moment from those late-night sessions. One of the engineers, Georges Harik, was sitting on one of the massive physio balls that Sergey would sometimes use as the end point of a running start and a big dramatic leap. (It freaked out visitors, and even some employees feared emergency room consequences.) Suddenly Harik bounded off it.

"I just want everyone to just savor this moment," Georges said. "Look at how much fun this is. Look at these *ideas*. No matter what happens from right now on, it'll never be as good as it is right now."

Many years later, Marissa Mayer, when she had become an incredibly wealthy and much-admired figure in technology, a subject of numerous magazine covers and a decision maker who almost every day made complex calls affecting hundreds of millions of people, would look back at that moment, when all of Google could just about fit in an SUV. "Georges is brilliant, and he's very rarely wrong," Marissa would say. "But when he said that, he couldn't have been more wrong."

It would get *much* better.

From the outside, Google behaved like hundreds of start-ups before it, some that succeeded and many more that fell off the earth. Its employees worked hard, went on ski trips, and had parties where everybody wore tropical clothes, drank garish mixed cocktails, and wound up sitting in the kitchen listening to John McCarthy, the crusty Stanford AI pioneer who miraculously showed up. But those who spent time talking to Larry and Sergey knew that there was something special about them and their company. The two founders had already sketched a road map that struck observers as ludicrously grandiose. But their determination and confidence when they explained their vision imbued an almost hypnotic plausibility into their wild expectations. And there was that search engine they built, so good it was scary.

Page was more of the driver of the vision. "Larry always wanted it to be a bigger thing—as soon as the opportunity presented, it was full speed ahead," says Craig Silverstein. "Sergey was consistent with that, but I don't think he has that drive to the same extent that Larry does. I don't feel as confident saying what would've happened had Sergey made all the shots."

Less than a year after Google moved to University Avenue, the company had already outgrown the space. This time Page and Brin figured they would move into a space they could barely fill, assuming that it wouldn't take terribly long to grow into it. They found a 42,000-square-foot space in Mountain View, just south of Palo Alto. It was one large building in a group, off a frontage road parallel to Highway 101: 2400 Bayshore Parkway. Through a contact they called on a real estate expert named George Salah, who handled facilities for Oracle. Only as a favor to his friend did Salah agree to eyeball the vacant building and give them some advice. He was surprised to learn that Google actually was looking for a full-time facilities manager, an unusual hire for a thirty-five-person company, as Google then was.

It was a summer day in 1999 when Salah dropped by after completing his day at Oracle. One cofounder, Page, was on Rollerblades. The other, Brin, was bouncing on a humongous red gym ball. Salah reported that the building needed some work but was generally fine. When the talk turned to his coming to work there, he challenged them. "What do you need *me* for?" he asked. "How do you see this company in five years?"

Their answer rocked him back on his heels. In five years, they said, Google would be half the size of Yahoo and have multiple international offices, data centers around the world, and a large cluster of buildings in Mountain View. "They're mathematicians, so they'd already done the calculations," says Salah. He took the job, and five years later, he compared their outrageous estimates to what actually happened. "They were right on," he says. "They knew exactly what was coming."

On August 13, 1999, everything was packed, from the monitors to the physio balls. Susan Wojcicki was monitoring the moving men from Graebal Van Lines as they trekked up and down the steps and lugged the boxes into the trucks. Followed by a video camera wielded by Harry the Spider-Man, she took one last spin around the Palo Alto offices, checking out the cubicles, the offices, the closet loaded with routers and telecom connections (already moved to Bayshore), and one office where the businesspeople had mistaken a white cork panel for a whiteboard and written sales figures on it. (Someone had draped a T-shirt over it to hide the numbers.) Her farewell tour was interrupted by one of the moving men, who had apparently been involved when Google had made its previous jump from her house to Palo Alto. He asked if she recalled how long it had been since that transfer.

"Six months," she said, a little wistfulness and even some anxiety in her voice. "Does it seem like shorter or longer?"

The moving man shook his head. "You don't like to stay in a place too long? Or is your company growing?"

"Our company is growing, that's why," she said.

"Now you can afford to get a place with an elevator," said the moving guy. "So you know you're doing good."

The Bayshore Googleplex, also known as Building Zero, or the Nullplex, was the staging ground for Google to build out its culture into a sustainable corporate structure. No matter what happened, engineers would have the run of the place: their Montessori-inspired freedom would be Google's distinguishing trait. One morning Salah came in and was startled to find that one of the engineers, Craig Nevill-Manning, had undertaken a midnight renovation. He had decided that he didn't like his wall. *His wall.* He had gotten some of his colleagues to help and removed huge slabs of drywall. Nevill-Manning greeted Salah with a big smile. "I love this!" he said. "This is so much better than it was before!" Despite the fact that he was now facing a corridor where people were constantly passing by, sometimes on Segways or Rollerblades, Nevill-Manning claimed that he felt liberated. "So we went back and took the wall apart properly, and everything was fine," says Salah. "And of course later he changed his mind and put the wall back. But he made it a more Googley environment." As did Craig Silverstein, who would come to the office with loaves of homemade bread and walk through the corridors calling, "Bread! Bread!" and people would run out and grab slices.

Even though Google's finances had improved after the $25 million infusion from the VCs, Salah was directed to buy cheaply. Brin and Page gloried in frugality and worried constantly about the opportunity costs of spending in areas that didn't directly benefit search. Though they spared no expense for engineers, in other matters they were cheap. Salah, an experienced negotiator, would buy some furnishings from a busted dot-com and think he'd done pretty well. But Page and Brin would say to him, "Why don't you see if you could get it for half that?" Salah would go somewhere else to get a price that pleased his bosses.

The sawhorse desks became a symbol of Google's parsimony. So did the convention of identifying the inhabitants of a cubicle or office not by embossing the name on a piece of plastic but by pasting a printout of the name on a CD jewel box. Google would often buy furniture from fire sales held at the sites of failed dot-coms. "The mishmash allowed us to create a variety of work settings," says Salah. To his relief, when Eric Schmidt arrived in 2001, the new CEO gave a thumbs-up to the mongrel style. "Don't change a thing," he told Salah. "Make sure it looks like a dorm room."

As Salah learned more about the company and began furnishing the buildings that Google would later populate, he roughed out a set of design guidelines that expressed what he saw as Larry and Sergey's values. The list centered on several "key performance principles." The very first one: "Create a 'Googley' atmosphere."

> Being truly Google goes beyond painting the walls with bright colors and liberally distributing lava lamps. A Googley space is one that reflects—and supports—our employees. We are a diverse team of committed, talented, smart, thoughtful hard-working individuals. Our core values should be manifested in our work environment.

It didn't take long for Google to begin growing out of Bayshore—the head count was doubling in size every few months as deals brought in new traffic, and the success of ads required a whole infrastructure of billing and business operations. Google began looking for more space in the vicinity. It leased a nearby building and moved in the business and sales operations; Googlers dubbed it the Moneyplex.

The center of gravity remained at Building Zero. It wasn't just that Sergey and Larry were there, sharing an office loaded with hockey equipment and the shells of discarded servers. It was where the *engineers* were, and they were royalty at Google. Those who had gotten jobs at Google without computer science degrees—the people churning out tasks such as communications, billing, human resources, and even building facilities administration—weren't exactly second-class citizens, but definitely a lower class of citizens. "There is an absolutely crystal-clear hierarchy at Google," says Denise Griffin, who was hired at Google for a nontechnical job in 2000. "It's engineers and everyone else. And if you want to be here, you have to, at some level, appreciate it."

Still, Larry and Sergey's mission to gather and organize all the world's information—and the messianic buzz that came from making it happen—bound all Googlers together. At 4:30 every Friday afternoon, there was the all-hands meeting dubbed TGIF. The early TGIFs were just a way for Larry and Sergey to relay the latest news, introduce new employees, and maybe give someone a birthday wish. A highlight came when Omid Kordestani would stand up on a carton and announce the week's financial results. The first time he was able to announce that Google made a profit, in 2001, the place went nuts.

Over the years the format of the TGIFs became more formalized, with better production values. Unless they are out of town, Larry and Sergey host the sessions. They always appear more comfortable addressing

Googlers than speaking publicly. (As Google began opening offices around the country and the world, TGIFs were webcast to those locations.) They engage in teasing banter, hitting their marks with clever, if a bit nerdy, humor. First there is a greeting of Nooglers, employees who had just begun their Google careers. They wear beanies with propellers on top and get a round of applause when they sheepishly stand up to be identified. Next there is often a demo of a new program or some corporate initiative. Projected screens of thank-yous always accompany those for all the Googlers involved in the project.

The highlight of the TGIFs is always the no-holds-barred Q and A. Using an internal program called Dory, employees rate questions submitted online, with the more popular ones rising to the top. Brin and Page respond to even seemingly hostile questions with equanimity, answering them in all seriousness with no offense taken. In a typical session, someone asked why the newly hired chief financial officer had gotten such a big contract. Sergey patiently explained that the marketplace had set salaries high for someone filling that role and Google couldn't fill it with a quality person if it underpaid. Someone else griped that the line at the café that served Indian food was too long and suggested that maybe Google should serve Indian food in additional cafés. Larry facetiously suggested that maybe the chefs should just make Indian food that didn't taste as good.

The only time beer is regularly served in the Googleplex is after a TGIF. Nobody drinks too much, because it is only 5:30, and most people slip back to their computers for a few more hours' work before the weekend.

By 2001, Google was looking for more space and began leasing buildings in the immediate area. In 2003, a bonanza came: an opportunity to take over the nearby campus of the troubled Silicon Graphics software company. At one time, SGI had been one of the hottest companies in the Valley. In the 1980s, it had built its headquarters as a statement of its success on the cutting edge of the effort to render the physical world into the pixilated bits of the new digital realm. Unexpected geometric shapes jutted from the buildings, as if a playful hacker had gone overboard with a CAD program, and sunlight hit the ample glass at odd angles. The four sprawling buildings encircled a long commons with a beach volleyball court and a spacious patio perfect for al fresco dining. According to a construction company that worked on the project, "This campus epitomizes virtual reality."

But now SGI could no longer afford to occupy its beautiful complex and was looking for a company to replace it. Google's offices were only a few hundred yards away. Salah did a walk-through and was impressed by how pristine the buildings were. He made a deal to lease the campus. (Google would later buy the property, along with the buildings that SGI had retreated to, a few blocks away on Crittenden Lane, for $319 million.)

The campus was located just east of the Permanente Creek, originally named Rio Permanente after the forces of Colonel Juan Bautista de Anza crossed it in 1776, on their way to establish a mission on what would later become San Francisco. To Googlers, though, the historic arroyo impeded shortcuts between the main buildings and later extensions of the campus to surrounding buildings that held other businesses. For a few days in 2008, some Google employees built and operated a zip line that let them coast over the ravine while hanging on to a tiny trapeze bar connected by pulleys to a cable bridging the gap. The city of Mountain View shut it down.

Salah was surprised that when Silicon Graphics occupied the building, all the cubicles had relatively high walls. And the desks were all oriented inward, with almost no one facing out. "So as you walk through the building, you couldn't find a soul," he says. "They were all there, you just didn't know it. It was dead space." His job, he felt, was to make it as alive as the company he worked for.

The key to vibrancy, he believed, was human density. Though the campus was built to accommodate around two thousand people, Silicon Graphics had had only 950 workers. Not long after Google took it over, it had more than nine hundred people in one building alone. Eventually there would be about 2,500 in those four large buildings. "We want to pack those buildings, not just because it minimizes our footprint but because of the interactions you get, just accidental stuff you overhear," says Salah. "Walking around, you feel good about being here. And that's what's Googley."

Page and Brin worked closely with Salah to make sure that the buildings expressed Google's values. Those included design features that would promulgate not only good feeling and efficiency but their growing environmental consciousness. In Building 43, which would house the search teams as well as Page and Brin's offices, Page insisted on sustainable and low-energy elements, including PVC-free Shaw carpets and automated solar MechoShade shades. (The building numbers on the new campus did not represent the count of Google's structures, but were holdovers from the SGI numbering.) Page made Salah take samples of the air inside and outside the building. The results were excellent—toxic emissions well within the approved levels of the Bay Area Air Quality Management Control District and other government standards. "It was, like, .0001 parts per billion," says Salah of the report he handed to Page. "Larry looked at it, handed it back and said, 'Can we get this to zero?'" Google wound up building superpowerful fans to power a high-end filtration system. It made for a higher electric bill, but the air quality met Sergey and Larry's standards. "They're two very sensitive people," says Salah. "They smell things most of us don't smell."

Until then Google's culture had informally emerged from its founders' beliefs that a workplace should be loaded with perks and overloaded with intellectual stimulation. The new campus formalized this inclination. The centerpiece and symbol of their view of the ideal work experience was free and abundant healthful food in an atmosphere that forged employee bonding and the sharing of innovative approaches to work. When new Googlers gathered for their orientation welcome session, the human resources person would explain that Google begins with the stomach. "We take our food very seriously—I've never seen an organization so fixated on food," a human resource exec told a crowd of a hundred Nooglers in May 2009.

Brin and Page had been thinking about a free cafeteria ever since Susan Wojcicki's house and had even talked to some local chefs about their working for the company when it moved to University Street. One of the candidates, Charlie Ayers, had asked Sergey why a company of twelve people needed a chef. As he had told George Salah, Brin said that the company was small at the moment but was destined to be huge. Nonetheless, the Palo Alto space was too small for food services, and the idea was shelved. 2400 Bayshore had sufficient space, however, so Google set up a café. Keeping employees on-site would not only save time but allow Googlers to mingle with all the newcomers who were arriving. Google posted an opening on its website for "an innovative gourmet chef." The ad ended with a scrumptious carrot: "The only chef job with stock options!"

Ayers won the competition for the job. Beginning in November 1999, he cooked for the Google workforce, then numbering around forty. Since his résumé included occasionally preparing meals for the Grateful Dead, press accounts often described him as a former full-time chef for the band. (Google never made much of an effort to disabuse the media of that notion, and as the years went on, Charlie was thought to have been as much a part of Deadhead culture as Mountain Girl or Rick Griffin skulls.) He began cooking in a modest café at the Nullplex, but when Google moved into its Silicon Graphics campus, a huge multilevel space in Building 40 was designated Charlie's Café. The food stations offered a dazzling bounty from various cuisines. And if the cafés weren't enough to stuff you, the work areas themselves had countless microkitchens filled with snack foods, vitamin-infused water and other beverages, and high-end coffees, some of them brewed in complicated espresso machines whose operation often required every bit of a Googler's IQ.

As huge as Charlie's was, soon Google's workforce grew too large to fit into it. Working with an outside caterer and a variety of chefs, Google built a cuisine complex that journalists loved to dwell upon. By 2008, it had eighteen cafés in Mountain View, spread over a couple of square miles of the campus, which continued to expand as Google snapped up nearby buildings abandoned by other Valley businesses. You could now drive down Charleston Road, which fronted the original Silicon Graphics campus, and for a half mile almost every building on both sides of the street sported the Google logo. Though Charlie's in Building 40 was the most spacious café, with the broadest menu, food-snob Googlers regarded it as a tourist attraction; it was the place Googlers took their guests to, and it was often populated by people attending conferences on campus. The other eateries were more like restaurants beloved by a neighborhood clientele. Walking around Google offices, you would occasionally see charts to help a product group keep track of their lunch venues: a foodie version of the celebrated Traveling Salesman Problem.

At all the cafés, the menu choices reflected a proscriptive view of nutrition. Google chef Josef Desimone once told a magazine, "We're here to educate employees on why agave-based soda is better for you than Coca-Cola." Café 150 limited its menus to items grown or produced within 150 miles of campus. A café called 5IVE in another building prepared its dishes with five ingredients or less.

How much did it cost Google to provide great food to its employees? "It's less than a rounding error," says Sergey Brin. Stacy Sullivan, Google's director of human resources, was a little more specific. When asked whether the rumored number of $17 a day per employee was accurate, she said, "I don't have the exact amount—it could be $15, it could be $17. It's some amount that's not totally outrageous but significant." (At $17, that's a total of about $80 million a year for free food.)

Food was only the most notable of the other Google perks. Without leaving the campus you could see a doctor, do Pilates, get a Swiss massage. (Google's masseuse, who wrote a book about her experience—she did not go the warts-and-all route—became a millionaire after the IPO.) Over time, Googlers would wind up with a closet full of corporate swag—jackets, caps, raincoats, umbrellas, fleece jerseys, prints, and more T-shirts than a U2 tour. At one point, Google gave employees backpacks full of survival gear in case of an earthquake.

"It's sort of like the corporation as housewife," wrote Googler Kim Malone in an unpublished novel. "Google cooks for you, picks up and delivers your dry cleaning, takes care of your lube jobs, washes your car, gives you massages, organizes your work-outs. In fact, between the massages and the gym, you'll be naked at work at least three times a week. It organizes amazing parties for you. And if all that is not enough, there is a concierge service; you can just send an email and they'll run any errand you want for $25 an hour."

Seen another way, Google was simply a continuation of the campus life that many Googlers had only recently left. "A lot of Google is organized around the fact that people still think they're in college when they work here," says Eric Schmidt. Andy Rubin, who came to Google in 2004 when the company bought his mobile-technology start-up, guessed that since Brin and Page had never been in the workplace before founding Google, "they structured things from what they were familiar with, which was the PhD program at Stanford. You walk between buildings here and see people interacting like they would at a university. When we hire people, we grade the way they answer each question on a 4.0 basis, and if the average scores are below 3.0, we don't hire them. We have these GPSs, Google Product Strategy meetings, that are run like PhD defenses."

The Google campus hosted a constant flow of technical lectures by employees and visiting computer scientists. Google also sponsored an author series that featured several book talks every week, sometimes several appearances in a day. It regularly showed movies on campus, and when geek milestone films debuted, such as new installments of the *Star Wars* series, Google often bought out a theater and sprang employees early for the showing. Politicians, actors, and musicians made it a point to include a Mountain View campus visit on their schedules. "You get an email at two in the afternoon saying, 'Hillary will be here at 5, drop by if you want to,' and you do come to expect it," says Devin Ivester, a longtime Googler. On a given day, you might hear Condoleezza Rice on foreign policy, Woody Harrelson on hemp farming, a reading from Barbara Kingsolver, or a Regina Spektor miniconcert. An otherwise obscure Googler, an engineer named Chade-Meng Tan—the job description on his card is "Jolly Good Fellow"—made it a point to get his picture taken with famous campus visitors. A montage of some of his greatest poses (with Bill Clinton, Muhammad Ali, Gwyneth Paltrow, Salman Rushdie, the Dalai Lama) was featured on a prominent wall in Building 43. ("I'm Chinese, so I give great Wall," he would joke.)

Google even had its own version of the Learning Annex, called Google University. Besides a number of work-related courses ("Managing Within the Law," "Advanced Interviewing Techniques"), there were classes in creative writing, Greek mythology, mindfulness-based stress reduction, and, for those contemplating a new career funded with Google gains, "Terroir: The Geology & Wines of California."

In April 2010, a software engineer named Tim Bray blogged his experiences as a Noogler on a single day at Mountain View. He woke up at a Google Apartment, a temporary arrangement while visiting from his home base in Seattle. He caught a Google Bus to the campus, doing a bit of work using the Google Wi-Fi supplied to the passengers, arriving in time for free breakfast at one of the Google cafés. For lunch, a companion took him to the Jia café across a few parking lots, known for its excellent sushi. (Thursday was Hot Pot day.) Later in the afternoon he wanted to buy a new camera, so he borrowed one of the free electric-powered Toyota Priuses available to employees and drove to a Best Buy to make his purchase. At 6:30 P.M. someone said, "Dinner?" and he accompanied coworkers to yet another Google café, eating al fresco at picnic tables as the sun set over the lap pool, the beach volleyball court, and the full-size replica of a *T. rex* fossil nicknamed "Stan."

Eric Schmidt loves comparisons of the Google lifestyle to the college experience. "The American university system is the greatest innovation engine ever invented," he says. The only problem, he conceded, was the employees who cook up stratagems to actually *live* on Google's campus. "But the fact of the matter is that for some people living here makes sense," he says. "Their friends are here, it's what they're familiar with, and the things they do here are very similar to what they did in college."

The personal perks are more than matched by Google's aggressive efforts to provide ideal conditions for employees to actually do their work. Joe Kraus, an early Internet entrepreneur (he cofounded Excite) who inevitably wound up at Google after it bought his start-up company in 2008, was pleasantly stunned at the relentless attention to removing the impediments to productive work time.

He saw particular genius in the way Google provisioned its conference rooms. There are hundreds of these rooms at Google, named mostly after far-flung locations around the globe (e.g., Ouagadougou, the capital of Burkina Faso), scheduled in sixty-minute slots with Google's web-based calendar software (many have small wireless displays by the door indicating who has booked the room for that day). Each room contains a large table with a slot in the center. Protruding out of that slot are snakes of cables from computer chargers for both Macintosh and Windows laptops. Thus no meeting will be delayed while someone dashes back to his office to get a charger. There are also cords that plug the computer into a projector that beams the display onto the wall—a standard companywide system so no one has to fumble while figuring out which protocol this room happens to demand. Likewise, for VC—which for almost all Googlers means "video conferencing," and not the moneybags types who fund companies—there's a single standard, and any Google employee could get a remote video connection going in her sleep. There is also a constantly replenished supply of pens and dry markers. Essentially, Google has eliminated a potential hundreds of thousands of downtime hours that employees would otherwise spend on housekeeping errands.

Even more time is saved by Google's ubiquitous "tech stops" spread about the buildings: these are, in essence, tiny computer shops, indicated by neon markers. When a piece of equipment fails or there is a sudden need for a new mouse or phone charger, all a Googler needs to do is walk no more than a few hundred feet to one of those locations, and almost instantly he or she will be made whole.

That attitude extends to some of the corporate protocols that at other companies have employees gnashing their teeth at unfriendly, complicated systems that divert their efforts to filling out forms instead of actually working. For instance, when Googlers complained that the expenses process was a time-wasting drudgery, Google set up a corporate "G-Card" that automated the work. (In a *Star Trek*–themed video to explain the system, a Mr. Spock–like character said, "The G-Card is a Visa card accepted galaxywide. The Federation pays the bill for you. The charges teleport directly into the new expense reporting tool.")

And if at any time a Googler had the urge to work standing up, podium style, or to use a physio ball as a desk chair, all that is required is to "file a ticket" on a site on the corporate intranet. Very quickly—often that day—someone appears to make the adjustments to the office to optimize the desk. "After trials and tribulations with many ergonomically correct chairs and exercise balls, I've found that just standing up while working is the best for me," says Matt Waddell, who filed a "magic ticket" and had his podium less than twenty-four hours later.

The business perks were of a piece with the fuzzier amenities such as free food, T-shirts, and lectures by Jane Fonda. It was a holistic effort to make sure that when a Googler stressed out, the cause would more often be fear that Larry would kill their project than a broken phone or the inability to get a video connection with a collaborating engineer in Moscow. Such largesse was costly. Companies that treated employees more conventionally—or asked them to endure spartan conditions because of tough times—would dismiss Google's approach as a spendthrift luxury possible only because of the company's profitable business model. But Google was convinced that the money was well spent. This raised the question of whether even a cash-strapped corporation might do better by budgeting money to make its employees happier and more productive. Was it possible that such a workforce might be more likely to turn around a troubled company? If you were a highly sought after recruit out of college, how could such a contrast not affect you? If you were an employee who saw evidence every single day that your company valued your presence, would you not be more loyal? The Montessori kids who started Google thought about those questions and asked, *Why? Why? Why?* If Google ever hits really hard times, it will be telling to see whether the sushi quality falls and the power chargers disappear from the conference rooms.

Google took its hiring very seriously. Page and Brin believed that the company's accomplishments sprang from a brew of minds seated comfortably in the top percentile of intelligence and achievement. Page once said that anyone hired at Google should be capable of engaging him in a fascinating discussion should he be stuck at an airport with the employee on a business trip. The implication was that every Googler should converse at the level of Jared Diamond or the ghost of Alan Turing. The idea was to create a charged intellectual atmosphere that makes people want to come to work. It was something that Joe Kraus realized six months after he arrived, when he took a mental survey and couldn't name a single dumb person he'd met at Google. "There were no bozos," he says. "In a company this size? That was awesome."

Google's hiring practices became legendary for their stringency. Google's first head of research, Peter Norvig, once called Google's approach the "Lake Wobegon Strategy," which he defined as "only hiring candidates who are above the mean of your current employees."

The basic requirements were sky-high intelligence and unquenchable ambition. A more elusive criterion was one's Googliness. This became explicit one day when Google was only a four-person company, still in Wojcicki's house, interviewing a prospective fifth. "It was someone we knew from Stanford who we knew was a smart guy," says Craig Silverstein. Maybe not *that* smart—he spent the entire interview lecturing the young founders on the mistakes they were making and the opportunity that they had, if they were sharp enough to hire him, to have someone in place to fix all those mistakes. "We really needed to hire people at that point," says Silverstein. But not at the expense of the culture. After the candidate left, Silverstein noted the obvious: this guy is not one of us. "Everyone understood that early employees set the tone for the company," he says.

The Googliness factor was something that Carrie Farrell learned about when she became one of the company's first engineering recruiters. She joined the company in 2001 and quickly understood that Page and Brin intended to make Google an exalted destination for the computer science elite. "We would have a list of the hundred best engineers around the world, and we basically had to call them and get them in," she says. But it wasn't only brilliance that would get a candidate a job at Google. When Farrell went to her first meeting of the hiring council (the group that vetted prospective employees), she assumed that she would present her case and, after a brief discussion, the council would accept her recommendation. Instead, she discovered a group determined not to permit unworthies to pass through the portals of geek heaven. Brin, Jeff Dean, Georges Harik, and other engineers began a tough analysis of the candidate, as if Farrell were peripheral to the discussion. Feeling she should be making a pitch for the candidate, Farrell pointed out her guy's credentials and coding acumen. They shut her down, saying that all that stuff was in the package. Then, after more heated conversation, they turned back to Farrell and began pelting her with questions: When he talked to the interviewers, what was he like? Good eye contact? Did he seem like a nice guy? Did he seem like someone you'd want to sit next to? Farrell was dazed.

She came to realize that they were schooling her on how to determine who would fit into Google's culture. One early employee called it "the Googliness screen." While the engineers involved in the process would evaluate the test code the candidate had to produce, it was her job to determine whether the person was both creative and sufficiently thick-skinned to defend her stance on a technical or strategic issue. "This is a tough environment," she says. "People need to know what they're talking about and be able to defend themselves, to communicate what they're thinking and feeling." If a candidate was rude to the receptionist, that was a deal breaker.

But Google's practices had a whiff of elitism as well. From the beginning, Google profiled people by which college they had attended. As Page said, "We hired people like us"—brainy strivers from privileged backgrounds who aced the SAT, brought home good grades, and wrote the essays that got them into the best schools. Google sought its employees from Stanford, Berkeley, University of Washington, MIT—the regulars. There were exceptions, but not enough to stop some Googlers from worrying that the workforce would take on an inbred aspect. "You're going to get group-think," warned Doug Edwards, an early marketing hire. "Everybody's going to have the same background, the same opinions. You need to mix it up."

Even more controversial was Google's insistence on relying on academic metrics for mature adults whose work experience would seem to make college admission test scores and GPAs moot. In her interview for Google's top HR job, Stacy Sullivan, then age thirty-five, was shocked when Brin and Page asked for her SAT scores. At first she challenged the practice. "I don't think you should ask something from when people were sixteen or seventeen years old," she told them. But Page and Brin seemed to believe that Google needed those . . . *data*. They believed that SAT scores showed how smart you were. GPAs showed how hard you worked. The numbers told the story.

It never failed to astound midcareer people when Google asked to exhume those old records. "You've got to be kidding," said R. J. Pittman, thirty-nine years old at the time, to the recruiter who asked him to produce his SAT scores and GPA. He was a Silicon Valley veteran, and Google had been wooing *him*. "I was pretty certain I didn't have a copy of my SATs, and you can't get them after five years or something," he says. "And they're, 'Well, can you try to remember, make a close guess?' I'm like, 'Are you really serious?' And they *were* serious. They will ask you questions about a grade that you got in a particular computer science class in college: Was there any reason why that wasn't an A? And you think, 'What was I doing way back then?'"

Google persisted in asking for that information even after its own evidence showed that the criteria weren't relevant to how well people actually performed at Google. The company sometimes even reinvoked undergrad grades when determining the position of Googlers well after their hiring. "They know there's no correlation between [performance and] where you went to school and your GPA, because we've done correlation studies," says Sullivan. "But we still like to ask, because it is an important data point."

Marissa Mayer was a defender of the practice. "A GPA is worth look-ing at, because it shows an element of diligence," she says. "Can you meet deadlines, do you have good follow-through? We know that good students will get their work done on time, they'll get their presentations done, they'll get their code done right." A score over 3.5 generally puts you in the clear; between 3.0 and 3.5 generated some concern in Google's hiring teams. Anything less was serious trouble. And even if your professional résumé shone, a lack of a degree at all was a major handicap. Another midcareer hire, Devin Ivester, who had been a creative director at Apple, thought his hiring was on track when he got a call from his recruiter saying that Google really liked him but there were some blanks in his application—specifically, his college graduation date. "I never graduated," he said. "I started a busi-ness." "That's going to be a problem," she said. That hurdle was overcome only because he had gotten the highest recommendation from an early Googler.

But Ivester's experience showed that Google could accommodate ex-ceptions to its standards. Just as in the case of elite institutions, the stray C or a non-Mensa SAT score could be trumped by an accomplishment that indicated that one was special. "It's like they did some crazy skiing thing or could do the Rubik's cube better than anybody," says early employee Megan Smith. Stacy Sullivan could recall having trouble hiring someone in inter-national sales—until she noted that his résumé cited a foosball champion-ship in Italy. "That's pretty good," said Sergey. "We can hire him." If the guy worked that hard at *something*, the logic went, he'd probably be pretty good at selling ads. And if you were stuck at the airport with him, you'd have the best foosball conversation ever.

Tales of the stringent Google hiring process gave rise to an entire genre of web literature, generally mini-memoirs about how the author had navigated (and, more often than not, failed at) Google's arcane hiring ob-stacle course. Generally, even those with dashed hopes expressed gratitude at a lesson well learned and a great meal at Charlie's Café.

As years went by, the company streamlined the process. After a period when candidates would go through a series of as many as twenty interviews, Google whittled down the number. Even though the company's metrics determined that after four interviews the returns diminished, candidates often had closer to eight. "It used to take forever—anywhere between six and twelve months—to get hired by Google. Now it takes, on average, something like forty-six to sixty days from start to finish," says Laszlo Bock,

Google's director of People Operations. (He describes his role as "HR with math.") If a hiring council wanted to go beyond eight interviews, it had to seek Bock's approval.

Still, even in its short form, landing a job at Google put you through a process that made a Harvard application look easy. The interviews, loaded with brainteasers that would challenge Gauss and computer-coding versions of *Jeopardy*, were only the first stage. The recruiters would comb the data, and, if they were high on the candidate, they compiled a detailed packet including all the interview feedback, academics, references, and so on. It could run twenty to forty pages. Then the application went to a hiring council made up of people with some expertise in the area—but *not* those who would directly manage the new employee. Otherwise, the temptation would be too great to give an offer to a substandard employee because "every manager wants some help rather than no help," says Peter Norvig. The council then did its own analysis. "We read through about eight pieces of feedback—each is more than a page—that discuss analytical ability, overall intelligence, technical skills, cultural fit, résumé, and sort of an overall summary piece," says Marissa Mayer. If the council gave thumbs up, an executive management group reexamined the packet to make the penultimate call.

The last word always went to Larry Page, who insisted on signing off on every employee hired at Google. For every hire, he was given a compressed version of the packet, generated by custom-made software that allowed Page to quickly see the salient data but also empowered him to probe into the gritty details should he choose. "It's sort of a nested electronic index of everything," he says. Page would get a set every week and usually returned them with his approvals—or in some cases bounces—in three or four days.

Page didn't think it unusual or a control-freak quirk that his personal seal was required for every hire. "It helps me to know what's really going on," he says. "I can get a pretty good feel for that in a short amount of time. I occasionally do a spot check, to ask what is the real quality of person we're hiring." On the day he spoke about this, in early 2010, he cited his most recent session, a few days earlier. "It only took me about fifteen to twenty minutes to do, and we hired probably over a hundred people."

2

"I look at people here as missionaries—not mercenaries."

It was Bill Campbell's idea to gather a few key Googlers together and hammer out a set of the young company's corporate values. He had no idea that it would be the source of a motto that would become a controversial self-definition of the company—a combination guiding light and curse.

Campbell was a Silicon Valley legend: if movers and shakers there were assigned human PageRanks according to important links, he'd be a rare 10. A former football coach at Columbia who had run Apple's software company in the 1980s, Campbell was the chairman of the software company Intuit. He was also best friends with Steve Jobs; in the Valley that was like being "1" on God's speed dialer. In early 2001, John Doerr had brought him into Google for an unofficial but critical role as an executive coach. A burly, profane straight shooter who mixed his macho with bearlike hugs and verbal wet kisses, Campbell improbably connected not only with Brin but with the not-so-huggy Page. Even more than Eric Schmidt, he became the father figure in Google's corporate family and was instrumental in easing the tensions in Schmidt's bumpy process of establishing his role in Google's ruling troika.

Brin and Page's idealistic views of a corporate culture impressed Campbell, but he worried that as the company grew, those values would be diluted, misinterpreted, or ignored as more layers wedged between the founders and a workforce of thousands. At Intuit, a group of employees had compiled a set of corporate values that could be shared both inside and outside the company. Campbell convinced the executives at Google that they should do something similar.

On July 19, 2001, Stacy Sullivan, who had come to Google to run human resources, pulled together a group for that purpose. They gathered in Charlie's, about fifteen of them from various parts of the company, including David Krane from communications, Paul Buchheit and Amit Patel from engineering, and Joan Braddi, VP of search services. Marissa Mayer was there, as was Salar Kamangar. And Campbell. Page and Brin were not in attendance. Charlie made smoothies. It was an unusual meeting.

Sullivan explained the format. People would identify Google's values, and she would write down the good ones with a marker on a giant pad she'd set up on an easel. Some of them were straight from the conventional playbooks of management and self-realization, such as "Play hard but keep the puck down." That was a riff on the twice-weekly roller hockey games that the Googlers played in the parking lot—since no one wore padding, there were frequent reminders not to emasculate anyone with a hard rubber disk. (Minor injuries were nonetheless common.) Another one stipulated, "Google will strive to honor all its commitments."

As Sullivan scrawled these nostrums on the big pad, Paul Buchheit was thinking, This is lame. Jawboning about citizenship and values seemed like the kind of thing you do at a big company. He'd seen enough of that at his previous job at Intel. At one point the chipmaker had given employees little cards with a list of values you could attach to your badge. If something objectionable came up you were to look at your little corporate values card and say, "This violates value number five." Lame. "That whole thing rubbed me the wrong way," Buchheit later recalled. "So I suggested something that would make people feel uncomfortable but also be interesting. It popped into my mind that 'Don't be evil' would be a catchy and interesting statement. And people laughed. But I said, 'No, *really*.'"

The slogan made Stacy Sullivan uncomfortable. It was so *negative*. "Can't we phrase it as 'Do the right thing' or something more positive?" she asked. Marissa and Salar agreed with her. But the geeks—Buchheit and Patel—wouldn't budge. "Don't be evil" pretty much said it all, as far as they were concerned. They fought off every attempt to drop it from the list.

"They liked it the way it was," Sullivan would later say with a sigh. "It was very important to engineering that they were not going to be like Microsoft, they were not going to be an evil company."

When the meeting ended, "Don't be evil" was just one of a number of broad statements on an otherwise timid list of values. But Amit Patel felt that when it came to corporate values, that phrase really said it all; follow that commandment, and the rest should flow. Patel, remember, was one of Google's first engineers. He had been an early keeper of the logs and had focused on the way they could be used to demonstrate Google's value as a barometer of public interest. Now he had a new crusade. He would imprint the phrase into Google's corporate subconscious. Making use of the whiteboards that were ubiquitous in the hallways and conference rooms in the Googleplex, he scrawled the phrase over and over in his distinct calligraphic style, a sans-serif, Tolkien-esque script. Amit Patel became Google's Kilroy.

"He wrote everywhere he could," says David Krane. "It became this atmospheric, pervasive reminder."

"It was just an informal sort of reminder that we're all here to do the right thing," says Cindy McCaffrey, head of PR at the time. "Everybody felt good about it, especially the engineers. It meant, 'Look, out in the world, there are all kinds of companies doing evil things and we have an opportunity here to always do the right thing.'"

It had a powerful effect within the company. Even in the kingdom of data, there was one thing that you could go on by gut: what was evil and what was not. The concept could impinge on your consciousness in small ways. You might be in a microkitchen eyeing someone else's leftovers in the fridge and then see the little note saying "Don't be evil." And, says David Krane, "You realize, it can mean, 'Don't take someone's food that looks appealing.'" But it also applied to much bigger things, like maintaining a stiff line between advertising and search results, or protecting a user's personal information, or—much later—resisting the oppressive measures of the Chinese government.

For months, "Don't be evil" was like a secret handshake among Googlers. An idea would come up in a meeting with a whiff of anticompetitiveness to it, and someone would remark that it sounded . . . *evil*. End of idea. "Don't be evil" was a shortcut to remind everyone that Google was *better* than other companies. Since the slogan was internal, no outsiders were talking about it. But then Eric Schmidt revealed Google's internal motto to a reporter from *Wired*. To McCaffrey, that was the moment when "Don't be evil" got out of control and became a hammer to clobber Google's every move. "We lost it, and I could never grasp it back," she says. "Everybody would've been happy if it could've been this sort of silent code or little undercurrent that we secretly harbored instead of this thing that set us up for a lot of ridiculous criticism." Elliot Schrage, who was in charge of communications and policy for Google from 2005 to 2008, concluded that "Don't be evil" might originally have benefited the company but became "a millstone around my neck" as Google's growth took it to controversial regions of the world.

Nonetheless, most people at Google continued to take pride in being associated with that risky admonition. "It's easy to take a cheap shot at them with that as a motto," says John Doerr. "But I think it's served them well." Doerr believes that the meme is so deeply implanted in the Google ethos because the rule became internalized. You wouldn't hear it much in the boardroom, he says, because "it doesn't need to be said—it's implicit."

Alan Eustace, Google's director of engineering, believed that the motto simply reflected what's in the souls of Googlers: "I look at people here as missionaries—not mercenaries," he says.

In any case, the founders themselves embraced "Don't be evil" as a summation of their own hopes for the company. *That* was what Google was about: two young men who wanted to do good, gravitated to a new phenomenon (the Internet) that promised to be a history-making force for good, developed a solution that would gather the world's information, level the Tower of Babel, and link millions of processors into a global prosthesis for knowledge. And if the technology they created would make the world a better place, so would their company; Google would be a shining beacon for the way corporations should operate: an employee-centric, data-driven leadership pampering a stunningly bright workforce that, for its own part, lavished all its wit and wizardry on empowering users and enriching advertising customers. From those practices, the profits would roll in. Ill intentions, flimflammery, and greed had no role in the process. If temptation sounded its siren call, one could remain on the straight path by invoking Amit Patel's florid calligraphy on the whiteboards of the Googleplex: "Don't be evil." Page and Brin were *good*, and so must be the entity they founded.

Which explains why Larry Page and Sergey Brin made the expression into the centerpiece of the initial public offering that transformed Google from a clever Internet start-up into a corporate phenomenon.

Neither Page nor Brin wanted to go public. The idea of hewing to the complicated reporting protocols of a public corporation was anathema to the secretive Page. And during the time when going public became a virtual imperative—in early 2004—the "hiding strategy" was still in effect. Talking to a reporter at that time, Page and Brin insisted that an IPO was not a foregone conclusion. "I think there's always the opportunity to screw it up, be it private or public," Brin said. "Perhaps I'm naïve, but I think that we could maintain Google being private or public."

But by that point, going public was inevitable. The previous year, Google had begun its path toward the public offering that was destined to be a Silicon Valley milestone. The venture capitalists, as one would expect, were forceful advocates; selling stock on the marketplace was their means of realizing the huge payback their investment had reaped on paper. And Page and Brin's arguments against the move had become progressively weaker. The attractions of remaining private were stealth and control. But regulations required a company with more than five hundred shareholders to reveal financial information anyway. In 2004, Google crossed that line. In any case, many of Google's employees deserved the opportunity to convert some of their own options to cash. It was almost sadistic to deny them.

Google would go public. But Larry and Sergey would do it their way. The process played out as a slow-motion conflict. It was the values of Google squaring off against the values of Wall Street, which embodied everything its founders despised about tradition-bound, irrational corporate America.

The first order of business was making sure that outside shareholders (who almost by definition would not be as smart as Googlers) would never be able to overrule LSE's decisions. Their model was Warren Buffett's Berkshire Hathaway, which was the most prominent example of the dual class ownership structure. In Google's case, ordinary investors would buy class A stock, which counted as one vote per share. Class B stock, restricted to founders, directors, and owners, would have a weight of ten votes a share. The vast majority of class B stock was owned by Page, Brin, and Schmidt. This way Brin and Page could maintain control even if their combined shares fell well short of 50 percent of the total.

Google warned investors that it intended to ignore short-term gains in favor of enduring value. Google also said that the information it provided every quarter would adhere to the minimum required by the law and generally be much less than other companies provided. In short, if you bought Google, you were taking a flier on its leaders. These specifications did not please VCs John Doerr and Mike Moritz—in theory, they would make shares less valuable to investors—but they accepted them. Even with those restrictions, Google's IPO would easily reap over a billion-dollar profit for each VC's fund.

Brin and Page decided that the IPO would be conducted by auction. Their impulses were both egalitarian and financial. In a typical IPO, the opening price is set much lower than the market would dictate. Opportunities to buy shares are available only to insiders—people connected to the investment banks organizing the offering or the company itself. Within hours the shares reach their true market price, often many times what the insiders paid for them. (When Netscape had gone public in 1995, shares had opened at $28 and been priced at $75 by the end of day.) That was unfair to the general public but also penalized the company, which wound up receiving less than the true value of its shares. In theory, an auction would eliminate those problems. The concept had been used previously, but never for a public offering the size of Google's, which would certainly sell over a billion dollars' worth of stock.

Eric Schmidt later said the tipping point for this decision was a letter "from a little old lady" who was griping in advance that whenever she tried to invest in an IPO, stockbrokers would get there first and she'd be shut out. But the real lure was the math of it. Logically, it seemed to be a better approach, and that meant a lot at a data-driven operation like Google. "We're an auction company—we're going to run an auction," Schmidt would later say, as if it were no big deal.

In 2003, Google started hiring people whose skill set was geared toward guiding a company through the IPO process. One was Lise Buyer, a former investment banker who'd moved to the world of Silicon Valley venture capital. She worked with Google's chief finance officer, George Reyes.

In early 2004, Google began contacting investment banks. The company felt it had the leverage to make sure that the ones involved would be on its wavelength. It began by limiting the field to investment banks that had sent it queries about an IPO before October 20, 2003. Those banks each received a solicitation asking for detailed answers to twenty questions on how they would handle the offering. It was Google's equivalent of the show-your-stuff essay that prospective students file with a college. Some bankers were offended at having to explain themselves and immediately got on the phone to try to talk their way out of committing themselves on paper. No waivers were granted.

Hypersensitive about leaks, Google worded each letter to a bank slightly differently, so that it could later identify which banks couldn't be trusted to keep their mouths shut. "It did not stop the leaks, but we were quite comfortable we knew where they came from," says Buyer, who added that Google cut the indiscreet parties out of the offering.

Typically, a bank would bring its heavy hitter—often its celebrity CEO—to the pitch meeting. Google demanded that it meet only with the bankers who would actually be handling the offering. The request was so unusual that some banks refused to believe it. "Goldman Sachs, Citi— pretty much all of them—said, 'Okay, we're going to fly in and bring Hank Paulson, we're going to bring Bob Rubin,'" says Lise Buyer. "And I'd say, 'I'm sure he's a great guy, but he's not going to do our deal—save us the time.'" Eventually, most of the banks got the message, but when Citibank showed up, there was its celebrated leader, Robert Rubin. "To be fair," says Buyer, "he didn't do the usual CEO grandstanding."

Credit Suisse, which had done a great job on the questionnaire, was a dark horse that became the co–lead bank, along with Morgan Stanley, which, as Google's team had expected, diligently answered the questions. Even though Hambrecht was known as the pioneer of the auction-based IPO, it was Morgan Stanley that developed the technology to run the Dutch auction that would determine opening prices.

Google wasn't the easiest client. For one thing, it specified that the fees it would pay would be 2.8 percent of the sale, about half the accustomed rate. (That sent Merrill Lynch running—no way it would allow Google to set *that* precedent.) There were also the complications of the auction, which would take much more time and attention than the normal IPO. And finally, there was the fact that this was *Google*, led by two Montessori maniacs who felt compelled to question traditional methods in every way.

Instances of Google's idiosyncrasies persisted throughout the process, beginning with the total value of shares originally to be offered: $2,718,281,828. Only the geekiest investor would understand that this was a mathematical joke, as those were the first nine decimal places in the irrational number e, known as Napier's constant. More striking was the prospectus. Normally such a document, known as the S-1, was a fairly dry packet that laid out financials, cited risk factors, and gave a straightforward but controversy-free account of what the company was all about. Since SEC regulations were specific, the document usually read as if it had been written by financiers and vetted down to the last dependent clause by lawyers—because it was.

Page and Brin instead drafted a personal letter to potential investors explaining in simple language why Google was special and therefore would have a different relationship with its shareholders than other companies did. It was in the spirit of the famous essays by Warren Buffett in Berkshire Hathaway's reports, as well as the "Owner's Manual" supplied by Buffett to his shareholders. Buffett's dispatches were distinguished by a homespun clarity and a core belief in a nourishing, steady-as-she-goes approach to the fundamentals of business. "We wanted to get people to know what to expect," says Brin. Brin and Page were so wed to an intimate missive, as opposed to committee-created documents, that they decided that the letter would be written mainly by one person, with the two founders alternating each year. The initial edition would be Larry Page's message.

"Google is not a conventional company," began Page's letter, released on April 29, 2004. "We do not intend to become one." It was an explicit warning to potential shareholders: fasten your seat belts!

In his "Owner's Manual to Google," Page put front and center the unofficial motto of Google, "Don't be evil." "We aspire to make Google an institution that makes the world a better place," he wrote. "We believe strongly that in the long term we will be better served—as shareholders and in all other ways—by a company that does good things for the world even if we forgo some short-term gains. This is an important aspect of our culture and broadly shared within the company."

The "Don't be evil" passage generated anxiety within Google's IPO team. "It was very clear that cynical Wall Street was going to rake them over the coals," says Lise Buyer. But once Buyer got past the weirdness of it, she came to agree with Page's approach. "What that letter did more than anything was, it really told people how the company thinks and operates," she says. Even five years later, Google CFO Patrick Pichette would tell potential shareholders, "Read the founder letter, and if you're comfortable, buy stock."

But when Google's S-1 appeared, the first-day news wasn't Larry's letter but the spectacular financial results that followed. "The day the prospectus was available to the public, it was 'Holy shit, somebody cracked the code of the age-old unsolved problem of the Internet,'" says David Krane. Newsrooms around the country began to deploy journalists to get to know this suddenly important force in global business. Google rebuffed the deluge of requests from journalists seeking context and color. It was the beginning of the quiet period mandated by the SEC.

Cindy McCaffrey was almost sick with frustration. She thought that the quiet period was some outdated artifact from the 1930s, when people barely had telephones and information dropped to outsiders was unlikely to spread. "Not being able to respond bred a permanent pattern of inaccuracy in Google coverage," says David Krane, years after the fact. "We're still digging out of that hole to some degree. And it had a tremendous impact on our founders and even our CEO on how they look at journalism and look at media."

Meanwhile, the Securities and Exchange Commission was unimpressed by the charms of Page's "Owner's Manual." "Please revise or delete the statements about providing 'a great service to the world,' 'to do things that matter,' 'greater positive impact on the world, don't be evil' and 'making the world a better place,'" they wrote. (Google would not revise the letter.) The commission also had a problem with Page's description of the lawsuit that Overture (by then owned by Yahoo) had filed against Google as "without merit." Eventually, to resolve this issue before the IPO date,

Google would settle the lawsuit by paying Yahoo 2.7 million shares, at an estimated value of between $260 and $290 million.

That set a contentious tone that ran through the entire process. The SEC cited Google's irregularities on a frequent basis, whether it was a failure to properly register employee stock options, inadequate reporting of financial results to stakeholders, or the use of only first names of employees in official documents. It acted toward Google like a junior high school vice principal who'd identified an unruly kid as a bad seed, requiring constant detentions.

From Wall Street, investment Brahmins waged a back-channel attack on Google's prospects. Their apparent intention was to drive down the price of the opening bid for the stock. Financial journalists—still feeling sheepish for having overplayed Internet companies during the late 1990s bubble—took the bait and filed innumerable stories expressing skepticism about the latest web darling. Google never figured out an effective way to respond.

An integral part of a public offering is a "road show," during which company leaders pitch their prospects to bankers and investment gurus. Brin and Page refused to see themselves as supplicants. According to Lise Buyer, the founders routinely spurned any advice from the experienced financial team they'd hired to guide them through the process. "If you told them you couldn't do something a certain way, they would think you were an idiot," she says.

The tone of the road-show presentations was set early, as Brin and Page introduced themselves by first names, an opening more appropriate for bistro waiters than potential captains of industry. And of course they weren't attired like executives—the day of their presentation of Google's case to investors was one more in a lifetime of casual dress days for them. Google had prepared a video to promote the company, but viewers considered it amateurish. It was poorly lit and wasn't even enlivened by the customary upbeat musical sound track. Though anyone who read the prospectus should have been prepared for that, some investors had difficulty with the heresy that Google was willing to forgo some profits for its founders' idealistic views of what made the world a better place. On the video Brin cautioned that Google might apply its resources "to ameliorate a number of the world's problems."

Probably the low point of the road show was a massive session involving 1,500 potential investors at the Waldorf-Astoria hotel in New York. Brin and Page caused a firestorm by refusing to answer many questions, cracking jokes instead. According to *The Wall Street Journal*, "Some investors sitting in the ballroom began speculating with each other whether the executives had spent any time practicing the presentation, or if they were winging it." The latter was in fact the case—despite the desperate urging of Google's IPO team, Page and Brin had refused to perform even a cursory run-through. Things went better on home turf a week later, at a presentation before a hundred Silicon Valley investors at San Francisco's Four Seasons Hotel. The best sessions of all were smaller meetings where a single member of the triumvirate would present. Lise Buyer accompanied Sergey on one of those trips and thought he was brilliant, connecting with investors one-on-one as he explained the way Google's business worked.

But that was a rare moment of connection in a process hampered by investors' failure to understand Google's unusual business model. Despite Google's release of its financials, Wall Street seemed to have no idea how the company really operated and what plans it had for the future. "We were asked on the road show why we were spending so much in capital," says Schmidt. "And Larry and Sergey looked at each other as if to say 'They don't know yet!'" Had the founders been candid, they would have explained that the capital was being spent on engineering talent, fiber-optic cables, and data centers, creating a nearly insurmountable advantage over their competitors. But they kept that to themselves, even at the expense of failing to persuade investors to buy the IPO.

As the auction date approached, an accumulation of further missteps hounded Google. Some of them involved the auction process. Google had spent a lot of time working out the details, using a team that included its chief economist, Hal Varian, and experts from academia. The company had come up with a way to implement a Dutch auction, in which the final bid—the amount paid by all winners—would be the lowest bid that would raise the required amount of money to buy the offered shares. Meanwhile, Page pushed for a test that prospective investors would be required to pass: answer three questions about Google, just to make sure that you understand the company and aren't just making a trendy bid. It was the closest he could come to demanding potential investors' SAT scores. The SEC nixed the idea.

Google had considerable experience with pleasing users, but in the case of the auction, it could not create a simple interface. SEC rules demanded complexity. So the Google auction was a lot more complicated than buying Pokémon cards on eBay. People had to qualify financially as bidders. Bids had to be placed by a brokerage. If you made an error in registering, you could not correct it but had to reregister. All those problems led to a few postponements of the start of the bidding period.

But the deeper problem was the uncertainty of Google's prospects. As the press accounts accumulated—with reporters informed by Wall Streeters eager to sabotage the process—the perception grew that Google was a company with an unfamiliar business model run by weird people. A typical Wall Street insider analysis was reflected by Forbes.com columnist Scott Reeves, who concluded that Google's target price, at the time pegged to the range between $108 and $135 a share, was excessive. "Only those who were dropped on their head at birth [will] plunk down that kind of cash for an IPO," Reeves wrote.

On August 12, just as the bidding process was about to begin, Cindy McCaffrey took a call from a reporter asking about a press release he had just received from *Playboy* magazine, whose September issue was just about to hit the stands. It featured a long interview with "The Google Guys."

McCaffrey knew that *Playboy* had done an interview with Brin and Page before the quiet period began. Google's PR people had been eager for exposure beyond the usual tech magazines and publications with weighty business sections, and had convinced Page and Brin to cooperate with *Playboy*. On April 22, the writer, David Sheff, had gone to the Googleplex for the first of what he believed would be several sessions. He'd seen this first interview as an icebreaker and held off on some of the more personal or critical matters that he planned to bring up when he'd established a rapport. He'd assumed he would return in a few days for more interviews and a photo session. But when Sheff called Google soon after his visit, he got nothing but evasion. A week later, Google filed its prospectus, and the quiet period officially began. Google told Sheff that if he wanted more time with Larry and Sergey, he'd have to wait until after the IPO was completed. McCaffrey assumed that the project was on hold. In any case, Larry and Sergey didn't want to sit down again with *Playboy*. The interview had been pleasant enough, but they felt that a single session had dispatched their obligation.

Sheff's editor, Stephen Randall, thought that the idea of more sessions was moot. "We had an opportunity to be more newsworthy because of the IPO," he says. "So I decided to crash it through, even though we only had a partial interview." *Playboy* thus had the Google Guys interview no one else could get. "It was a very, very big day for us," says Randall. "You couldn't have asked for anything better."

For Google, though, it was a disaster. Even Google's finance team was stunned. Out of nowhere a photocopy of the issue appeared—the cover story promised "The Women of the Olympics—12 Pages of Spectacular Nudes"—and was being passed around like a social disease. "It made us look like idiots," says Lise Buyer. Google had to contact the SEC to clarify what seemed like a violation of its rules. For a while it looked as though the entire IPO was in jeopardy. Google came up with a compromise that defused the situation: it included the entire *Playboy* interview as an amendment to the S-1. Still, it was yet another indication that these people asking shareholders for billions of dollars looked like a bunch of idiot savant kindergartners. "It has no bearing on my plans to bid in the auction," one banker told *The Wall Street Journal*. "But it's certainly consistent with the lack of adult supervision that seems to go on there."

All the fumbles, postponements, and adjustments took their toll. Articles from that summer had headlines like "Whiz Kids' Blunders Blacken IPO's Eyes," "Google's Way May Not Be the SEC's Way," and one that summed it all up, "How Miscalculation and Hubris Hobbled Celebrated Google IPO." It became obvious that the targets Google had set for the auction would not be met. Brin and Page cut in half the number of shares they planned to sell. Kleiner Perkins and Sequoia announced that they wouldn't sell any of their shares. (They feared the IPO price would be lower than what their shares would fetch on the open market later on.) And the projected price range for winning bids fell from the range of $108 to $135 per share to an estimated $85 to $95. Essentially Google's projected value fell by about 30 percent, to $25.8 billion.

Google stumbled to the finish line on August 19. When the computers calculated the explicit bids, it was determined that the opening price would be $85—every bidder who submitted that price or more would be allocated shares at that sum. It was much higher than the opening price of a typical IPO but less than Google had hoped for.

Sergey stayed in Mountain View that day. "I was tired and didn't want to take the red-eye," he later explained. Instead, he did some code reviews. "This is a great opportunity to make a lot of decisions without Larry or Eric to disagree," he joked to his colleagues at the Googleplex. Charlie Ayers served ice cream in Building 40 all day. In New York City, Larry Page, wearing a suit purchased at Macy's, rang the opening bell at NASDAQ with Eric Schmidt, then went to Morgan Stanley to see how the stock would move. It finished the day at $100, quieting the doubters—somewhat. *The Wall Street Journal*'s headline was "Google Shares Prove Big Winners—For a Day." (In fact, Google stock would never be that low again.) Page and Brin each ended the day worth $3.8 billion.

Those people dropped on their heads at birth who were dumb enough to bid more than $100 for the shares did pretty well. The shares they purchased for $85 realized an 18 percent profit in a single day. Though Wall Street had gotten its licks in, Google could claim success insofar as the auction process gave equal access to all investors. None of that mattered in the ensuing months and years as the stock took off. The stock price climbed to $280 a year later, $383 a year after that, and a little more than three years after the IPO, topped $700.

The Monday after the IPO, Schmidt hosted a postmortem at the weekly executive meeting. "Everybody yelled and screamed for a while," he says. After all the venting, Schmidt turned to Omid Kordestani for his comment. In 1999, Kordestani had spurned other opportunities to join two brash Stanford kids, and now he was unfathomably rich. Maybe a more successful IPO would have made him a little richer at that very moment, but now his financial fate depended on what happened to the share price, not the opening bid. His response played on a convention of the Olympics, currently under way in Athens.

"I would like to declare the closing of the IPO," he said.

Schmidt was delighted. "I hereby declare the IPO is over," he said.

The *Playboy* interview, the SEC, the sniping from Wall Street—none of it mattered now.

The sudden enrichment of Google's workforce presented a serious threat to a culture that aspired to a certain public humility. (Matt Cutts expressed the unspoken code this way: "I like to drive fast, so I don't have any Google-related stuff on my car. I don't want to cut someone off and as I go zooming off have someone say, 'What a jerk! Oh, he's a Googler!'") Its executives took some steps to stem the toxic behavior seen during the recent tech bubble, where newly coined millionaires paid more attention to lucre than product development. In the Googleplex, one's personal wealth could now be constantly monitored on the same computer screens that engaged everyone's attention at every moment. On the day of the IPO, Wayne Rosing, the head of engineering, addressed an all-hands meeting. In his hand he held a baseball bat. He told the Googlers that if he looked in the parking lot in the next few days and saw new BMWs or Porsches, he would use the bat to smash the windshields.

Marissa Mayer told her team that she didn't want them checking the stock price during the day. When her workers did not respond with full compliance, she instituted another policy: if anyone who worked for her spotted someone else in the group looking at the stock ticker, all he or she had to do was walk over and tap that person on the shoulder. Then that person would have to buy you a share of stock. After a number of involuntary exchanges, people either stopped checking or learned to hide their peeking more effectively.

But Googlers *were* affected by stock ownership. (They were, after all, human.) Bo Cowgill, a Google statistician, did a series of studies of his colleagues' behavior, based on their participation in a "prediction market," a setup that allowed them to make bets on the success of internal projects. He discovered that "daily stock price movements affect the mood, effort level and decision-making of employees." As you'd expect, increases in stock performance made people happier and more optimistic—but they also led them to regard innovative ideas more warily, indicating that as Googlers became richer, they became more conservative. That was exactly the downside of the IPO that the founders had dreaded.

Regulations stipulated that Google employees could not sell stock for ninety days after the August IPO. By that time, the stock price had risen to $175 a share. During a press interview at the Googleplex that November day, Eric Schmidt did his best to convey that Googlers were going to remain the same down-to-earth geeks they always were. "Somehow there's this assumption that the people at Google made money and are going to retire on their boats," he said. "*These people don't sail.* Some of them do need to buy a house—they've been living in itty-bitty apartments." He turned to David Krane, a onetime English major who was now a tech millionaire. "Do you sail a lot?" he asked.

"I don't sail," said Krane.

"You see what I'm saying?" said Schmidt. "Look around—everybody's here!"

Indeed, that day the people at Google were improving search quality, selling ads, and figuring out how to work the espresso machine—not sailing. Six years after the IPO, an impressive number of Google's most important early employees—executives such as Susan Wojcicki and Salar Kamangar and core engineers such as Amit Singhal, Ben Gomes, and Jeff Dean—were still working hard at Google, even though they had the wealth of Saudi princes.

Still, that personal wealth would inevitably change the lifestyles of early Googlers. How could it not?

Not long after the IPO, Marissa Mayer shared a recent revelation with a reporter. Previously if she were in a department store and there was a pair of slacks that cost a hundred dollars, she would ask herself whether or not she should buy the slacks. Now she would just buy them. Mayer would later purchase a house in Palo Alto in addition to a penthouse suite in the San Francisco Four Seasons Hotel, and Oscar de la Renta would tell *Vogue* that Mayer was "one of his biggest customers." If you spent time with other early Googlers, it would sometimes slip out that they owned lavish homes in posh Atherton, California, vacation retreats in Hawaii, pied-à-terre brownstones in New York City, and other indications of brimming bank accounts. Eric Schmidt, who was already a tech magnate when he joined Google, owned several airplanes and a yacht. Larry Page would buy his own $60 million pleasure boat. (Not all Googlers eschewed sailing, it seems.) The key was keeping it on the down low. When someone failed to maintain that discipline, colleagues would note it.

Even the Google masseuse noticed the impact of money, especially when it came to the divide between early employees holding valuable options and those who came later. "While one was looking at local movie times on his monitor, the other was booking a flight to Belize for the weekend," she said in a book she wrote. "Don't think everyone wasn't aware of the rift."

Schmidt came to see the IPO as a necessary rite of passage for Google. "I don't understand, and will never understand, some of the specific trade-offs that were made, and to be honest, we don't need to. We were never going to do it the way anybody else did," he said that November. Framed on the wall in the room where he spoke was a poster-sized certificate from Morgan Stanley congratulating Google on the sale of 22,534,678 shares of stock in its August 2004 initial public offering, at the opening price of $85 a share. On the glass covering the poster someone had stuck a yellow Post-it note saying, "SHOULD HAVE BEEN $135."

Five years later, the Post-it note was still there.

3

"People don't want to be managed."
"Yes, they *do* want to be managed."

By the time of its IPO, Google had grown to the size where a company usually sets aside its loose structures and adopts well-established management structures. But Google, in Page's words, was "not a conventional company." Page and Brin wanted it all: a company with thousands of engineers that ran smoothly while still indulging the creative impulses of its people. Every time the head count doubled, the question came up again: could Google's bottom-up style of management actually scale? Page and Brin never doubted it. They envisioned an organizational map of Google as looking like a huge sheet covered with polka dots: small teams, flat organizations. The sheet would just get bigger, that was all.

Both Page and Brin believed that the company should run like the Internet itself: fast-moving, bottom up, going to work every day to make yesterday obsolete. "We were born in the Internet time," says Megan Smith, "so our company's like our products in some weird way."

Google, however, had been through an early ordeal that showed that this flat-org ideal was unattainable. In 2001, Google had more than four hundred employees, reaching the point where it was impossible to pretend that it was an intimate company where everyone knew everyone else. Worse for Page and Brin, despite their best efforts, a layer of middle management was creeping in. Worse still, some of the newcomers were experienced product managers from companies such as Microsoft, whose training made them un-Googley—and those newcomers had difficulty adopting the often heretical approaches of the founders.

Brin and Page came up with a solution: *Google would no longer have managers*. At least not in engineering. Instead, they figured, the engineers could self-organize. That approach worked well in the nascent days of Google. If something needed fixing, people would figure out on their own what was wrong, and what was broken would be fixed. Other people would identify interesting problems in computing, and from those insights new products would arise. At the time Google had just hired Wayne Rosing to head engineering. Brin and Page figured that everyone could just report to him. The engineers would arrange themselves in pods of three, work on projects, and check in with Wayne.

That struck some of Google's executives as madness. Stacy Sullivan, the head of HR, begged Page and Brin not to go through with it. "You can't just self-organize!" she told them. "People need someone to go to when they have problems!"

The newly arrived Schmidt and the company's unofficial executive coach, Bill Campbell, weren't happy with the idea, either. Campbell would go back and forth with Page on the issue. "People don't want to be managed," Page would insist, and Campbell would say, "Yes, they *do* want to be managed." One night Campbell stopped the verbal Ping-Pong and said, "Okay, let's start calling people in and ask them." It was about 8 P.M., and there were still plenty of engineers in the offices, pecking away at God knows what. One by one, Campbell and Page summoned them in, and one by one Page asked them, "Do you want to be managed?"

As Campbell would later recall, "Everyone said yeah." Page wanted to know why. They told him they wanted somebody to learn from. When they disagreed with colleagues and discussions reached an impasse, they needed someone who could break the ties.

Nonetheless, Page and Brin were determined to go through with the plan. They called an all-hands meeting and announced it to a baffled workforce. For a few people it meant leaving the company. Others scrambled to find new roles. On the other hand, the move was welcomed by the engineers, who had been chafing at the creeping management restraints. For example, Eric Veach, who at the time was trying to invent the auction-based AdWords, later said that losing a manager had liberated him to make his breakthrough.

Ultimately, however, the plan petered out. After the initial turmoil, there was a quiet backslide where Google's managerial class reassembled and regained a place in the structure. You just couldn't have more than a hundred engineers reporting to Wayne Rosing. Google was taking on new engineers at a furious rate, and, brilliant as they were, the new people needed some guidance to figure out what to do. "I don't remember Larry and Sergey saying that they were wrong and that we were right, but they agreed we could start to hire managers again, as long as the managers were good culture fits and technical enough and could be highly respected by the engineers," says Sullivan.

Another organizational crisis at Google centered more specifically on product managers—the people who led the small teams of engineers. At Google, teams would typically have a tech lead (the smartest engineer) and a product manager. But it didn't seem Googley to have lesser minds tell the brainiest engineers what to do. Unlike other tech companies, as late as 2001, Google didn't have a top executive focusing on product management, and Schmidt kept suggesting candidates. Not convinced that the job should exist at all, Page and Brin kept rejecting them. Then Schmidt heard that Jonathan Rosenberg, a former executive at Excite@Home, had once impressed the founders during an interview for a VP of marketing job he'd turned down.

Schmidt begged Rosenberg to come in and talk. To get a sense of

Rosenberg's skills, he was asked to audition by delivering a test briefing. At one point in his canned presentation, Rosenberg stared at a spreadsheet calculation in his PowerPoint deck and corrected a subtle mathematical error. Everyone was blown away. (In fact, Rosenberg, knowing that Sergey Brin was supposed to be some sort of math Olympian, had planted the mistake and faked his spontaneous discovery.) Schmidt showed Rosenberg Google's astounding financials, convincing Rosenberg that the job was the opportunity of a lifetime.

But his first year was awful. Larry Page would sit in meetings and second-guess every move Rosenberg made. "I would come to the staff meeting with my structured agenda, the market research we needed to do, the one- and two-year road maps that we needed to develop, and Larry would basically mock them and me," Rosenberg later said.

For Rosenberg, whose leadership style was based on aggression and self-confidence, it was a crushing experience. Google's executive shrink, Bill Campbell, suggested that Rosenberg ask Page what *he* thought Rosenberg should do. Page said that instead of working with schedules and plans, Rosenberg should just listen to the engineers. They were the ones with the ideas that mattered. After taking the advice to heart, Rosenberg finally got it: *engineers rule*. Page wasn't out to get him—he and Brin were just adamant about not wanting product managers telling engineers what to do. He reevaluated his view of Page. Larry wasn't ignorant of management processes; he was simply not an effective communicator. It wasn't until a couple of years later that Rosenberg got the acknowledgment from Page he really sought. Page was showing his mother around Google one day, and he introduced her to Rosenberg. "What does *he* do?" she asked Larry. "Well, at first I wasn't sure," he told her. "But I've decided that now he's the reason I sometimes have free time."

Even as he sorted out his role, Rosenberg had another problem, a difficulty in getting product managers hired. His usual modus operandi was to go to places like Stanford and Harvard and bag the Baker Scholar or the R. J. Miller Scholar. But Page would meet such people and send them home jobless. "They would talk about paradigm shifts and competitive advantage and all that shit Larry wasn't interested in," Rosenberg says. "They weren't *technical*." It was Marissa Mayer who told him the obvious—Page wasn't looking for project managers who were smart enough to understand engineers—he wanted them to *be* engineers.

Mayer suggested that Google look for computer science majors who saw themselves not just as engineers but as future CEOs. Her idea was to assemble a legion of "associate product managers." Google would get them straight out of school, young people with no preconceptions derived from working elsewhere. Their careers would coevolve with Google. "We value insight over experience," says Mayer. "We take people who we think have the right raw skills and insights and put them into roles with a lot of responsibility. And while that happens with APMs, it also happens all across the company. People here might not really be accomplished or have a long career before coming to Google, but they have the right data instincts about their area."

It took months to find the first APM, a Stanford grad named Brian Rakowski. But what would he do? Mayer decided to put him in charge of launching an important product, a web-based email system. On Rakowski's first day, she met him in the Ping-Pong conference room. "You're going to be working on Gmail," she said. Rakowski was speechless. "I was twenty-two years old," he says. "I was shocked that they were going to let someone that young and inexperienced do that job."

A lot was riding on Rakowski—if he flamed out, the program would be tarnished. The engineers on the project didn't welcome a kid coming in as their PM. They asked Mayer if they could interview him first. She reminded them that he was already hired. The situation was defused a bit when the engineers checked out Rakowski's web page. There was a picture of him taken after he'd had dental surgery, and his cheeks were puffed up like some sickly bunny's. This was an indication that the kid had a certain wit and humility. But they still had to submit him to a technical gauntlet, just to make sure that his Stanford CS degree wasn't just some anomaly. Even then, the job presented Herculean challenges. A product manager at Google didn't give orders. His (or her) job was to charm the engineers into a certain way of thinking. It was a Mensa form of cat herding.

The way to do that, of course, was by hard numbers. Information was the great leveler at Google. "Because the APMs work with people who are so much more senior and more experienced, they don't have the authority to say, 'Because I said so.' They need to gather the data, lobby the team, and win them over by data," says Mayer. That process made the managerial weakness of the APM an asset for Google, by making sure that data was at the center of decision making. (Google further cemented this hierarchy by creating a position called UTL, or über tech lead—a wizard-level engineer on a bigger team who *really* calls the shots.) If an APM had an idea, he or she could order up a 1 percent A/B experiment (in which one out of a hundred users gets a version of the product with the suggested change), then go to the über tech lead and the team and say, "Users with this new experience are doing 11 percent more page views and clicking on ads 8 percent more." With ammunition like that, a decision to include the new feature in the product wouldn't be based on a power struggle but on a mathematical calculation. Nothing personal. It was *data*.

The APM program was a huge success. Google provided its young managers support in the form of regular meetings with Mayer and her staff and even regular sessions with executive coaches. Ultimately, the program helped Google maintain its team approach while still focusing on engineering as opposed to the kind of more elusive un-Googley skills that an MBA brings. (One might also note that Google, in its management practices and hiring preference for freethinkers, has achieved a complete turnaround from the ethic posed in William H. Whyte's 1956 classic *The Organization Man*, which describes the perfect corporate employee as "obtrusive in no particular, excessive in no zeal"—the polar opposite of a Googler.)

Executives at Google were still worried about keeping the company's teams lean. "Google still does try to keep things small and have teams that are really motivated, who feel they own the project," says Urs Hölzle. But when a team begins to get too big, Google breaks the project into smaller pieces to keep the teams smaller—it refers to this practice as "load balancing," as if its people were servers in a data center.

Another form of corporate load balancing assures that engineers' dreams won't mess with the bottom line. Around 2005, Google determined a simple formula to distribute its engineering talent: 70–20–10. Seventy percent of its engineers would work in either search or ads. Twenty percent would focus on key products such as applications. The remaining 10 percent would work on wild cards, which often emerged from the 20 percent time where people could choose their own projects. For all the talk about its other, well-publicized fraction—the 20 percent of free time that supposedly gestated Google's big innovations—70–20–10 became Google's magic allocation algorithm.

As the years passed and Google's management system became formalized, a corporate amnesia seemed to envelop Brin and Page's 2001 kill-the-managers caper. Ask Larry Page about it, and he professes only a vague memory. "We were two years old as a company," he says. "You try different things, and we learned things that worked and things that didn't."

One thing that did seem to work was a management trick suggested by John Doerr, not long after the VC made his original $12.5 million investment in Google and joined its board. Doerr was a fan of a complicated system called Objectives and Key Results, usually referred to by the acronym OKR. It was something Andy Grove had devised at Intel (he'd called it Management by Objective), but Doerr believed it was even more useful for start-ups. "It's really important in rapidly growing companies because it allows you to be superclear about what priorities are," he says. His efforts to start OKRs at previous start-ups had met with mixed results, so he had no idea what reaction Larry and Sergey would have. But they were enthusiastic enough to have Doerr come and present it to the company.

So one day in 1999, Doerr took Googlers into a conference room and did a PowerPoint presentation on how OKRs worked. The idea was not just to identify what one wants to do but to break down the task into measurable bites ("key results"). In his book *High Output Management*, Grove imagined the OKR system applied to Christopher Columbus. The explorer fell short of his objective of finding a trade route to India, but he did carry out some subsidiary OKRs: he gathered a crew; he bought supplies; he avoided pirates; and by discovering the New World, he brought riches to Spain.

Doerr had Google at metrics. "Google did more than adopt it," says Doerr. "They embraced it."

OKRs became an essential component of Google culture. Every employee had to set, and then get approval for, quarterly OKRs and annual OKRs. There were OKRs at the team level, the department level, and even the company level. (Those last were used sparingly, for important initiatives or to address gaping failures.) Four times a year, everything stopped at Google for divisionwide meetings to assess OKR progress.

An outsider might have wondered if this were a sign of Dilbertization at Google, an annoying program that diverted energy from real work. But Googlers didn't seem to think so. They saw the OKRs as data, a means of putting a number on the traditionally gooey means of assessing performance. It was essential that OKRs be measurable. An employee didn't say, "I will make Gmail a success" but, "I will launch Gmail in September and have a million users by November." "It's not a key result unless it has a number," says Marissa Mayer. The OKR embodied ambition. "It sanctions the ability to take risks," says Doerr. Even worse than failing to make an OKR was exceeding the standard by a large measure; it implied that an employee had sandbagged it, played it safe, thought small. Google had no place for an audacity-challenged person whose grasp exceeded his reach.

The sweet spot was making about .7 or .8 of your OKR. (Geekily enough, the metric was measured by a decimal representation of how close an employee came to the OKR, with the integer 1 being an exact hit.) At the end of every quarter, employees set their OKRs for the next quarter, and six weeks later, they saw their managers and gave a progress report, using a traffic-light system for grading. "Green light, I'm good to go on that one. Red light, I'm having serious issues. Yellow, possible danger," says McCaffrey. Toward the end of the quarter, all the OKRs were graded, and if an employee was hitting 100 percent, he or she needed something else to do.

What's more, OKRs were not private benchmarks shared only with managers. They were public knowledge, as much a part of an employee's Google identity as the job description. The OKRs appeared on every employee's biographical information on MOMA, Google's internal website. (The name didn't stand for anything in particular—according to Marissa Mayer, Larry Page just wanted something fast and short and easy to type.) You could even see Larry and Sergey's OKRs. "We needed to run our company somehow, and I think having an organizing principle makes sense," says Brin. "We really like transparency and like the idea that we communicate to everybody on roughly one or two pages of paper every quarter what we want to accomplish."

That kind of sharing was another hedge against the creeping impersonality endemic to big companies. At a start-up, everybody knows all their colleagues and what they are working on. Even as Google grew to more than 20,000 employees, it tried to maintain the ability to keep up with everyone else. In addition to MOMA, Googlers could access Project Database (PDB, as it was referred to at the Googleplex) to follow all the things the company was up to—engineering allocations, product manager allocations, product definitions, engineering documents, and specs. Also, Googlers looking for a cool new project could access a section called simply "Ideas," where their colleagues pitched promising concepts that needed manpower.

The internal transparency was especially startling because Google had a phobia about leaks that rivaled that of the Nixon White House. The company was an information lobster, hard-shelled on the outside but soft and accessible on the inside. Sometimes employees didn't get the distinction, as was the case with Mark Jen, a twenty-two-year-old Noogler who started a blog in 2005 called "ninetyninezeros" about his experiences; among the items that apparently displeased his bosses was a comparison of his salary and benefits to those at his previous employer (Microsoft), which paid more. He also noted that Google's business was booming; even without his mentioning numbers, that was interpreted as data best withheld from competitors. Jen was fired before he completed a month at Google.

Google's OKR system was only one of many processes, many imposed by Schmidt, intended to bring a sense of order to a company growing to 20,000 employees. "Google's objective is to be the systematic innovator of scale. Innovator means new stuff. And scale means big, systematic ways of looking at things done in a way that's reproducible," Schmidt says. So Google spent a lot of effort on actual bureaucracy—a regular set of launch meetings and reviews, weekly meetings of the Operating Committee of the top leaders, global product strategy meetings, and a companywide peer review system that consumed enormous time.

"We try not to expose all those things," Schmidt would joke about the organizational scaffolding, "because we want it to look chaotic."

Perhaps the best illustration of Google's creative denial of its Brobdingnagian size was a startling move that its founders made in 2007. For a number of years, Brin and Page drew organizational and clerical support from a pool of four sharp young women known as LSA, or Larry and Sergey Assistants. (Googlers referred to LSA as if it were a single organization. You would say, "I'll check with LSA to see if Sergey can come to this meeting.") The system seemed to work well, but Brin and Page felt constrained. By having assistants, they noticed, it was easier for people to ask things of them. "Most people aren't willing to ask me if they want to meet with me," says Page. "They're happy to ask an assistant." When a meeting request came, an LSA would have to see if Page or Brin actually wanted to do it. In truth, the founders almost never wanted to do it. So one day, Brin and Page abruptly dissolved LSA. They would thereafter have no assistants. Whatever they felt was important at the moment would be their work. Sergey sometimes liked to move his workplace right in the middle of a project he found interesting. And sometimes he or Larry would just take off somewhere. Even the communications people would have no idea where they were.

On one hand, the shift offloaded a lot of menial work to the assistants of other executives. Sergey wasn't about to spend his time mailing packages, so one of Eric's assistants wound up doing it. Using Google's calendar application, which allowed people to share their schedules, certain Google executives and their helpers would make appointments for the founders. Larry and Sergey would regularly attend the key weekly meetings—the Operating Committee on Monday, the global product strategy sessions on

Monday and Tuesday, product reviews at the end of the week, and TGIF at 4:30 on Friday. You could expect them to be present when the board convened. But they wanted to keep much of the week open. "My favorite meeting," says Page, "is the absence of meetings."

It went without saying that Page's least favorite meetings were one-on-one press interviews. "Larry can be a very, very sensitive and good person," says one former Google PR hand, "but he has major trust issues and few social graces. Sergey has social graces, but he doesn't trust people who he thinks don't approach his level of intelligence."

Googlers learned to adapt to this system. If someone needed the founders' approval for a purchase or project, the accepted strategy was stalking. Like the network of amateurs who sit with binoculars at airports and track the peregrinations of private planes, an informal Google pipeline delivered a steady stream of Larry or Sergey sightings. Canny Googlers hoarded knowledge of key interception points. "If I want an opportunity to meet with them, my best option is to go to Building 43 and just plop myself on a couch somewhere," says George Salah. An APM named Jini Kim once got a key approval from Larry by gathering intelligence on his movements and loitering in his expected trajectory. Googlers also knew that there was an elusive window of access in the few minutes following a TGIF. But sometimes you could carefully plot a collision course with a founder and be frustrated when one of them was engaged in deep conversation with the Mexican mogul Carlos Slim or some other visiting dignitary. Or they would simply be in a hurry. Page in particular was a master of the drive-by greeting, flashing a wide, happy-to-see-you smile while slightly picking up his pace, so that if you attempted to follow up with anything more than a quick hello, you found yourself talking at his receding back. "Larry got rid of his assistants so that he would never meet with anyone who couldn't figure out how to get a meeting with him," says product manager Wesley Chan. "If you wanted a meeting with him, you had to find out where he was and harass him."

Larry's and Sergey's peripatetic ways could drive Googlers crazy. Even Eric Schmidt sometimes viewed them acerbically: "Larry will call and say, 'I'm going to go visit Android,'" he says, referring to Google's mobile phone project. "He's not going over there to inspect—he's going over there to have fun." But Maria Montessori might approve. "To be . . . helpful," she wrote, "it is necessary rigorously to avoid the *arrest of spontaneous movements and the imposition of arbitrary tasks.*"

PART FOUR

GOOGLE'S CLOUD

Building Data Centers That Hold Everything Ever Written

1

> "Hi, here I am, and I've got to explain this thing that seems creepy and weird, and convince you it's not so bad."

Paul Buchheit looked like a fourteen-year-old when he joined Google in 1999, his cherubic face crowned with wisps of blond hair. He had grown up just outside Rochester, New York, a typical hacker kid driven by silicon and curiosity, and by the time he entered Case Western Reserve University in Cleveland, he was full of ideas and projects, one of them being a web-based email program. After graduation, he took a job with Intel. But the chipmaker was big and bureaucratic. "I wasn't really loving Intel," he later said, meaning he hated it. He started looking around for an interesting start-up. He'd read about Google on Slashdot, an online discussion site that was like *Entertainment Tonight* for geeks, and started using its search engine. He was impressed by Google's imaginative stab at an interesting technical problem. He sent his résumé to jobs@google.com. The email bounced—the server was down—but he persisted and eventually was granted a phone screener, followed by a face-to-face interview.

Unlike at the other companies he was talking to, the Google people asked smart, technical questions. The one he remembered was "If you have a server that's performing too slowly, how do you diagnose the problem?" On one hand, it was straightforward, but when you thought about it, the question was almost spiritual in its depth. "Surprisingly, it's something that people don't really get," says Buchheit, years later still engaged by the profundities. "Your site is slow, what do you do? What resource is being restrained? Because it's always a bottleneck. Is it CPU-bound? Is it disk-bound? You have to understand the fundamentals of what makes things fast or slow. That's a pretty good question."

Google made him an offer. He didn't have much confidence in the company's future—"I thought they would probably get crushed by Alta-Vista or something," he says—but he viewed it as a learning experience. Even if the company didn't last long, he'd learn about start-ups. He was employee number 23.

In mid-2001, Buchheit found himself liberated from his assignment by the management putsch Page and Brin launched that year, doing away with all the product managers. So he unilaterally decided to revisit his college project and create a web-based email product for Google. He would have the benefit of something that was only just invented when he was at Case Western: the dynamic JavaScript computing language, which could, if you pushed it, help you create a web-based application that behaved like a desktop application running directly on the computer. (That would make it more responsive and flexible than the current web-based mail systems run by Microsoft and Yahoo) "He was writing with the technology that would later be called Ajax, but that term didn't even exist then," says Keith Coleman, who would later head the email product at Google. "Internally, there were a lot of questions about whether this would work at all for a Google project." Within months, Ajax would become a core technology in thousands of web-based computer applications, and Buchheit would look like a prophet.

But what would really distinguish Buchheit's email product from its competitors was storage. He wanted a lot of it. One of the frustrations of people who used email was the constant need to clear out the cramped digital inboxes and archives, products of an era when email use was sparse and storage costs were sky-high, two factors that no longer applied. Of the existing web-based systems, Microsoft's Hotmail offered 2 megabytes of storage and Yahoo only 4. For people with even moderate needs, those mailboxes would fill up in a few days. Almost as soon as you received an email, you had to consider whether to delete it. Weirdly, this problem also plagued people who worked for corporations. Even though storage was increasingly inexpensive, the information technology (IT) people in charge of the corporate systems policed disk space as if it were made of platinum. They would commonly impose impossibly low ceilings on the amount of disk storage allotted to a given account, and if you exceeded the limit, you were unable to access your mail until you weeded nonessential messages out of your inbox.

Buchheit wanted to eliminate that problem. "It was fundamental to the way the product actually worked that I need to be able to save my mail. Otherwise, it's a different product. And then, the other thing is that I thought it would be cool." His mailboxes would have a *gigabyte* of storage—more than a hundred times what competitors offered. For free. This was enough for more than 10,000 emails. And that would be only the start. As storage got even cheaper (an inevitability in the age of Moore's Law), Google would offer more and more space.

An email product was a departure for Google, which to date had concentrated on search. Analysts and business writers continually praised the company for "sticking to its knitting," a practice obviously regarded as a virtue. Anyway, by what logic could the company's mission include offering email service? Even Buchheit's colleagues thought that making a web-based email product was too problematic. They thought that implementing the scheme would be expensive and complicated and were especially doubtful that the JavaScript approach would work well. "Almost everyone thought it was a bad idea," says Buchheit. "Except Larry and Sergey."

Indeed, Page and Brin were thrilled at the prospect. They saw email as a search problem. Your email, after all, was a crucial information corpus. How ridiculous was it that you could find the most obscure item among billions of web pages but it was a tortuous—or impossible—process to dig up an interesting comment you had made a few weeks ago or relocate a book recommendation someone sent for you last year? The most popular desktop email application—Microsoft's Outlook—had a search function so slow and cumbersome that no one used it. So what company better than Google to allow you to easily access your information? The founders wanted to use the system Buchheit proposed for themselves, and volunteered to test it. Soon Buchheit and his team (including his office mate Sanjeev Singh, who became a colead on the project) had a prototype, dubbed Caribou. The name was an homage to "Project Caribou," a doomed initiative in a *Dilbert* cartoon. "Larry and Sergey literally became our first users," says Buchheit. "It was not only key to the product surviving but also becoming a good product."

The first suggestion from the founders was rather obvious. "All the first version did was store and search email—Larry and Sergey said it would be nice to be able to *reply* to emails," says Buchheit. "I said, 'Okay, I guess I can add that.'"

From the start Buchheit wanted revenues. The product could have ads, the same kind you saw on Google search results pages. Instead of relying on the relevance of keywords, ads in Caribou could relate to something you talked about in your email. "People always asked how things could make money, and putting in ads was the obvious thing to do, because that's how Google made money," says Buchheit. "And if we were going to do it, we should do it from the start, so that people wouldn't feel tricked."

Remember, it was Buchheit who originally came up with the slogan "Don't be evil."

A lot of people at Google hated the idea of ads, saying that users would be repelled at seeing ads alongside their emails, especially ads that related to the content of the messages. Opponents also claimed that it was too hard to match ads to the content of emails—it wasn't like search, where people started with keywords. Marissa Mayer, who was the product manager at that point, was particularly opposed. Mayer told Buchheit, who shared an office with her at the time, that targeting ads to email "is just going to be creepy and weird," warning him that people would mistakenly assume that Google had a bunch of drones in some room who were reading your email and matching ads to the private expressions contained therein. Buchheit was on the fence, but his colleague Sanjeev made some back-of-the-envelope calculations and concluded that even a small percentage of people clicking on the ads would produce more than enough revenue to pay for Gmail.

Buchheit figured, why not try it out? The two engineers sat down by Sanjeev's computer and went through his email, trying to pick out a subject and then typing the word into the search engine to see which ads came up. They discovered that Google had plenty of ads in its inventory to produce ads relevant to at least some emails. Then he began figuring out how to automate the process. He downloaded a program from the web that used semantic analysis to distill blocks of text into a few keywords. Then he accessed Google's AdWords system, replacing the keywords that advertisers requested with the keywords he'd extracted from the text analysis. When he was done, a series of sponsored ad links appeared to the right of the body of an email—presumably, linking to products relevant to the email's content. "It was a very basic thing, and I implemented it in a few hours," Buchheit says. (Eventually, Gmail would use the same semantic analysis system as AdSense, based on Georges Harik's Phil project.)

"It took people by surprise," says Buchheit. "It was by far the most negative backlash of any feature release we'd done on Gmail." The annoyed Marissa Mayer asked, "Why are you building this?" But Brin and Page thought the idea was cool and useful, an unbeatable combination. "We were really entranced by it," says Page. "We really felt like, 'Wow, something was mentioned in my email and I actually got an ad that was relevant!' That was amazing. We thought that was a great thing." As for the potential blowback, Brin says, "We didn't give it a second thought. There were plenty of things to question, but I never batted an eyelash at that. It never occurred to me as a privacy thing."

Even Mayer came around. While testing the system, she was in an email thread where she was arranging a hiking date. Up popped an ad for hiking boots. This can actually be useful, she thought, and from that point she was on board.

Caribou took forever to develop. Part of the problem was that Larry and Sergey were so invested in the project. They adopted it as their primary email system and would often drop by to give criticisms and suggestions. Buchheit would often take a working prototype to the weekly Google product strategy meeting, where product managers submit their products to a human wind tunnel of executive criticism. Products have been known to die at GPSs; there are stories of teams entering the conference room, exhausted and hopeful after long hours of getting a demo *just right*, and Page saying, "You're wasting our time" and ordering the project dismantled. Larry and Sergey liked Caribou too much to kill it but dished out very tough love. At one point Page told the group, "I'd rather be doused with gasoline and set on fire than use your product." But finally it was ready to be released in beta version. (Google often kept its products in beta much longer than other companies, signaling that users should be tolerant of faults and that an update was probably around the corner. In the case of Gmail, which became the public name for the project, the beta label was not removed until five years after Google released it, when it had tens of millions of users.)

Brin and Page both thought Gmail was special, so they thought it appropriate to launch it on a day that was special for them: April 1. It was a definite stumble. When your main competitor allows only 2 megabytes of storage, people think you're goofing when you boast a service with *1,000* megabytes and announce it on the day you usually unveil phony products. Even years later, Brin still relished the reverse spin—tricking people by *not* hoaxing. "I liked doing it on April Fool's Day," he says. "We learned some things, but that doesn't mean that we don't want to do audacious things on April 1."

The launch was problematic for a number of other reasons besides the question of whether the whole thing was a spoof. Even though Google was making a public announcement of its new product, the public couldn't sign up for it. Google limited the number of users by declaring that it was by invitation only. At launch, it gave away 1,000 accounts to outsiders, allowing each new user to invite a few more people. Those left out were frustrated.

But much more serious was what happened when people saw how Gmail operated. They were shocked when, alongside the text of emails, they found ads that seemed related to the content. It was as if Google were looking over their shoulder and snooping on their mail.

A second, related complaint came from Google's boast that with Gmail, you could keep your email forever. People were accustomed to having files of email on their own computers, in locations they could identify. And here was Google, the harbinger of a new age where everything—be it business confidential or searingly personal—would be stored on computers owned by Google that were physically God knew where.

Those complaints hit Google's engineers by surprise, because they *wanted* their mail kept forever and believed that in a connected world information was best kept in some futuristic version of safety-deposit boxes, maintained by professionals. They considered the privacy concerns illogical. They trusted machines, and their own intentions were pure—ergo, people should have trusted them.

Inside the bubble of the Googleplex, that made sense, but the engineers failed to understand how, from the user's point of view, Gmail was different. With Microsoft's Hotmail and Yahoo's Yahoo Mail, the low ceiling on storage meant that only a small fraction of mail would be kept by those companies. Google, on the other hand, would keep a comprehensive archive. And though it was true that Microsoft and Yahoo also automatically scanned mail in their systems for viruses and other things, users actually saw the evidence with Gmail. By serving ads related to content, Google seemed almost to be reveling in the fact that users' privacy was at the mercy of the policy and trustworthiness of the company that owned the servers.

And since those ads made profits, Google was making it clear that it would exploit the situation.

But it wasn't just Gmail that disturbed people. Suddenly, Google itself was suspect. Until 2004 Google had been seen as a feisty start-up performing an invaluable service. But it was sitting on a privacy tinderbox. One key issue was Google's retention of user requests and responses when they visited its search engine. You can't get more personal than that. A search history can reveal your health problems, your commercial interests, your hobbies, and your dreams. What would your health care insurer think about your search for "chest pains"? What would your investors think if you searched for "bankruptcy lawyers"? What would the cops think if you searched for "hydroponic equipment"? What would your spouse think if you searched for "afternoon sex encounters"? What would the government think if you searched for "tax resistance"? In 2006, the government, in a fishing expedition for information to help efforts to regulate pornography, would demand that Google and other search engines hand over logs of millions of searches. Google alone fought the subpoena. But when privacy advocates demanded that Google not retain any logs at all, the company balked. Those logs were the lifeblood of Google's persistent drive to improve itself, the oxygen of its effort to become an unprecedented learning machine.

In a sense, Google had been fortunate in postponing the inevitable privacy showdown until Gmail's arrival. The excellence of Google search had been exposing personal information ever since Brin and Page first started spelunking in the caverns of the web. It wasn't Google that put information on web pages and other online repositories, but it was Google that dislodged it all. Like it or not, Google had a role in the process. Though the issue hadn't exploded into an outcry such as Gmail created, it had been simmering constantly. Larry Page recognized early on that "there's going to be large changes in the world because of all this stuff," and those Internet benefits might have a cost. "People will have to think when they publish something online, 'This might be forever associated with me.' Because Google exists." But the problem wasn't just what people published—Google was relentless in finding out everything about them, whether it was an address previously hidden in a database or a twenty-year-old article about a criminal charge that may or may not have resulted in a conviction.

Denise Griffin, a Googler who joined in 2000 and worked in the tiny marketing department, was the person charged with handling complaints. It was often heartbreaking to hear stories of how the things that Google dug up caused hurt feelings and sometimes caused actual harm to people. Google's official stance, with some justification, was that it was simply delivering information that resided on the web. That explanation did little for those who felt exposed; without Google, all that information would have remained buried. "It's very tough for people to conceptually understand that it's not our website [exposing them], it's the web," she says. "We had a few different canned responses that we would send people, trying to explain, and when they would write back cursing, then we would try again with a slightly different version and then a slightly different version."

The worst situation was when someone was put into physical danger from information unearthed by Google—for example, people who had gone to great lengths to hide personal information from abusive ex-spouses and found their efforts undone in a 400-millisecond Google search. "I would feel terrible," says Griffin, who would try to suggest remedies, such as contacting the webmaster where the toxic information lay. But unless there was a legal justification for removing the information—copyright infringements, child pornography, libelous information as determined by a court—Google said it couldn't do anything. And philosophically Google was perfectly fine with not doing anything except in those cases. Brin and Page both believed that if Google's algorithms determined what results were best—and long clicks indicated that the algorithms were satisfying the people who did the searching—who were they to mess with it? That was essentially the message they gave to Denise Griffin when she shared her concerns with them. "They were very frustrating conversations for me," she says. "I lived this. It was really hard to get these emails."

It was a problem that Googlers themselves often saw firsthand. At one point, a search engineer named Jessica Ewing challenged the search team to do something about the fact that the first search result under her name was a mortifying picture of her as a thirteen-year-old Michigan all-state mathlete. "I will never have a date again!" she wailed. But there were less frivolous complaints. When you did a search for Google executive Susan Wojcicki, for instance, the second result was a posting from the Silicon Valley gossip blog Valleywag, inaccurately charging her with stealing the credit for developing AdSense. Wojcicki knew why Valleywag's posting was ranked highly—"to link to a well-read article is not a crazy thing," she says. But she didn't like it. "Yes," she would say when pressed on the issue, "it does bug me."

At least those Googlers understood that their status as employees should give them no privilege to censor the company's indexes when other people could not. One day Denise Griffin got a call from Eric Schmidt's assistant. "There's this information about Eric in the indexes," she told Griffin. "And we want it out." In Griffin's recollection, it dealt with donor information from a political campaign, exactly the type of public information that Google dedicated itself to making accessible. Griffin explained that it wasn't Google policy to take things like that out of the index just because people didn't want it there. After she hung up the phone, she freaked out. *Doesn't Eric know that we don't do that?*

She called her boss, Sheryl Sandberg, and they had several conversations before they finally trudged up to Eric's office and told him it wasn't Google's job—nor should it be—to filter his personal information. Griffin understood how he felt, because she came across upset people all the time. You could explain forever how making obscure but damaging information available in milliseconds was at the core of Google's lofty mission. "Principles always make sense until it's personal," she says. (Schmidt, through a spokesperson, later said that the incident did not happen.)

Then in July 2005, a CNET reporter used Schmidt as an example of how much personal information Google search could expose. Though she used only information that anyone would see if they typed Schmidt's name into his company's search box, Schmidt was so furious that he blackballed the news organization for a year. "My personal view is that private information that is really private, you should be able to delete from history," Schmidt once said. But that wasn't Google's policy. If Google's own CEO had trouble dealing with privacy, how could ordinary people cope?

Google's Gmail conflagration needed dousing. Fortunately for Google, the company had recently beefed up its policy and legal team. Google's original counsel, David Drummond, who came to the company from the big Silicon Valley law firm of Wilson Sonsini Goodrich and Rosati, preferred more of a business development role to a purely legal role, and he hired a group of people with experience in protecting civil liberties to help shape and defend Google's policies.

A big part of the task fell to Nicole Wong, an attorney who had been hired only four months before the Gmail release. She had a joint passion for news and law—she earned a master's in journalism at the University of California at Berkeley while getting her law degree there—but eventually decided on the law. She sent résumés only to law firms with First Amendment practices, winding up at a San Francisco firm with media clients. In 1997, she began to move into Internet-related issues and moved to a Seattle firm that did some privacy work for Google. At a breakfast meeting with Drummond one day, she was pitching her firm for a bigger role at Google when Drummond asked if she'd like to do those things as an employee. The carrot was the ability to write her own job description, which turned out to be a list of legal problems that would trouble Google for the rest of the decade: intellectual property challenges, defamation, invasion of privacy, and content regulation.

Starting at Google on the same day as Wong was another lawyer named Andrew McLaughlin. With a background in Internet administration—he'd worked for the Internet governance organization ICANN, requiring him to deal with a passionate constituency of geeks and freaks—he became Google's first policy director. He didn't know much about Gmail until the day before the product release, when the whole company was summoned to Charlie's Café for a demo. Everyone left with a Gmail account and a T-shirt. McLaughlin left with a headache. Oh, crap, he thought, I better get in on this.

The reaction was all that he feared, best summarized in a CNET headline: "Why Gmail Gives Me the Creeps." Simon Davies, the head of a group called Privacy International, put out a press release saying, "Google looks at privacy the way a worm looks at a fishhook." Google had gone from cuddly Internet icon to Big Brother in one day. From that point on, instead of the introduction McLaughlin had hoped for when meeting legislators and industry groups—"Hi, I'm Andrew from Google, let's talk about policy"—he had to use a different opening line: "Hi, here I am, and I've got to explain this thing that seems creepy and weird and convince you it's not so bad."

When the outburst hit, Page and Brin called for a war room. Buchheit's troops were joined by engineering teams, PR people, and Google lawyers. Brin got on the phone to a sympathetic writer at Salon.com. "We will use good judgment," he promised, after laying out why people should not be outraged.

The most serious challenge came from a California state senator from Fremont, barely out of Wi-Fi range from the Google campus. Liz Figueroa, McLaughlin would later recall, was exploring a run for lieutenant governor and was on the hunt for issues. One of her top staffers had become a father a few months earlier, and he and his wife had begun receiving free samples of baby lotion and other products. The staffer had been horrified that corporations had used personal information to solicit him. "It made a real jihadist out of this man," says McLaughlin. The staffer clearly saw Google's new product—it was reading citizens' email!—as a threat to society.

Figueroa appears to have had a minimal grasp of technology and apparently didn't realize or didn't care that many of her constituents worked at Google. She introduced a bill that would ban advertising targeted to email. "Telling people that their most intimate and private email thoughts to doctors, friends, lovers and family members are just another direct-marketing commodity isn't the way to promote e-commerce," she said in a statement.

But McLaughlin had a card to play. "I mobilized the Big Al," he says.

That meant Al Gore, the former vice president. In the years since losing, or maybe not losing, the 2000 election, Gore had taken comfort in a warm reception in Silicon Valley. "I was trying to figure out what the hell I was going to do with my life," he says of this period. His geeky side led him to Page and Brin, and Google asked him to join its board of directors. But still undecided about another campaign, he was avoiding such offers. (Later, when he'd made up his mind not to make another run at the White House, he joined Apple's board.) But at Google he agreed to become a "virtual board member," with the formal appellation of senior adviser, consulting with the five or six top leaders at Google and occasionally helping pull a lever or two with a government contact. McLaughlin, who didn't have much clout with Larry and Sergey, spoke to Gore regularly and would sometimes implore the former VP to talk to the founders when it looked as though they were about to make a wrong call on a policy issue. In this case, McLaughlin asked Gore to speak to the Democrat state legislator who was giving Google a privacy hotfoot.

Figueroa agreed to meet with Gore at the Ritz-Carlton in San Francisco, where the former vice president was staying. Gore was ready for her. He launched into a defense of Gmail that was nearly as elaborate as the climate change slide show that would later help him share the Nobel Peace Prize. "He was incredible," says McLaughlin. "He stood up and was drawing charts and did this long analogy to the throw weight of the ICBM, the Minuteman missile."

"It was a full and candid discussion," Gore would later recall, while claiming not to recall the ICBM analogy. (He did cop to the use of "a whiteboard, large-scale Post-it notes, and diagrams.") "We talked through the fairly complicated nature of the advertising model that had the robotic analysis, without giving any human being any access to email." Eventually, Figueroa modified her bill to permit the kind of automated scanning Google performed in Gmail.

Nonetheless, McLaughlin and Wong spent a lot of time in Sacramento educating legislators on the fine points of Gmail. At Sergey Brin's suggestion, Google gave Gmail accounts to all the legislators and their aides. At the time that was a valuable commodity, since the service was invitation only. (Invitations were going for $100 on eBay.) The Figueroa bill passed the California senate but never became law.

Even though the legislative challenge fizzled, Gmail became a permanent bête noire to privacy rights organizations. One bone of contention was that Gmail didn't seem to have a delete button. (It actually did have an option to delete an email, but that choice was buried under several nested menus.) Buchheit later said that that approach had been his idea. Omitting a delete button was supposed to teach you to view email—and information itself—the way Google did. The implicit message was that the only thing that should be deleted was the concept of limited storage. Not everybody at Google subscribed to this philosophy—Eric Schmidt had long before instituted a personal practice of making his emails "go away as quickly as possible" unless specifically asked to retain them. To most people at Google, though, automatic archiving was a cause for celebration, and gripes from privacy do-gooders were viewed as misguided or even cynically—exploiting a phony issue for their own status and fund-raising. "Even to this day, I'll read people saying that Google keeps your [deleted] email forever. Like, totally false stuff!" says Buchheit. Buchheit called his critics "fake privacy organizations" because in his mind "they were primarily interested in getting attention for themselves and were going around telling lies about things."

But to millions of people whose perceptions were framed by the traditional nature of storage and the control it provided, Gmail was a shrieking alarm that in this new world, privacy was elusive. And Google's policy people knew that from that point on, everything Google did would have to withstand scrutiny from the angle of privacy, whether or not its engineers thought the charges were valid. "Gmail was game-changing," says Nicole Wong. Google would now have to figure out answers to questions—mostly legitimate ones—of what happens to personal information stored on Google's servers.

Ironically, even as the Gmail privacy conflagration moved off the news pages, there was another source of frenzy around Gmail—people who were desperate to get accounts. The strong demand for Gmail accounts confirmed Buchheit's instinct, supported enthusiastically by Page and Brin, that giving people huge amounts of storage and letting them search all of their emails with lightning speed would be irresistible—even if the service came with sometimes-creepy ads.

Why did Google see this when its competitors who had web-based mail products first didn't? About six months after Gmail came out, Bill Gates visited me at *Newsweek*'s New York headquarters to talk about spam. (His message was that within a year it would no longer be a problem. Not exactly a Nostradamus moment.) We met in my editor's office. The question came up whether free email accounts should be supported by advertising. Gates felt that users were more negative than positive on the issue, but if people wanted it, Microsoft would offer it.

"Have you played with Gmail?" I asked him.

"Oh sure, I play with everything," he replied. "I play with A-Mail, B-Mail, C-Mail, I play with all of them."

My editor and I explained that the IT department at *Newsweek* gave us barely enough storage to hold a few days' mail, and we both forwarded everything to Gmail so we wouldn't have to spend our time deciding what to delete. Only a few months after starting this, both of us had consumed more than half of Gmail's 2-gigabyte free storage space. (Google had already doubled the storage from one gig to two.)

Gates looked stunned, as if this offended him. "How could you need more than a gig?" he asked. "What've you got in there? Movies? Power-Point presentations?"

No, just lots of mail.

He began firing questions. "How many messages are there?" he demanded. "Seriously, I'm trying to understand whether it's the number of messages or the size of messages." After doing the math in his head, he came to the conclusion that Google was doing something wrong.

The episode is telling. Gates's implicit criticism of Gmail was that it was wasteful in its means of storing each email. Despite his currency with cutting-edge technologies, his mentality was anchored in the old paradigm of storage being a commodity that must be conserved. He had written his first programs under a brutal imperative for brevity. And Microsoft's web-based email service reflected that parsimony.

The young people at Google had no such mental barriers. From the moment their company started, they were thinking in terms of huge numbers. Remember, they named their company after a 100-digit number! Moore's Law was as much a fact as air for them, so they understood that the expense of the seemingly astounding 2 gigabytes they gave away in 2004 would be negligible only months later. It would take some months for Gates's minions to catch up and for Microsoft's Hotmail to dramatically increase storage. (Yahoo Mail also followed suit.)

"*That* was part of my justification for doing Gmail," says Paul Buchheit of its ability to make use of Google's capacious servers for its storage. "When people said that it should be canceled, I told them it's really the foundation for a lot of other products. It just seemed obvious that the way things were going, all information was going to be online."

People would quickly identify that concept as a core value of "cloud computing." The term came from the phenomenon where data—even private, proprietary information once stored on one's own computer—would be accessed via the Internet, no matter where you were. As far as the user was concerned, information lived in a huge data cloud, and you pulled it down and sent it back up without regard to its actual location.

The term originally wasn't popular at Google. "Internally, we thought of 'cloud computing' as a marketing term," says Urs Hölzle. ("Marketing" being pejorative in this context.) "Technically speaking, it's *cluster computing* that you do." (At Google, people refer to a "cluster" as a large number of servers—well into the thousands—usually representing the minimum number of machines needed to serve search results from a query.) But the aptness of the metaphor, as well as the fact that it became standard industry jargon, eventually led Google to accept it. Gmail was a cloud application. "For the first time you said, 'Gee, there's a product that could conceivably replace your desktop client,'" says Hölzle. He meant that instead of using Microsoft applications, people might switch to advertising-supported products, with ads supplied by Google. Even more important, the psychology of the cloud matched Google's worldview: network-based, fast, operating on scale. "On one level, [the cloud is] the business we've been in since the day Larry and Sergey founded Google," says Dave Girouard, a company executive in charge of Google's cloud-oriented business software. "We have an amazing advantage because we're a company that was born of the web that has never done anything else."

What's more, Google was a company that benefited from the massive adoption of that web. The sooner people migrated to all-digital worlds—where Google could mine the information, deliver it to users, and sell ads targeted to their activities at that very moment—the more Google would be intertwined in their lives. After Gmail, a corollary was added to the all-the-world's-information axiom: the sooner everyone moved to the cloud, the better it would be for Google.

2

"My job was to get in the car, get on a plane, go find data centers."

Google's own cloud would come to reside in a constellation of huge data centers spread around the world, costing more than a billion dollars each, each of them packed with servers Google built itself. Of all of Google's secrets, this massive digital infrastructure was perhaps its most closely held. It never disclosed the number of these data centers. (According to an industry observer, Data Center Knowledge, there were twenty-four major facilities by 2009, a number Google didn't confirm or dispute.) Google would not say how many servers it had in those centers. (Google did, however, eventually say that it is the largest computer manufacturer in the world—making its own servers requires it to build more units every year than the industry giants HP, Dell, and Lenovo. Nor did Google spokespeople deny reports that it had more than a million of those servers in operation.) And it never welcomed outsiders to peer into its data centers.

But in 2002, before Google firmly closed the shutters, I was offered a rare glimpse of the company's data storage. Jim Reese, then the caretaker of the company's infrastructure, was the guide. He drove to the Exodus colo (colocation center) near San Jose in his car, apologizing for a flapping patch of upholstery on the interior roof as he steered. On the way over, he shared the kind of information that in later years Google would never divulge: real numbers about its servers and its searches. Google, he said, had 10,000 servers to process the 150 million searches its customers launched every day. A sleepy guard waved us in, and we entered a large darkened space with "cages" of servers surrounded by chain-link fences. Air conditioners churned out a steady electronic hum. Reese pointed out who owned the servers in each cage. The cages of companies such as eBay and Yahoo held symmetrically balanced racks of pizza box–style servers, with all the cables tidily secured and labeled. Google's servers looked half finished—without cases they seemed almost uncomfortably naked—and sprewing from them was an unruly tangle of cables. If you could imagine a male college freshman made of gigabytes, this would be his dorm.

Components built to fail, supersophisticated software schemes, and a willingness to discard conventional wisdom would grow Google's storage capabilities from this puzzling rat's nest to the world's biggest data cloud.

A neurosurgeon by training, Reese had drifted to corporate computer maintenance when he applied to Google in June 1999. Google had eighteen employees then. Urs Hölzle conducted an initial interview by phone. In Reese's interactions with other companies, he'd gotten a few cursory questions about a technical point or two, and then the interviewer would pitch the job. "But in this phone screen, absolutely no recruiting went on," says Reese. "He questioned me for an hour and a half. Really grilled me." It was disorienting, even more so with Hölzle's gruff, accented voice barking one question after another, with never an acknowledgment that Reese's answers were satisfactory or not. Then Hölzle abruptly thanked him and hung up. The next day, Reese got an invitation to the Palo Alto office, where he went into a tiny conference room with Larry and Sergey, who asked him more technical questions. They paid special attention to his answer concerning the best way to install Linux on bare, white-box (unbranded) computers with blank disk drives and from there scaling the process to huge numbers of new machines. The founders looked at each other and nodded. Then they invited him into their tiny office.

Larry sat in his desk chair. Sergey sat in *his* desk chair. Then the Google leaders sheepishly realized that there were no other chairs. "Why don't you pull up a ball?" they asked him. So Reese was perched on a red physio ball when they asked him to work at Google. The $70,000 salary was the lowest offer of any company he talked to, but he took it anyway. It hadn't escaped him that between the time of his first interview and the employment offer, Google had announced its $25 million venture capital windfall.

Reese quickly realized that the question about massive Linux installations was not rhetorical—it was his job to get Google's jury-rigged machines up and running. At the time Google had about 300 servers, all located at a single colocation facility in Santa Clara, a few miles south of Palo Alto. They occupied about half a cage, which in this facility was a space about the size of a New York City hotel room, bounded by chain-link fence. Reese's first assignment, and pretty much every assignment after that, dealt with expansion. But he had to do it in the most economical way possible. Larry Page understood why the square-footage rate at colos was so high—"You're paying for security, fire suppression, air-conditioning, interruption of power," he noted at the time. "The square-footage cost is extremely high—it's maybe a hundred times what I pay for my apartment." He told Reese to double the number of servers and fit them into a cage. Reese managed to exceed that spec, squeezing not 600 but 800 servers into the cage.

Google was a tough client for Exodus; no company had ever jammed so many servers into so small an area. The typical practice was to put between five and ten servers on a rack; Google managed to get eighty servers on each of its racks. The racks were so closely arranged that it was difficult for a human being to squeeze into the aisle between them. To get an extra rack in, Google had to get Exodus to temporarily remove the side wall of the cage. "The data centers had never worried about how much power and AC went into each cage, because it was never close to being maxed out," says Reese. "Well, we completely maxed out. It was on an order of magnitude of a small suburban neighborhood," Reese says. Exodus had to scramble to install heavier circuitry. Its air-conditioning was also overwhelmed, and the colo bought a portable AC truck. They drove the eighteen-wheeler up to the colo, punched three holes in the wall, and pumped cold air into Google's cage through PVC pipes.

When Brin and Page hired Reese, they made it clear that they expected an exponential growth in Google's computer power and infrastructure. "They told me that whatever I do, make sure it will work not just for 500 or 5,000 computers but 50,000—that we should build in massive scalability now and that we would have that many computers in just a few years. Which we did," says Reese.

The key to Google's efficiency was buying low-quality equipment dirt cheap and applying brainpower to work around the inevitably high failure rate. It was an outgrowth of Google's earliest days, when Page and Brin had built a server housed by Lego blocks. "Larry and Sergey proposed that we design and build our own servers as cheaply as we can—massive numbers of servers connected to a high-speed network," says Reese. The conventional wisdom was that an equipment failure should be regarded as, well, a failure. Generally the server failure rate was between 4 and 10 percent. To keep the failures at the lower end of the range, technology companies paid for high-end equipment from Sun Microsystems or EMC. "Our idea was completely opposite," says Reese. "We're going to build hundreds and thousands of cheap servers knowing from the get-go that a certain percentage, maybe 10 percent, are going to fail," says Reese. Google's first CIO, Douglas Merrill, once noted that the disk drives Google purchased were "poorer quality than you would put into your kid's computer at home."

But Google designed around the flaws. "We built capabilities into the software, the hardware, and the network—the way we hook them up, the load balancing, and so on—to build in redundancy, to make the system fault-tolerant," says Reese. The Google File System, written by Jeff Dean and Sanjay Ghemawat, was invaluable in this process: it was designed to manage failure by "sharding" data, distributing it to multiple servers. If Google search called for certain information at one server and didn't get a reply after a couple of milliseconds, there were two other Google servers that could fulfill the request.

"The Google business model was constrained by cost, especially at the very beginning," says Erik Teetzel, who worked with Google's data centers. "Every time we would serve a query it cost us money, and generating ad money didn't happen until later, so Larry and Sergey and Urs set out to build the cheapest infrastructure they could. They didn't buy the prescribed notion that you must buy your servers from HP and couple it with a Cisco router and software from Linux or Windows. They looked at it holistically, to have control from soup to nuts. That set the stage for this holistic picture where we could do very efficient computing."

By having only one data center, Google was vulnerable. First, it moved to make sure that it had multiple fiber links into the building—otherwise an errant public works crew could take Google down. "When it comes to a backhoe versus fiber, the backhoe always wins," says Reese. "So we made sure that we had fiber coming in from different routes." More significantly, Google needed redundant data centers to keep operating if a catastrophe struck the Exodus center. So the company also took space in a nearby colocation facility in Sunnyvale.

But it wasn't only redundancy that Google needed at that point; it was speed. Speed had always been an obsession at Google, especially for Larry Page. It was almost instinctual for him. "He's always measuring everything," says early Googler Megan Smith. "At his core he cares about latency." More accurately, he despises latency and is always trying to remove it, like Lady Macbeth washing guilt from her hands. Once Smith was walking down the street with him in Morocco and he suddenly dragged her into a random Internet café with maybe three machines. Immediately, he began timing how long it took web pages to load into a browser there.

Whether due to pathological impatience or a dead-on conviction that speed is chronically underestimated as a factor in successful products, Page had been insisting on faster delivery for everything Google from the beginning. The minimalism of Google's home page, allowing for lightning-quick loading, was the classic example. But early Google also innovated by storing cached versions of web pages on its own servers, for redundancy and speed.

"Speed is a feature," says Urs Hölzle. "Speed can drive usage as much as having bells and whistles on your product. People really underappreciate it. Larry is very much on that line."

Engineers working for Page learned quickly enough of this priority. "When people do demos and they're slow, I'm known to count sometimes," he says. "One one-thousand, two one-thousand. That tends to get people's attention." Actually, if your product could be measured in seconds, you'd already failed. Buchheit remembers one time when he was doing an early Gmail demo in Larry's office. Page made a face and told him it was way too slow. Buchheit objected, but Page reiterated his complaint, charging that the reload took at least 600 milliseconds. (That's six-tenths of a second.) Buchheit thought, *You can't know that*, but when he got back to his own office he checked the server logs. Six hundred milliseconds. "He nailed it," says Buchheit. "So I started testing myself, and without too much effort, I could estimate times to a hundred milliseconds precision—I could tell if it was 300 milliseconds or 700, whatever. And that happens throughout the company." (Page himself considered it unexceptional to be able to detect lags of 200 milliseconds, generally thought of as the limit of human perception.)

Sergey Brin even put a label on his cofounder's frustration at the tendency of developers to load more and more features into programs, making them run way too slowly. Page's Law, according to Brin, was the observation that every eighteen months, software becomes twice as slow. Google was determined to avoid this problem. "We want to actually break Page's law and make our software increasingly fast over time," says Brin.

"There's definitely an obsession with speed here," says Buchheit. "With most people in the world, when you complain that something is too slow, they might say, 'Well, you just need more patience.' At Google, they're like, 'Yeah, it makes me want to tear my eyes out!'"

The data in Google's logs justified the obsession with speed. When things go slowly, says Urs Hölzle, "people are unconsciously afraid of doing another search, because it's slow. Or they are more likely to try another result than rephrase the query. I'm sure if you ask them, none of them would tell you, but in aggregate you really see that." On the other hand, when you speed things up, they search more. Hölzle would cite Google's experience when the company boosted the performance of its Picasa web-based photo service, making slide shows run three times as fast. Even though there was no announcement of the improvement, traffic on the site increased 40 percent the first day it was implemented. "It just happened," says Hölzle. "The only thing we changed was the speed."

In 2007, Google conducted some user studies that measured the behavior of people whose search results were artificially delayed. One might think that the minuscule amounts of latency involved in the experiment would be negligible—they ranged between 100 and 400 milliseconds. But even those tiny hiccups in delivering search results acted as a deterrent to future searches. The reduction in the number of searches was small but significant, and were measurable even with *100 milliseconds* (one-tenth of a second) latency. What's more, even after the delays were removed, the people exposed to the slower results would take a long time to resume their previous level of searching.

(Microsoft found a similar effect when it conducted its own tests with its Bing search engine. The Bing experiments also showed that when results are delayed, users respond with their own latency, taking longer to click on links after a search is completed. Presumably, during the half second or more that the results are delayed, the users have begun to think about something else and have to refocus before they get around to clicking on a result.)

In 2008, Google issued a Code Yellow for speed. (A Code Yellow is named after a tank top of that color owned by engineering director Wayne Rosing. During Code Yellow a leader is given the shirt and can tap anyone at Google and force him or her to drop a current project to help out. Often, the Code Yellow leader escalates the emergency into a war room situation and pulls people out of their offices and into a conference room for a more extended struggle.) This Code Yellow kicked off at a TGIF where Hölzle metered the performance of various Google products around the world, with a running ticker on the big screen in Charlie's Café pinpointing the deficiencies. "You could hear a pin drop in the room when people were watching how stunningly slow things were, like Gmail in India," says Gabriel Stricker, a Google PR director. After the Code Yellow, Google set a companywide OKR (the objective key result metric Google uses to set goals) to fight latency. To help meet its goals, the company created a market-based incentive program for product teams to juice up performance—a cap-and-trade model in which teams were mandated latency ceilings or maximum performance times. If a team didn't make its benchmarks, says Hölzle, it accrued a debt that had to be paid off by barter with a team that exceeded its benchmarks. "You could trade for an engineer or machines. Whatever," he says.

The metric for this exchange was, oddly enough, human lives. The calculation goes like this: average human life expectancy is seventy years. That's about two billion seconds. If a product has 100 million users and unnecessarily wastes four seconds of a user's time every day, that was more than a hundred people killed in a year. So if the Gmail team wasn't meeting its goals, it might go to the Picasa team and ask for ten lives to lift its speed budget into the black. In exchange, the Gmailers might yield a thousand servers from its allocation or all its massage tickets for the next month.

But you couldn't keep borrowing forever. "People have definitely been yelled at," says Hölzle. If a team got too deep in the hole, the latency police would close down the casino. "There's a launch gate where if you're too far in the negative, you can't launch features. From that point on, you need to focus on latency alone until you're close to your goal."

Back in 2000, Google wanted to get speedier by setting up data centers in locations closer to its users. Its first priority was getting servers on the East Coast of the United States. By the spring of that year, Google was occupying space in a colo in northern Virginia. The tricky part of setting up in a new facility was loading all those thousands of servers with the indexes. That involved terabytes of data, which was potentially going to force Google to pay a huge amount of money to the bandwidth provider that owned the fiber. "Networking was very expensive," says Hölzle. "And our data push would take twenty hours at a gigabyte per second—that would cost us something like $250,000 a month." To save money, Google devised a trick that exploited a loophole in the billing system for data transfer. Broadband providers used a system known as the 95th Percentile Rule. Over the period of a month, the provider would test how much information was moving, automatically taking a measurement every five minutes. In order to discard unusual spikes in activity, when the billing rate was calculated the provider would lop off the measurements in the top five percentiles and bill the customer at the rate of the 95th percentile.

Google's exploitation of the rule was like the correct answer to a trick question in one of its hiring interviews. It decided to move all its information during those discounted spikes. "We figured out that if we used zero bandwidth all month, except for thirty hours once a month, we would be under that 5 percent," says Reese. For two nights a month, from 6 P.M. to 6 A.M. Pacific time, Google moved all the data in its indexes from west to east. "We would push as fast as we could, and that would cause massive traffic to go across, but it was during the lull hours for them. . . . And of course, the bill came out to be nothing," says Reese, "because when they lopped off the top 5 percent, our remaining bandwidth was in fact zero, because we didn't use any otherwise. I literally turned off the router ports for twenty-eight or twenty-nine days a month."

Eventually, the contract expired and Google negotiated a plan where it actually paid for its bandwidth. But by that time it had decided how to end the need for such contracts entirely: it began to buy its own fiber.

Fiber-optic cable was the most efficient, robust, and speedy means of moving data. Just as Google had taken advantage of the oversupply of data centers in the wake of the dot-com bust, it had a great opportunity to buy fiber-optic cable cheap. In the 1980s and 1990s, a raft of optical networking companies had made huge investments in fiber optics. But they had overestimated the demand, and by the early 2000s, many were struggling or going broke. Google began buying strategically located stretches of fiber. "We would want to pick up pieces that would connect our data center, so we'd identify the owner, negotiate, and take it over," says Chris Sacca, who did many of the deals. "Then we'd put optical networking equipment on one end in our data center, the same equipment on the data center at the other end, and now we're running that stretch of fiber," says Sacca. "We were paying ten cents on the dollar." Since fiber-optic cable had huge capacity, Google then made arrangements with broadband companies to fill in the gaps it didn't own. "We swapped out strands with other guys," says Sacca.

By the time Google finished with its fiber push, it was in a unique situation. "We *owned* the fiber. It was ours. Pushing the traffic was nothing," says Sacca. How much fiber did Google own? "More than anyone else on the planet."

In 2001, Exodus suffered financial disarray, and some of its data centers fell into the hands of private investors. Google began renting entire data centers from the new owners. As the sole tenant, it had the opportunity to revamp everything that went inside the shell. Its biggest operation was in Atlanta, a former Exodus facility with 200,000 square feet of floor space. It was big enough for Google to maintain an assembly operation where workers could build the servers on the spot.

But there was only so much that could be done when someone else owned the facility. Google's engineers knew that if they had a chance to design their facilities from the ground up—beginning with the site selection—they could be much more efficient. By mid-2003, Google reluctantly began planning to build its own data centers. "It was a big step," says Hölzle, "but not a welcome truth. It's nice if you have something you don't have to worry about, and we'd been very successful in buying space in bankrupt data centers." Looking into the future, though, Google saw that the period of oversupply in data center space was coming to an end, and after the current cheap contacts expired, prices would rise to perhaps three times what Google was currently paying. Those high costs would more accurately reflect the true costs that the hosts paid, particularly in terms of power.

Google considered the existing data centers horribly inefficient, particularly in the way they gobbled up power. "They wasted power, both by bad practice and bad buildings," says Hölzle. If Google designed and built its own data centers, it would be free to innovate new ways to keep costs down. In some cases, all it had to do was apply existing ideas that no one had yet put into practice. There was a lot of unheeded literature about how to cool computers. One paper outlined a potential back-to-back arrangement of servers where the exhaust pipes faced each other and created a warm aisle between the racks. These would alternate with cool aisles, where the intakes on the front of the servers would draw on cooler air. Google tried to implement such arrangements in its colos, but the facilities managers complained. Their job, they would insist, was keeping the temperature in the building at a steady 68 degrees.

In its own data centers, Google could not only implement these energy-saving ideas, but take extreme measures to separate the hot and cold air. Its own data centers would have enclosed rooms that segregated the hot air. Inside those separate rooms, the temperature would be much higher—perhaps 120 degrees or even more. If someone had to go into one of those hot rooms, you could temporarily cool the area down so the person wouldn't melt while trying to swap out a motherboard. Even in the cold aisles, Google would raise the temperature. "You can save just 20 percent by raising the thermostat," says Hölzle. "Instead of setting the cold aisle temperature to 68 you can raise it to 80."

Doing so would put a lot of stress on the equipment, but Google's attitude was, so what if stuff broke? "You counted on failure," says Chris Sacca. "We were buying nonspec parts [components rejected for commercial use because they were not rated to perform at high standards], so we didn't need to coddle them."

With all these hot and cold rooms, Google had a modular approach to data centers, and it even wondered whether it would make sense to build a data center without a traditional shell, just a scaffolding for stacking truck-size weatherproof containers. For a while, Google even ran a test of a containerized data center in the underground parking lot under Building 40, where Charlie's Café was located. It was covered with a big tarp to hide its purpose, and a special security guard was posted to make sure no one except the very few Googlers permitted to visit could get a glimpse of the experiment. (Eventually Google would adopt a plan where the modules would reside inside a huge building shell, and a peek inside its centers would reveal what looked like an indoor trailer park. In ensuing years, other companies, including Microsoft, would adopt the container model for some of their data centers.)

Google also mulled over some radical approaches to save energy. What if you put a data center in Iceland and used only native geothermal power? Could you put a data center above the Arctic Circle and use outside air to keep temperatures down? How about buying an old aircraft carrier and cooling it with seawater? There was even one suggestion to use a big old blimp filled with helium as a data center.

Google was still reluctant to take the big step—and the enormous capital expense—of building its own data centers, so it explored the idea of having one of the companies currently involved in hosting to build a facility especially for Google, collaborating with the company to implement all the efficiencies. None was interested. "People just didn't believe they should change, basically. There wasn't a willing partner," says Hölzle. It was a challenge even for Google to find an engineering firm flexible enough to violate the standard methodology and build things Google style. "We interviewed a number of companies, and they would say, 'This is crazy talk. We're professionals. We know how to build facilities,'" Hölzle recalls. Ultimately Google hired a small East Coast company called DLB Associates. "I think they were actually not convinced at all in the beginning, but they were willing to collaborate," says Hölzle.

So Google, a company that had once focused entirely on building Internet software, prepared to begin a building program that would lead it to construct more than a dozen billion-dollar facilities over the next few years. A key Googler in the process was Chris Sacca. Not quite thirty at the time, Sacca had already been through several careers. Born to a working-class family in Buffalo, he'd been a ski bum, a stock speculator, and a lawyer. During law school at Georgetown, he'd taken a three-month break to help El Salvador's telecom privatization project and after that thought he could make extra money as a consultant. (To buff up his status, he gave himself a fancy name: The Salinger Group.) When his stock trading put him $4 million in the hole, he took a job at a Silicon Valley law firm, where insistent networking put him on Google's radar. "They wanted one person who could identify, negotiate, draft, and close data centers," he says. "My job was to get in the car, get on a plane, go find data centers to buy, lease."

Now Sacca was charged with finding sites where Google could build its centers. It was a process conducted with utmost stealth. In 2004, prior to the IPO, the company was still hiding its success. "Google didn't want Microsoft to know how big search was," says Sacca. "And if you knew how many computers Google was running, you could do some back-of-the-envelope math and see how big an opportunity this was."

There was also the additional consideration that if people in a given locality knew it was Google they were dealing with, they might be less generous in giving tax breaks. In any case, when seeking out locations for a Google data center, Sacca and his colleagues did not let on who employed them. Sacca frequently used the name of his made-up consultancy operation, The Salinger Group. Other times he'd say he was from Hoya Technologies. ("Hoya" is the name of the sports teams at Georgetown, where he went to law school.) At some point, Larry Page noted that the flaw with those names was that people could all too easily Google them; something vaguer was needed. So Sacca became a representative of Design LLC. ("LLC" stands for "limited liability corporation.") It was so generic that there were millions of search results for that name.

The basic requirements for a data center were clear: land, power, and water. The last was important because the cooling process was to be done by an evaporative process that required millions of gallons of water through refrigerator-style "chillers" that drop the temperature and then run the cool water through "jackets" that hug the server racks. Then the water—heated up by now—gets run through massive cooling towers, where it trickles down, evaporates, and gets collected back in the system again. (The air-conditioning is generally reserved for backup.) All of this requires massive power, and before a shovel can be stuck into the ground, it has to be determined whether the local electric utility can provide sufficient amps to power a small city—at bargain rates.

Focusing on Oregon, Sacca and a colleague used maps of power grids and fiber-optic connections to find potential locations. Then Sacca would drop into the local development office and power utility. To make sure someone was at the office that day, he would call from the previous town. "If we were in Coos Bay on Monday, we'd call Tillamook—'Hey, I'm going to be there Wednesday, will you be there?'" And on Wednesday, a ragged six-foot-tall guy in shorts with his shirttail out—Sacca—would go to some double-wide trailer where the development people worked. "How's it going?" he'd ask, "I'm up here doing some site selection." Soon into the conversation he would identify himself as being from a company called Design LLC. And eventually he would reveal his intent to build a massive, *massive* utility. *Uh, do you have any property in this town that has a contiguous fifty to sixty acres with access to power from Bonneville?* "It was hilarious," recalls Sacca. "There's no reference check you can do, but here's this kid rolling in there claiming he's going to spend millions and millions of dollars and he needs your help."

Officials in some localities didn't take Sacca and his coworkers seriously; others had nothing to offer. One township, freaked out by the scruffy guys asking about high-voltage lines, worried that they were terrorists and called the Department of Homeland Security. Others busted a gut to help out. Sacca remembers that the people in Coos Bay flew them around in a helicopter to survey potential sites. "They figured the community needed it and they were going to take a chance that we were legit."

It was in a Columbia River town seventy miles east of Portland, near the Washington border, that Sacca hit pay dirt. "It was an ugly site," he says. Rough land. Rocks jutting from barren ground. Big power lines. The site was on the bank of the river, but not the pretty part—the view wasn't beautiful Mount Hood but semidesert terrain. Nearby was the abandoned headquarters of a wood-chipping plant. But Sacca had retrained his eye for a different kind of beauty, and to him the adjoining power lines were as alluring as a majestic vista. As was the state of the town—sufficiently run-down and desperate to woo a massive building.

The town was The Dalles, population 12,000, described by one local reporter as "a hamburger pit stop between Portland and Pendleton." Lewis and Clark had camped there in October 1805. French fur traders had later made it a trading post. (*Dalles* is French for "flagstones.") For a few years, Les Dalles was the end of the Oregon Trail. But by the early twenty-first century, the town seemed at the end of the trail in a metaphoric sense. The smoke-belching industries that had propped up its economy were gone forever. "The town was beat up, the downtown kind of abandoned," says Sacca. "It was a big aluminum town and they lost the smelter, and that was it."

To Sacca's astonishment, the town government had laid a fiber-optic ring around the town. "It was visionary—this little town with no tax revenues had figured out that if you want to transform an economy from manufacturing to information, you've got to pull fiber," says Sacca. The town had already won status as an enterprise zone, meaning that all sorts of enticements and tax breaks were available to any business willing to locate there.

Of course, Google had more stringent demands that would eventually require gubernatorial approval. As a potentially large employer with leverage, it wanted tax relief and other concessions. The key player in The Dalles was a Wasco County judge with a day job as a cherry farmer. He looked like a younger Wilford Brimley, complete with mustache and an appealing country drawl. The judge understood Design LLC's goals, and once he heard that the project would bring in three hundred people to build its plant and leave the town with fifty to a hundred long-term jobs—and boost every local business, where the newcomers might spend their paychecks—he was committed. Even though the jobs in question would generally be on the level of technicians, as opposed to pampered Google engineers, they would pay around $60,000, double the average county income.

The Dalles had one more little perk: a local airport with a runway to accommodate some of the planes in the Google air force. "That wasn't a major factor but an interesting one, since Eric is such an aviation enthusiast," says Sacca. "It was fun to say, 'Hey, Eric, there's an airstrip nearby.'"

The local congressman set up a conference call and mediated between Google and the Bonneville Power Administration. Then Google worked with the state to get fifteen years of tax relief, only the second time in Oregon history that a company had received a break of that length.

On February 16, 2005, the commissioners approved the land sale to Design LLC. The cost of the land was $1.87 million for just over thirty acres, with an option to buy three more tracts, including those where the Mountain Fir Chip Mill had once stood. At a certain point, the Googlers swore the townsfolk to secrecy and revealed the entity behind the mysterious Design LLC. "They were stunned," says Sacca. "At that time Google still really had a beautiful, angelic reputation." Even after the local paper outed the benefactor as Google, the company still insisted that local people not make reference to that fact and had local officials sign a confidentiality agreement. When they talked about it, they used the code name Project 02. When visitors came asking, the locals clammed up like bay mussels; *New York Times* reporter John Markoff traveled to the site in 2006 and was stonewalled by the city manager. An official in a nearby town, free to make sour-grapes jokes at the lucky municipality across the river, said, "It's a little bit like He-Who-Must-Not-Be-Named in Harry Potter." Indeed, as local reporters found out when Google finally allowed them a glimpse of the compound (only the cafeteria and the public area—not the vast area where the servers resided), outside the security fence was a sign that read VOLDE-MORT INDUSTRIES.

To show goodwill, Google spread a few dollars around The Dalles, including a donation toward a new Lewis and Clark Museum. The company also gave a few thousand dollars' worth of AdWords credit to local nonprofits. More significantly, Google delivered on jobs. And best of all, Google's data center put the township on the map.

After its construction, the building dominated the landscape, a massive shell the size of two football fields with a pair of four-story cooling towers. According to Sacca, the shell cost about $50 million, but its contents were valued close to a billion dollars. There was more than 200,000 square feet of space for the servers and infrastructure and another 18,000-square-foot building for cooling towers. In addition, there was a 20,000-square-foot administration building that included a Google-esque cafeteria and a dormitory-style building almost as large for transient workers. The exterior gave no clue about its contents.

Not until 2009 did Google tip its hand publicly, during its first Efficient Data Center Summit. A Google engineer described a setup in one of its buildings that seemed to be one of the cluster of structures at The Dalles. Forty-five containers, each holding 1,160 servers, are arranged in a two-story setup. The cold aisles on those buildings ran at 81 degrees. When the news of the event hit the web, people weren't sure whether it was a joke, since the summit took place on April Fool's Day. Urs Hölzle added to the confusion by making an actual April's Fool's joke: Google, he said, was going to convert old oil tankers into petroleum-cooled seagoing data centers. It was tough to tease out what was true. Some people didn't believe about the cold aisles and others were asking to take a tour of the fictitious U.S.S. *Sergey*.

Google never revealed how many servers it could pack into a center like the one at The Dalles, but it surely was more than 100,000. The company could handle such huge numbers because the system required very few human beings to keep it running. Google's data centers didn't have big control rooms like the one in *The Simpsons* where guys in short-sleeved white shirts sat in front of big displays and flipped switches. "When you have very large numbers of computers in multiple data centers, it's probably risky to attempt to manage this with human beings at the control panel," Google's onetime engineering head Wayne Rosing once explained.

Instead everything was monitored by a series of software scripts. The computer scientists remained in Mountain View, while a skeleton crew of local technicians was on site. When a metric deviated from the norm, the software checked out what was happening in other data centers to compare. At some point, someone in Mountain View would be alerted. "We had written enough scripts and basic infrastructure so that the data centers all over the world could be run from Mountain View," says Jim Reese. "It didn't matter whether you have 500 or 500,000 computers—you could run them remotely. We designed it for scale. We need physical hands only to get computers in place and replace the hard drives and motherboards when they fail. Even at the point where we had 50,000 computers, there were maybe six of us maintaining them."

Even before construction at The Dalles was finished, Google gathered teams to scout out new locations. Their business cards identified them as being from Zenzu Consulting. Google had set up a website under that company name to deflect attention. It didn't take a genius to suspect a Google hand, but the Zenzu people wouldn't even wink at the implication. "We made it very clear that our client did not want anyone to guess who they were, and that if any of this stuff went out, our client would essentially walk away," says Cathy Gordon, a Google business development employee who'd joined the data center group as a lark, a chance to do something different.

Gordon's first deal was in Atlanta. The site had previously been developed for a large trucking facility, but after the pad for the building had been laid, the deal had fallen apart. It seemed like a good deal for Google, since the grading had been done, roads had been built, and permits had been issued. Gordon focused on getting state revenue bonds passed. It was a typical request of a Google employee, requiring a person with no experience in an esoteric field to not only keep up with experts but essentially outsmart them. Gordon remembers sitting in rooms with lawyers droning about codicils and amendments to these bizarre documents and thinking, *I don't know what you're talking about, mister.* In lots of ways the job was stressful, requiring her to travel three weeks out of four, staying in economy motels, feeling almost like she was an undercover agent. But she figured it out, and beat the experts. Google would add to its southern presence with huge data centers in Goose Creek, South Carolina, and Moncks Corner, North Carolina.

For a long time, Google had feared a doomsday scenario where a calamity at one of its locations could bring down a Google product or even all of Google. Its billions of dollars' worth of investments and its failure-tolerant infrastructure now made that scenario unlikely. "We could lose an entire data center, and everything would just spill over to the other data centers and we'd still have excess capacity," says Jim Reese.

Google also made it a priority to build centers overseas. Not long after she found the location in Atlanta, Cathy Gordon went to Europe, where Google wanted to build a giant data center similar to the ones in the United States. Google had studied the laws and business practices of every country and narrowed the field to a few that might be able to provide the power and water required, as well as a friendly governmental hand. Some of the proposed locations were predictable—Switzerland, Belgium, France—but a couple were not.

One of those was Latvia, which Gordon had never visited before. The Google team flew into a ramshackle little airport and met the economic development committee, a cadre of what seemed to be stereotypical Soviet bureaucrats, only now they were Latvian bureaucrats. Their hosts escorted them to the potential data center site, an abandoned Soviet minibus factory. The building was cavernous and gloomy. In the center of the building was a giant pit, filled with some acidic liquid, and Gordon couldn't help but wonder whether any bodies were quietly decomposing in the stew. The group went to the area where the power facilities were located, and it looked to Gordon like they were on an old horror movie set, a *Gulag Archipelago* version of Dr. Frankenstein's lab. One of the hosts leaned over and spoke in a confidential whisper, heavy with Slavic accent. "Don't get too near those things," he said. "Basically we don't know if they could kill you."

"We eventually ended up doing a deal in Belgium," says Gordon.

The center in Saint-Ghislain, seventy-five kilometers from Brussels, was a test bed for some new ideas about data center energy conservation. Even though Google had always attempted to minimize its power consumption, its centers gobbled up many, many megawatts, a humiliating flouting of Page and Brin's vision of a cleaner planet. A study funded by the chip company AMD (and vetted by other firms including Intel, HP, IBM, and Dell) estimated that in 2005, data centers accounted for 1.2 percent of all power consumption in the United States. More than twenty states used less power than the nation's data centers. That was double the amount of power that data centers had used five years earlier, and the rate of growth was increasing. Since no one had more data centers than Google, the company was one of the world's greediest power hogs. "We use a fair amount of energy," says Bill Weihl, a computer science PhD who came to Google in

2005 to become its conservation czar. "Some people say 'massive amounts.' I try to avoid 'massive.' But it's a lot."

He would not put a number on it. "The fact that we're not transparent about it causes us embarrassment," he says, explaining that "competitive reasons" justify the reticence. By not knowing what Google is spending, Microsoft CEO Steve Ballmer, for instance, will have no target to aim at when apportioning his own cost estimates for infrastructure. "If I'm Ballmer, I'm probably going to pick a number that's too high, in which case it bankrupts Microsoft—and that's good for Google," says Weihl. "Or he'll pick a number that's too low, in which case it can't really compete. And *that's* good for Google."

One of the most power-intensive components of the operation is the huge chillers that refrigerate water to keep the temperature in the building no higher than around 80 degrees F. Google augmented these chillers with much more efficient systems that take in fresh air when outside temperatures are cool. The data center in Saint-Ghislain, completed in 2008, actually eliminated chillers entirely. The average summer temperature in Brussels is around 70 degrees, but during the occasional scorcher, Google would shift the information load to other data centers. "Most data centers run chillers a lot, but we use free cooling, for the most part," says Eric Teetzel, who works on Google infrastructure.

The Belgium center was the first where Google didn't need access to relatively clean water; it had discovered ways to use more readily available tainted water. In Belgium the water is drawn from a polluted canal. "We literally build treatment plants and run the water through our evaporative cooling towers," says Teetzel. "That's the beauty of energy efficiency—it will save you money."

The operation in Saint-Ghislain was a milestone for another reason: it was the first data center that Google publicly acknowledged upon completion. In June 2009 King Albert II made an official visit. He wasn't allowed in to see the servers.

Organizing Google's hundreds of thousands of computers was one of those "hard problems" that make PhDs want to work at Google. It was definitely the lure for Luiz Barroso. He had been yet another colleague of Jeff Dean and Sanjay Ghemawat at Digital Equipment Corporation's Western Research Lab. Born in Brazil, Barroso had a PhD in computer architecture and had worked at DEC on multicore processors, which put the "brains" of several computers onto a single chip. (Radical then, this technique later became the dominant design of virtually all PCs.) When Dean urged him to come to Google in 2001, he worried that as a "hardware guy" he'd be out of place in a situation where he'd be working on software system designs. But because of his hardware expertise, a couple of years after he arrived, Urs Hölzle asked him to help design Google's data centers.

Barroso realized that in order to meet the demands of search, handle the constant experiments the company ran, and accommodate the rapidly growing number of projects at Google other than search, the company had to basically reinvent the computer. "Suddenly, you have a program that doesn't run on anything smaller than a thousand machines," he says. "So you can't look at that as a thousand machines, but instead look at those thousand machines as a single computer. I look at a *data center* as a computer."

Indeed, a 2009 publication by Barroso and Urs Hölzle that described Google's approach (without giving away too many of the family jewels) was called *The Datacenter as a Computer.* It explained the advent of "warehouse-scale machines" and the Google philosophy of tolerating frequent failure of components. It outlined the organizational hierarchy of its machines, each server situated in a rack of eighty, with about thirty of those racks in a cluster. The document explained that Google works like one machine, an omnivorous collector of information, a hyperencyclopedic vault of human knowledge, an unerring auctioneer, an eerily skillful student of languages, behavior, and desires.

What it *didn't* say was what outside observers had already concluded: that by perfecting its software, owning its own fiber, and innovating in conservation techniques, Google was able to run its computers spending only a third of what its competitors paid. "Our true advantage was actually the fact that we had this massive parallelized redundant computer network, probably more than anyone in the world, including governments," says Jim Reese. "And we realized that maybe it's not in our best interests to let our competitors know."

One reason Sanjay Ghemawat loved Google was that when researchers were looking to solve problems a year out, Larry Page demanded that they work on problems that might be a *decade* out, or maybe even a problem that would come up only in a science fiction novel. Page's point of view seemed to be, If you are ridiculously premature, how can people catch up to you?

Spurred by Page's ambition, Ghemawat and Jeff Dean came up with a dramatic improvement in handling massive amounts of information spread over multiple data centers. It split tasks among machines in a faster manner, in the same way a programmer performing an operation on large collections of data can spread the work over many computers without worrying about how to apportion the work. The program worked in two steps—first by *mapping the system* (figuring out how the information was spread out and duplicated in various locations—basically an indexing process) and then by *reducing the information* to the transformed data requested. The key was that the programmers could control a massive number of machines, swapping and sharing their contents—a cluster's worth or more—as if they were a single desktop computer. Ghemawat and Jeff Dean called their project MapReduce.

"The engineers only have to think about the data," says Christophe Bisciglia, a Google engineer who became an evangelist for cloud computing. "The system takes care of the parallelization. You don't have to think about what machine the data is stored on or how to synchronize what happens when the machine fails or if there's a bad record or any of that. I just think about the data and how I want to explore or transform the data, so I write code for that, and the system takes care of everything else." What's more, with MapReduce Google could easily build out its system—adding thousands more machines, allowing for much more storage and much faster results—without having to change the original code.

Sanjay and Dean cooked up a version in a few weeks, then rewrote it, and within a few months completed the first revision of the product. Google policy requires engineers to write in tandem, doing code checks of each other's work. Not all Google engineers like the process. (One noted Google engineer categorizes programmers as either Code Nazis or artists and dreads projects where he—an artist—is paired with one of the other variety.) But Sanjay and Dean liked the process, having been close colleagues since their time together at DEC Western Research Laboratory.

MapReduce was a blueprint for a different kind of computing, one that gave Google an edge in the cloud computing era. Add that to Google's preexisting edges in free fiber and more efficient data centers, and it's easy to understand how Google can do everything cheaper than its competitors, from providing huge mailboxes for free on Gmail to hosting billions of video views on YouTube, which Google bought in 2006.

In 2006, Bisciglia came to realize that MapReduce had potential even beyond Google's ambitious computing plans. He often interviewed college students vying for jobs at Google. The interview would be humming along, with the prodigies from Yale or Stanford posing clever solutions to problems until Bisciglia asked them the question "What would you do with a thousand times as much data?" And they would stare at him blankly. Which was a problem, because, although they didn't know it, Google was *already* working on a thousand times more data than anyone suspected. But information on that scale was going to be more common as storage got cheaper, people generated more information, and ubiquitous sensors sucked up even more data that could be mined. Bisciglia realized that MapReduce offered a way to do what was otherwise unthinkable: empower a single programmer to efficiently make use of those humongous, googolesque data sets.

Ghemawat and Dean published a paper on MapReduce, and other computer scientists used the concepts to produce an open-source version of MapReduce called Apache Hadoop. This program guaranteed that Google's ideas would spread throughout the world and made it easier to implement cloud computing. Even though competitors would benefit, this wasn't seen as a negative in Mountain View. If everyone adopted this new computing paradigm, people would always be just a click away from Google's services—and Google's ads.

What was good for the cloud would be good for Google.

3

"They're created by machines. And that is what makes us powerful."

In its earlier days, Google had taken pains not to draw the attention of the world's biggest software company. But everyone knew that eventually the Silicon Valley search kings would wind up in a death cage match with Microsoft. With the development of Google's cloud computing strategy, it became clear just how that would happen.

Microsoft's revenues flowed largely from two cash cows, both of which were monopolies. The first was its Windows operating system, and it was almost unthinkable that anyone could challenge that. In any case, an operating system was far from Google's mission. The second was Microsoft Office, its applications suite with components including Word, the Excel spreadsheet, and the PowerPoint presentation software. The threat to Microsoft was that Google would apply its Internet-centric approach to attack the older company's desktop-bound products. And that is exactly what it set out to do.

The person in charge of Google's strategy was the person who had first come up with the company's business plan, and had been later instrumental in AdWords, the product that would make virtually all of Google's money: Salar Kamangar. With AdWords bringing in several billion dollars a year, Kamangar thought he'd try something different. "I was very excited about what was happening in the applications area, and I saw there was a need for product management that I could bring," he says.

Google began to buy small companies producing web-based applications. One of the earlier ones was JotSpot, a creator of collaborative, wiki-style tools. It turned out to be what is called a "talent acquisition," since the value Google derived from the purchase lay in JotSpot's founders, Joe Kraus and Graham Spencer. A founder of the early Google competitor Excite, Kraus had developed into a visionary executive with significant start-up skills. Spencer was a brilliant engineer, the tech power behind Kraus's ideas.

As far as software was concerned, a more significant purchase was a start-up called Upstartle. It had been cofounded in 2004 by Sam Schillace, a former product manager for Intuit, and two friends. Looking for a good idea for a start-up, they began playing with some emerging Internet technologies, including Ajax, which lets users create web-based programs that behaved like the ones people usually installed on their computers. They found that it was possible to build a simple web-based word-processing program. Such a cloud-based word processor allowed users to work on documents from any computer in the world. Schillace and his partners called their program Writely.

"We encountered an unbelievable amount of negativism," says Schillace. Skeptics asked, "What would you do when you *weren't* online?" To Schillace and his colleagues, the question was shortsighted. It was like condemning an appliance for using electricity. They believed that as a matter of course cloud computing would eventually become as ubiquitous as the power grid. In the meantime, people could back up their documents and use cheap lightweight client apps to view and edit them.

Writely had barely shipped when Google bought the company. Schillace understood why Brin and Page's company wanted it. Applications were moving to the cloud. Google was a cloud company. Google understands, he told himself. Still, he would later note, after the sale the doubters said that Google was crazy for believing that one could do word processing via the cloud. "Eric had a vision before everybody else," says Schillace.

After the deal closed in March 2006, the Writely team began migrating its product to the Google code base. The product became part of a project code-named Tricks, a web-based alternative to Microsoft Office. Google had already started developing a web-based spreadsheet that would be a companion to the word processor. The company was also developing a product called Google Gears that would let people keep working on their documents while offline, but the program lacked the bedrock reliability that would be required.

When Schillace went to Google in 2006, he had to struggle to get resources in the data center. "They had this crazy hand-cobbled system where there was one guy in the middle doing the planning—it was, like, put a bottle of vodka on his desk, and you'd get your machines for the service." That un-Googley system was replaced by something very Googley—an auction-based allocation.

Google's chief economist, Hal Varian, would later explain how it worked when new data centers open: "We'll build a nice new data center and say, 'Hey, Google Docs, would you move your machines over here?' And they say, 'Sure, next month.' Because nobody wants to go through the disruption of shifting. So I suggested we run an auction similar to what airlines do when they oversell a plane—they keep offering bigger vouchers until enough customers are willing to give up their seats. In our case, we offer more machines in exchange for moving. One group might do it for fifty new ones, another for a hundred, and another won't move unless we give them three hundred. So we give them to the lowest bidder—they get their extra capacity, and we get computation shifted to the new data center."

Google eventually devised an elaborate auction model for divvying up existing resources. In a paper entitled "Using a Market Economy to Provision Computer Resources Across Planet-wide Clusters," a group of Google engineers, along with a Stanford professor of management science and engineering, reported a project that essentially made Google's computational resources into a silicon Wall Street. Supply and demand worked here not to fix stock prices but to place a value on resources. The system not only allowed projects at Google to get fair access to storage and computational cycles but identified shortages in computers, storage, and bandwidth. Instead of the Vickery auction used by AdWords, the system used an "ascending clock auction." At the beginning, the current price of each resource would be displayed, and Google engineers in competing projects could claim them at that price. The ideal outcome would ensure sufficient resources for everyone, in which case the auction stopped. Otherwise, the automated auctioneer would raise the prices for the next "time slot," and remaining competitors for those resources had to decide whether to bid higher. And so on, until the engineers not willing to stake their budgets on the most contested resources dropped out. "Hence," write the paper's authors, "the auction allows users to 'discover' prices in which all users pay/receive payment in proportion to uniform resource prices."

To round out its suite of web applications, Google began developing a cloud-based alternative to Microsoft's PowerPoint. In early 2007, it heard about an innovative start-up that was working on a web-based presentation program that had some even niftier features than the one Google was developing internally. Wayne Crosby and Robby Walker had begun a company called Zenter. Funded by $15,000 from a start-up incubator called Y Combinator, they set out to create their web-based program in four months. They were working out of a small apartment in Mountain View with almost no furniture: their dining room table was a large Styrofoam box that had once held a case of Lean Cuisine meals that Walker's father had sent them so they wouldn't starve. Back in his home state of Arizona, Crosby's wife was about to give birth to their first child. In ten weeks they wrote 40,000 lines of code, creating a program that let users alter their presentations on the fly. And then Google called, eventually buying the company for several million dollars.

By the time it bought Zenter, Google had already released a beta version of its web-based productivity suite, Google Docs. Google Docs had one huge advantage over Microsoft Office: it was free. Google also began marketing a version to corporations, universities, government agencies, charging $50 a year "per seat" (i.e., for each user) for a license. Adoption was slow but steady. Googlers, however, gobbled it up. It was as though their brains were already in . . . the cloud. "Ninety-five percent of the company was using it in, like, a month, with no pushing at all," says Schillace. "It just took the company over."

When Schillace began talking to outsiders in 2007, the first reaction he got was "Are you frigging nuts? This will never work." Some months later, people would say, "Maybe it's going to work." By 2010, the qualifiers had been deleted. "Every conversation I have acknowledges that cloud computing is clearly going to happen," Schillace says, "and the only interesting thing is whether we're going to win or someone else is."

The surest sign that Schillace was right? In 2010, Microsoft rolled out an online version of its Office product—for free. Even if only a small percentage of the marketplace used Google's own productivity apps, the company had achieved its larger goal—moving work onto the web.

Google's next step would put it even more squarely into Microsoft's sights: it was going to build its own version of the web application that had been at the center of Microsoft's government antitrust case, a browser.

The idea long predated Google's plans for web-based applications. In 2001, Page and Brin had told Schmidt they wanted Google to build its own browser. Right away. Schmidt understood the impulse: browsers were important. They were the vehicles by which people navigated the web, and it made sense for Google to have an alternative to the Microsoft Internet Explorer browser in case Bill Gates and company built in features that would favor Microsoft. But Schmidt originally nixed the plan. "I said, 'Give me a break,'" he recalls. "'We don't have any cash!'" Most of all, he felt that a Google browser would arouse the ire of Microsoft. "I did not believe the company was strong enough to withstand a browser fight," he says. "I didn't want to moon the giant."

Schmidt brokered a compromise with Sergey and Larry to forestall the inevitable. Google would begin a partnership with the Mozilla Foundation, the nonprofit founded with money from Netscape's sale to AOL. The foundation's key product was an open-source browser called Firefox. Google was already the biggest source of revenue for the foundation, paying it millions of dollars to ensure that the search box in Firefox was powered by Google. In the new arrangement, Google hired some top engineers from Mozilla, including Ben Goodger and Darin Fisher. While their employer would be Google, their job would be the same: making improvements in Firefox. Another hiring coup came with Linus Upson, a thirty-seven-year-old engineer with browser experience from Netscape, Steve Jobs's company NeXT, and Palm, where he created the browser for the PalmPilot. "This was very clever on Larry and Sergey's part," says Schmidt, "because, of course, these people doing Firefox extensions are perfectly capable of doing a great browser."

The Mozilla refugees worked in what was known at Google as the Product Client Group. This group covered all of Google's applications that were not web-based but hewed to the more traditional model, where a user installs the program on a computer and thereafter runs it on that machine.

The first Google client app was the Google Toolbar, an application that let users put the Google search box onto their browsers. John Doerr was a big supporter, urging that Google should aggressively push the product so that the company would not be vulnerable if Microsoft built its own search engine into its Internet Explorer browser. "I was quite nearly panicked that Google was getting to all the world's people through Microsoft's browser," says Doerr. But the product was languishing until a new associate product manager, Wesley Chan, arrived and was assigned to the team. Chan would later develop Google Analytics. Larry Page approached Chan on his first day. "I'm so happy you're thinking about this," he said, "because this is a disaster. If we don't fix it, we'll cancel the project."

Chan realized that users were ignoring the Toolbar because it provided no value to them. His idea was to implement a feature that would allow people to block annoying pop-up windows, which at the time were a plague on the net. But when he presented the idea at a meeting, Brin and Page, who had tied water bottles to the venetian blind cords and were playing a game of water-bottle tetherball, nixed the idea. "That's the dumbest thing I've ever heard!" said Page. "Where did we find you?" Chan built the pop-up blocker anyway, and surreptitiously installed it on Page's computer. ("He'd leave the computer on in his office," says Chan.) Not long afterward, Page remarked that his browser was running faster. Chan told him that he'd installed the pop-up blocker.

"Didn't I tell you not to do that?" asked Page.

"Oh, it was a 20 percent project," said Chan. Page dropped his suspicions and okayed the feature, which helped spur millions of Toolbar downloads.

In subsequent years, the client group added more products: Google Desktop, which allowed users to use Google technology to search the contents of their own hard drives; the Google Pack, a set of applications from other software companies that Google bundled together and let users download all at once; and a not-yet-released project called GDrive, which would let users store documents in Google's data centers.

The head of the Product Client Group was an intense engineer named Sundar Pichai. Born in Madras, India, he was among many Googlers who had attended the Indian Institute of Technology. After graduation, he followed the well-trod path to the United States and earned an M.S. in computer science at Stanford. But Pichai left academia in 1995. "The PhD just seemed like too long a commitment," he says. "I just wanted to work." He took various jobs in semiconductors and came to enjoy product management and business management, so he went to business school. He was working at McKinsey & Company in 2003 when one of his younger colleagues announced that he was going to take a job at Google. Pichai tried to talk him out of leaving until he realized that the arguments in favor of joining Google were actually much stronger. Ten months later, Pichai became a Google employee. It was April 1, 2004, and Google was in war room mode because of the Gmail announcement.

In spring 2006, Pichai's client group was working in Building 44, across Charleston Street from the core campus. They were preparing for the Firefox 2.0 launch, but not unexpectedly, there were conversations about designing an ideal browsing app of their own. The team believed that there was a flaw in the current generation of browsers. Microsoft's Internet Explorer and Mozilla's Firefox had been conceived in the 1990s, before the cloud computing era. Now the web was expected to become not just a means of delivering information but also a platform for running programs. Those creaky old browsers could not easily adapt to the new reality. The conclusion was obvious: only by building its own browser could Google bring the browser into the cloud age. Even if it didn't catch on, it might jar the current browsers into radicalizing their own approach, triggering a spiral of innovation not seen since the 1990s browser wars between Microsoft and Netscape.

The Google engineers began informally discussing what a totally new browser should look like. One key change they had in mind was something called multiprocess architecture. This is the system that helps a computer keep going when an application crashes or freezes. Why not extend that idea to browsers, so if one tab crashes, the other tabs would be unaffected? Starting from scratch had other advantages. The program could be designed to look cleaner and run faster. This fit with the corporate religion of making software with spartan interfaces that run with the speed of Usain Bolt.

Google had gotten a lot of flak for its impersonal interface style—some thought its programs and search pages so plain as to be ugly. "It's like they almost *want* it to be insipid," says Andy Hertzfeld, a former Macintosh wizard now at Google. Many decisions were made by testing rather than aesthetics—sometimes a minor tweak in spacing or the shade of a color could result in millions of dollars lost or gained in AdWord clicks. Also, Larry Page, wary of anything that would degrade performance, would routinely bounce any interface element with clever frills such as animation. "Artsy" designers seldom lasted long in the company, and one defector left behind a blistering blog post on Google's visual shortcomings. The fact was, Google didn't want to be beautiful. Marissa Mayer, the fierce protector of Google's look, once quelled an incipient revolt by designers by finally defining what rankled her about a stunning design submitted to her. "It looks like a *human* was involved in choosing what went where," Marissa told them. "It looks too editorialized. Google products are machine-driven. They're created by machines. And that is what makes us powerful. That's what makes our products great." In other words, the message Google wanted to convey was that its products had no human bias. "It was like this lightbulb went off," says Margaret Stewart, a key curator of the Google interface. "Marissa said Google products are machine-driven. It was the locked-up principle that had never been expressed, and that was of enormous assistance to us."

The essential spec of a new browser was high speed. "Larry and Sergey wrote an OKR saying we should make the web as fast as flipping through a magazine," says Pichai. "If things could be instant and there's just no latency at all, the sky is the limit. I mean, we haven't even scratched the surface."

In June 2006, the former Mozillans created a small prototype. Though Brin and Page had yet to give an explicit go-ahead, it was clear that they were quietly rooting the effort on. Schmidt no longer opposed the browser idea. But if Google did undertake the project, the CEO said, the result would have to be something that differed significantly from other browsers. In addition, it would have to be fast, it would have to be open source, it would have to be secure. The Executive Committee green-lighted the project to begin in earnest.

"I remember one Friday, there was a meeting called with, like, an hour's notice," says one engineer. "It was kind of mysterious. And we were told, 'The management is thinking about doing our own browser—what do you think about that?' It was a crazy question, and everybody was a combination of excited and freaked out." The engineers knew that building a competitive browser was a massive undertaking. There were also mixed feelings due to the group's strong attachment to both the technology and vision behind Firefox, an icon of open-source development and a hedge against Microsoft's dominance of the browser market. Particularly for the Googlers who had come from Mozilla, this was a case of digital fratricide. "The fear was that people were going to read this as sabotaging Firefox," says engineer Erik Kay, who joined the team in October 2006. That would be *evil.*

The Googlers were eventually mollified by the assurance that their browser would be 100 percent open source. With the open-source system, Google's code would be publicly available, and if people wanted to use it to create variations, that was fine. It was even possible that Google's innovations could find their way into the Mozilla code base.

It was Pichai's unhappy duty to break the news to Mitchell Baker, the chairman of the Mozilla Foundation. Baker was tough; trained as an attorney, she could passionately argue the open-source cause. She also cut a memorable figure with her asymmetrical punkish coiffure. She would have fit right in at Google, except for the fact that she was wary of all commercial enterprises. And as a veteran of the browser wars, she knew that every point of market share was as toughly contested as a football goal-line stand.

Since a Google browser had been rumored for months, Baker wasn't shocked. But Google had been a partner and benefactor of Mozilla. Now it was her competitor.

Was it a betrayal? Evil? With the pride of a jilted lover, Baker would later shrug it off. "To be betrayed, you have to expect something different," she says. "I expect Google to pursue its economic interests. I have never had illusions. We're not a toy. Google doesn't control us." But she could not mask the bitterness when, after the Google browser came out, Google began promoting it with AdWords delivered to people who searched using the keyword "Mozilla." "They're actively trying to take people away from Firefox," she complained.

After the usual flurry of crazy alternatives for a code name, the team decided to call its browser Google Chrome. The moniker came from the term used to describe the frame, toolbars, menus, and other graphic elements that border a browser window. In a way, the name was counterintuitive, because Google wanted to strip off a lot of the decorative chrome seen in other browsers and create a sleek sports car of a browser. The idea was to make the interface so minimal that people wouldn't feel they were using a browser at all but interacting directly with the pages and web apps. An unofficial motto became "Content not chrome," a bit bizarre considering the product's name. "We've learned to live with the irony," said engineer Mark Larson during the development process.

Page and Brin wanted Chrome optimized to run web applications—fast. When you run a program faster by an order of magnitude, you haven't made something better—you've made something new. The crucial element in speeding up a browser was a component called a JavaScript engine, a "virtual machine" that ran web application code. In previous browsers, JavaScript didn't run quickly enough to make web applications seem as nimble as desktop apps; Google felt that if it changed that, people would use the web more and thus use Google's services and ads more. Google hoped to kick-start a new generation of web-based applications that would make Microsoft's worst nightmare a reality: the browser would become the equivalent of an operating system.

There was an ideal person to supercharge the virtual machine, a Danish computer scientist named Lars Bak, whose virtuosity in virtuality had established him as the master in the field. But after more than twenty years of nonstop labor designing virtual machines, the forty-five-year-old Bak had returned to his native country and had been planning to take some time off to work on his farm outside Aarhus. When he got Google's call in September 2006, however, the opportunity was too tempting to resist. Bak set up a small team that originally worked from his farm, then moved to some offices at the local university. He understood that his mission was to provide an engine faster than any previous browser. He called his team's part of the project "V8." "We decided we wanted to speed up JavaScript by a factor of ten, and we gave ourselves four months to do it," he says. A typical day for the group would begin between 7 and 8 A.M.; they'd program constantly until six or seven at night, when they'd call Mountain View to debrief. The only break was for lunch, when they would wolf down food in five minutes and spend twenty minutes at the game console. "We are pretty damn good at Wii Tennis," Bak noted.

They were also pretty good at writing a JavaScript engine. As the project progressed, Bak's benchmarks showed that V8 was running JavaScript ten times as fast as Firefox. And how did it compare in those same benchmarks to the market-share leader, Microsoft's IE 7? Fifty-six times as fast. "We sort of underestimated what we could do," Bak says.

Sundar Pichai and his team had an OKR of 20 million users by the end of the year. "It was a very aggressive OKR," he says. "A classic." He didn't make it. "We got there, but not in the time frame we had in mind." A lot of people downloaded Chrome in the early weeks and found that it didn't work. Because the online behavior of Googlers was not typical of the general public, there had been many websites and apps that went untested. "We had five thousand internal users, but not one noticed that Hotmail didn't work," says one engineer. But after Chrome shipped to the public, Hotmail users *instantly* found that it wouldn't run their mail—and deleted Google's browser.

Also the Macintosh version was months late, even though an early Mac version was in the plans all along. In fact, after Steve Jobs's keynote presentation in January 2008, when Apple's CEO introduced a slim new computer called the MacBook Air, Sergey Brin gave Pichai one of the first units and said, "I want Chrome running on a Mac." The Mac version didn't ship until late 2009.

But Chrome's numbers grew, to over 120 million by the end of 2010. What's more, every one of Chrome's competitors made it a point to speed up *their* browsers. That was exactly what Google wanted: browsers that provided a better experience for people to run applications on the web.

In fact, Google began to believe that people already had reached the point—with web apps such as Google Docs and all the myriad services on the web—that there was almost nothing you *couldn't* do with a browser. Pichai gave a netbook to his father and noticed that once his dad opened Chrome, he never opened another application. He came to think that the word "application" didn't apply to a browser—it was more like a gateway to everything in the world that really mattered, the stuff in the cloud. "It was very clear to us a lot of people were buying these devices with the goal of spending their entire day in the browser. So we all started talking about a natural course: designing an end-to-end experience around the browser. Think about it."

In fact, the thought had already occurred to the team. "We didn't want to use the OS word, but Chrome was always thought of as an operating system for web applications," says Linus Upson. But once Chrome was launched, the team began thinking of it literally that way, building it so that if you bought a netbook—or eventually any other kind of computer—there would be no Windows or Linux operating system, just Chrome.

"From eight P.M. onwards is when you have really interesting conversations," says Caesar Sengupta, an engineer on the team. "We started challenging ourselves to think about how we would build an operating system." They got Upson and Pichai on board and began ticking off what a Chrome operating system should be: blisteringly fast, totally free of malware. "It should just feel like the web," says Sengupta. They put together a proposal that they took to a meeting with Larry and Sergey in October 2008. Since Brin and Page had been wanting to do an OS for ten years, they instantly embraced the idea. "I'm all for it," said Page.

As the Chrome team brainstormed its operating system, they realized that there was a chance to redefine computing itself, in terms of the cloud. As web applications got better, they figured, why have any client applications? In fact, why not jettison the entire concept of storing a file and running a program with it? It was a startling concept, as few thought that cloud-based computing was far enough along to replace the current paradigm. Privacy advocates might worry about the security of cloud-based data—but Google believed that it had proved its trustworthiness with Gmail. IT experts might worry about what happens if web services had outages. But Google was confident that its unmatched infrastructure had sufficient power and redundancy to be as dependable as the electricity from a power outlet. In any case, an ambition junkie like Larry Page wasn't about to argue with such an audacious premise.

Besides, if Chrome OS could move people more rapidly toward cloud computing—or just make computers so easy to use that people used them more—Google's business would boom. In fact, Upson argued, Google had more at stake in improving computers than did companies that actually make computers. "Google makes money with advertising online, but that's about 20 percent of total advertising spent," Upson says. "Eighty percent of the time, people's attention is offline. To the extent that we can make computers better, everything will go online, and Google can participate in that advertising space. There are four more Googles to be had here. That's why we have incentives to make computers better. Computer manufacturers want to figure out how to get the most money out of you. We want to make you happy. If we can do it free, so much the better."

At the time, Google was about to launch a project it had been developing for more than a year, a free cloud-based storage service called GDrive. But Sundar had concluded that it was an artifact of the style of computing that Google was about to usher out the door. He went to Bradley Horowitz, the executive in charge of the project, and said, "I don't think we need GDrive anymore." Horowitz asked why not. "Files are so 1990," said Pichai. "I don't think we need files anymore."

Horowitz was stunned. "Not need files anymore?"

"Think about it," said Pichai. "You just want to get information into the cloud. When people use our Google Docs, there are no more files. You just start editing in the cloud, and there's never a file."

When Pichai first proposed this concept to Google's top executives at a GPS—no files!—the reaction was, he says, "skeptical." Upson had another characterization: "It was a withering assault." But eventually they won people over by a logical argument—that it *could* be done, that it was the cloudlike thing to do, that it was the Google thing to do. That was the end of GDrive: shuttered as a relic of antiquated thinking even before Google released it. The engineers working on it went to the Chrome team.

"We're taking a fairly radical position," said Upson. Netbooks running Chrome OS—and Google had already contracted with computer makers to produce them in late 2010—would have no storage. None. You would never install any application. The idea was that you would turn on your computer, and it would boot up instantly (forget about the three-minute wait one must endure with Windows) and connect you to your world, which resided in some cloud somewhere. You wouldn't have to bother where. And you could enter that world through any computer once you entered your proper passwords. "We will be your IT department," says Upson. "You never need to worry about software updates, anything like that. We will take care of it all for you."

Upson and Pichai believed that a wave of new technologies would allow a cloud computer to do everything one did with a desktop machine, only more reliably, more simply, more securely, and much faster. A new protocol called HTML 5 was beginning to roll out, and it enabled web applications to run offline. Google had also been working on a project called Native Client that would allow web-based programs to run as nimbly as those written specifically for a given computer—it would allow even hard-core gamers to get the performance they needed from a web app, something previously unthinkable. And it would all run on the web—you would never install software on your computer again.

That was so startling to the public that the Chrome OS team members often had to repeat it several times before it sank in. The conventions of the desktop were so ingrained that they felt like gravity. But the Googlers had an answer for everything. What about those times—and there were a lot of them—when there was no Internet broadband available? The prototype Chrome OS released to a few thousand testers had a cellular 3G modem built in, as a backup for those times when Wi-Fi wasn't around. (It wasn't a great solution, but it was better than nothing.) What about drivers, those little pieces of software that allow your particular computer to connect smoothly with printers and other plug-in devices? "We're saying *no drivers*. We're done," says Upson. What he meant was—*they're* done, *they're* the current model of computing.

Google had declared that the cloud was its destiny. And ours.

PART FIVE

OUTSIDE THE BOX
The Google Phone Company and the Google TV Company

1

"They *already* hate us—what's the downside?"

You might say that the seeds of the Google Telephone Company took root right after the company moved out of its Palo Alto office to Mountain View in August 1999. The tenant moving into the space Google vacated was a start-up company named Danger.

Danger's cofounder, Andy Rubin, was a veteran of Apple in the early 1990s and a fabled start-up called General Magic. He'd started Danger to make a mobile communications device called the Sidekick, less a cell phone than a tiny computer—arguably the first smart phone with a measurable IQ. Instant messaging, not phone calls, was the Sidekick's main purpose; you held it sideways, slid out a keyboard, and began thumb-punching IMs, which appeared in colorful pop-ups on a bright screen. It became popular with teenagers and rap musicians. The Sidekick's built-in search engine was Google. "The engineers just liked Google," he says. In 2002, Rubin was demo'ing the Sidekick for a class at Stanford when someone approached him to tell him how cool it was. That was Larry Page.

A couple of years later, Rubin made it a point to visit Google when he was seeking partnerships and funding for his next start-up. (He'd left Danger, and eventually Microsoft bought the company.) Rubin's new idea was to create an operating system that would power whole families of smart phones—then give the system to the big network carriers (like Verizon or Sprint) for free. This would save the carriers money, since they wouldn't have to license an operating system from a company like Microsoft or build their own. (Typically a carrier pays 20 percent of the per-phone cost for an operating system.) The system would be written under the rules of open-source software, with the code available to any software authors who wanted to write applications. Rubin's plan was to make money by selling back-end services to go with the operating system, such as storage, support, and security. It was the familiar model of giving away the razor and making money on the blades.

Rubin, who was a maniacal robot aficionado—he would haunt the Akihabara district of Tokyo for weird Japanese toys, and build a few of his own—called the company Android. He gathered a team of eight to begin working on a prototype. He had a good contact at the handset manufacturer HTC, which provided him with a top-secret new device that he could use just for demos. After a few months, Android had a working model with a set of slick features such as contacts, email, and a camera. (One nice touch was that Android's photo software could recognize faces.)

Rubin began pitching carriers in 2004. He also went to the Far East to sell the idea to other handset manufacturers. Even though he was offering something for free, it was a tough sell. The mobile phone world had a profitable business model and was loath to consider disruptive new schemes. He would later vividly recall the trip he had made to Korea—"on my own dime!" he said—to present the concept to Samsung. He and two colleagues found themselves in a huge boardroom. Standing along the wall were about twenty carefully manicured executives in blue suits. (Rubin was in blue jeans.) The division head arrived, and, as if on cue, everyone sat down. Rubin gave his presentation, and the division head rocked with laughter. "You have eight people in your company," said this executive. "And I have two thousand people working on something that's not as ambitious." It wasn't a compliment.

Rubin pressed on, but he needed more money to keep going. He had funding prospects on the line when he took a meeting with Larry Page. Maybe Page would write an email saying that Google wanted to place custom versions of search and Gmail on Android phones; that might help with the venture capital firms. "We really weren't there to pitch Google," says Rich Miner, Android's cofounder. They gave their standard presentation.

Page had an idea: what if Google *bought* Android? It was a classic Larry Page moment: ask him to consider a toothpick, and right away, he was thinking about a forest. Later, Page would explain that he and Sergey had been thinking about getting deeper into mobile for a while. "We had that vision," he says. "And Andy came along and we were like, 'Yeah, we should do it. He's the guy.'"

It was 2005, and Google's mission was to access and organize the world's information. To most people, that seemed plenty. Explaining how a company that made an operating system for mobile phones fit into this mission would eventually present a challenge for Google's publicists. But Larry Page interpreted Google's mission in the broadest sense. What was good for the web was good for Google. What was good for the cloud was good for Google. So it made sense that what was good for the growing universe of wireless communication over mobile phone carrier networks would also be good for Google. Because the carriers tightly controlled the software that ran on phones using their networks, Google had reason to worry that it might not have the opportunity to place its services on those nets. An open network would give Google unlimited opportunity, so that even if Google spent millions of dollars to develop an operating system— and then gave it away for free—it would still come out ahead.

If the move wound up putting Google in the path of a few more competitors, so be it.

Before Rubin committed to Google, he had to take the measure of his potential employer. It wasn't easy, because he found Google crazy. He was accustomed to companies such as Apple and Microsoft, where you'd meet with someone, go over the corporate org chart, and figure out where you'd fit in. "At Google, it was impossible to figure that out," he says. "I met with everybody multiple times, and I'm pretty good at extracting information— and I couldn't find out." But he did at least learn that Alan Eustace, Google's director of engineering, would be his boss. Rubin asked Eustace about the process Google used to improve itself. He expected to hear about quality assurance teams and focus groups. Instead Eustace explained that Google's brain was like a baby's, an omnivorous sponge that was always getting smarter from the information it soaked up. When a Google user searched for Nike shoes, he was told, there were sets of algorithms that determined search results and another set that figured out which ad should appear alongside the results; then another set of algorithms would run an instant auction. But the system was always learning. Rubin liked hearing that; his own companies had evolved from protean ideas. Danger had originally been centered on digital cameras before becoming a cell phone company.

So in July 2005, Android went to Google. The biggest adjustment Rubin had to make was keeping his limited-edition German sports car in the garage—in 2005, ostentation was still discouraged in the Google parking lots.

At first Android was Larry's thing. "Early on, Sergey opted out, just saying he really didn't understand mobile yet. Eric was supportive of what Larry was doing," says Rich Miner, who went to Google with Rubin. The acquisition actually contradicted Schmidt's frequent proclamations that there would be no Google phone. "We're not going into the phone business, but we're going to make sure Google is on those phones," Schmidt emphatically said in October 2004, nine months before Google bought Android—and got into the phone business. "But it wasn't very long before Sergey and Eric were experts on mobile, and could speak very competently about it," says Miner. At product reviews, Brin and Page would throw ideas at the team. Some were worth thinking about: Why don't we have a keyboard on the other side that mirrors the one on the front? Others not: Why don't we put solar panels on it? Schmidt was tough about some aspects, too. At one GPS, unhappy with a prototype keyboard, he looked straight at one of the product managers. "First impressions really matter here," he said. *"Don't fuck it up."* At another meeting he expressed impatience that Android hadn't responded quickly enough to his request for five thousand units so Googlers could "dogfood" the product. ("Eating your own dogfood"—that is, letting Googlers use product prototypes in their everyday lives to detect flaws and identify possible improvements—is a sacrosanct principle within the company.) "You're not taking my request seriously!" he said, just about pounding the table to punctuate his words. The line assumed legendary status in the Android building and became a kind of punch line.

Rubin appreciated the interest of his bosses, but he appreciated even more the unusual degree of autonomy he was granted. He managed to get a special concession for his Android team: he could do his own hiring. His basic team consisted of the group he'd imported from Android, merged with new hires snapped up from two groups abandoned by other companies. One contingent came from Palm, where they'd worked on a system called PalmSource; they were devotees of the open-source software movement and were drawn by Google's promise that Android would be an open-source project, open to hacking and improvements by the geek community that avidly participated in such projects. The other was a bunch of people from Microsoft's ill-fated WebTV project. "We had these three groups with very strong ideas about what Android should be, so there were a lot of heated debates," says Dianne Hackborn, who had come from PalmSource. Rubin also drew talent from within Google.

Now that Google was running Android, the former start-up's business model changed. The razor part of the equation—the operating system—would still be free to carriers, but the blades were no longer boring things such as back-end services. Android would be a Trojan horse for Google's consumer apps, chief among them mobile search. "They already existed, so I didn't have to do any work," says Rubin. "And it's not boring. It's stuff like Gmail, maps, all this cool stuff. The boring back-office stuff went away, and it became stuff that delights consumers." Better yet, the partner reaction to Android changed. Not long after Rubin joined, he returned to Samsung. This time, backed by an Internet giant, he left with a contract. He had similar experiences with other companies he approached. One deal was made with an executive who had previously told Rubin that only in his dreams would such an agreement materialize. "We had to try really hard not to let decisions be affected by that," says Rubin.

Rubin tapped a new Google employee named Erick Tseng to manage the product. Tseng had a CS master's from MIT and had spent a few years as a McKinsey & Company consultant before going back to school to get an MBA from Stanford. He'd been about to take a job as a venture capitalist with Sequoia when Eric Schmidt, who lectured at the business school at Stanford, took him to lunch one day. "Imagine a world," Schmidt told him, "where a company like Google can provide cell phones to everyone in the world for free. Now imagine the possibility of what that can enable. It's not just about the phones. Whether you're in the U.S. or you're in Africa, you will be connected to your family, your friends—and to all the content on the web. *That* is something Google is possibly working on," he said.

"That's what sold me on Android," says Tseng.

At first the Android team worked on two different systems. One was called the Sooner; it was based on the existing Android prototype. With a keypad sitting underneath the screen, Sooner was designed to get into the market quickly. Sooner absorbed most of the energy in Android's early days at Google. For the long term, Rubin's group wanted to develop a more advanced platform with a touch screen. He dubbed that version the Dream. But in January 2007, Apple's new iPhone redefined the smart phone. With its touch screen, tightly integrated software, and sharp display, the iPhone had delivered the future ahead of schedule. Sooner became never, and Android went straight to the Dream.

Early that year the press began reporting rumors that Google was indeed working on a "Gphone." Brin and especially Page were furious at the leak, ominously informing employees at a TGIF that Google had launched an investigation and even accidental breaches would not be tolerated. When an employee noted that the publicity about the project seemed positive, suggesting that the company was going overboard in a Nixonesque mole hunt, Page was unyielding. "I think that's a decision for the team to make, not you," he said. But Rubin wasn't too surprised that the news of a Google phone project had leaked out—"If you get a guy who started a company that built a phone, what else are you going to do?" he says. In any case, he said that people didn't have the imagination to see what Google was really up to, so the secret was safe.

But as one person in particular began to understand what Google was up to, a bitter rivalry was born. That person was Steve Jobs, the Apple CEO.

Since Jobs's original meeting with Page and Brin—the one where the Google kids had decided that he would meet their CEO requirements—the relationship between the two companies had blossomed. The Google founders were entranced by Jobs's vision and decisiveness, and Jobs was excited by the opportunity to hook up with a business whose activities were entirely complementary to Apple's—there seemed to be no competitive overlap. The two firms embarked on a potentially glorious, industry-changing alliance in which the veteran Jobs would lend his expertise and wisdom to the smarty-pants Internet kids and the two firms together would take down Microsoft. All sorts of concepts were discussed. How about a free version of the Mac OS, supported by Apple ads? What about a Google-ized version of Apple's Safari browser? Jobs bonded especially with Brin; both lived in Palo Alto, and the pair would take long walks around the town and up in the hills . . . current and future kings of the Valley, inventing the future.

In August 2006, Jobs invited Eric Schmidt to sit on Apple's board of directors, which included Google board member Arthur Levinson, CEO of Genetech; and Bill Campbell, Google's corporate coach. Al Gore sat on Apple's board, while he was the self-described "virtual advisory board" at Google. Intel CEO Paul Otellini, who was on Google's board, had started supplying the chips for Macintosh computers. There was so much overlap that it was almost as if Apple and Google were a single company.

Smart phones seemed to be the logical nexus of the unofficial partnership. Google had a bustling mobile division apart from Android, intended to put Google squarely into the world of smart phones, mainly by way of making mobile applications of products like Gmail, Google Maps, and especially search. Apple's iPhone looked to be the showcase for what those apps could do when liberated from the desktop.

Google's mobile division was headed by Vic Gundotra, who had previously been a high-level Microsoft executive. In 1976, at age seven, he had been fascinated by the term "Information Age," which set a course for his life that led him to work for Bill Gates. For twelve years, Gundotra had bled Windows. But in 2002, sitting with family and friends at a restaurant, his four-year-old daughter accidentally overheard him say the words "I don't know." She broke into the conversation with a suggestion: he should get out his phone and find out whatever it was he didn't know. In her reality, after all, when someone is stumped on a question, the place to look for answers was that hand-size device. It was a eureka moment for Gundotra. "It dawned on me that the culmination of the Information Age was not going to be at Microsoft," he says. "It wasn't about a computer on every desktop but making the world's information accessible and available." After trying to sound alarms at Microsoft about the paradigm shift, he concluded that the company could not accept the reality that Windows was no longer the center of the universe; the web was. By 2006, he was at Google.

Gundotra's team worked with Apple to make sure that the iPhone, shipped in the summer of 2007, launched with two crucial apps: a slick implementation of Google Maps and a special version of YouTube that enabled the iPhone to access its millions of videos. One Thursday Google's mobile group called an emergency meeting at 7 A.M. to discuss how Google had to push more. Six weeks later, there was a new Google mobile search, rolling out first on the iPhone. Making use of the voice recognition knowledge gleaned by Google's voice-powered, 1-800-GOOG-411 directory assistance project, the app let you dictate search terms into the phone with startling accuracy.

But as Android developed, Google's mobile efforts looked more toward the company's own technology. "If you love Google, then the Android phone is a phenomenal phone for you," says Gundotra. "Because it allows us to get innovation out to the phone very quickly." Google still put a lot of effort into working with other platforms. After all, as people used phones more and more, the number of searches on phones was growing. Eventually the number of searches performed on a phone would exceed those on computers. "I don't think that anyone at Google has a doubt that the day is coming," says Gundotra of that milestone. Google professed to have a permanent nook in its heart for the iPhone, which was an unofficial Google cousin, but when Google shifted from Sooner to Dream, Google's focus turned to its own child.

Apparently, it took a while for Jobs to understand that Google was becoming his competitor. It was almost a year after the Android acquisition that Schmidt joined Apple's board. "I feel I fully disclosed it when I joined," says Schmidt, who adds that he also informed Jobs about the impending Chrome browser. But at that time, Jobs apparently believed that Google's phone plans rested with the Sooner version, which was more of a competitor to Microsoft's Windows Mobile than an iPhone rival. When Apple introduced its iPhone in January 2007, Jobs didn't seem to be worried about Android, at least judging by the mutual good feeling when Jobs called Schmidt to the stage at the product launch. Schmidt joked that the collaboration was so close that the two firms might as well combine. "If we merge the companies we can call it AppleGoo . . . but we can merge without merging."

By 2008, however, the trajectories of the two companies, at least with respect to phones, was less a merger than an impending collision. An implicit acknowledgment came from a decision to bar Schmidt from hearing product plans for Apple's phone. "It's not like it was a new discovery—it was an evolution," says Schmidt, apparently referring to Google's accelerated plans to launch a device that behaved like an iPhone. "So at the end of my second year [as a board member] Steve and I agreed without discord that I would recuse myself from the phone [discussions]." When the iPhone came up at Apple board meetings, Schmidt would leave the room. (He would later say that he had been kept totally in the dark about the evolution of Apple's tablet computer, the iPad.) Schmidt also kept his distance from Android, something that Rubin regretted. "There were decisions along the way where I could have used Eric, and I was left to fend for myself," says Rubin. Meanwhile, Schmidt would joke to Googlers that he treated every Apple board meeting as if it were his last.

Still, Schmidt insisted that it was a mild case of "frenemy," with no animus between the two companies. "It's a model-based tension, not a personal tension," he would say. His point of view was that the competition was good for users, and if there were losers, they would be other competitors: Microsoft, Oracle, Yahoo

Nonetheless, insiders say that over a period of months, Jobs concluded that he was a victim of deceit. The first alarming sign of Google pursuing its vision regardless of its effect on Apple was the Chrome browser. It competed with Apple's Safari browser and also with the open-source WebKit technology that Apple had developed for Safari. It was all kosher from both a legal and an industry practices standpoint, but Jobs wasn't happy, especially since Google had tried to hire some of his Safari developers.

Android, though, was much worse. As he learned more about how the benign competitor he had envisioned was actually a full-blown alternative to the iPhone, Jobs became increasingly upset. Yet for months he was reluctant to break with Google. From all accounts, Jobs prided himself as a canny observer not only of business but also of human character, and he did not want to admit—especially to himself—that he had been betrayed by the two young men he had been attempting to mentor. He felt the trust between the two companies had been violated. After increasingly contentious phone calls, in the summer of 2008, Jobs ventured to Mountain View to see the Android phone and personally judge the extent of the violation. He was reportedly furious. Not only did he believe that Google had performed a bait and switch on him, replacing a noncompeting phone with one that was very much in the iPhone mode, but he also felt that Google had stolen Apple's intellectual property to do so, appropriating features for which Apple had current or pending patents.

While Jobs could not stop Google from developing the Dream version of Android, he apparently was successful, at least in the first version of the Google phone, in halting its implementation of some of the multitouch gestures that Apple had pioneered. Jobs believed that Apple's patents gave it exclusive rights to certain on-screen gestures—the pinch and the swipe, for example. According to one insider, Jobs demanded that Google remove support of those gestures from Android phones. Google complied, even though those gestures, which allowed users to resize images, were tremendously useful for viewing web pages on handheld devices.

That omission became particularly glaring when another competitor, Palm, implemented those gestures on its own phone. (Palm's team was led by a former Apple executive, Jon Rubinstein, whose new job was regarded by Apple as a heinous defection.) Rubin later tried to shrug it off. "Everything's a barter," he says.

Google had already publicly announced its phone initiative in November 2007, in conjunction with the formation of the Open Handset Alliance, a group of device manufacturers and carriers committed to supporting Android. In a blog post, Rubin stipulated, "We're not announcing a Gphone." Instead, he promised something more significant: a "truly-open and comprehensive platform for mobile devices . . . without the proprietary obstacles that have hindered mobile innovation." Skeptics noted that absent from the alliance were the two biggest U.S. cell phone networks, Verizon and AT&T. Both giants seemed satisfied to maintain control of the software of devices that ran on their networks.

But for the longer term Google had a broader plan to open them up—it would lobby the Federal Communications Commission to permit openness in mobile networks.

In 2007, Google had hired its first telecom lobbyist, a former Verizon lawyer named Richard Whitt. His job focused on fighting for net neutrality—regulation to assure that Internet providers could not slow down or block services or websites because of their content or competitive status. (He had support in this public campaign from Google's Internet evangelist, Vinton Cerf, a renowned figure in the development of the net.) But Whitt also alerted the company to an opportunity: the FCC's early 2008 auction of wireless spectrum. Up for bid were some valuable slices of the airwaves that would host the next generation of mobile communications, allowing faster Internet access, not just from handheld devices but from computers and TVs inside homes, since the waves on these frequencies could penetrate walls more easily. Various coalitions were pushing the FCC to declare that, unlike the current spectrum, this platform would be designated as "open." That would mean that the winning bidders had to accommodate outside innovators. Requiring that the spectrum be open would reduce the value of the prize for the winning bidder, so it would stand to reason that the ultimate bid amount would be less than if the spectrum were unrestricted. Thus the Treasury would see fewer dollars from the auction. But presumably, the payback to consumers would far exceed the few billion dollars' difference.

At Whitt's suggestion, Google became an active proponent for open spectrum. His team wrote up four conditions that the FCC should impose on whoever won the spectrum in the most valuable block of frequencies up for auction. One demanded that a phone made by any manufacturer should be able to run on the network. A second would dictate that any software developer could write applications that ran on the network. That meant that if, say, Verizon won the auction, it could use that spectrum exclusively to serve its customers, who would still pay monthly bills to Verizon for the connectivity—but Verizon would have to let Google and others sell phones and write applications that worked on its network. (This was in contrast to current regulations, where Verizon could deny those companies access.) The other two conditions were more complicated restrictions on the network that Google never thought would be approved. "We didn't want them," says Whitt. "We figured if you asked for four, you might get two."

During one conference call among Google's wireless team, Whitt suggested a more emphatic means of making a point: what if Google actually participated in the auction? "It would be great," he said, "if we could really shut up those [carriers] by sending a letter to the commission that said, 'If you adopt those four openness conditions, we at Google will put our money where our mouth is. We will bid the amount necessary to trigger the conditions.'" That meant a minimum of $4.6 billion, the designated reserve price. But winning the auction would be a disaster. It would be like the dog who chased the car: what will he do if he catches it? Nonetheless, Google decided to go ahead. It really wasn't that big a risk, since it was unlikely that the FCC would grant all four conditions. Indeed, when the FCC responded, it agreed to only two conditions. But they were the key ones, which would require the winners of the most valuable slice of spectrum, the piece in the 700-megahertz range, to open the airwaves to different device makers and software developers. That gave Google exactly what it wanted: some big telecom company would have to spend billions of dollars on a wireless network that Google would be able to exploit.

But there was one hitch. According to the rules of the auction, if no one bid the minimum $4.6 billion, the process would end. There would be another auction, almost certainly without the openness requirements that Google wanted. The only way to ensure that the airwaves would be friendly to Google would be for the company to participate.

So Google became a player in a telecom auction. It gathered consultants and experts—its chief economist, Hal Varian, headed a team of auction wizards—to help it negotiate the unfamiliar territory of an FCC spectrum sale. That put Google directly in the sights of a host of new competitors, virtually every big telecom company interested in spectrum, particularly Verizon and AT&T. Google had already aroused their pique by supporting free or very cheap municipal wireless broadband Internet service, a commodity those companies sold for high monthly fees. Google had actually attempted to provide the service for the entire city of San Francisco, but the experiment had flopped. Now Google was messing with the airwaves themselves.

Though Google's presence in the auction put it on dangerous ground, the founders took to the task with relish, seeing it as a rare chance to experience video-game action blended with a multibillion-dollar gamble. It was like Maverick meets the electronic frontier. The company set up war rooms in Washington, D.C., and Mountain View, with computers hot-wired to the FCC auction site. As befit a multibillion-dollar risk, the room in Mountain View was a top secret facility, a windowless space with access severely limited. Larry and Sergey repeatedly dropped by as the auction progressed. At one point, Varian and Sergey wanted to visit, but Varian didn't have a key that would open the room. Sergey tried his, and it worked. They entered the empty room and monitored the site for a while. Before they left, Sergey pulled a prank, writing on the whiteboard "AT&T WAS HERE!" "When people came back, they were totally freaked," says Varian.

The auction process was complicated. It proceeded by a number of rounds, each requiring a bid exceeding the previous high by a certain minimum. If the bidding stopped before the top offer reached the $4.6 billion reserve, the auction would be invalid. Google's strategy was to bid early each round, even if that meant that the bid it topped was its own. That way, it would have the option to drop out if someone else outbid it. "It's a nerve-racking experience," Whitt says. But Larry and Sergey were totally into it, even having a photo taken of them as they pressed the trigger on one of Google's multibillion-dollar dice rolls from the Mountain View war room.

The bidding proceeded until the point was reached where the next round would require a bid over the reserve price, meaning that the spectrum would actually be awarded. If Google made the bid and no one else topped it, Google would become a telecom company, like it or not.

Page was gung ho on making the bid. But before presenting the issue to the board of directors, Eric Schmidt did a videoconference with the entire auction team. The key question was the likelihood of being stuck with the spectrum. What were the odds that Google's bid would be topped? Everyone made a guess, and they ranged from 15 percent on up. Finally Schmidt asked Whitt.

"Eighty-seven percent," he said.

Schmidt was taken aback. "Not 85? Not 90?"

Nope, said Whitt. He had learned that nothing swayed a Googler more than what looked like specific data, even if it had been somewhat concocted from the gut. "There's an 87 percent chance that Verizon will top this." (Later he explained his reasoning: "There was no way in hell that Verizon was going to let us walk away with spectrum that would destroy its business model.") The board okayed the bid, and on Thursday, January 24, 2008, Google's $4.71 billion bid made the spectrum auction official.

At that moment Google owned the valuable C block licenses. It still owned them the next day and through the weekend, as no other bidder emerged. "The realization was growing that 'My God, maybe we were all wrong,'" says Whitt, who was starting to regret his brash 87 percent prediction. The probable fallback within Google would be to lease out the spectrum to partners, but that would have been an unholy mess and a massive distraction from its business. In any case, says Whitt, "we had no clear definite plans what to do with it."

Finally, on Tuesday, the Googlers in the war room were looking at the display when suddenly the screen lit up with a cluster of bids. Verizon had topped Google by about $200 million. Google was off the hook.

Or was it? "Larry was disappointed," says Whitt. It seems that Google's cofounder really wanted to keep going. The D.C. team hurriedly presented the alternatives to Schmidt. A higher bid would keep them in the game, but then Verizon (which hadn't identified itself but was the obvious bidder) could up the ante. The bidding might not stop until $9 or $10 billion! Schmidt told the team to stand down.

Google would later insist that it had played a perfect bluff. "Google definitely wanted to lose," says Hal Varian. But Page would later confirm that he had seriously been considering a higher bid, with the justification that auction theory demanded it. "It was an unusual auction," he says. "Obviously, you wouldn't have made the bid if you thought you were wasting your money, but if someone else bids, you know you're probably not wasting your money. So that means you might be willing to pay more. And so you've really got to think about that." He says that Google had begun thinking of what it might do with the spectrum: "We'd figured it out already, because we'd already committed to buying it."

In any case, Google's economics teams managed to keep Page from engaging in a bidding war that would instantly have made it a major telecommunications player. But the next time around, it would not be so surprising if Google were bidding to win.

2

"Apple didn't enter the search business—so why did Google get into the phone business?"

With its successful bid in the FCC auction Google ensured that when Verizon developed the spectrum it had secured, any competitor could develop devices to exploit the new bandwidth. But in the shorter term, Google still had a lot rolling on Android. For much of 2008, the success of that investment was in doubt. Google kept saying that there would be no single Gphone but a whole array of different Android-powered phones from different companies. But the public didn't seem to understand this and kept asking for a Gphone. The message became even more obscure when Google decided to launch the system with a single device running on a single network, instead of a small army of phones appealing to different constituencies running on separate networks. The first Android device would be called the G1, and everyone involved with Android winced when people called it the Google Phone. The carrier was T-Mobile, chosen mainly, says Rubin, because of his long-term relationship with the company. T-Mobile had been the first carrier to launch Sidekick. "There was a trust," he says. Similarly, the first handset was made by the company Rubin trusted most, HTC.

Rubin later explained that one phone on one network was almost more than Google could handle. The team worked frantically for its release in October 2008. If it missed that window, even by a couple of weeks, retailers would not get the phone for the holiday season and the product would have to be killed. "I personally thought we weren't going to make it," says Rubin. "Three months before we were supposed to ship, nothing worked. Crashed all the time. Couldn't receive an email. Superslow. And over time it got more and more unstable."

Googlers were dogfooding the phone, constantly reporting elements that needed tweaks. Larry Page was all over the Android team about various problems, including a snag involving his massive list of contacts and schedules. "It was a big calendar sync that affected Larry only," recalls engineer Brian Swetland. Sergey also had an idea he wouldn't let go of—he liked the idea of scrolling down a list of contacts by tilting the phone, letting the accelerometer do the work. It would be as if the names were affected by gravity, sliding down a slope. How cool would that be? The engineers tried to explain that, in practice, it would be more likely to cause vertigo than be seen as a useful function. "We actually wound up having an engineer build it," says Erick Tseng. "Then we showed Sergey that it wasn't a good user experience." Faced with the data, Brin agreed. (Generally, however, the Android team says that the founders were helpful with resources and guidance—and that they also knew when it was important to get out of the way.)

To the amazement of even the Android engineers, the team managed to make the deadline. "It was a happy mess, but it worked," says Android engineer Omar Hamoui. Indeed, the G1 was a solid if not compelling entry into the phone market. Its most attractive features were the ease with which you could run Google products such as the Android browser, Gmail, and Google Maps. Unlike the iPhone, it offered multitasking, a way to run more than one application at a time. But the G1 lacked the slick comprehensiveness of an Apple product. Also, Google's cloud bias showed—when an iPhone was connected to a computer, it automatically synchronized the phone with data on the computer, everything from contacts to music. Getting this information onto a G1 was an awkward process. Clearly, Google was impatient with those who still subscribed to the antique concept of having files on their computers, even though this category included nearly everyone.

The T-Mobile G1 phone, "powered by Google," was unveiled in New York City on September 23. Compared to the Broadway sophistication of an Apple launch, this event was community theater. It was held in an obscure catering facility underneath the Queensboro Bridge on the eastern edge of Manhattan's Midtown, rendered even harder to get to by a United Nations summit meeting of world leaders that day. Instead of a dramatic demonstration of the phone's capabilities, the main presentation was a list of boring self-congratulatory speeches by representatives of the partners with shockingly little product information. Andy Rubin had a glazed grin throughout. "The last thing I wanted to do was talk about it," he says. "The only thing I wanted to do was make sure it didn't crash when it powered on."

Halfway through the presentation, Larry and Sergey Rollerbladed into the building. They went straight to the stage. Standing awkwardly among the business-suited executives, they looked like gate-crashers at an awards ceremony. (Indeed, their appearance had not been rehearsed.) In the Q-and-A period after the formalities, reporters directed most of their queries to them. When asked for an example of a cool application, Sergey mentioned one he'd written himself, making use of the built-in accelerometer.

"You throw your phone in the air, and it tells you how long it takes before you catch it."

While the example nicely reflected Google's obsession with milliseconds, the demo provoked near coronaries from the HTC people. The last thing you want to do with an expensive phone whose most fragile component was a large glass touch screen is throw it into the air.

"Ad hoc," Andy Rubin later characterized the performance with a shrug. "That's Larry and Sergey, and that's pretty much how the company's run."

The G1 phone didn't rack up huge sales, but it set the stage for subsequent Android models made by various hardware manufacturers, running on different networks. After a while, Android came to be seen by the telecoms as a poor man's iPhone. Since only Apple made iPhones and only one U.S. carrier, AT&T, had the rights to sell it, this was an important market niche. And as Android kept improving, it became a genuine iPhone alternative. Google made frequent upgrades, and in some cases it introduced features the iPhone lacked. Android people felt strongly that because of Google's aversion to marketing, few consumers understood an advantage you'd get from their phone: superior integration with Google's cloud services. "Trying to chase Apple for pure glitz is kind of silly, because they totally own that market," says Brian Swetland. "But we're much better placed to synchronize mail and calendar and other back-end things."

Another potential Android advantage was the open nature of its system. A vibrant community of software developers had embraced the iPhone, creating hundreds of thousands of apps. Apple exercised tight control on those submitting applications to the store and rejected an app if, for instance, it felt the content was objectionable; Google welcomed almost everyone. The contrast reflected the differing philosophies of the companies and also the difference between the web-centric Chrome operating system and Apple's hermetic operating system for its iPad tablet computer. Nonetheless, Apple raced to an early lead in the number of apps, while Android emerged as clear runner-up.

Developers even began to think of the Android operating system as a platform for bigger devices such as tablet computers or even small laptops. Barnes & Noble designed its Nook e-book reader around Android, and Asian manufacturers began making plans for Android-based netbooks. (This placed Android at odds with Google's Chrome OS plans. When asked in 2010 how it had come about that a company founded to focus on search had wound up with two computer operating systems, Larry Page responded, with a smile, "Only two?")

Perhaps the breakthrough Android device came about a year after the original, when Verizon introduced an Android handset made by Motorola called the Droid. (This was a significant partnership since Verizon had become a fierce opponent of Google on technology policy issues. The thaw in relations was probably attributable to Verizon's need to market a competitor to AT&T's iPhone.) The Droid took advantage of new Android features that Google had developed, most impressively the ability to convert dictation into text in various applications. The accuracy of the transcription resulted from the data Google had gathered from billions of callers to its 1-800-GOOG-411 directory assistance service. Some critics wondered whether Android was actually superior in some ways to the iPhone.

The Droid was also the first Android phone that used another feature Google recently introduced, a high-quality implementation of the "turn-by-turn" navigation that various companies offered in stand-alone GPS devices and other phones. While those competitors charged a monthly fee of $10 or $15 for the service, Google's version was free. As with other cases when Google had decimated an entire subindustry by offering a product for free, the company was anything but apologetic. "We don't monetize the thing we create," Andy Rubin says. "We monetize the people that use it. The more people that use our products, the more opportunity we have to advertise to them."

Surely one would have thought that the line Google would not cross would be going into competition with Android partners who made phones and sold them. But in mid-2009, while discussing ideas for a new Android model with the head of HTC, Andy Rubin asked, why not break the usual procedure where Google created and gave away the software, the handset maker designed and manufactured the hardware, and the carrier ran the device on its network and sold the device along with a contract? The phone contract was universally despised by customers. It was not Googley. A better way, Rubin felt, would be for Google to make its *own* great phone, "unlocked" so it could be used with any carrier, and let consumers buy it via a browser, using the company's payment service, Google Checkout.

"We fundamentally believe in the online business," he explained. "It's what we stand for, it's what we participate in."

Rubin pitched the idea at a GPS that summer, outlining a plan for Google to sell its own phone, unlocked, on the website. (Google wouldn't physically make the phone, he explained; HTC would manufacture the device to Google's specifications.) If all went well, this method, called direct to consumer, would smash the unfriendly system that bound users to carriers and prevented them from easily switching, for example to the latest Android phone. By removing nasty impediments, Google would be encouraging more phones, more phone uses, more mobile searching, and more ads. What was good for mobility was good for Google.

Google's Operating Committee signed on—good thing, because Rubin had already set the project in motion. "That's the way Google works," Rubin later explained. "Don't ask for permission for an idea, just go and do it. And then, when you're way beyond the point of no return, you're like, 'I need $200 million.'"

The initiative was a two-step process. The first was to build "the best possible phone with the latest hardware, the latest technology, to push the limits of innovation of mobile applications for that phone," said Mario Queiroz, an Android executive who came to the team from Google Europe. This was bound to be seen as hostile by partners who were using Android to build their own phones. The second part was selling the phone on the website. Users would buy an unlocked phone for a high price—$529—but then, at least in theory, would not have to bind themselves to a carrier for a long contract. If they wanted to sign up for a contract, that was okay, too, and Google expected Sprint, Verizon, T-Mobile, and AT&T to offer big phone discounts for those who wanted a more traditional arrangement.

The phone itself would be called Nexus One. "Nexus," explained Queiroz, "is a convergence of connections." But the real origin of the name was Andy Rubin's robot fixation: in the movie *Blade Runner*, the model name of one of the humanlike robots was Nexus 6. "We're not at six yet, we're at one," said Queiroz. "This is our first device." Inside Google, however, there was a different code name: the Passion Device.

Google's playbook had gaps. One of them was customer support. Though buyers of $500 phones were accustomed to having human beings accessible on help lines when something went wrong, that concept was alien to Google. Early in its history, Google had decided that human customer support was something that should be left behind with the twentieth century. Back in 2000, some of Google's millions of users had begun filling its inboxes with questions, comments, and even love letters. But there was not a single person in the company whose job was to communicate with those users. Grudgingly, Google came to accept that it should have at least one regular employee to do this. Denise Griffin arrived that year to face a backlog of several thousand emails. "It was never manageable from the first day," she says.

At one point in 2003 Griffin and Sheryl Sandberg went to ask Larry Page for more people. He told them that the whole idea of support was ridiculous. "Why do we even do it?" he asked. Instead of Google assuming the nonscalable task of answering users one by one, it should let users help one another! The idea ran so counter to accepted practice—it was almost as if you were stranding customers on a desert island and asking them to form their own society to get off—that Griffin felt lost. But Google implemented Page's suggestion; a system called Google Help Forums allows users (with an occasional Googler dropping in) to share their knowledge about the system. To Griffin's surprise, it worked, and thereafter she cited it as evidence of Page's instinctive brilliance.

"There's a very strong belief at Google that if the product is better, people will use it anyway," says Griffin. "You might not like not having support; you might want to talk to somebody. But are you going to stop using it? If we create better products, support isn't a differentiating factor."

Griffin wound up heading a bare-bones customer support team of people numbered "in the low three figures," many of them spread around the globe. (A lot of email seemed to be handled in Hyderabad, India.) Even though, a few years later, Google did offer some phone and email support to corporations that paid for its productivity software, by and large it had managed to keep its products going without customer service. But with the Nexus One, Google was selling a physical product where user problems were inevitable. When people bought a Google phone from Google, they would naturally expect support from the company. But when they tried to call, they could get no one to help. The resulting outcry reverberated in every corner of the net.

Nexus One had a bigger problem: offering a good financial deal to the customer. For some reason, Google hadn't figured out that in order to offer users an attractive package, it would need the cooperation of the telecoms. As hateful as the current contracts were, they offered a way to buy a phone at a discount, though the ultimate costs were hidden by the long, overpriced connection contract. Google, not having its own network, could not counter. Google hoped that networks would offer users who bought an unlocked phone a significant discount on their normal rates. But none did, and that hurt the adoption of the product. Google sold very few units.

The irony was that the Nexus One was an excellent phone. At the time of its release, it was easily the best Android handset available. It was especially impressive in the way it used voice recognition. It superbly ran a new version of Android software, which included some interesting advances. For instance, Google had devised an app that fulfilled a long-held dream of its founders. Called Google Goggles, it was a visual search engine. The user could take a picture of something—a wine bottle, a movie poster, a book cover, an Eames chair—and Google would return search results as if you typed the relevant information into the search box. It was effective, even a bit scary. (It could have been scarier: the Google engineers who devised it built in a component to recognize faces. After a spirited discussion at an October 2009 GPS, Google's executives decided that such a feature was too radioactive to include.)

Goggles was definitely a portent of the future—the same future that Page and Brin had been talking about since the early days of their company, when speculating about how Google would become an information prosthetic, always available, a brain appendage that would instantly provide you with the world's knowledge. "A mobile phone has eyes, ears, a skin, and knows your location," said Vic Gundotra while demo'ing the phone one day before its release. "Eyes, because you never see one that doesn't have a camera. Ears, because they all have microphones. Skin because a lot of these devices are touch screens. And GPS allows you to know your location. Those things have caused us to change our development goals to do things that are relatively like magic." Gundotra picked up his Nexus One and dictated, "Best Italian restaurant in Schenectady, New York." He smiled. "Now, clearly, that's not something you're going to type in." Then he showed the screen. Ferrari's Ristorante, 1254 Congress Street. Nice.

But further advances would have to come through phones not made directly by Google. On May 14, 2010, barely five months after Google introduced its direct-sales model, Andy Rubin posted an official "never mind" blog item announcing that Nexus had reached its exit. He brightly noted that "innovation requires constant iteration," while admitting that the web store for its phone was no more than "a niche channel for early adopters." Thus ended the experiment, and thereafter those seeking Nexus One phones would have to buy them from carriers, which would presumably station sufficient numbers of human beings on the phone lines to help buyers with a problem. At a Google event in May 2010, Rubin said that the experiment "didn't pan out."

If all of this hadn't sufficiently tainted Google's relationship with the telecom giants, another initiative would. Google, it seemed, would not rest at making mobile phone operating systems and even phones. It had embarked on another initiative that actually made it a virtual phone company: giving users a single telephone number that would work for all their various devices while authorizing Google to be their communications terminus. All, of course, for free.

As was common at Google, this project didn't start from an executive strategy but in the brain of a product manager, in this case Wesley Chan. He was the restless product manager who had enjoyed successes with the Toolbar and Google Analytics. One night he and Salar Kamangar were talking about Internet phone calls and the huge number of people using the free Skype service. "Let's figure out how to get in on this," says Chan. It was a classic expansionist Google move—on the surface it had nothing to do with search, but since more free calls could popularize the web, Google would get more search customers and more ad clicks. "So I went shopping again," says Chan.

Not long after, he was at a conference in Boston and a Google biz-dev person asked him if he'd go to a demo by Craig Walker, the founder of a start-up called GrandCentral. It was an amazing piece of software. Its motto was "One number for life." You would pick a telephone number, and the service would automatically link to all your office, home, and mobile numbers, direct callers to your locations, and screen them with the deftness of an efficient secretary. Launched in September 2006, it had won a small but devoted following, whose enthusiastic recommendations elevated GrandCentral accounts into a precious commodity. Even though Wesley Chan was suffering from food poisoning (he would blame a toxic hot dog) and was sprawled on a bench doing everything he could not to vomit, he understood enough of the demo to see that GrandCentral was special. "Why can't I have this?" he thought. Walker didn't want to sell, which was the exact response Chan had hoped for. "You don't want to buy companies that want to sell," he explains. "The ones who want to sell have problems."

Chan was persistent, and he wore Walker down, convincing him that with Google his idea would be amplified by other services and reach tens of millions of people. "Google had all these cool properties that GrandCentral could really work with—Google Talk [web-based chat], Gmail, Calendar, and the Android project," says Walker. "If we were going to be acquired by anyone, Google was at the top of the list." (The payout, estimated at

$50 million, wasn't bad, either.) Chan had a bigger problem: getting the Google brain trust to sign off on the deal. "No one wanted it," he says. "It was branded as another crazy Wesley product." Chan said that Nikesh Arora, then the head of Google's business operations in Europe, opposed it because he felt it would upset the carriers in Europe.

Even Page and Brin were wary. *Voice* calls? "I don't make phone calls anymore—nobody does," Brin told him. Larry Page, who at one point early in Google's history argued that there should be no landlines in the company, agreed. He also seconded Arora's notion that GrandCentral would cause too many troubles with carriers—he was worried about AT&T and Verizon. "Larry," Chan recalls saying, "they *already* hate us—what's the downside? If we fail, we fail." He appealed to Page's and Brin's sense of guilt about having objected to his previous projects, Google Toolbar and Google Analytics, when Chan had proved them wrong. They gave him the okay, and Google announced the deal in August 2007.

Thus began an eighteen-month process to improve and Googleize the service into something called Google Voice. In the very first GPS, with Chan as his consigliere, Walker presented a project road map. Larry Page laid out his own vision: Google Voice should become an Android application that would do everything that GrandCentral did—but it would also make Internet voice calls, like Skype. You wouldn't even know it was any different from making regular phone calls. The plan would essentially make Google into a stealth phone carrier. (Chan liked the idea—he thought that Page was brilliant on innovation but not so much on the details of product design. "Larry's the worst person you want designing your product—he's very smart but not your average user," he says. To avoid this situation, Chan had a strategy of "giving him shiny objects to play with." At the beginning of one Google Voice product review, for instance, he offered Page, and Brin as well, the opportunity to pick their own phone numbers for the new service. For the next hour the founders brainstormed sequences that embodied mathematical puns, while the product sailed through the review.)

Halfway through the development cycle, an opportunity arose that Google's leaders felt compelled to consider: Skype was available. It was a onetime chance to grab hundreds of millions of Internet voice customers, merging them with Google Voice to create an instant powerhouse. Wesley Chan believed that this was a bad move. Skype relied on a technology called peer to peer, which moved information cheaply and quickly through a decentralized network that emerged through the connections of users. But Google didn't need that system because it had its own efficient infrastructure. In addition, there was a question whether eBay, the owner of Skype, had claim to all the patents to the underlying technology, so it was unclear what rights Google would have as it tried to embellish and improve the peer-to-peer protocols. Finally, before Google could take possession, the U.S. government might stall the deal for months, maybe even two years, before approving it. "We would have paid all this money, but the value would go away and then we'd be stuck with a piece of shit," says Chan.

Chan was desperate to stop the acquisition, so he went to his friend Salar Kamangar. By then Kamangar, though almost totally unknown to the outside world, had become a hugely influential force in the company. He was a key member of a quiet cabal of Googlers who weighed in on crucial issues and influenced the final decisions of Brin and Page. Some were top executives, and others had "influence beyond their title," says one insider, who said that quite often the conflicts aired in GPS meetings were settled by conversations and email among this loose cabal. The group included some of the very early people, such as Susan Wojcicki, Marissa Mayer, and Lori Park, who had been one of the first twenty employees and had been influential in activities such as protecting the logs, China policy, and fulfilling odd personal assignments for Larry and Sergey. It wasn't a formal club, and you didn't have to have been at Google from the very early days—sometimes people like Chan could work their way in by being supersmart in a very Googley way, such as coming up with great ideas that promoted the company in general. Everyone in that inner circle really cared about Google both as a company and as a concept. Of all the people in that cohort, none was as respected as Kamangar. "Salar is like the secret president of Google," says Chan, who laid out the reasons why a Skype acquisition would be a disaster. Kamangar agreed. Then the two of them talked to Sergey and won him over as well.

With those allies on board, Chan devised a plan to kill the Skype purchase. As he later described it, his scheme involved "laying grenades" at the executive meeting where the purchase was up for approval. Chan tricked the business development executive who was pushing the acquisition into thinking that he was in favor of the deal: he had even prepared a PowerPoint presentation with all the reasons Google should buy Skype. Chan says that halfway through the presentation, though, the trap sprang. Brin suddenly began asking questions that the deck didn't address. "Who's going to run this?" he demanded. "Not me," said Kamangar. Craig Walker said he had two kids in school and wasn't about to make regular runs to Eastern Europe. "What are the regulatory risks?" A lawyer said it might take months to get approval. Finally, Brin looked at Chan and asked why Google would want to take the risk to begin with. Chan dropped his defense entirely and began explaining why Google had no need for Skype.

"At that point," recalls Chan, "Sergey gets up and says, 'This is the dumbest shit I've ever seen.' And Eric gets up and walks out of the room. The deal's off."

Not long after, eBay sold Skype to a group of investors, taking a loss from its original purchase price.

In March 2009, Google Voice made its debut with a thunderclap. In addition to all the services GrandCentral offered, such as one number for life, the company had added others, including integration with Gmail and Google Calendar. Best of all was the way the service handled voice mail. Using Google's sophisticated voice recognition technology, the service translated voice-mail messages into text and sent them to the recipient by email. Google Voice also made phone calls—web and domestic calls for free and international calls for a pittance. While carriers made billions of dollars charging people to send text messages to other mobile phones, Google Voice let you do it for free. People clamored to grab the limited number of accounts available. (It wasn't until early 2010 that Google was able to satisfy all the people who wanted to use Google Voice.) Once again, the press seized on the fact that Google was giving away a service that people would be happy to pay for.

"We want to be the good guys," said Craig Walker. "Telecom companies are notorious for hidden fees and long-term contracts with penalties—fine print everywhere. We're not going to screw you. We want to have a bunch of happy users. We want you to enjoy being on the Google properties and loving Google for it."

Predictably, one company that did not embrace Google Voice was Apple. In addition to implementing Voice as an Android application, Google submitted it for consideration as an iPhone app—and was denied. Reporters and industry analysts speculated that Apple had slammed the door at the request of its exclusive network carrier, AT&T. The FCC demanded an explanation, and on July 31, 2009, Apple haughtily explained that it had not rejected Google Voice but was continuing to study it, to make sure it did not negatively affect "the iPhone experience."

Ironically, this conflict played out as another government agency, the Department of Justice, was examining whether Apple and Google were too closely tied, specifically questioning Schmidt's presence on Apple's board.

But by then the relationship between the two companies had deteriorated so much that even Bill Campbell could not mitigate the tension. In August 2009, Schmidt left the Apple board, explaining that the departure was motivated not by government pressure but by the fact that the competition between the two firms, particularly in phones, made it too difficult for him to continue. In addition, Art Levinson left Google's board. (Al Gore remained on Apple's board while retaining his advisory role at Google. "It hasn't been uncomfortable," says Gore on negotiating potential conflicts. "All that's required is common sense, really.")

Now that Schmidt was off the board, hostilities became more overt. The iPhone was still the royalty of smart phones. But as Android became the fastest-growing smart-phone operating system—by mid-2010, Google partners were selling 200,000 a day—Jobs increased the pressure. He sued the handset manufacturer HTC, alleging that its Android phones used techniques patented by Apple. Within days, Google rolled out a change in Android's operating system: it would now support the pinch and stretch multitouch gestures that Jobs had demanded that Google remove. The capability had been hibernating inside the code base, and all Google had to do was switch it on in the next upgrade.

Schmidt maintained that those developments were part of the normal course of competition. "I admire Apple," says Schmidt. "It's a very well run company. Steve is the best CEO, the most clever leader, that maybe we'll ever see. I was honored to be a part of it."

But Jobs felt compelled to reveal his impression that Google itself was a fraud—that beneath the warm and fuzzy exterior was a company that could not be trusted. What's more, he felt personally abused by what he considered its misbehavior, and numerous sessions with Brin or Page in which he pressed his case had given him no satisfaction. He expressed his feelings in a semipublic performance in January 2010, at an employee question-and-answer session in the Town Hall Auditorium on Apple's campus. Ostensibly the event was a victory lap to celebrate the iPad, announced just two days previous. Jobs took the opportunity to send a message to the people at Mountain View, just a few miles north of Cupertino. All it took was one open-ended question about Android to unleash a fusillade of anti-Google invective. "Apple didn't enter the search business," he said, "so why did Google get into the phone business?" That wasn't all. "Google wants to kill the iPhone," he said. "We won't let them." Even as the next question came on a different topic, Jobs felt he hadn't sufficiently vented. He reminded his minions of Google's "Don't be evil" mantra. Then he shared his thoughts on the motto that Google used to define itself.

"It's bullshit," he said.

3

"We saw YouTube building an edgy fun brand, in a way that Google Video wasn't."

Google's Android plans were only part of an energetic expansion into every corner of the digital world. There seemed to be no limit to the categories that Google would deem relevant to its mission. At a November 2009 tech conference called Web 2.0 Summit, an interviewer ticked off some of the staggering bounty of Google products and initiatives to Brin (who had decided only earlier that day to appear on the stage and was of course immediately accommodated). "Can you succeed in every one of these, or is your strategy to bat .350?" he asked. Brin frowned. "I'm not familiar with baseball," he said.

"That's very good," said the interviewer. "Three-fifty is very good."

"Like *35 percent*?" Sergey asked with a trace of mockery in his voice. "Out of what? Out of a *thousand*? I think we can do better than that."

(Brin's lack of baseball knowledge was typical; his ignorance of popular culture was legendary. Once he asked a colleague if he had ever heard of a musician named Carlos San-*tain*-a; Brin had been asked to introduce him at a concert. "Sergey," the Googler said, "*everyone* knows who Carlos Santana is." "I'll just say he needs no introduction," said Brin.)

Brin and other Google executives were sensitive to the charge that the company was a "one-trick pony," unable to come up with anything that even closely matched the success of its core combination of search and ads. Google contended that there was a holistic aspect to its activities: the companies it bought, the new areas it colonized, built a bigger Google ecosystem. Google would often point to a putatively unprofitable area and claim data that showed a positive impact on search and subsequent clicks on its ads. Even a tiny increase in the percentage of searches meant many millions of dollars of revenue. Nonetheless, the breadth of its expansion reflected Larry Page's unfettered ambition. Some of the Google projects the interviewer referred to indicate the breadth of its efforts:

▲ Relatively early in its history, Google invented a search-related algorithmic news service called Google News. The idea came from early Google engineer Krishna Bharat, who was stuck in a New Orleans hotel room when planes were grounded right after the September 11, 2001, terror attacks, and was frustrated in his web searches for fresh information. "I really wanted one place where all the reporting on one issue was collected, so I started thinking about one way to do this, to extract the content of the articles and cluster it," he later said. He used his 20 percent discretionary time to create a news search engine. Using the tools of search, he was able to identify news sources and algorithmically determine their quality. (For instance, a site that used the full names of news subjects—for example, "Hillary Rodham Clinton"—was probably more reputable than one that used only a first name.) Other algorithms enabled him to cluster stories by subject. Bharat believed that an engineering approach to the news would provide an alternative to skewed coverage. "If you had a human editor providing that mix, it's going to be difficult to explain to people why that is unbiased. With an algorithm, that argument becomes much easier, because the algorithm has no personal interest in either the Israelis or the Palestinians. And it's measurably so." Even though Google took years to put any ads into the product (they would appear when people used a keyword to search for news), Google News instantly became the bête noire of the troubled news industry. To little effect, the company would note that newspapers' problem was the Internet itself and services such as craigslist, which offered classified ads for free, not a search engine that provided links to news sites.

▲ In 2004, Google bought Picasa, a Santa Monica company that stored users' photos online. Though not as popular as the leading cloud-based photo-sharing site Flickr (a start-up bought by Yahoo), Picasa steadily gained customers, in part because of increasingly seamless integration with Google's other applications. Google also used its billions of images as data fodder for its learning machine. And unlike Flickr, Google did not charge monthly fees for a "pro" version.

▲ Also in 2004, Google purchased a web service that stitched together high-resolution satellite images of the earth's surface as if they were a huge virtual environment in a video game. Keyhole had been the brainstorm of John Hanke, whose résumé included a stint at "foreign affairs" for an unnamed branch of the U.S. government; his company was partially financed by the CIA's venture capital unit. Keyhole combined the techniques of video games and satellite photography to give its subscribers powerful geographical observations that previously had been limited to military leaders in situation rooms. When Sergey saw it, he went bonkers. Googlers recall meetings when a product under discussion or a PowerPoint deck was shunted to one side while Sergey projected a Keyhole screen on the other side, swooping from the sky to peek on this location or that. He totally disrupted one meeting by zeroing in like a smart bomb on the lavish homes of every executive in the room. "We thought it was too fundamental to let somebody else control it," says Eric Schmidt. So Google bought it, changed the business model from a $1,000-a-year subscription to free, and integrated it into its Google Maps application—and into its mirror world. By 2009, 300 million people routinely peered down on the earth from space via Google Earth.

▲ Google launched its Knol project in 2008, when the head of search engineering, Udi Manber, an aficionado of *New Yorker*–style cartoons, found unsatisfactory results for a query on that magazine's wry artist Peter Arno. He began thinking of a project that would encourage people with expertise on a subject to create online encyclopedia-style articles on their specialties or just things they knew a lot about. (That would contrast with the hugely popular crowd-sourced Wikipedia items, which garnered reliably high rankings in Google searches.) Manber had a team set up protocols for creating "knols" on items—which could be financed by AdSense. (The term derived from "knowledge.") He recruited his MD wife to write a prototype knol on insomnia and got Google to pay handsome sums to the country's best medical specialists for seeding the service with succinct descriptions of their specialties. But Knol never took off, and Wikipedia remains the web encyclopedia of choice. Manber never did write his knol about Peter Arno.

(As an example of Google's Darwinian product development process, even a minor project like Knol had a direct competitor within the company: a team in Google's Zurich office was working on a similar project called Wooki. But the Zurich engineers had no formal way to determine whether their project was viable. On a trip to Mountain View, the project lead, Gabor Cselle, went on a corporate quest to seek an answer. He grabbed Sergey Brin after a TGIF, who sent Cselle to Larry Page's office in Building 43. Cselle found Page there, sitting in front of a Windows netbook that provided the only illumination in the room. The intimidated—"scared shitless" was the term he'd later use—engineer asked Page if he'd heard about Wooki. Page hadn't. Cselle quickly came to understand that his project was doomed. But the two men spoke for half an hour. At one point Cselle asked Page if he had problems with Wikipedia. "Yes," said Page. "I have problems finding really good information about nuclear fusion." That's when Cselle had his insight about Larry Page. What Larry asks himself in situations like this is not *How can I help this person?* Instead, he's asking himself, *Ten years from now, what thing can we build at scale that's going to have the maximum impact on humanity?*)

▲ Google routinely snapped up a number of back-office technology companies. One of the biggest deals was its $625 million purchase of an email spam-fighting company called Postini in 2007.

▲ Google saw itself as part of the energy business. Though the massive amounts of energy consumed by its data centers seemed a good reason to pursue that course, Brin and Page were also motivated by a fuzzy sense of eco-activism. When Google set up its nonprofit foundation Google.org, it announced that one of its goals was to make investments and inventions to make renewable energy cheaper than coal. In 2009 Google secured a federal license to engage in the electrical power transactions that were limited only to energy companies.

Those were only the highlights of a dense constellation of acquired and homegrown products and projects. They came with such frequency that reporters couldn't keep up with them. Not a week went by without a few launches of some new Google project that rendered a traditional business obsolete or mowed down some digital enterprise that had pinned its existence on charging for its products. For instance, in one unexceptional week in November 2009, Google announced that it had acquired volumes of information on court rulings and would offer a free alternative to expensive legal research services such as Westlaw; and a blog item unveiling a computer language written by the industry legends Rob Pike and Turing Award recipient Ken Thompson.

Even Googlers couldn't keep track. During that week Google's PR person in charge of search was driving to the Googleplex from his San Francisco home when his BlackBerry lit up with queries from reporters concerning a new proprietary dictionary service, dealing harsh blows to other online services offering similar functions. He'd never heard of it. As soon as he blew into the office, he began frantically emailing people on the search team for information on the product.

To Brin and Page, the distractions, the confusion, the cost, and the disruptions were all secondary to what they saw as Google's key criterion: benefit to the end user. Time and again, when asked if the company was overstepping or gaining too many enemies, they would say that their yardstick was not revenues, advertisers, or even their own employees. "We started this company to bring this technology to the user," Brin said when asked about the issue at a Google event in 2008. "I don't feel comfortable denying it to users." Schmidt concurred: "To hold back because we're worried is not a good way to run a business." Another statement Schmidt made illustrated the distance that the once careful corporate planner had traveled since surrendering to the ethos of the founders: "Disorganization is a feature."

But none of Google's postsearch initiatives would be more significant and have a bigger impact on the world at large—and draw a bigger lawsuit—than its movement into online video. The key was a 2006 corporate acquisition, the biggest the company had made to date, of a company whose name would become almost synonymous with the explosion of Internet video, a brand almost as recognizable as Google itself: YouTube.

Google's original effort in the world of online television was a dud. Jennifer Feikin was a onetime entertainment lawyer who became a business development executive at AOL and then moved to Google, working under Omid Kordestani. Her initial job involved complicated AdSense deal agreements. Before embarking on yet another one, Feikin got Omid to promise that on completion she could work on a different idea she called Google Video. Her concept was that Google's search should deliver links to movies, TV shows, and even news clips as well as it did to web pages. In late 2003, she began pulling together a team.

Feikin believed that in addition to providing links, Google Video should offer users a chance to view professionally produced work in categories such as television news, sports, documentaries, movies, and network television shows. Such programming would be legally licensed and would be available for free for promotional purposes or would be ad-supported or sold. Selling videos would give a boost to the company's perpetually struggling payment system, Google Checkout, which had never quite gathered the huge number of credit card sign-ups that competitors such as PayPal, Amazon.com, or iTunes had amassed. "It was very important to find a way to monetize content for the entertainment industry," Feikin says. "Putting stuff on the Internet was very new, and there were lots of clips and promos and stuff like that, but putting the full shows online was a very interesting thing to our partners."

Not as crucial to the Google Video approach was the long tail of Internet video. The web, along with new and powerful digital tools for making and distributing videos, offered an opportunity for the most obscure video auteur—meaning anyone with a cheap camera and a modem—to reach an audience of billions. It was a perfect opportunity for Google. But someone else was seizing it.

In December 2004—just as Feikin and her team were finalizing plans for a January launch of Google Video—Jawed Karim, a twenty-five-year-old engineer at PayPal, began thinking about web video from the bottom up. How, he wondered, could you make it supereasy for people to upload their homemade videos to a site where anyone could see them? What he had in mind was a video version of the website HOT or NOT, where users looked at people's photos and made decisions on their desirability. He shared his ideas with two colleagues at PayPal, Steve Chen and Chad Hurley.

In February 2005, Karim, Chen, and Hurley formed a company called YouTube. (Karim, who wanted to return to academia, soon went back to school and turned over the leadership to his partners.) They set up shop in a second-floor office over a pizzeria in San Mateo, halfway between San Francisco and Palo Alto. They made a few decisions early on that proved brilliant in retrospect. First was a revelation that seemed elusive to Google Video: success in a video site hinged on making it easy for users to actually *view* the videos. (Google Video didn't launch a player until that June, and it required a separate download.) "It was important when you come to YouTube that within a few clicks you are watching video," said Chen. The second decision was to include YouTube in a budding movement described as Web 2.0, where online activities were seen as participation in a self-defined community. YouTube built tools to make its videos viral; by copying and pasting a few lines of HTML code, you could stick a YouTube video into your blog or website, email it to a friend, even post it to a social network such as MySpace.

In April 2005, the founders began uploading some videos of their own—inane stuff such as Karim rolling down a snowy hill or the antics of Chen's cat, Stinky—and awaited the deluge. It didn't happen instantly. In May, the impatient founders took out an ad in craigslist offering "hot" women $100 for every ten videos they'd post displaying their charms. But once the snowball started rolling, it was an avalanche. That summer, someone named Matt Harding began posting videos of himself dancing (spastic, cringe-worthy nerd dancing but so unself-conscious that it was infectiously joyful) in various vacation spots. He became a global celebrity.

YouTube also benefited from taking a tolerant stance toward users who uploaded music videos, snippets from TV shows, and scenes from movies without the permission of those who owned the copyrights. In an email sent in September 2005, Hurley worried about the "truckloads" of copyrighted content. Chen successfully argued that YouTube should just press forward. Even though YouTubers knew that people who were uploading videos didn't really have the right to do so, they believed that YouTube would be all right as long as there weren't complaints from copyright holders about specific videos, in which case they could respond. Otherwise, they would simply assume that copyright holders permitted their content to appear on YouTube. Chen's instinct in this case turned out to be a canny interpretation of the Digital Millennium Copyright Act, which promised a "safe harbor" to sites hosting uploaded content. But the decision to take a lax view of policing copyright was less likely a legal judgment than one determined by the carpe diem ethic of a start-up.

The giant entertainment conglomerate Viacom would eventually sue YouTube, its attorneys arguing that the copyrighted content uploaded by users was the main reason for YouTube's success. More likely, it was the *combination* of the copyrighted content and the millions of videos created by the users themselves that made YouTube a unique and valuable property. YouTube was a magnet for videos old and new, and its very existence led people to create their own. In tandem with an emergent library of (mostly unauthorized) professionally produced clips, YouTube became an unbeatable destination where the short videos on the site (YouTube limited contributions to ten minutes, and most were under three) were consumed like potato chips. As soon as one was finished, the site offered suggestions for similar diversions, or maybe watching that clip reminded you of something else you wanted to see. Could YouTube provide video evidence that a long-haired hairdresser turned rock singer named Monti Rock III had actually been a frequent guest on early 1970s talk shows? Or was that some hashish dream you had? *There he is, on Johnny Carson and Merv Griffin!* What's more, there's a clip recently uploaded from Monti, alive and well, doing a cabaret act in Miami Beach!

In short, YouTube was beginning to become a video version of Google search. In mid-2005, Google Video instituted its own system for users to upload content. "Response has been great," Feikin said at the time but took pains to add that such uploads—which did not get the viral boosts so often given by YouTube's happy fans—were only one component of Google Video, which would deal with "the whole gamut of content." And when it came to enforcing copyright, the difference between YouTube and Google Video was as stark as the contrast between Ferris Buehler and his principal. To keep on the sunny side of the studios it was wooing, Google took pains to avoid hosting pirated content. But there was also the feeling that copyright violations, when you came right down to it, were *evil*. For much of 2005, Google's policy was to police videos over two minutes long to make sure they didn't infringe. Even that was deemed too much for a public company to tolerate. In December 2005, Feikin sent a memo to her team saying that the two-minute restriction was gone and Google would now do a sweep to find copyright violations of any length. She included a list of the top twenty search terms of copyrighted material, starting with "*Family Guy*" and ending with "*Dragonball Z.*"

By that time, Google was finally ready to roll out what it called the Google Video Store, an attempt to offer an online bazaar where users could get high-quality content. The offerings were a mishmash of content obviously organized by the principle of "this is what we got." Unlike the iTunes store, where television shows all cost $2, Google's prices were all over the lot. Its big attractions were CBS shows—prime-time episodes, and some "classics" from the archives, which seemed to be chosen at random, cost $2. (A couple of old Ed Sullivan shows cost $10 each.) There were one-dollar episodes of *Charlie Rose*, but no Jon Stewart or any other late show. NBA games were available for sale a day after they concluded—for the price of $3.95. You could see Bullwinkle cartoons, but forget about Mickey Mouse or Daffy. Music videos from Sony were on the service ($2) but no other major music company licensed its music videos. The most prominent movie studio Google convinced to show full-length movies on the service was an independent operation, GreenCine—the highlights of its meager inventory were films by the Polish director Andrzej Wajda and the documentary *Mau Mau Sex Sex*. The only way you could watch any of these offerings was with Google Video's finicky player.

In contrast, YouTube was dead simple: everything was free, you could find clips from just about anything, and it played inside your browser. God knows where its users had gotten access to some of the stuff they put up there, but because of the company's lax policy of policing its archives, YouTube managed to have just about anything you were looking for. YouTube users had uploaded a popular clip from *Saturday Night Live* called "Lazy Sunday," which became a phenomenon—5 million people streamed it until NBC demanded that YouTube remove the clip seven weeks after its appearance. The clip jacked up YouTube's traffic by 83 percent. Later, it was cited as the event that restored luster to the aging *SNL*. Content providers were confused about how to deal with YouTube, but they were beginning to realize that its popularity made it impossible to ignore.

Google had an auspicious opportunity to launch its video store in January 2006: its first ever keynote presentation at the annual Consumer Electronics Show. In an uncharacteristic display of enthusiasm for public speaking, Larry Page volunteered to do the presentation. Keynotes at CES were carefully choreographed, almost as if they were artifacts from the era of auto shows in the 1950s. Page had his own ideas. Ever the AI enthusiast, he had become enamored of Stanford University's winning entry in a 2005 competition for autonomous robot vehicles; its modified Volkswagen Touareg, nicknamed Stanley, was the first across the finish line in a 183-mile driverless desert trek. Page wanted to ride onto the Las Vegas Hilton stage (where Elvis once reigned) on Stanley's roof while the car itself did the driving. Even when the Google planners told him such a stunt was impossible—try getting insurance for an autonomous SUV driving a billionaire into a crowded auditorium—Page insisted. He backed down only when the head of the Stanford AI lab, Sebastian Thrun, confirmed that the plan was madness. They compromised by having Stanley's human test driver take the wheel.

Unlike other tech execs in well-tailored suits, Page gave his speech in a lab coat, spending much of the keynote ranting about the incompatibility of power supplies in consumer devices. By the time he got to a description of the Google Video Store, people were scratching their heads. When celebrities representing partners in the store did quick walk-ons—there were an NBA player and CBS's head, Leslie Moonves—they seemed to have dropped in from some different planet, where cars didn't drive by themselves and corporate executives didn't wear lab coats. And as Page tried to explain the product details, it was clear that he was fuzzy on the complicated payment structure.

The keynote did end on a high note. Page had insisted that there be a question period, almost as if he were running a Google TGIF. This was almost unheard of in CES keynotes. The people at Google in charge of the speech came up with an inspired idea: they spent a bundle to book the comedian Robin Williams (a huge Google fan) as Page's sidekick for the Q and A. The conceit was that Williams would be a human Google. The comic's manic improvisations made people instantly forget the awkwardness of Page's presentation. The funniest moment came when a French reporter began to ask a tough question of Page but could not finish due to

Williams's relentless, politically indefensible, and utterly hilarious mocking of the man's accent and nationality. The unfortunate Frenchman sputtered with rage. The moment fit Google perfectly: corporate presentation turned as anarchic as a Marx Brothers skit.

After the launch came the reviews of Google Video; they were uniformly dismal. Google Video was clearly a hobbled entrant into a race where one dog was already circling the track in a blur. Yet for the next few months the Google Video team pressed on. In the spring of 2006, the group spent weeks preparing an elaborate strategy to fend off YouTube, but the numbers presented in their slides undercut the delusional promises that a new approach could lead it to "win" the online video market. The Google Video team acknowledged that "the user-generated trend is huge" but didn't seem to grasp how dominant YouTube was becoming—the little start-up located over a pizza shop was streaming 25 million videos every day, more than three times as many as Google. The Google Video team seemed to take comfort in reporting that premium content owners—which it still considered the key players in the field—viewed YouTube as "a small start-up with no cash," "perceived as trafficking in mostly illegal content."

But some of their bosses saw YouTube as something else: an acquisition target. "They had beaten us—we had underestimated the power of user-generated content," Google's counsel David Drummond would later say. "And so we looked up one day and saw YouTube building an edgy fun brand, in a way that Google Video wasn't. We imagined that if you put that on the Google platform, and, you know, with Google distribution, Google machines, and everything, you'd take it, you'd really, really accelerate."

Google wasn't the only suitor; Yahoo was interested as well, as were a number of more traditional media companies, hoping to defibrillate their flatlined Internet sites. But for most of 2006, YouTube's Hurley and Chen professed not to be terribly interested. "They were talking a few hundred million dollars, and we thought there was a bigger opportunity. Our whole idea was that we were going to take this thing as far as possible," says Hurley, neatly summing up the dynamics of YouTube's vacillation. Hurley and his partners were building a company for the long run, while simultaneously poising themselves to accept the right offer from the right company. In an August 2005 video the founders made after visiting Sequoia (Mike Moritz's venture capital firm)—a clip definitely not uploaded to YouTube—the giddy Karim asked, "At what point would we tell them our dirty little secret, which is that we actually just want to sell out quickly?"

As the months went on, Hurley and Chen determined that the time to sell was now. YouTube was *too* popular: it was overwhelmed by traffic. To build up infrastructure would require a lot more money than the original $3.5 million in venture capital it had received from Sequoia. YouTube got another round of funding for a total of $11.5 million, but even then it would struggle. Serving millions of videos a day was just plain expensive.

Grappling with this reality in the early fall of 2006, Hurley and Chen concluded that they had to sell. Yahoo and Google were the front-runners. Hurley and Chen barely knew the Google ruling troika, having met them only once at the previous summer's Sun Valley mogul conference. But once Google realized that YouTube was truly in play, Salar Kamangar sent out the alarm. "I was building a case for why it would be worth it to us to buy them at the price they were then asking for, which we'd previously thought was too much. We heard that they were going to be sold, most likely to Yahoo" says Kamangar, who teamed up with Drummond as the biggest advocates of the deal. They set up a series of meetings at the Denny's in Redwood City, between Mountain View and YouTube headquarters in San Mateo. The YouTubers told Schmidt that their goal was to democratize the video experience online, and they felt that the idea resonated with him—after all, wasn't that what Google wanted to do for the whole web? The meeting with Brin and Page went well, too. At one point Page turned to Hurley and asked, "Are you sure you want to sell your business?" That impressed Hurley—it meant that Larry cared about a good match, too. "They were authentic," says Hurley of the founders.

Hurley and his partners had gone by their instincts all along, although Hurley had gotten some advice from his father-in-law, Jim Clark, the entrepreneur who had founded Silicon Graphics and Netscape. Now their collective gut was telling them that Google was the right match. So they trusted their instincts one more time.

The "few hundred million" that Hurley originally mentioned didn't come out of the air—it was probably a fair valuation of the company. In fact, Schmidt would later say in a deposition in the Viacom lawsuit that he estimated that YouTube's worth at that point was between $600 million and $700 million. "It's just my judgment," he said. "I've been doing this a long time." But Google wound up paying $1.65 billion to close the deal with YouTube. "I'm not very good at math," said the deposing attorney, "but I think that would be $1 billion or so more than you thought the company was, in fact, worth." Schmidt provided an excellent summary of deal making in Internet time, embodying the Google principles of speed, scale, and minimizing opportunity cost.

This is a company with very little revenue, growing quickly with user adoption, growing much faster than Google Video, which is the product that Google had. . . . In the deal dynamics, the price, remember, is not set by my judgment or financial model, or discounted cash flow. It's set by what people are willing to pay. And we ultimately concluded that $1.65 billion included a premium for moving quickly and making sure we could participate in the user success in YouTube.

If Google had been inclined toward remorse about the price, such worries were surely mitigated by a letter sent by Rupert Murdoch's Twentieth Century Fox as the deal was closing. It declared that whatever Google was paying, Fox would pay more. In early October, as both parties scrambled to complete negotiations, both camps spent all-nighters working out the term sheets. As it happened, Google was hosting the Google Zeitgeist conference on its campus, to which partners, tech luminaries, and some press were invited. Hurley and Chen had long ago been invited, and when Drummond and other Google executives interacted with them at the conference, they all pretended that they hardly knew one another. "We were like, 'Good to meet you,' even though we'd been up all night negotiating this thing," says Drummund. Google's board convened to approve the deal in the middle of the conference, and Drummond had to smuggle Hurley and Chen individually into the meeting past curious onlookers. (Since Sequoia Capital had funded YouTube—and stood to rack up $516 million from its $9 million investment—Google board member Mike Moritz recused himself, but he was obviously ecstatic. "I always felt that YouTube done right was the fourth horseman of the Internet," he says.)

"This is the next step in the evolution of the Internet," said Schmidt in the conference call announcing Google's biggest deal to date.

In the euphoria that came with winning YouTube, Google didn't dwell on a disturbing implication: the purchase was necessary only because its own initiative had failed. Barely a year after going public, some of its fears had been realized: when it came to plotting certain revolutions, the company was now at a distinct disadvantage. The emails and internal presentations from both companies revealed a striking contrast. The Google Video team had spent an enormous amount of time getting approval and advice from executives. Also, Google Video—whose product manager was herself a lawyer—was constrained by oversight by a legal team all too aware that a deep-pocketed public company could not behave with the insouciance of a start-up. The YouTube team, however, didn't have to create multiple drafts of slide shows for bosses. They did what felt right. "It's all 'bout da videos, yo," wrote Karim at one point to his cofounders.

But after the purchase, Google did something very smart. Almost as if acknowledging that overattention from the top had hobbled Google's original video effort, the company made a conscious decision not to integrate YouTube. "They were edgy and small, and we were getting big," says Drummond. "We didn't want to screw them up." (Google was also smarting from its $900 million acquisition of dMarc Broadcasting, a company dealing in radio advertising, which had not gone well. "They had tried more of a top-down approach with dMarc and considered that a disaster," says Hurley.) YouTube would keep its brand and even stay in the building it had recently occupied in San Bruno, a former headquarters of the Gap. Though some aspects of Googliness would find their way up Route 101 to YouTube (such as free food and a climbing wall), the culture of YouTube— more Hawaiian shirt than T-shirt, with a dash of New York hipster vibe and guilty-pleasure subscriptions to *Entertainment Weekly*—would persist. One open area had a putting green, more in the miniature golf spirit than as an aid to lowering one's handicap. The conference rooms were named after TV shows that had gone off the air before much of the workforce was born.

Not that Google was hands off. Part of the deal's logic was that the bigger company would lend its expertise and resources to YouTube to help it grow and, eventually, turn a profit. Now that YouTube could tap Google's resources, it could do things even better. Chen and YouTube's engineering team worked with Google's experts on data centers and fiber, as well as product management. And certain Googlers used the YouTube acquisition to reboot their own careers in a company that seemed bigger and more impersonal than the one they had joined only two or three years before. Chad Hurley welcomed them, at least those simpatico with the YouTube microculture. Unlike Android, YouTube didn't have autonomy in hiring, and Hurley was frustrated when candidates he liked were nixed by Mountain View. "It slowed us down," he admits. "Google gave us the freedom to fight for people we really cared about, but over time it gets a little tiring to fight." It was much easier to bring in Googlers who wanted to reexperience life at a smaller company.

In San Bruno, they would call the 2007 holiday the YouTube Christmas, where all sorts of devices—iPhones, other phones, set-top boxes— came with YouTube inside. The consumer electronics manufacturers loved it, because adding YouTube was a signal to customers that it was time to buy new gadgets that could do new tricks. "Watch YouTube on your phone, that's a value I can understand," said Hunter Walk, who was a key Googler-turned-YouTuber.

Under Google's benign management, YouTube had the luxury of continuing to build an audience and a cultural presence without having to worry too much about the bottom line. "We could have spent more time on how we're going to monetize the system, but we continued to focus on more growth, more users, better experience," says Hurley. Meanwhile, Google's legal team did its best to extricate YouTube from its difficult copyright situation. Google created a system that would allow it to quickly remove infringing video once its owner identified it as such. At the same time, YouTube struck a number of deals with studios like Warner Bros. and Sony. Studios had grudgingly come to accept that it was better to have their intellectual property on the site, even for free, than to be out of sight of YouTube's hundreds of millions of users.

In June 2010, Judge Louis L. Stanton basically affirmed Steve Chen's gamble on the copyright violations when he granted summary judgment to Google, dismissing Viacom's lawsuit. As long as YouTube wasn't given "red flags" about the content from the actual owners, he wrote, the safe-harbor provision of the DMCA allowed YouTube to accept uploaded clips without prescreening them. Though copyright absolutists complained and Viacom set about drafting its appeal, it seemed that the law performed a useful function. A new business had been given leeway to grow, and when it flourished under the guidance of a bigger company, its more questionable practices were tempered. Thousands of people had jobs in a new, thriving industry.

YouTube may not have become as significant a phenomenon as Google search, but it had a huge impact on the country and the world. With the ubiquity of cheap camcorders and video recorders on mobile phones, it became easy to upload clips to YouTube, and soon it was certain that any major goof—whether it was the comedian Michael Richards snapping at black people during a stand-up performance or Virginia Senator George Allen referring to an Indian-American opposition researcher as a "macaca"—would find its way onto YouTube, sometimes with seismic consequences. Cannier politicians would use the service for campaign messages and town hall meetings. A clever video could launch a band or an acting career. Formerly private moments, from schoolyard fights to an overweight kid swinging a laser-sword toy, generated instant celebrities. And millions of people watched cats do silly things.

Even while their company was suing YouTube, some Viacom employees secretly uploaded content under pseudonyms. After Google itself, YouTube was the most popular search engine in the world.

Even someone like David Drummond, who pushed hard for Google to come up with the cash to buy YouTube, would later admit he'd had no idea of how huge a purchase it was. "The impact YouTube has had on the culture, on politics, wasn't on my radar screen at all," he says. Nonetheless, two years after the purchase, some analysts and observers were still unconvinced that Google's YouTube deal was a smart one—because the service wasn't making money on its own. And in a recession, that would not do.

4

"You can still get braised beef cheek ravioli and lobster bisque!"

As every new year approached, Eric Schmidt would write a letter outlining the company's status and goals coming into the new annus. When Schmidt wrote his memo for 2009, he had a conundrum. It was a recession year. Though Google had consistently warned shareholders not to fixate on stock price, the serious dip in the price of a share of Google stock—down as much as 50 percent from its high of over $700—cast a pall over the company, especially among those who had arrived at the company too late to be awarded shares at much lower prices. But money was still flowing, and opportunities still abounded. The trick was to foment innovation and ambition while somehow putting a halt to giddy spending. Schmidt saw the situation as an opportunity to acknowledge that Google was now a big company—and no denying it, Google *felt* like a big company—and could no longer operate with some of the slipshod recklessness of a start-up.

"We had managed to built a company of $20 billion of revenue without operating budgets," Schmidt explained at the time. "It's not obvious to me that having budgets prevents the creative mind, especially since we are all over the creative thing. So I reject that argument. I've taken a position that we have so many people that I want to know what they are doing." Schmidt gave an example of what he was talking about: a group had come into an executive meeting the previous week and said it needed $10 million to do a deal. Eric asked why. The answer was, basically, that it seemed like the right thing to do. "They had no budget, no concept of what they were trading off," says Schmidt. "For them it was free money. Sure, we *could* do it—but Larry, Sergey, and I looked at it and said no. Just stopped it."

While much of the country worried about buying bread, Google employees still nibbled free bruschetta in the cafés, although in some locations service hours were cut. For the first time, Google took a hiring breather. Its revenues continued to rise, but the rate of growth leveled off.

Brin and Page actually welcomed the downturn. They saw it as time for Google to recapture some of the hungriness of a start-up. They had never stopped claiming that the hunger was there all along, but as Google had grown, it had developed sleepy backwaters. Bureaucracy and defensive practices had crept in. You could even spot an occasional *Dilbert* cartoon on a cubicle. Many cheeky activities that had once seemed so refreshing began to assume an aura of calculation when they became routine. How many scavenger hunts can you attend before it becomes a chore?

Page and Brin themselves had grown in the decade since they founded Google. Both were now married and within a year of each other fathered sons. Brin's wife, Anne Wojcicki, was a cofounder of 23andMe, a company involved in personal DNA analysis. Brin defied corporate propriety when he shifted his personal investment in the firm to a company one. Google's lawyers made sure the transaction passed formal muster.

The normally gregarious Brin could turn icy when an unfamiliar person referred to his private life—for example, when a reporter offered congratulations at a Q and A at the Googleplex soon after his wedding, he changed the subject without acknowledging the remark. It took the web gossips months to figure out the name of his son. But Brin was genuinely open and emotional during a session of the 2008 Google Zeitgeist. Brin put aside talk of commerce to explain that he had examined his own genome with the help of his wife's DNA-testing enterprise. Since his mother, Eugenia, had previously been diagnosed with Parkinson's disease, he had looked specifically for an anomaly on the genetic location known as LRRK2—and discovered a mutation known as G2019S, associated with Parkinson's. His mother, also a 23andMe customer, had the same mutation. ("She's okay," he assured everyone. "She skis.") Brin immediately began researching the implications of this signal; "I found it fairly empowering," he said. He also became involved with charities trying to find a cure for Parkinson's, such as the Michael J. Fox Foundation. He showed rare public emotion as he thanked his wife for her help, support, and genomic expertise. It was a display of candor that one seldom saw in public from a top officer of a huge corporation—motivated in part to thwart the press from reporting on it first. "I viewed it as kind of unavoidable—either you talk about something, or somebody else will talk about it and it will end up in the tabloids," he later explained. "I viewed it as impractical and not worthwhile to keep it a secret."

Brin would subsequently attempt to stave off the onset of Parkinson's with a self-determined regimen of physical activity—he took up diving—and by imbibing gallons of green tea. "This is all off the cuff," he told *Wired* reporter Thomas Goetz, "but let's say based on diet, exercise, and so forth, I can get my risk down by half, to about 25 percent." Of course, he continued researching the issue, seeking solutions in data.

Page married Stanford graduate Lucinda "Lucy" Southworth and worked even harder to keep his personal life out of public view. It was a life much different from the modest one of a grad school dropout that he had led for the first few years of Google. He held his wedding free from web snoops on the isolated Caribbean island owned by a fellow billionaire, Richard Branson, the British head of the Virgin group of companies. There was one moment when he shared his feelings—with an audience of more than 30,000 in the football stadium of the University of Michigan. He had agreed to be the 2009 commencement speaker. The speech was a tribute to his dad; he wore the same velvet hood his father had worn upon graduating from that university. He told the story of how he had decided to search the entire web and recounted the saga of Google, but kept returning to his family, mentioning how happy his dad would be that "Lucy and I have a baby in the hopper." He ended his speech by invoking family: "They are what really matters in life."

"Sergey and Larry are not kids anymore," Eric Schmidt noted in early 2010. "They are in their midthirties, accomplished senior executives in our industry. When I showed up, they were founder kids—very, very smart, but without the operating experience they have now. It's very important to understand that they are learning machines and that ten years after founding the company, they're much more experienced than you'll ever imagine."

From Schmidt's comments, it was reasonable to wonder when the inevitable would occur—when Larry Page, now middle-aged and officially seasoned, might once again become Google's CEO, a job he had been reluctant to cede and gave up only at the VC's insistence. When asked directly if he was eager to reassume the role, Page refused to engage. "That's all speculation," he said.

In 2008, Google hired a new chief financial officer, the first whose job was not to manage explosive growth and stage-manage epochal events such as an IPO. Patrick Pichette was a French Canadian in his midforties who was the operations manager at Canada's dominant phone company, where he cut operating costs by $2 billion. He had Googley credentials as well: a passion for fly-fishing had taken him as far as Russia, and unless a blizzard hit, he always rode his bike to work. When offered the job, he worried that it would represent a step backward for him—his current post was a higher rung than CFO, a job he'd held at two different firms. But Schmidt told him that as a key voice on Google's Operating Committee (OC), he'd be a big part of running the company. But maybe a bigger factor in his accepting was the conversation he'd had with Larry Page during the courtship stage of the process. Pichette was at the end of a long day of a tough labor negotiation, and Page called him to have their first discussion ever. Pichette asked if they could have the conversation in two hours, then immediately regretted it, knowing it would be past midnight and he'd be exhausted. In the car driving home that night, he returned the call, and Page asked him what was going on. Pichette shared the details of the negotiation and was surprised to be drawn into a problem-solving negotiation in which Page— theoretically a naïf when it came to labor, since Google has no union employees—intuitively grasped the dynamics. From there, it turned into a discussion about the complicated issues facing Google. "It was like a great table tennis game," says Pichette. As a result, when he accepted the job, "I didn't feel like I was being hired as an employee. Larry was really looking for partners in crime."

In this case, the "crime" would include ushering in a degree of discipline that Google hadn't previously experienced. Though Pichette professed to hate headlines about him such as "The Axman Comes to Google," his charter was indeed to do some trimming, albeit, perhaps with an X-Acto knife instead of an ax.

Oddly, whereas Google had built its data infrastructure to reroute around failure, it had no human infrastructure to deal with failed projects. "We didn't know which ones they were, because we never paused to ask ourselves that question," says Pichette. "The people working on that project know it's failing—as senior management you have to say, 'Let's declare failure—let's get the champagne out and kill this puppy. Then we can put you on stuff that's really cool and sexy.'" That had always been part of Google's philosophy, but whether from lack of rigor or just distraction, the company had been lax in actually issuing execution orders. One of the first puppies Pichette helped drown was a virtual-reality-style communications program called Lively.

Google's sudden austerity was contradictory in a sense. While there was indeed an international financial meltdown and Google's growth had slowed, the company was in no serious danger. Indeed, soon into his tenure, Pichette went to the OC and told it frankly that at Google, there was no crisis. "We generate so much cash that we were always going to make payroll. Our data centers were always going to run. We were always going to pay our suppliers. We were sitting on eleven billion dollars in cash," he later recalled. But Pichette told the OC that it still made sense to cut. The woes of the financial world outside the Googleplex created a great atmosphere to make tough decisions to cut waste. "And because we're Google, we'll do it differently," he says. "If we were GM or Exxon, we'd set up a committee full of people wearing ties, hire consultants, and come back with a memo saying 'Here's the answer.' At Google, we said to our employees, 'You live it every day, you tell us where the waste is.'" Google set up an array of web-based tools for the task and recruited the workforce to a data-driven scavenger hunt for waste. Googlers attacked the problem like a math puzzle and came up with answers. Some of them seemed trivial: for instance, instead of Google's ubiquitous refrigerators being stocked with upscale bottles of designer water, employees would now drink filtered tap water from cups. "We have the best water in the world here in Mountain View," Pichette said. "And we're using bottles from Sierra-something and burning CO_2 to bring in bottles that end up in landfills!" Did something like that make a difference? "It was a meaningful savings," says Pichette, while not sharing the number. Other cuts: lavish Christmas gifts to suppliers and the company-wide annual ski trip. Just telling Googlers to think twice before booking trips led to a 20 percent decrease in travel. "It's not about memos and top down," says Pichette. "Because people here share values, they get it."

Googlers also took a wonky approach to cutting the food costs, gathering data on consumption and traffic at all the cafés, as well as consumption patterns in microkitchens, and analyzing the data in spreadsheets and pivot tables—what's the wasabi consumption in Oasis?—to discover underperforming cafés. "We had a couple places where we had full staff, full chef, and nobody in there," says Pichette. This led to the closing of one café in Mountain View and reduced hours in others. Also, the days of unlimited invites for friends and family were over. A new rule said that at the end of the workday, employees were not to stop into a café to scoop up a free take-home dinner. Even the volume of food a server put on the plates was cut back. "If you make a portion size 10 percent smaller, people won't overeat so much," says Google's director of People Operations, Laszlo Bock. "And it has the benefit of not gaining weight!" According to Bock, Google's food austerity program reduced food costs by a quarter to a third. But, he noted, "You can still get braised beef cheek ravioli and lobster bisque!"

Brin felt that the cuts addressed a creeping sense of entitlement he'd noticed. "I actually thought carefully about all the benefits," he says, "and they did start to proliferate out of control. It was a two-year battle to essentially cut down the microkitchens."

More serious cuts affected Google's head count. Normally Google's new hires numbers looked like a rising fever chart; for much of 2008 and 2009 that line turned into a plateau. Judy Gilbert, Google's director of talent, says that when she joined the company in 2004, the message was "We're going to hire all the fantastic people you bring up, and don't stop until we tell you to stop." Now a directive to proceed with caution went out. The company decided it could get by with fewer engineering offices; some were consolidated, and some plans for new ones were shelved. Google also cut down on the thousands of contract workers it used. During one week in late 2008, for instance, Googlers noted that many of the workers posted at reception desks at buildings around campus had suddenly disappeared, as swiftly and unceremoniously as Google deletes spam from its search rankings. Those wishing to visit Googlers in buildings with vacated lobbies were asked to go first to one of the buildings where receptionists remained and there perform the visitation ritual (digitally sign a nondisclosure form and get a badge printed out).

Also affected by Google's brief belt-tightening session was its foundation, Google.org, called DotOrg within the company. Larry Page had announced the company's intention in his original 2004 letter to shareholders, vowing that the company would devote 1 percent of its equity and profits toward philanthropy. Urs Hölzle would remark, "It was launched with the thought that one day it might eclipse Google.com," reflecting a sentiment Page himself had expressed in the 2004 letter.

In October 2005 Google announced its intentions with almost comical fanfare. Among its goals were to solve the energy crisis by finding ways to make sustainable energy cheaper than coal. Other areas it hoped to transform included "climate change, global poverty, and threats like epidemic diseases," said Sheryl Sandberg. But though Google had roughly made good on its promise to set aside 1 percent of its equity to philanthropy, the 3 million shares—then worth about $918 million—would not go directly to Google.org. Instead an equivalent amount, spread over twenty years, would be devoted to its social goals. These would also include beneficiaries such as investments in "socially progressive corporations" and money spent "influencing public policy." Though Google's intent was laudable and its goals in keeping with its usual pursuit of big dreams, its actual amount of charitable spending did not seem on a scale with its usual ambitions.

In February 2006, Google appointed Larry Brilliant to head DotOrg. Brilliant was a charming man with a medical degree and a mind-blowing résumé that included a key role in eradicating smallpox and a close relationship with the Grateful Dead. DotOrg's biggest successes were modest compared to its aspirations. It worked best when it tapped Google's unique assets to take on a problem at scale. Its archetypical success story was Google Flu Trends, which data-mined the behavior of search users to quickly locate outbreaks of the disease. At a dinner during the TED Conference in 2009, one early Googler, Lori Park, approached the head of the Bill and Melinda Gates Foundation and asked for his opinion of Google's efforts. Bill Gates said that DotOrg "is the most publicized foundation in the world, and it's *tiny*. Expertise and analysis is *this* much of what's needed." He made a gesture with his thumb and index finger a half inch apart to indicate how insignificant that amount was. "You make an impact with *money*," he continued, referring to DotOrg's outlays, in tens of millions compared to his own foundation's billions. "Your analysis won't help sick people or save people's lives! You do that with *monnnn-ney*."

In April 2009, Brilliant resigned his post and Google installed Megan Smith to head the division. She helped curtail DotOrg's wildly ambitious agenda, promising to focus on the measurably useful projects such as Google Flu Trends and other ventures that leverage the company's assets. Smith explained the change to Googlers at a TGIF. "Money really matters," she said. "We don't have the kind of money that Ford and MacArthur have. But they don't have the engineering talent we have."

The corporate cut that most disturbed employees was Google's first significant layoff, involving a hundred people in a recruiting operation in Phoenix. "I was always worried that day would come," says Judy Gilbert. Though it made impeccable sense—hiring was stagnant, so who needed all those recruiters?—laying off Googlers simply wasn't Googley. Page, Brin, and People Operations executives had to endure hostile questions at the TGIF interrogation after the layoffs, and they assured people that there would not be larger cuts to come.

Google didn't stop recruiting the best people it could find, especially engineers. In fact, the effort became more urgent because there were vacancies at Google created by valued employees who either joined tech firms that were newer and more nimble than Google or started their own companies. And every so often, an early Googler would simply retire on his or her stock-option fortune. The defections included high-ranking executives and—perhaps scarier to the company—some of its smartest young engineers. The press labeled the phenomenon Google's "brain drain." Sheryl Sandberg, who had built up the AdWords organization, left to become the chief operating officer at Facebook. Tim Armstrong left his post as head of national sales to become CEO of AOL. ("We spent all of Monday convincing him to stay," said the grim Sergey Brin at that next week's TGIF, expressing well wishes toward its valuable sales manager.) Gmail inventor Paul Buchheit joined with Bret Taylor (who had been product manager for Google Maps) to start a company called FriendFeed. Of the eighteen APMs—Google's designated future leaders—who had circled the globe with Marissa Mayer in the summer of 2007, fewer than half were still with the company two years later. All of them left with nothing but respect and gratitude for Google—but felt that more exciting opportunities lay elsewhere.

Bret Taylor, while specifying that he cherished his time at Google, later explained why he'd left. "When I started at the company, I knew everyone there," he said. "There's less of an entrepreneurial feel now. You have less input on the organization as a whole." When he announced his departure, a procession of executives came to his desk asking him to reconsider. "I didn't know Google *had* so many VPs," he said. But he'd made his mind up.

Google tried to respond. "As we shift from the crazy days of backing up the truck and hiring as many people as we can, we're focusing more on career development," said Judy Gilbert. At a TGIF in October 2009, Laszlo Bock tried to explain the new reality. "Googlers don't care about microkitchens or how we pay," he said. "It's about how we think." Bock elaborated on how his team was shifting focus. Whereas People Operations had previously concentrated on maintaining the overtaxed Google hiring machine, now it would concentrate on "keeping people happy." And how would it do that? With data, of course. Just as Google supplied analytics to website owners and advertisers, People Ops would develop a set of metrics to generate data to "inform people decisions." There would even be a "people analytics team." Bock's group would conduct experiments and simulations in areas such as interviewing, hiring, compensation, and performance. They would construct statistical analysis curves to determine factors influencing Google's attrition rate.

Judging from the questions from the Googlers in attendance at Charlie's that day, the reaction was skeptical. One Googler complained that with the newly static workforce, the traditionally quick promotions were slowing. Sergey Brin remarked that since Google's organization was so flat, promotions were always hard.

That was something employees were well aware of. Left to figure out how to handle the complexities of a 20,000-person company—"Larry and Sergey definitely don't want to talk about career ladders," says Judy Gilbert—Google's People Operations team had constructed a system with nine levels of employee status below the top executives (who were tens and elevens on that scale). Some of the distinctions were vague. Often, Google didn't even share with employees what level they occupied on the ladder, an odd departure from its usual internal transparency. Bock would explain that the stealth was due to "cognitive heuristics." These were the deep-seated mental processes that made people think that they should defer to someone with a higher title. "That might help you on the savannah and it might help you in big companies, but it doesn't help us at Google," says Bock. "Eric and Larry want *anybody* to be able to tell someone, 'You're wrong,' and give ten reasons why." Titles got in the way of that.

In February 2008, Eric Schmidt sent word to Chad Hurley that it was time for YouTube to get more serious about the bottom line. As Hurley put it in an email that month, the unit was "redirecting our efforts from user growth to monetization." The biggest personnel change was the arrival of Salar Kamangar in the San Bruno office, where he would spend "three and a half days a week" (as Kamangar would say in his usual clipped deadpan) on YouTube.

Hurley had been bugging Salar to make the jump for a while—even in meetings before the acquisition, he felt there was kind of a glow of success around Kamangar, a result of his work in developing Google's ad system. Hurley thought how awesome it could be if Salar could do the same thing at YouTube. Now that there was more urgency to make money, it was a perfect time for Kamangar to arrive. Best of all, even though internally he was almost as much a Google icon as Larry and Sergey, Kamangar also appreciated that YouTube worked best while at arm's length from its parent.

At the same time as Google was stepping up its efforts to make profits with YouTube, it argued against the common perception that the service was bleeding money. Some commentators were calling the purchase an outright blunder and comparing YouTube unfavorably with Hulu, a website that combined selected programming from its owners, several television networks and studios. (Hulu was closer to the Google Video concept than to YouTube.) Some analysts figured that Google was burdened by sky-high video-serving costs. One widely circulated report by Credit Suisse in April 2009 calculated that YouTube was spending more than $350 million a year to stream an estimated 75 billion video plays to users. Google would privately tell journalists that those guesses were based on what *others* had to pay to move such massive numbers of bits. With its superefficient cloud infrastructure and its private fiber-optic network, Google's costs were less, much less. (Exactly how much less, the company wasn't saying, but Ramp-Rate, another company conversant with infrastructure costs, made its own assessment of $83 million.) In addition, because of the combination of Moore's Law and Google's infrastructure improvements, Kamangar would note that the costs of streaming always went down. "I think it's halving every year," he says. (Of course, Google could have silenced the critics by simply sharing the actual numbers; the congenitally secretive company chose not to do so.)

It was trickier to manage the costs of licensing from studios and other content holders. "In order to get it now, in some cases, we have to do things that are unnatural, like offering guarantees we can't expect to recoup," Kamangar says. "But we've made some good trade-offs and brought the costs down, so that's helping with profitability." The key was both breaking the ice with content companies and making the deals. Kamangar was boggled when he began to unravel the complicated tapestry of rights, permissions, and claims that governed licensing agreements in Hollywood and in the music industry.

Without music rights, millions of homegrown videos created by YouTube users violated copyright—an amateur director would use music from a personal collection as a sound track on a video, or sometimes the sound track would simply be music playing ambiently. (If you captured your child's first steps on video and in the background a radio was playing a song, the entire clip infringed copyright.) Kamangar didn't put a value judgment on the way the labels and studios worked but tried to crack their code, talking to executives, producers, agents, and managers. One day he happened to be in New York and was invited to meet with the CEO of Universal Music Group, Doug Morris. Kamangar was escorted by bodyguards to a private elevator and ushered to a fancy office high above the city. He couldn't help thinking of the contrast with Google, where you stumbled in and went to the microkitchen for coffee. Kamangar didn't dwell on the irony that it was the scruffy kids in shorts, munching energy bars and writing analytics programs, who were pushing aside the old power structure. While he put the pieces of YouTube together, though, he always kept in mind that he was documenting a traditional media system on the verge of collapse. He had to deal with the music world as it was but also plan for the way it would be after disruptions, which Google and YouTube were accelerating.

Kamangar had some specific ideas for improvement of YouTube. He urged a simpler user interface and a smarter recommendation system to point users to other videos they might enjoy. He urged more flexibility with producers of professional video so YouTube would get more commercial content. He also emphasized how some of Google's key attributes—notably speed—had a huge impact on the overall experience. If Google could reliably deliver videos with almost no latency, he reasoned, users might not balk so much at the "preroll" ads that come before the actual content, especially if the video was one of a series that users subscribed to and so were already eager to see what was coming.

But maybe the biggest contribution that Kamangar made was putting an end to the "silver bullet" theory—that lurking in someone's imagination was a multibillion-dollar idea that would enrich YouTube as dramatically as AdWords had transformed Google's bottom line. Since Kamangar had cocreated AdWords, he was able to declare that no such equivalent existed and YouTube should develop a broader, multifaceted revenue strategy, making use of some of the concepts of Google's ad model but hitting some corner shots as well.

A lot of his ideas for monetization, though, had the spirit of AdWords. Just as with Google search keywords, sometimes it was appropriate to show relevant ads with videos, sometimes not. "If I'm watching a kite-surfing video, it's very likely that I'd be interested in buying the board that the kite surfer is on or taking a lesson from that person," he says. Taking advantage of this symbiosis would open the door for bigger advertisers selling sports equipment or bathing suits, as well as small, long-tail advertisers, such as kite-surfing teachers looking for students in their zip code.

In addition, people uploading videos for free viewing might be willing to pay Google to promote them as sponsored links—a one-click connection would then appear alongside organic search results like an AdWords ad, in either the search results page or the results page from a YouTube search. YouTube also began experimenting with "interest-based" advertising, in which ads would be personalized to the subjects that users had previously accessed. (This would be something that privacy-conscious users could opt out of.) Finally, YouTube was exploring something that Google Video had tried without success: paid viewing for premium videos.

It was essential, says Kamangar, for YouTube videos to find their place in an advertising-centric ecosystem. "If we don't figure out how to advertise this correctly, we're not going to bring users a lot of the content that they would want." But if Google did figure this out, people would produce movies, shows, and clips that would never have otherwise existed, just as people made videos of their cats because YouTube provided a venue for airing such digital folk art. Kamangar was amazed that documentary filmmakers had to scramble for a measly million dollars to make a movie that could profoundly affect people. If YouTube could make it worth their while, there would be many more such documentaries! "The previous model was built on scarcity, where you see things in windows—the movie window, the DVD window, the cable window," says Kamangar. "The Internet is completely different, where you expect to have everything available to you at all times. But you relate to other people based on the similarity of content that's now so niche that you self-identify with that."

Personally, though, Kamangar was cautious in sharing his video likes—or uploading his own videos—with a wide community. "I'm kind of private and only want to share with people that I know," he says. But that didn't mean that he wasn't an enthusiastic supporter of YouTube's community. "There's an aliveness to YouTube, a set of values that make it less of a platform machine and more of a living, breathing set of people."

Google also became more aggressive in connecting sponsors for popular videos. A paragon of YouTube's business model was "Fred," a video channel created by a Columbus, Nebraska, teenager named Lucas Cruikshank. The teen pretended to be a six-year-old kid named Fred Figglehorn in a series of two-minute videos. "Fred is the George Clooney of YouTube," says Hunter Walk. "He was the first one with a million subscribers. He uploads videos, and we put ads against them. Sometimes he sells product placement ads. Fred makes a million dollars a year. He just signed a movie deal." The Fred videos—generally manic rants in which Cruikshank portrays a hyperactive, possibly brain-damaged child who speaks like one of Ross Bagdasarian's chipmunks—often sported commercial messages for sponsors such as Samsung, the Food Channel, and Bratz on an overlay at the bottom of the window. Since he started in 2008, at age fourteen, Fred's

YouTube videos have chalked up over half a billion viewings. Though Fred's success was solely a product of YouTube, people in the company never met the phenom. "We sent him a cake once," says Walk.

YouTube helped Fred's youthful creator not just by selling ads but by providing analytics, the same way it did for AdSense publishers. (This was a result of an initiative called the YouTube Insight project, developed by engineers in Google's Zurich center.) Such data helped creators learn what was working and where. "They're like, 'Oh my God, I'm big in the U.K.! I never knew I had a London following!'" says Walk. Superusers such as Cruikshank were so successful in exploiting YouTube's business initiatives that corporations such as Sony were studying their methodology and even paid some of them consultant fees to help them understand the digital world.

The dynamic between Kamangar and Hurley was interesting to watch. Hurley was still YouTube's CEO, while Kamangar considered himself "a facilitator." (YouTube cofounder Steve Chen left his role as YouTube's chief technology officer in June 2009, still working at Google on various engineering projects.) Kamangar loved to stay behind the scenes; he had to be dragged to a magazine photo shoot that paired him with Hurley in the lead photo. But Hurley clearly respected Kamangar's opinions to the point of deference. Consider the behavior in a meeting of YouTube's lead managers one day in 2009. Under discussion was the question of when YouTube should show its videos in high definition. Brin had sent word that he was pushing for it. But it would be expensive for YouTube to stream those bigger files over the network. Kamangar held back during the discussion of costs until the room paused to allow him to speak. "I thought we were going to stay within our budget," he said. That deflated the advocates for making HD the default mode for playback. YouTube's engineering director suggested that maybe they could just test making HD the automatic choice, so YouTube could measure the impact. Kamangar wondered whether such a choice would shift users' expectations, making it impossible to reverse the move. Finally he suggested a compromise: Google would stream HD as the first option in the professionally produced, copyrighted videos known as "partner content." Later, as Google delivered more broadband, it would focus on countries where a larger percentage of videos produced ad revenue. As he made this suggestion, Hurley and the rest nodded in agreement, and that was it. (Kamangar would become the official CEO of YouTube in October 2010, with Hurley assuming an advisory role.)

YouTube didn't become profitable in 2009, but it was making back enough of its expenses for Google executives to consider Kamangar's tenure successful. Advertisers were paying for a billion "monetized views" a week. "We've done an incredible job in bringing costs down and revenues up," Kamangar says. "It's obvious that the basic model is correct."

In September 2009, the top executives of Google decisively agreed that was the case. YouTube's leaders ventured down to Mountain View for a GPS meeting, and after assessing the numbers, the verdict was unanimous: YouTube had made it. "Basically things are fine," said Eric Schmidt. "You're at the point where the question is what to do next."

Kamangar said that with the profitability push on track, it was time to refocus on user growth and work on more social features. But Schmidt had another suggestion. That previous weekend, he had seen a tennis match streamed over the Internet by CBS and was impressed at the quality of the video. That was the direction that YouTube should take. "I want you to create a new kind of broadcast," he said. "It's so obvious what the product should be. Your goal should be to have a million quality broadcasts of . . . what knows what?"

Not long after that, YouTube began streaming live events, including a U2 concert at the Rose Bowl and a Barack Obama press conference. It also streamed its version of Google Goes to the Movies—a full-length version of *Taxi Driver*. These were apparently the first examples of Google's intended millions of broadcasts.

Earlier in that same GPS session where YouTube had presented in September 2009, Google executives had seen a demo of another television-based product dubbed Google TV. They had okayed the project back in 2007, when a French engineer named Vincent Dureau had explained that by 2010 there would be many television devices connected to Internet broadband and "Google wants to be on those devices." Dureau's idea was to provide a Google operating system for televisions—a sort of Android for TVs. Instead of a program guide, users would get the equivalent of a video dial tone via the Internet, directing them to a wealth of content. Google TV would originally be included in devices such as Blu-ray players, and eventually in television sets, which would presumably give users instant access to the millions of high-quality YouTube channels that Eric Schmidt envisioned—all paid for, certainly, by a video equivalent of AdWords.

The ambitions of the two video-based projects were so audacious that you would never know that there was a recession on. Indeed, at an October 2009 press roundtable in New York City, Schmidt would declare that, for Google at least, the economic bad times—as mild as they had been for his company—were officially over. Google was hiring again. It would also step up its rate of acquiring companies, big and small. Expect one a month. "We are increasing our hiring rate and our investment rate in anticipation of a recovery," he said. The company would prosecute with vigor its efforts to dominate in the phone world and the television world, as well in the field of software—Microsoft, Apple, and cable companies be damned.

PART SIX

GUGE

Google's Moral Dilemma in China

1

"I feel like I shouldn't impose my beliefs on the world. It's a bad technology practice."

"DO KNOW EVIL!"

That was the legend on the back of the cool black T-shirts printed by the geeks, scientists, pager-bound technicians, and former break-in artists on the Google Security Team.

But the failure to know evil—or more accurately, the failure to navigate around it without falling into its dark orbit—would come to haunt the company in its most serious moral crisis. When the revelation came that a security breach had compromised the company's intellectual property and additional attacks had exposed the Gmail accounts of dissidents critical of the Chinese government, Google's "China problem" became front-page news. After weeks of struggling with the issue, Google's Executive Committee, including Schmidt, Page, and Brin, finally agreed on the most significant and embarrassing retreat in the company's history. On January 12, 2010, they changed course in the country with the world's biggest Internet user base, announcing an effective pullout of their search engine from mainland China.

Though the underlying issue of Google's China pullout was censorship, it was ironic that a cyberattack had triggered the retreat. Google had believed that its computer science skills and savvy made it a leader in protecting its corporate information. With its blend of Montessori naiveté and hubris that had served it so well in other areas, the company felt it could do security *better*. Until the China incursion, it appeared to be succeeding.

As with other aspects of the company, Google's security team had evolved as the enterprise grew. In May 2002, Google hired its first person dedicated specifically to protecting its operations from intruders, vandals, and thieves. Heather Adkins had wound up in the field almost by accident. She'd been a marine biology major at Humboldt State University, where she'd stumbled on computers, then switched her major to CS. It was the mid-1990s, and the Internet craze had spawned hundreds of companies desperate for engineers. Even before Adkins could graduate, the Internet company Excite lured her to Silicon Valley, where she ran its huge email system. She obtained an education in computer security on the fly and left Excite to run security for a short-lived start-up. She survived Google's interview process to become the top security enforcer of one of the world's most visible cybertargets. She was twenty-five years old.

Google's existing sysops (systems operations) teams, staffed by engineers familiar with best practices in the field, had been diligent in using security software to defeat what was already a constant series of probes and outright attacks, so Adkins wasn't facing a crisis. Instead, it was apparent that a big part of her job would be making sure that security was baked into the products and services Google would introduce. Some cyberattacks would inevitably involve not just Google's security but the personal information of Google's users. An early challenge came when Adkins learned about the Gmail product in development. Google would be responsible for billions of emails, loaded with personal information and confidential business materials. Atkins called for a complete design review from the security perspective. She took the entire Gmail team to an off-site meeting, and for a couple of days they whiteboarded every possible vulnerability. That began Google's practice of working on security with engineers while projects were in the design stage. The security team also ran training sessions, including a mandatory secure programming class that every Noogler had to take, and had regular office hours where engineers could work out knotty security problems with the team.

Google's security team grew substantially from the day when Adkins arrived as employee 451. It hired three different kinds of security workers. There were academic computer scientists; responders, who wore pagers and were prepared to address intrusions or denial-of-service attacks instantly (for instance, a giant attack of hacker bots during the 2003 Google ski trip); and "breakers," people whose job it was to don the mental cloak of dark-side hackers and reverse-engineer and probe Google's systems to see if there were holes that some malfeasant might be exploiting. Sometimes Google paid outside consultants—their murky résumés notwithstanding—to search for vulnerabilities. Other times, it worked with skilled amateurs who were more than happy to be paid with a T-shirt for locating a bug in Google's software. (There was a discussion whether the garment should read, I FOUND A FLAW IN GOOGLE AND ALL I GOT WAS THIS LOUSY T-SHIRT, but the security people worried that the message might encourage even more attacks, so the shirt had only the standard company logo.)

In 2003, the company hired Alma Whitten. She'd earned the first doctorate in computer security and human factors at Carnegie Mellon. Her focus was internal security—in part to make sure that Google's security protocols were sufficiently easy to manage that the company's engineers wouldn't bypass them with shortcuts. Her job was not only to encourage a security-conscious mind-set but, in the worst case, to catch any Googlers who proved to be disloyal crooks.

"Google's been described as sort of the inmates running the asylum," says Brandon Downey, who works with Whitten in Security Operations. "But it's a little more than that—it's more like the inmates all have real guns." There was precious information to be protected, as well as hundreds of thousands of servers that could be turned into useless junk. And then there was the looming nightmare of espionage.

Early in Whitten's tenure, Google had been rewriting its system for handling user logs. Those were the crown jewels of information, containing precious and sometimes pernicious information about what Google users searched for and yearned for. Google wanted increasingly to use that information to improve its search and ad systems, but the company had a strict rule that no one examine logs to glean information about any individual user.

Whitten realized that Google needed what other big information technology companies already had: an explicit policy about security. But the policy had to be Googley. So Whitten and others formed a seven-person group to hammer out a commonsense internal security policy—something written in plain English that could be described in a couple of pages.

One issue proved to be a devil for the committee. "Specifically, it was about whether Google's physical security people would have the right to ask people to submit to a search," she says. "The set of people who were on this team were quite uncomfortable with the idea that this would be part of the employer-employee relationship." The people charged with physical security wanted a license to check out anyone anytime the security team's wrongdoing antennae twitched. "I was concerned that within the corporate environment the incentives would be perverse—it would always be janitors who got searched and never the research scientists."

This discussion dragged on for months, a glaring anomaly in a company that measures things in milliseconds. ("The analogy to childbirth was certainly mentioned a number of times," says Whitten.) Ultimately, the group reached an arrangement that all sides could live with. A Google security officer could search employees without probable cause in issues where physical well-being was threatened—such as looking for weapons—but not to safeguard information. "You can do it to keep people safe, not to keep property safe," says Whitten.

That was the way Google security in Mountain View would work. As crucial as security was, Google could not bear the idea that its employees could not be trusted. In accordance with best practices, there would be "reasonable audit trails," in the words of Alma Whitten. But Google would not submit itself to a lockdown mentality. Could you really be a Googler if the company eyed you like a shoplifter and rummaged through your bag as you left?

As 2009 approached, Heather Adkins was asked about her OKRs for the approaching year. "Number one is, don't get hacked," she said. "That's always my first one." She was particularly concerned with attacks from overseas. Palestinian hackers were emerging. Iran was a rising threat. But one country presented the biggest worry for Google's security team. "Of course," she said. "China."

Page and Brin always saw Google as a global corporation. In the company's first few years, Omid Kordestani established beachheads in a number of countries. But those were sales operations. In 2004, Google began to get serious about starting engineering centers overseas.

To help set them up, Google turned to a recent hire from Hewlett-Packard. Kannan Pashupathy had been schooled in his native India before traveling to the United States for graduate work at Stanford. (This is so common a biographical fact at Google that there should be a keystroke shortcut to invoke it.) Pashupathy was a deft leader as well as an engineer, and HP moved him up its organizational ladder rung by rung—to lead engineer, architect, and ultimately senior manager.

Pashupathy was just about to return to the United States after a long stint abroad when Google's head of engineering, Wayne Rosing, recruited him. The university-like atmosphere at the Googleplex charmed Pashupathy, but an expertly baited hook by Rosing clinched the deal. "Kannan, if you're confident about your abilities and you know you'll be successful at whatever you do, Google is the place for you. If not, then don't come."

"That got me," says Pashupathy. "It appealed to my machismo." He arrived at Google just as the company was beginning an era of international expansion of engineering offices. Currently the company had only three small overseas outposts—in Zurich, Bangalore, and Tokyo. Larry Page wanted to build a hundred engineering offices in the next five years.

That was the situation in which Pashupathy found himself as a brand-new Googler sitting in a conference room in Building 43 with Larry Page, Sergey Brin, Eric Schmidt, and Alan Eustace, who had replaced Wayne Rosing after the latter's retirement. "It was almost like it was the first time they were talking amongst themselves about how Google was going to grow as a company internationally, from an engineering perspective," says Pashupathy. Larry Page was standing by the whiteboard, and Eric turned to him and said, "Okay, Larry, what do you want to do? How fast do you want to grow?"

"How many engineers does Microsoft have?" asked Page.

About 25,000, Page was told.

"We should have a *million*," said Page.

Eric, accustomed to Page's hyperbolic responses by then, said, "Come on, Larry, let's be real." But Page had a real vision: just as Google's hardware would be spread around the world in hundreds of thousands of server racks, Google's brainpower would be similarly dispersed, revolutionizing the spread of information while speaking the local language.

Pashupathy and Eustace worked out a plan for expansion that they would take to a GPS session for approval. They ranked countries into tiers, organized by suitability for Google engineering offices. Before the meeting, Pashupathy was warned not to *ever* bring cost into the discussion—not to talk about return on investment. He was simply to look at the talent and the user value the project would bring. "That was brand-new to me, because all my years at HP, I'd be standing on budgets, trying to cut costs." Even so, his ambitions proved too timid for the founders. Part of his strategy was to move deliberately into the new countries. In Google's cathedral of speed, this was a cardinal sin, and Page ripped into him for the transgression. "You're thinking like a big-company guy," he said. Google had become a big company by thinking like a small company.

Google began to open engineering offices overseas. As soon as Google made a decision to pursue a country, Pashupathy would go in and do a lightning round of meetings, gatherings, and interviews. "It was a very streamlined process," he says. "Talk to a bunch of people, including government, companies, students, professors, the whole bit. And then come back and make a call of whether we were going to invest. If we were, we'd immediately look for a director."

Some countries were natural fits. Zurich was a central location for European operations. Israel's entrepreneurial character led Google to establish a center in Haifa as well as the more expected Tel Aviv. The Haifa office was a move to accommodate Yoelle Maarek, a celebrated computer scientist who had headed IBM's labs in Israel. Google hired another world-class computer scientist, Yossi Matias, to head the Tel Aviv office. (In 2009, during Google's austerity push, the company would merge the engineering centers and Maarek would depart.)

Pashupathy's native country, India, was an obvious choice for an engineering office. But finding a director proved difficult. Eventually, an early employee, Krishna Bharat, volunteered for the job. The India offices became among Google's most productive. "When you're outside, you've got the auto rickshaws, the poverty, the honking horns . . . India," says Roy Gilbert, who helped set up the offices. "And then you walk into our office in Hyderabad and it's like you're in Mountain View. Like any Google office around the world." (One difference: in India, the electricity was erratic.)

Different countries presented different challenges. In India the politicians demanded penalties and censorship when users of the Orkut social-networking service, very popular in that country, launched epithets at officials. In Thailand, the king could not be insulted. In Germany, denying the Holocaust is illegal. Generally, in cases where officials ordered that Google filter its search results, the company would push back. It was a constant struggle.

But nothing like that in China.

Before Pashupathy's time, Google's history in China had been brief but not without tumult. In 2000, as part of its general effort to make Google search available worldwide, Google began working on a version of its flagship service in Chinese. Google was way late to the game—a year before, Yahoo had offered Chinese search and had actually opened an office in Beijing. Google would notice the originating country of a user's Internet address and deliver its home page in the native language. All the indexes were in the United States, and Google had no operations in China itself. Substantial numbers of Chinese users, particularly well-educated ones, began Googling, and its market share rose to an estimated 25 percent. It became the favorite among well-educated people who wanted information from outside of China. This ascent came to an abrupt halt on September 3, 2002. That day, Chinese visitors who typed "www.google.com" into their browsers got only error messages. The Great Chinese Firewall had blocked Google. That was how outsiders referred to the technology behind the Chinese government's sweeping censorship. China realized that the Internet was a commercial necessity but the potential freedom of speech it offered was deemed a threat. So the country built an elaborate censorship infrastructure to block disfavored sites or pages.

The outage caught Google by surprise. But by that time Google's leaders were accustomed to extreme reactions to their products. Making all the world's information accessible was a fairly disruptive goal, with particularly low appeal to authoritarian regimes. "Pretty much every possible contentious political issue comes up at Google," Brin said in September 2002, ticking off other recent conflagrations involving gun ads and neo-Nazi websites. It was Brin who made the calls on those situations. "I've generally been the one to do that, because you can debate these things forever," he said. "It's between Larry and Eric and myself, and they sort of say, 'Sergey will take care of it.'"

Or, as Eric Schmidt told a reporter when asked just how Google determines the application of its famous unofficial motto, "Evil is what Sergey says is evil."

The problem that September was that Google didn't know *why* China had blocked its search engine or what it could do to fix things. (Brin hinted to one media source that he suspected that the government had acted at the instigation of the leading Chinese-based search engine, a company called Baidu, which had begun operating in 2000.) Brin ordered a stack of books about China from Amazon.com to educate himself and asked tech luminaries with international experience for advice. Google had never established a relationship with the government, and it pulled every string it could to try to connect. The diplomacy initiative had barely begun when, two weeks later, on September 12, Google was mysteriously unblocked.

At the time Brin tried to present the situation as just one more knotty consequence of tapping into the disruptive force that made Google Google. "As for China, I want to be respectful about all the kinds of issues they have, with the Falun Gong and so forth," he said. "They also have their own set of laws. We didn't have explicit communication [with the Chinese government] at that time. And we've tried to establish channels since then. But we felt that we should simply continue to provide the service we were providing, and eventually the site became unblocked. It just illustrates how Google is viewed as a really important tool for information."

Left unspoken was Brin's own history. His family had been victims of anti-Semitism under the Soviet regime. Sergey's father, Michael Brin, had dreamed of being an astrophysicist, but the state had blocked his efforts. He became a mathematician, but though he graduated with honors from Moscow State University, his Jewish background made it impossible for him to continue his studies. (He would later sneak into research seminars and find advisers who helped him as he wrote a dissertation, for which he received a PhD.) He found work as an economist for Gosplan, the government planning agency. After a decade at the agency, he earned only a modest salary. Instead of using data to illuminate the reality behind statistics, Brin was forced to churn out misleading propaganda. "Much of that time I devoted to proving the Russian living standards were much, much higher than the American living standards," Brin said to a reporter. Sergey's mother, also a mathematician, worked as a civil engineer.

In 1977, Michael Brin attended a conference in Poland and for the first time socialized with Westerners, who gave him a sense of life outside the Soviet Union. It was possible, he realized, for his son to have a better future. "We cannot stay here anymore," he said upon his return and with much trepidation began the risky process of applying for permission to emigrate. The family managed to leave Moscow in 1979, but not before a stressful waiting period. They spent several months in Paris waiting for visas before entering the United States, where Brin secured a teaching post at the University of Maryland.

The experience profoundly shaped Sergey Brin's consciousness. "Just applying to leave the Soviet Union branded us with a scarlet letter," he would later write in a blog posting. "My father lost his job, and we had visits from the police." His personal saga left him with a visceral appreciation of the personal freedom provided by a democratic system—and the burden suffered by those whose freedom was constrained. Before Sergey entered college, Michael Brin led an exchange program of students back to the

USSR, and Sergey accompanied the contingent. After two days of exposure to the soul-crushing landscape of his early childhood, he turned to his father, and said, "Thank you for taking us all out of Russia."

Sergey shared with Larry a clear belief that data were the trump card in corporate decision making. But it troubled him when pure analytical criteria triumphed over vital humanistic concerns. In April 2004, Google had one of its countless minicrises, over an anti-Semitic website called Jew Watch. When someone typed "Jew" into Google's search box, the first result was often a link to that hate site. Critics urged Google to exclude it in its search results. Brin publicly grappled with the dilemma. His view on what Google should do—maintain the sanctity of search—was rational, but a tremor in his voice betrayed how much he was troubled that his search engine was sending people to a cesspool of bigotry. "My reaction was to be really upset about it," he admitted at the time. "It was certainly not something I want to see." Then he launched into an analysis of why Google's algorithms yielded that result, mainly because the signals triggered by the keyword "Jew" reflected the frequent use of that abbreviation as a pejorative. The algorithms had spoken, and Brin's ideals, no matter how heartfelt, could not justify intervention. "I feel like I shouldn't impose my beliefs on the world," he said. "It's a bad technology practice."

What seemed to shake him most was the fear that people would believe that Google was somehow endorsing Jew Watch. "I don't want people to be under the impression that these are decisions we somehow make," he said. (Google's eventual response to the problem was to serve its own sponsored link to the search term "Jew"—Google's ad, titled "Offensive Search Results," said, "We're disturbed about these results as well" and offered a link to a fuller explanation of how Google's algorithms could produce the occasional abomination.)

Google found itself in similar tough positions with Holocaust deniers and Scientology documents, which courts had ruled were protected as trade secrets. The company had to carefully abide by national laws while preserving its mission to make the world's information accessible.

All of those controversies dealt with the delicate balancing act Google had set out for itself. Its business and its mission were pitched on the disruptive platform of the Internet; riding on the updraft of this tornado, Google was able to deliver the life-changing benefits of its search engine to users, but the company also paid the price of appearing to be the force behind the destruction of traditional models that the net leveled like so many trailer parks. Inevitably, Google drew critics, but guided by its motto, "Don't be evil," it managed its mission with a clear conscience. Until China.

2

"I choose Google. I choose China."

While Google was growing in the 2000s, so was the People's Republic of China. China was the most exciting business story of the decade. The once-isolated Red giant was not just transforming its economy but its people, who were rising from poverty to taste the fruits of capitalism. The Chinese government continues to squash political dissent, most notably in the technological barricade that prevents Chinese Internet users from access-ing websites and services whose messages conflict with the government's propaganda. (For instance, the government diligently blocks news accounts and web pages that refer to the 1989 Tiananmen Square massacre. And if a Chinese user happens to look for a website referencing the dissident Falun Gong group, his or her Internet service might mysteriously go down for several hours.) Nonetheless, it became an article of faith in Silicon Valley—and some quarters of Washington, D.C.—that China's adoption of the digital advances of the twenty-first century would inevitably erode those controls.

In any case, an internal company presentation at Google declared in January 2004, "China is strategically important to Google." The country was too big to ignore. "Larry and Sergey were depressed by the idea that if we just stayed out of China, we would be giving up on a billion plus people," says Andrew McLaughlin, who joined Google in 2004 as its policy director. McLaughlin had gained some previous experience in coping with China, helping out some nonprofit groups that wanted to make their infor-mation available in spite of China's firewall. Not long after McLaughlin got to Google, the vice president of corporate development, David Drummond, took him aside and explained that Google had never really understood what had happened in the 2002 blockage and that it still had not established use-ful relations with the government. Google had sent an employee to Beijing, a Chinese-born Silicon Valley businessman named James Mi, to explore a more serious presence. He was essentially surveying the territory to see if it was plausible for Google to set up an engineering center there. Later that year Mi contacted McLaughlin and asked him for help.

In the spring of 2004 McLaughlin took a small Google delegation to China, the first of several journeys there he would undertake. "It was kind of a scouting trip," he says. They met with government officials, of course—formal interviews in big, overstuffed chairs—but also with businesspeople, techie nerds, academics, and some people who had ambiguous connections to power and were quietly interested in the potential of a company like Google to help China make the transition to a more open and wired society. One of them was a woman named Hu Qiheng. Madame Hu's father had been an associate of Chairman Mao, and her brother had been a top Communist official. She became a government expert on the Internet. She expressed excitement that Google's entry into the country would work out for the company and would be a positive force for China as well.

McLaughlin presented his findings at a GPS, laying out the benefits and risks—he was still skeptical about the perils of dealing with the government. Everyone agreed that Google should look into putting more energy into China. Schmidt asked McLaughlin to perform an ethical analysis. McLaughlin remembers his mission very clearly: "Forget about revenue, assume that business considerations play no role here whatsoever, and come up with the best analysis: 'Will Google accelerate positive change and freedom of expression in China by being there, or will we accelerate it by staying out?' That was the question."

McLaughlin worked on his report for nearly a year, spending one week of every six in China. Sometimes he included Larry and Sergey in his interviews. At one point the three Googlers met with Qiang Xiao, a Chinese human rights activist who was teaching at Berkeley. He told Page and Brin that if he were advising almost any business—an auto company, for instance—he would tell them not to invest in China, as the business would just contribute to the oppression of its people. But the Internet was a different matter. People in China wanted to connect with one another, and the net would help them do that. Xiao told them that Google's presence could help fight censorship by increasing communication.

But McLaughlin heard plenty of the other side as well. Censorship aside, Google would have to face the maddening process of dealing with bureaucrats. Kannan Pashupathy, for instance, had had experience with China while working for HP. "If you only wanted to start an engineering organization, you could do it rather easily," he later said. "But if you wanted to actually start operating a business where you made money, you couldn't do it without a certain type of license. It was a multiweek, multimonth time frame we could never depend on. Every month, it moved to the next month. We really couldn't bank on that."

In October 2004, Brin and Page were scheduled to go to Italy to receive the Marconi International Fellowship Award for computing innovation. At McLaughlin's urging, they decided to continue traveling east to make a complete global circuit, visiting India and China. In India they met with the president, rode in rickshaws, and bantered with reporters (Sergey gabbed about his desire to see monkeys on the street). *The Times of India* wrote that in comparison to the serious demeanor of Bill Gates, Brin and Page "have been more like a couple of sophomore backpackers doing India."

McLaughlin thought that approach would be a terrible error in China, making Google's founders look like frivolous geeks who could easily be played by clever Communists. McLaughlin couldn't get his bosses to listen to him, so he got Al Gore to speak to them. "I advised them to keep it low-key, because of the way Chinese react to Westerners, particularly Americans, who go over there and are full of themselves," says Gore. Gore worried that the politically naïve Google founders might find themselves manipulated. He shared an experience he'd had as vice president, when he'd visited a Chinese factory. During the protocol negotiations, Gore's representatives had made it clear that there would be no toasts—he would not clink glasses with Chinese officials. But at the actual event, a waiter with a tray full of champagne glasses made a beeline for Gore and handed him a glass. Gore quickly handed it off to an assistant, but a photo of that moment made it look like he was indeed raising a glass with the butchers of Tiananmen Square. He got ripped up for it in the press. Gore's warning had its effect, and Page and Brin kept a low profile.

The trip was exciting—to a point. They visited all the major Internet companies—Baidu, Sohu, and Sina—to see what they were like. "We were treated warily," says McLaughlin. "They couldn't tell if we were a friend or a foe." Despite the fact that Google was about to make an investment in China's leading search engine, Baidu (a $5 million toe in the water), CEO Robin Li held the meeting on a national holiday so that Brin and Page could not see how many engineers he employed. The Google cofounders offended Li by refusing to eat the Subway sandwiches that Baidu provided.

The trip awakened the founders to how fast things were moving there and gave them a glimpse of the impact Google might have if it went all in. "They definitely were interested," recalls McLaughlin. "But Sergey's background as a refugee of the Soviet Union made him inherently suspicious of doing business in an environment like that." The bigger question remained: should Google begin the process of cooperating with the Chinese government to get a license to operate in China?

The advantage was clear: Google could offer a speedier, more satisfying experience than existing search engines offered. Page and Brin were startled and upset by the difficulty people in China had getting access to the Internet in general and Google in particular. But in order to get a license to operate, Google would have to follow the Chinese government's restrictions. Which meant that Google, which had always strived for purity in its search results, would have to alter its very nature in order to hew to the government's Orwellian demands.

McLaughlin thought that Google should stay out, and his formal report made that clear. He acknowledged that Google's presence might benefit China. His concern was with what the experience would do to Google. "My basic argument involved the day-to-day moral degradation, just dealing with bad people who are badly motivated and force you into a position of cooperation," he says. "It's degrading to the company. Life is short, focus on other markets. Don't go into countries that are going to force you to censor to do business there, even if you could do good by being there."

The entire executive team participated in the debate, though the call would be made by Google's reigning troika. Schmidt was all for entering. Brin was troubled at the prospect. But Page, a natural optimist when it came to the potential of technology to transform society, believed that Google's entry would be a boon to China.

Because the good that Google would do was hard to predict and impossible to measure, the China decision would be determined not by data but by gut. Nonetheless, the Google executives came to a decision using a form of moral metrics. The evil of censorship was balanced with a number of other factors, many of them involving the benefits that would come from Google's participation in China. It was as if Google had created a kind of spreadsheet, with some cells (censorship) showing a loss and others, relating to more information, increased use of the Internet, and Google's determination to eventually decrease censorship, winding up on the profit side. The global calculation of this virtual spreadsheet indicated that, morally, Google would wind up in the black. As Schmidt later explained, "We actually did an 'evil scale' and decided not to serve at all was worse evil." All three leaders signed off on the concept.

To what degree did business considerations affect the outcome? You would have needed a psychologist, or a polygraph, to figure out whether the rush to China was fueled by self-interest. But even years later, Larry Page would insist that the evidence indicated that the right thing—the *moral* thing—was to help the people of China by giving them access to Google. "Nobody actually believes this, but we very strongly made these decisions on what we thought were the best interests of humanity and the Chinese people," says Page.

In some respects, setting up Google China was a similar process to the one Google had used in Zurich, Tel Aviv, and Bangalore. There would be a business operation that handled the local marketplace and took care of marketing and ads, and an engineering center where Googlers would create products for both the specific region and the world at large. It would be housed in a Googley office, with accommodations to the national culture. But some aspects of the China operations were unique. No other Google center had to deal with anything like China's strict licensing requirements. No other Google country had such disregard for civil liberties that building a local data center (vulnerable to government seizure of information) was out of the question. And no other country required Google to censor its results for a broad range of content, especially content that contained a mere whiff of dissent.

If Google's Chinese service, running on the .cn Chinese Internet domain, was to earn its license, it would have to follow those laws. But Google had some ideas on mitigating the abhorrent practice of censorship. In an October 2004 presentation, "China Entry Plan," the company proposed that it explicitly inform users when results were blocked. A December 23 "China Launch Update" elaborated that Chinese users should be given "the greatest amount of information possible." When a search query listed a result that required filtering, Google would indicate at the bottom of the results page that there were results missing. Meanwhile the company would continue offering its Chinese-language version of the global search engine (which appeared when someone inside the country typed "www.google .com"), though it knew that the Chinese government would often block it and Google could not get a license to make money from it.

A different problem was determining what information should *not* be given to Chinese users. Though the government demanded censorship, it didn't hand out a complete list of what wasn't allowed. Following the law required self-censorship, with the implicit risk that if a company failed to block information that the Chinese government didn't want its citizens to see, it could lose its license. That was actually an interesting problem, and if nothing else, Googlers loved to solve such brain-twisters. In this case, they came up with an elegant solution. Google would exhaustively examine and probe the sites of competitors, such as China's top search engine, Baidu, testing them with risky keywords, and see what *they* blocked. It was a speedy means of determining forbidden information, and best of all, it scaled. Just as the people who created Google's machine learning algorithms didn't have to know Urdu or Greek to be able to write software that could be translated into those languages, Google's .cn programmers would not have to deal in the unpleasant intricacies of denying freedom to customers. The algorithms could do the censoring. In practice, the Google divination of what terms must be censored was only a baseline and was augmented by regular calls from the government demanding that Google block links to various other sites or not provide any links involving certain events or themes.

Plans for Google.cn were well under way by May 7, 2005, when an unexpected email arrived in the inbox of Eric Schmidt. It was from a computer scientist and executive named Kai-Fu Lee. "I have heard that Google is starting an effort in China," he wrote. "I thought I'd let you know that if Google has great ambitions for China, I would be interested in having a discussion with you."

Lee mentioned that he was a corporate vice president at Microsoft who had started its research and R&D efforts in China, and thoughtfully provided a link to an article in *Technology Review* that described Microsoft's Beijing center as "the World's Hottest Computer Lab." The biographical information was unnecessary. Kai-Fu Lee was a celebrated computer scientist—he'd worked for Apple before Microsoft—who had become a phenomenon in China. Lee, who had grown up in Taiwan and gotten his doctorate at Carnegie Mellon, was the embodiment of the "sea turtle"—an Asian-born engineer whose success in America was a prelude to a homecoming that allowed him to contribute to China's drive to the pinnacle of the world economy. Lee was perhaps the most famed of all sea turtles. Hundreds of thousands of people went to his website and wrote to him for advice, as if he were a combination of Warren Buffett, Bill Gates, and Abigail Van Buren.

Google immediately recognized how Kai-Fu Lee could accelerate its plans to make a mark in China. "I all but insist that we pull out all the stops and pursue him like wolves," Senior Vice President Jonathan Rosenberg wrote to his fellow executives. "He is an all-star and will contribute in ways that go substantially beyond China." Alan Eustace responded to Lee's email, urging him to "call me as soon as possible, 24 hours a day, on my cell phone." Lee flew down to Mountain View to meet with Google executives on May 27, 2005. The session was a love fest. That didn't stop Google from conducting a series of job interviews. "How would you write a short program to tell if an image was a banana or an apple?" one engineer asked him. But these were really formalities. When he met Brin and Page—Lee was startled when Sergey, who had arrived by skateboard, asked him, "Do you mind if I stretch?" and then asked questions while doing body motions on the floor—Lee overheard them as they left the room. "People like Kai-Fu don't grow on trees," one founder said to the other. When Lee returned to Seattle, he was greeted by a huge box of Google swag, including a basketball, a chair, and a coin-operated gumball machine with a Google logo. When Google's offer came a couple of weeks later, he decided to accept.

Lee resigned from Microsoft on July 18 and officially accepted Google's offer the next day. It was worth over $13 million, including a $2.5 million signing bonus. Lee posted an explanation on his Chinese-language website, with the headline "I need to follow my heart." He said that Google had given him "a shock" by its fresh approach to technology and postulated that in China, his new employer's youth, freedom, transparency, and honesty would produce a miracle. "I have the right to make my choice," he wrote. "I choose Google. I choose China."

Microsoft rushed to the courthouse and charged Lee with violating a noncompete agreement that was part of his employment contract. The Washington state judge filed a temporary restraining order preventing Lee from joining Google or even talking to its employees. "I had one meeting with him to transition my China duties to him," says Pashupathy. "I said, 'Kai-Fu, welcome to Google. Here's all I know about China.' And the next day I couldn't talk to him."

By going to Google, Kai-Fu Lee had hit a soft spot in Microsoft's psyche. Ironically, in early 2002, Kai-Fu Lee, who was an early enthusiast of Google search, had once recommended to Bill Gates that Microsoft buy Google. After looking into it, Gates told Lee that the cost would be too high. "It's a company without revenue but asking for a billion dollars," he said to Lee. "Those two kids are crazy!" After it became clear that Google was not just an innovator but a financial powerhouse with resources to take on Microsoft, the rivalry took on a bloodlust. Just how intensely Microsoft's CEO, Steve Ballmer, despised his competitor to the south became clear in depositions that would be filed in the Lee lawsuit. The year before, in November 2004, a top Microsoft executive named

Mark Lucovsky had gone to Steve Ballmer with the unwelcome news that he was leaving Microsoft. "Just tell me it's not Google," said Ballmer, according to Lucovsky's sworn testimony. Lucovsky confirmed that it was indeed Google. Lucovsky testified that Ballmer went ballistic: "Fucking Eric Schmidt is a fucking pussy! I'm going to fucking bury that guy! I have done it before and I will do it again. I'm going to fucking kill Google." (The reference to having "done it before" seemed to refer to Microsoft's anticompetitive actions during the browser war, when Schmidt was aligned with the Netscape forces.) For good measure, Ballmer threw a chair across the room, according to Lucovsky. (Ballmer would later say that Lucovsky's account was exaggerated, but the CEO's denials were not made under oath.)

A little-noticed aspect of the litigation was a declaration made by Kai-Fu Lee. He claimed that Microsoft didn't understand how to deal with the Chinese and that its employees "repeatedly angered and embarrassed various officials in the Chinese government." He told of an episode when Bill Gates had yelled at him that the Chinese government had "fucked" Microsoft, and concluded, "It was a statement my work had been in vain." (Gates denied the episode.) That comment indicated that Lee saw his role in leading a corporation's China effort as one that brought the company into harmony with the demands of the government.

Despite Microsoft's saber rattling, Lee would get his chance to work with Google. On September 13, Judge Steven Gonzalez ruled that while Lee was prohibited from sharing proprietary information with or helping Google in competitive areas such as search and speech technologies, he could participate in planning and recruiting for Google's effort in China. Ultimately, the two companies would settle, and the restrictions on Lee's activities would be lifted in 2006.

Google.cn went live on January 27, 2006. Earlier in the month, Brin and Page had showed the product to Googlers at a TGIF. The question-and-answer session "was honest and frank," says Sunny Oh, an American who had helped pull together the presentation. She remembers one employee in particular standing at the microphone and aggressively challenging Larry to say just why this was a good thing for Google.

It was something that people outside Google wanted to know as well. Just before the launch, Schmidt, appearing before the annual gathering of string pullers at the World Economic Forum in Davos, explained the company's reasoning: "We concluded that although we weren't wild about the restrictions, it was even worse to not try to serve those users at all." On Google's official blog, Andrew McLaughlin (whose hellish job it was to become the chief defender of a policy design he had argued against) allowed an apologetic tone to creep into his prose. "To some people, a hard compromise may not feel as satisfying as a withdrawal on principle," he wrote. "But we believe it's the best way to work toward the results we all desire."

As soon as Google.cn went live, Google's critics made their own assessments on the "evil scale." The verdict was that Google's algorithms had done a scary-good job in preventing Chinese citizens from accessing forbidden information. *The New York Times* described what awaited people who tried to seek out the truth from Google.cn:

> [T]he first page of results for "Falun Gong," they discovered, consisted solely of anti–Falun Gong sites. Google's image searching engine—which hunts for pictures—produced equally skewed results. A query for "Tiananmen Square" omitted many iconic photos of the protest and the crackdown. Instead it produced tourism pictures of the square lighted up at night and happy Chinese couples posing before it.

On the other hand, Google had stuck by its intention to inform users when it blocked information to conform to Chinese law. It had done so without seeking permission from the government. To Larry Page, that extra bit of explanation—making explicit what was perfectly obvious to all but the densest Chinese users—had the potential of a snowball rolling down a mountain. Maybe rubbing the censorhip in the faces of the Chinese users would make them so mad that they would no longer tolerate it.

There was an alternative interpretation, however: the rulers of China had managed to get even the freedom lovers at Google to compromise their principles, sending a message that resistance was hopeless. You could take your choice.

Christopher Smith had no difficulty making that choice. A representative from New Jersey who chaired the House Subcommittee on Human Rights and International Operations, he had been following the activities of U.S. technology companies in China for some months. What he had found appalled him. Yahoo had provided the Chinese government the identity of a dissident journalist—whom the Chinese had thrown in prison. Microsoft had shut down a dissident blog at the Chinese government's request. Cisco had provided the Chinese with Internet tools that had become critical components in its Great Firewall. And now Google—the warm, fuzzy company that wore its morality on its T-shirt—was China's partner in political censorship. Since the unofficial company motto presented him with a large bull's-eye, he could not resist a shot.

"It is astounding that Google, whose corporate philosophy is 'don't be evil,' would enable evil by cooperating with China's censorship policies just to make a buck," he said in a press release. ". . . Many Chinese have suffered imprisonment and torture in the service of truth—and now Google is collaborating with their persecutors."

On February 1, 2006, Smith's subcommittee held a hearing, but none of the offending Internet companies chose to attend. Smith and similarly indignant representatives scheduled a second hearing, this time with a more coercive approach. The title of the session was "The Internet in China: A Tool for Freedom or Suppression?"

Besides Smith the committee included California congressman Tom Lantos. As the only Holocaust survivor ever elected to Congress, his personal mission was to stamp out genocide and suppression and to dole out retribution to those who tolerated oppressive foreign regimes. There was no doubt where he stood on the issue of the Internet and China. "The launch last week of the censored Chinese Google website," Lantos said at the February 1 hearing, "is only the latest sign that the companies that make strong and impressive corporate claims, such as Google's motto, 'Don't be evil,' cannot or do not want to respect human rights when business interests are at stake."

The Google representative at this hearing would have to endure hostile questioning alongside punching bags from Microsoft, Cisco Systems, and Yahoo. Who at Google would take the bullet? The recently hired vice president of communications and policy, Elliot Schrage.

"My background was the most relevant," he would later say to explain why he was chosen. He had once represented the Gap when it was defending itself against charges of labor violations. Schrage had never testified before Congress before, but he knew what was in store for him. No matter how cogent his arguments, his role was to act as Tom Lantos's piñata. Complicating matters was his personal history. Schrage's grandparents had died in the Holocaust. So even though he disagreed with Lantos, he felt a connection with him.

On February 15, Room 2172 of the Rayburn House Office Building was packed. Reporters were approached by a stream of people from various human rights groups distributing leaflets and reports documenting the misguided or just plain immoral cooperation that these companies were lending to the regime that had murdered its citizens in Tiananmen Square. (By the end of the day there were enough pages to fill a Russian novel.) Less than five minutes after calling the session to order, Chris Smith was praising a recent book entitled *IBM and the Holocaust*, which had documented with devastating detail how Big Blue had sold the Germans technology that had allowed them to murder 6 million Jews and other targets more efficiently, including Tom Lantos's family.

"U.S. technology companies today are engaged in a similar sickening collaboration," Smith said. Whoa. He cited Yahoo's despicable act in providing the identity of an anonymous blogger. What if Yahoo had been operating during World War II and had been asked by the Germans to turn over Anne Frank? he asked. Then he got to Google. "Should businesses enable the continuation of repressive dictatorships . . . by cooperating with laws that violate basic human rights?" he asked somewhat rhetorically. Google, he charged, could no longer lay claim to its "Don't be evil" standard. "Indeed," he said, "it has become evil's accomplice."

The technology executives had to stand and be sworn in with upraised hands, knowing that a photo of them doing so would appear in the next day's news. Thus the darlings of the information economy—who assumed that their companies were boons to society—were presented as no different from tobacco executives or mobsters. Each company representative entered written testimony on the record and gave brief verbal summaries. Schrage's was a well-argued treatise that summarized the paradox of a nonevil company conducting an evil act: "The requirements of doing business in China include self-censorship—something that runs counter to Google's most basic values and commitments as a company." The rest of the document explained the circumstances that, he argued, justified that transgression.

During the questioning, the legislators asked Schrage to explain how Google determined which sites it would block from the organic results produced by its algorithms. Schrage outlined Google's clever learning process that identified which sites the Chinese wanted to block. Congressman Jim Leach was appalled. "In all industries, we have heard the term 'best practices.' I think you have just affirmed a novelty in American commerce—*worst* practices," he said. "So, if this Congress wanted to learn how to censor, we would go to you, the company that should symbolize the greatest freedom of information in the history of man?"

At that point Representative Lantos entered the room; he had been at the hearing for the opening remarks but had left for some unexplained business. His colleagues immediately turned the floor over to the star interrogator. Lantos was an old man, and he was an angry one. The poison tip to his darts was the Hungarian accent he still retained, a constant reminder of his origins. As his questioning proceeded, his volume rose until he was almost shouting. It was reminiscent of the scene in the movie *Marathon Man*, where an elderly Jewish survivor spots the war criminal played by Laurence Olivier on 47th Street and dogs him, howling, "Stop him! He's a beast! He's a murderer!"

"Mis-ter Schrage," said Lantos. "You have just indicated that you are not proud, and are not enthusiastic. Can you say *in English* that you are ashamed of what you and your company and the other companies have done?"

Schrage did his best to answer unemotionally. "Congressman, I actually cannot."

"*Cannot*," repeated Lantos, barely able to contain his contempt.

One by one, Lantos asked the other representatives of the high-tech firms the same question: were they ashamed? None would admit it. There was more than a bit of theater in the presentation—and it was certainly easier to flog technology companies that were trying to navigate this difficult international dilemma than it was to pass laws to help them. (No legislation emerged from the hearings.) Nonetheless, Lantos had once stared down the devil, and when he said that the behavior of these companies was abhorrent and disgraceful and professed not to understand how its leaders could sleep at night, he was articulating concerns that Google itself had been debating. Lantos died two years later, but his words rang in Google's ears for a long time.

3

"Most Chinese don't speak English. They will never use Google."

In 2006, Google China had a coming-out party. The occasion was Google's adoption of a new name. Since names are accorded tremendous significance in China, a lot of care was devoted to the process. An exact transliteration of Google was out of the question: it sounded too much like Gou-gou, which meant "dog-dog." Culturally, this was humiliating. After months of research, in 2004 Google settled on something pronounced Goo-go-a. It seemed to reflect the quirkiness of the original name. The first syllable evoked a bird call, and *go-a* means "fruit." But critics immediately seized on the name as being overly cute. Also, one translation of the name meant "wandering and enough," which implied a lack of initiative. Like every actual or perceived misstep Google would make in China, the misguided name was viewed as proof of the American company's inability to grasp the intricacies of Chinese culture. (And how could such a company provide the essential information that a Chinese person would look for in a search engine?) So in 2006, Goo-go-a was replaced by GuGe, which translated to "valley song." "It didn't have any negative meaning, and the priority was to get a Chinese name as soon as possible," says Dandan Wu, a member of the "landing team" that helped establish Google China.

For the launch, Google produced a video that showed animated nature scenes in the style of traditional ink brush painting. Over a sound track of wooden flute and tweeting birds, a gentle female voice made the connection between a song of the valley and the seething digital infrastructure that makes up Google's products.

> In this sowing season Google takes the name Valley (grain) Song. Using the grain as a song, it is a song of sowing and expectation. It's also a song of harvesting with joy. Welcome to GuGe. Let's search for you, let's harvest for you.

The video only vaguely referred to Google's algorithms, nothing too technical: "It is our expectation to put a very big server on the boat and just let the ever-flowing water be the energy to drive the integration of information. It seems like a beautiful and romantic picture, but it shows our drive to pursue our ideals day and night."

The name "Valley Song" didn't please everybody. In a poll conducted by the popular Sina portal, 85 percent of respondents thought GuGe was a bad idea. A website called NoGuGe.com, supposedly consisting of Chinese Google fans unhappy with the new name, collected thousands of signatures protesting the change. Commentators charged that Valley Song was a weird, unsophisticated, and embarrassingly clueless effort to evoke China's rural past to embody an exciting futuristic venture.

But GuGe it was. To celebrate the new name, Eric Schmidt and other executives went to China in April, and the Google CEO defended its policy. Schmidt was perhaps the most enthusiastic supporter of the company's China strategy. "I think it's arrogant for us to walk into a country where we are just beginning to operate and tell that country how to operate," Schmidt said to reporters at the event. Later that year in business meetings, he framed a more poetic promise: "We will take a long-term view to win in China," he said. "The Chinese have five thousand years of history. Google has five thousand years of patience in China."

A few months later, Google moved into its new offices. It occupied several floors of a gleaming building that appeared as if it were made out of giant white Lego blocks and glass. It was one of several similar structures in the Tsinghua Science Park on Zhongguancun East Road in the Hardan District of north Beijing. Close to two top universities—Beijing and Tsinghua—the district was known as China's Silicon Valley. Google shared the development with other high-tech firms, and there was even a Starbucks around the corner. Occupying several floors of the high-rise, Google's headquarters was outfitted with the usual frills: physio balls, foosball tables, a fully equipped gym, a small massage room, and (in a nod to local recreational activities) a karaoke room and a Dance Dance Revolution video game. As with other Google offices, the centerpiece was a huge cafeteria with free meals. Kai-Fu Lee was a notorious foodie and took as much care in hiring a chef as the original Googlers had devoted to choosing Charlie Ayers. "I'm a demanding taster," he admits. After several weeks of competition, the winner was a Shanghai chef, Rohnsin Xue. Lee made him go through numerous iterations of a recipe for beef noodle soup that Lee's mother used to cook. Ultimately, he would declare that Xue's beef noodle soup was superior to his mother's. "It's been served to the president of Taiwan," he would boast.

Kai-Fu Lee had been busy. For several months, the restrictions of the Microsoft suit had prevented him from engaging in product strategy, but, as he told the landing team already in place in Beijing, his priority was recruiting. Finding applicants wasn't a challenge. As soon as the news broke that Lee would be heading Google China, résumés began arriving by the hundreds. The best incentive was Lee himself. He went on a recruiting trip that had aspects of a rock-and-roll tour. Students were actually bootlegging counterfeit tickets. Alan Eustace accompanied him on one trip and couldn't get over how people mobbed Lee. It was like some weird Asian form of Beatlemania. "He'd give a talk at a university, and it would be like a basketball game, two thousand people in the audience," he says. "He would be surrounded by literally hundreds of students. People would get close to him, just to touch him."

Kai-Fu Lee's celebrity status had a downside. He became as much a part of the rumor mill as the celebrity female pop singers who dominated bulletin board discussions. Every time Google had a setback, word would appear that his departure was imminent. The Chinese press would often slam Google by going negative on Lee. At one point, reports spread that Lee was a tax evader. "That was completely personal, even though there was no tax issue," Lee says. "The company pays my Chinese taxes."

At Microsoft, the hiring had focused on experienced computer scientists. But at Google, Lee wanted young graduates. "He was worried that once people worked for a Chinese company, it would be hard to culturally fit into Google," says Ben Luk, a Hong Kong–born Google engineering director who began working in China in 2005. Lee said at the time that Google China's atmosphere would be exactly as it was in the United States.

While appreciating the difficulties censorship posed for the company, Lee believed that inside the walls of Google China, the filtering question wasn't all that important. The Chinese people themselves didn't see censorship as something so onerous. Some of the smartest people in China had confided in him that in a time of dramatic economic change, it made sense to keep some control over society. In any case, it was not an issue that engineers should be involved with, in his view. "We're technologists," he said. "We're not politicians. We don't care about all this mumbo-jumbo." Most of the Chinese engineers he spoke to were hardly aware how controversial the matter was. When they heard that it was a big issue, they would say, "Oh, is that how Americans think?"

The young Chinese engineers were to be augmented, and generally led, by experienced Googlers. Lee was looking for a Google variation on sea turtles.

Typical of those who heeded his call was Xuemei Gu. A Beijing native, she'd graduated from Tsinghua University and, like many of the top graduates, had gone to the United States to attend graduate school at Carnegie Mellon—Kai-Fu Lee's alma mater, where his name was still invoked with awe. After her doctorate, she went to Silicon Valley to work for Inktomi, a company that handled web infrastructure. When her part of the company was acquired by AOL, she jumped to Google. Hearing about Google's new venture in her hometown stirred conflicting emotions. She still had deep ties to China and had watched its economic transformation over the last decade feeling very much like an athlete relegated to the sidelines. On the other hand, she enjoyed life in California. She and her husband had a one-year-old son. She had just bought a BMW. "A lot of Chinese engineers were very excited, but I didn't think many of them would have the determination to come back. They have everything already set up in the U.S.—house, kids, and all," she says.

Yet she went to China. She later recounted her thought process: "If I stay in the U.S., what's my future? I'll probably become a better engineer, doing more complicated work, but my life will be the same every day—very peaceful life, go shopping on the weekend, go hiking. That's not what I was looking for. I was just thirty-three then. I needed some change."

Another Googler who joined the China team was Wesley Chan, straight from his triumphs with Google Toolbar and Google Analytics. Soon after arriving, he sensed there would be trouble. "I'm really blunt, and that's not the norm there," he says. He felt that Chinese citizens were suspicious of people like him, who came from headquarters. "Everybody saw me as a spy from Mountain View, so I couldn't be successful there." Though Chan got along with Kai-Fu Lee personally, he felt that something very un-Googley was happening in Beijing: "A bunch of people built a cult of personality [around Lee]," says Chan. According to Chan, at one meeting a number of people Lee hired in China began squabbling about what their titles should be. "Your title," Chan told them, "is *product manager.*" They objected that in China no one knew what that meant, and they preferred the official appellation of "special assistant to Kai-Fu Lee," so everyone would know that they had the ear of the esteemed leader of Google China. Chan almost fell over. "This isn't the White House!" he told them. "Our job is to be focused on users, not Kai-Fu." But they insisted and told him that it was important for them to sit within a hundred feet of Lee, a geographic honor that would cement their status as special assistants. Worst of all, he says, "It was this weird culture of kiss up or kiss down, and I really don't do that. So I said, 'Okay, I'm done.'" Besides, the air pollution in Beijing was killing him.

He left expecting little to come from Google's great experiment in China. "We'd get these edicts from the Ministry of Information every day about what thing we had to remove every day, and I had to sit there. We hired some of the smartest people in China, but between the leadership issues and the government Wild West situation of all that arbitrariness, it was really difficult to operate," he says.

Lee considered his role as navigating his team through a landscape full of treacherous conflicts—Chinese law and Google morality, Chinese culture and Google hubris, Chinese nationalism and Google's disruptive ambition. He believed that his celebrity could help. "I felt that if I put my reputation behind Google, it was good for Google and I did that," he says.

Others weren't so sure. Xuemei Gu recalls a remark by an executive visiting from Mountain View. Gu asked him what he thought the biggest difference was between Beijing and the other international engineering centers he had visited. "Other offices think they are Google," he told her. "The Beijing office thinks it's Google China."

Kai-Fu Lee was gratified that China's top students strove to win posts at Google. But winning consumers was another matter. "Google is clearly number one with computer science students," he said in early 2006. "But if you go out on the street and say, 'Who makes a good search engine?' most people will tell you, 'Baidu.' They've done a good job of marketing."

Baidu ruled search in China. It was founded by Robin Li—the Chinese native who had discovered the power of web links in Internet search at the same time that Larry Page and Jon Kleinberg had. He had left the United States in 2000. "I didn't have a Stanford degree, and I didn't know many VCs at the time, so I went back to China and started to develop our own search technology," he says. (Despite this, his new company was funded by Silicon Valley VC money.) Working out of a hotel room that overlooked Beijing University, he began Baidu. Its name was drawn from the first words of a Chinese poem that translates as: "Hundreds and thousands of times, for her I searched in chaos; suddenly I turned by chance to where the lights were waning, and there she stood." Originally, Li found users for Baidu by licensing his technology to the big Internet portals in China. But he quickly found that they were not willing to pay him enough to maintain the high level of technological effort he wanted. So Baidu decided to put its efforts into its own website.

Some Googlers believed that Baidu shamelessly borrowed from Google's interface; on its debut in September 2001, it looked like a Chinese-language version of Brin and Page's search engine. ("If you find similarities between Baidu and Google that means the market demands the same things," Li would later explain.) And its search results sometimes included links that it served not because of their relevance but because of fees paid by advertisers. (A search for "cancer" delivered top results not for information on the disease but for hospitals eager for patients.) But it also took advantage of a freedom that Google did not have, particularly in flouting copyright regulations. A significant percentage of its searches were for music, and the links that came up on results connected users directly to free downloads of songs. It was such a dominant music distribution tool that Chinese people call MP3 players "Baidu devices." And because, unlike Google, Baidu did not have objections to turning over the names of users to the Chinese government, it could run services that let Chinese citizens express themselves. Its bulletin boards promulgated discussion of popular cultural issues. Items on Chinese celebrities would commonly generate more than a million comments.

Also, Baidu had none of the moral qualms about censorship suffered by Google or the U.S. Congress. In 2001, when the Chinese government had informed Robin Li that Baidu had to filter results, he was at first shocked. "I didn't understand—we're a search engine, we don't create content, we shouldn't be responsible for what's on the web," he later recalled. "But we were told we were the entry point." Li spent a sleepless night considering whether he should move the service to Hong Kong. His objections were not moral, but practical. "It's a cost issue," he says, noting the drain in resources it would take to implement such a system. "I thought, if the servers are in Hong Kong, then it's not subject to Chinese law and we can save this kind of cost." In the light of morning, he realized that as a Chinese citizen, he had no choice, and from that point he implemented the government's request without complaint. "It's not an issue to me," he says. "It's just Chinese law. I'm not in politics. I'm not in a position to judge what's right and wrong."

When the Chinese government first blocked Google's search engine for a period in 2002, Baidu had only a single-digit market share. But in the ensuing years it grew to over half the market. (Google sold its $5 million investment in Baidu in 2006. The 2.6 percent stake was worth $60 million by then.) Generally, Google was the favorite of English-speaking, highly educated Chinese consumers; the newly wired, less educated consumer class in China was less familiar with Google. "When I first told my family I am going to come to China and work for Google, they asked, 'What is Google?'" says Mark Li, a Chinese-born, schooled-in-America engineer hired by Kai-Fu Lee who had previously worked at Oracle. "It's Baidu's competitor," he told them, and only then did they understand.

Kai-Fu Lee felt strongly that Google's underlying technology could whip Baidu's in a head-to-head competition. But Baidu was not a pushover. Robin Li was a smart computer scientist, and he had hired a thousand engineers to work solely on Chinese search. He professed that he was not threatened by Google's new rock-star hire. "Kai-Fu is very smart and probably the best that Google could find at that time," says Li. "But Google understands search, and Kai-Fu did not." (Lee disputes that, writing in his book that he thought about search every waking hour.) The Baidu founder was particularly unimpressed with Kai-Fu Lee's recruiting strategy. "I had been very afraid of Google hiring away my engineers by doubling or tripling their salaries. Instead, they hired a lot of fresh graduates and brought Chinese engineers from Mountain View to train them. That gave me some relief," he says.

Google China's top engineer—hired from Microsoft, where he'd worked with Lee in the Beijing research center—was a scientist named Jun Liu. He arrived at Google's office in June 2006 and conducted a comparative study of the competitors. To his horror, "we realized that even on the technology part, we were actually behind, though publicly we didn't want to admit that. I was a bit shocked by how advanced their systems were." The difference lay in one of the key components of search: freshness. In a study of top-rising queries, the ones that included new names and phenomena, Google lost. Once those new terms were around for a couple of days, Google's other signals, including PageRank, handled them effectively; for familiar queries, Google's quality surpassed Baidu's. But by that time people had lost interest in the rising queries. "For the first eight days [of a rising query], our search quality was worse than Baidu," Liu says.

"It was so obvious that there was something wrong that we spent one and a half years basically fixing our entire infrastructure," says Liu. "We initially devoted 80 percent of the energy of our entire office to fixing search problems." (Google search in general benefited from this work, as some of the ideas found their way into Google's next general update of its indexing system.) Eventually Google's studies showed that the company had caught up to and passed Baidu. By the time it introduced new improvements such as Universal Search, Google was confident that its superiority was obvious.

But by then the comparison in the minds of Chinese consumers was seriously clouded. Baidu had succeeded in transforming the competition into a test of patriotism. Its message was that Baidu, being local, understood China and Google did not. Its nationalistic campaign was embodied in a television commercial that defined the two companies for many Chinese. A tall, bearded American in a top hat, accompanied by an Asian woman in a wedding gown, squares off in a knowledge contest against a young Chinese man dressed in bright yellow traditional garb. While the Chinese man is glib and brainy, the American's grasp of Chinese is halting, and he butchers his pronunciation. A group of spectators gleefully taunts the American greenhorn. His bride bolts and joins the Chinese man. The American is last seen spitting up blood. "It was very unprofessional, but very funny, so it caught on," says Kai-Fu Lee.

But Baidu's biggest boost came from the Chinese government. The government would often slow or block Google's service and at one point even redirected Google traffic to Baidu. An apparent whispering campaign attributed the problem to Google's alleged ineptness in serving China. The most charitable fiction was that an undersea cable had broken, cutting off service from the United States.

Google had hoped that its decision to create a search engine in the .cn domain—one that followed government rules of censorship—would lead to a level playing field. But even as Google had rolled out its .cn web address, there were indications that its compromise would not satisfy the Chinese government. Unexplained outages still occurred. And not long after Google got its operating license in December 2005, the Chinese declared that the license was no longer valid, charging that it wasn't clear whether Google's activities made it an Internet service or a news portal (foreigners could not operate the latter). Google then began a year-and-a-half-long negotiation to restore the license.

On the one hand, Lee saw the episode as a positive sign—since the government did not go public and announce a crackdown, that meant that the bureaucrats Google were dealing with had a certain degree of trust in the company. On the other, Google had two strikes against it. The government was giving it the benefit of the doubt but also signaling that if anything went wrong, China would not protect it.

Google finally got its license in June 2007. The dispute had been resolved in secret. And to a large degree, the level of service stabilized. Another boost that year was that Google was granted a valuable concession: simply typing "g.cn" would take Chinese users to the Google.cn site. But by then, many Chinese had written off Google as an unwelcome outsider with less reliable service. In the summer of 2007, a group of young associate product managers from the United States spent an afternoon interviewing Chinese consumers. One woman in a T-shirt that read BRASIL SOCCER seemed surprised that she'd even be asked what search engine she uses. "Baidu." Why? "Because it is the product of Chinese people who naturally know more about China than Google," she said. Though she conceded that some people with advanced education and familiarity with English may want to use Google, "Most Chinese don't speak English. They will never use Google." A young man told them, "Google needs to be more close to the Chinese people." And another young woman said that she likes Google but doesn't use it much because it often stops working. Did she know why? "A broken cable under the ocean," she said.

When Google set up in a country, it typically would have two leaders, one to head the engineering operations and the other to run the business side. In China, Google's business head was Johnny Chou. Officially, he was the equal of Kai-Fu Lee, but Lee's celebrity and exalted status as the man who had started Microsoft's China Research Lab far outweighed Chou's reputation. Ultimately, Google China was not big enough for both of them. Chou's replacement was an even-tempered executive named John Liu, who formerly had headed the China operations of SK Telecom (Korea's dominant mobile network). Liu was content to let the more celebrated man take the spotlight. "I respected Kai-Fu as the in-country leader," he says. "I think we needed one. I'm not an ego guy." In any case, Lee told Liu that he wasn't a businessman and was perfectly happy for Liu to act on his own in generating sales and revenue in the Chinese marketplace.

Liu found that though Baidu's nationalistic sales pitch worked well with consumers, advertisers wanted results and Google—with its superior AdWords technology—could offer that. Chinese businesses also liked the idea of a competitor to Google. "Baidu did a great job of building up local Chinese search, but the Chinese will never accept that there's only one search engine," he says. "They want Google to be here, they want Google successful."

But Liu believed that to compete in China, Google had to try harder to get its message across. "A lot of normal users in third- and fourth-tier cities don't really know Google," says Liu. It depressed the Google China people to see Baidu's name everywhere. When you used an ATM machine, the log-in screen often showed a Baidu ad. When you ate at a KFC restaurant, the paper on your tray would have the Baidu logo on it. Google China's leaders—including Kai-Fu Lee—wanted the sort of aggressive marketing that Google never had done in the United States. But the people in Mountain View, perhaps because they were still conflicted about the entire China effort, would not give those efforts full blessing.

Early on, Google's marketing team spent six months on a big media campaign, including print, radio, and television. They'd hired Ogilvy & Mather to coordinate and shoot television commercials with real Chinese Google users. In one, a teenage boy couldn't find the Nike sneakers he wanted anywhere—until he used Google. Google made six variations of those success stories. But at the last minute, the bosses at Mountain View pulled the plug. This was disheartening to the China Googlers, who felt that the company should cover the third- and fourth-tier cities to tell people of the existence of Google. But that wasn't the Google way.

Google was already at a disadvantage because its ethics prevented the company from practices that were common in China but too unsavory to pass the "evil test" applied in Mountain View. Some of these were as simple as paying expense money (known as "red pockets," typically fees that exceeded cab fare) to reporters attending press conferences. Google angered the local press by not paying.

More complicated were fees paid to managers of Internet cafés. A substantial percentage of Chinese users accessed the net in these basement operations, smoky parlors that looked like a cross between a telemarketing boiler room and a video poker casino, with hundreds of terminals active at any hour. The large companies that franchised these establishments preloaded the computers with their chosen software, and Google and Baidu paid for the privilege of being the default search engine. But often the managers of individual cafés would take money under the table to replace one search engine with another. Google generally avoided such arrangements. But the company sometimes used representatives who weren't as finicky and looked the other way.

Navigating these precarious situations was especially tricky for Google because it presented itself in China as a righteous force, a trustworthy avatar of the digital age. "In my mind there's a new kind of China—the WTO and the Olympics, where there's a rising middle class that expects justice and expects things to work," said Sunny Oh, who became Google's director of marketing in Beijing. "We represent this new China, a trustworthy institution that's not going to fiddle with the results because someone's paying us to insert search results or suppress results because there's bad publicity." (Apparently this was a distinction from suppressing results to accommodate government censors.)

Google had a chance to trumpet its incorruptible search standard when its competitor Baidu was embarrassed by a commercial arrangement in its own search results. In 2008, the Chinese company Sanlu Group sold baby formula containing melamine, which caused kidney stones to form in hundreds of thousands of babies, killing six of them. Chinese news agencies reported that Sanlu had paid millions of renminbi to Baidu for its program called PR [page rank] Services to remove news articles about the scandal from search results. Baidu denied the story, but on September 12, a reporter for 21st Century Economic Report found that Google delivered

11,400 search results for the incident, while Baidu had 11. Even CCTV, the government-controlled television network, reported the story, thus reprimanding Baidu.

"We saw this problem as a great opportunity to drive our core values," says Sunny Oh. "It was a chance to say, 'Why does integrity matter?'"

But Baidu had its revenge. A couple of months after the Sanlu flap, Robin Li undoubtedly enjoyed Google's discomfort when CCTV criticized Google for serving search ads for unlicensed medical products for keywords such as "diabetes." That year, Baidu won the sponsorship of one of the hugest events in the country's television schedule, the CCTV Chinese New Year gala, watched by more than 400 million people.

It was as if the government was sending Google a message: you can be in our market, but you must not be the leader. As Google's market share inched into the twenties and approached 30 percent, some Google executives believed the number was hitting an artificial ceiling: the government would never allow Google to accumulate more than a 35 percent share.

Meanwhile, Kai-Fu Lee and his directors were organizing their smart young engineers to do great work. It took a while for some of the Chinese to adjust to the Google style. For instance, many had difficulty with the concept of 20 percent time—despite assurances, they did not feel comfortable pursuing a part-time project on their own initiative. At one point a visiting Mountain View executive called an all-hands meeting and asked for all the managers to leave the room. When only the engineers remained, he emphasized that they did not need permission to do a 20 percent project. Even that wasn't sufficient, so Lee set up brainstorming sessions where people could talk freely about cool ideas and then vote on the best. "It gives you more confidence if your idea was voted number one in a group of ten," says Lee. Another impetus for engineers to pursue 20 percent projects was to pair them, on the theory that having a partner would build confidence.

Because Google had a firm policy against storing personal data inside China—to avoid the problems of having the government demand that Google turn over the data—it did not offer a number of its key services for local Chinese users. No Gmail. No Blogger. No Picasa. Other services had to be drastically altered. YouTube was blocked entirely.

In 2007, Kai-Fu Lee assigned Mark Li to head the Google Maps team. At the time Maps was judged the worst product in Google China. In large part this was due to the government restrictions Google labored under. It had no license to gather geographical data and had to buy information from other companies. Li began working closely with the government to get various functions approved. Google also shared its information and technology with other companies. For instance, one of Google's partners had a service that identified the best restaurants in an area but did not have a license to show the restaurants on a map. Under the arrangement, Google could pinpoint the restaurants on its maps—both helping the partner's business and making Google Maps more useful. As more information came online, Google began to draw more users.

The breakthrough for Google Maps came during the 2008 Chinese New Year, when a huge, unexpected snowstorm hit. Millions of people were stuck in their home provinces; more than 100,000 people were stranded at the Guanxou train station alone. A group of seven or eight Googlers who regularly ate dinner together brainstormed on how they could help and returned to the office to start on a project inspired by the fire maps around San Diego during forest fire season. By the end of the next day, the Google team published a detailed interactive snowstorm map that aggregated information from dozens of different sources—things like news, weather reports, airport closures, and road status. It was wildly popular, and Google did a variation on other holidays. When a major earthquake hit China, the Googlers combined the system with Google Earth to bring in satellite images. Google provided the Chinese government information it had not gathered on its own. The government actually presented Google with an award for its efforts. By 2009, Google was the market leader in maps.

But arguably the most important project at Google was the Pinyin Input Method Editor (IME), a system that sped up and streamlined the often awkward task of producing Chinese-language ideographs on a computer keyboard. (Pinyin is a phonetic system that generates Chinese characters from Latin alphabet input.) Google's system took smart guesses from minimal keystrokes and suggested which characters the user might want to use. It was able to make these predictions by applying user behavior data it had collected from its search engine. As people began to use its IME system more, Google would get even better data (by noting which suggestions the user accepted and rejected), and the system would presumably get even better. Thus Google's system had the chance, when it debuted on April 10, 2007, to become a huge asset in the company's crusade to win market share in China. "We were really proud of this product," says Yonggang Wang, who headed the project. But the launch was one of Google China's worst disasters.

Google had invited the Chinese business press to attend a roundtable where the engineering director and product manager would announce the product. During the presentation, Jin Cui, the Google PR rep, got a call to go to Kai-Fu Lee's office. Apparently, some of the Chinese bulletin boards were reporting that Google's IME was based on intellectual property stolen from a local company. Google's engineers discovered that there was indeed a problem with rogue information inside the IME product but weren't sure how widespread it was. Jin Cui returned to the meeting, pretending that all was fine, and the first day's reports on Google's new product were positive. But over the next few days, the bulletin board reports accusing Google of theft only accelerated.

After a couple of days, Google found the problem. One of its student interns had been working on the IME product, and during the testing process, he had taken a shortcut. Instead of using original data, he had gone to a competing search engine called Sogou (which translated to Search Dog) and drawn from Sogou's search results, which in turn had drawn from an internal dictionary that had originally come from its parent company, the Internet portal Sohu.

"He was an intern, and he just wanted to find a work-around to speed up the process," says Wang. "So he borrowed the data to provide a work-around way. It was a bad thing." Wang explained that such acts are not uncommon in China, where there's a "more fluid" view of plagiarism. Google's routine new-employee training did address such issues, but in this case it had apparently failed to make an impression on the intern. ("He went to Microsoft," says Wang.)

People at Google were convinced that the early discovery hadn't happened by accident but had been planted on the bulletin boards by competitors, who had come across the problem by testing Google's IME as soon as they got their hands on it. Nonetheless, Google had screwed up, and before it formed its response, Sohu was attacking it in the first of what would be a series of almost daily press conferences over the next two weeks. "It was a smart decision on Sohu's part," says Cui, "because they had a competing product and they could say, 'Our product is so good that the mighty Google is stealing from us.'"

All Google could do was admit its error and apologize. "The Chinese journalists really believe Google values, so they cannot believe Google would do this kind of thing," Cui says. "All they wanted to know was, is it true?" And it was. The company that had hoped to instruct China on moral business practices had stolen code.

▼ ▼ ▼

The number one concern of Google's engineers was not unfair competition or the pressures of censorship. It was an issue that spoke to the place Chinese employees—and the Chinese business itself—occupied in Mountain View's estimation. The situation infuriated and humiliated the Chinese engineers every day of their working life. It was their access, or lack of it, to Google's production code.

Google was a collaborative company that wanted its engineers around the world to innovate on its existing products and create exciting new ones. It empowered them to do so by giving them access to its production code base. Without such access, engineers were limited in what they could do. But unlike Google's employees in other locations—Zurich, Tokyo, Tel Aviv, Bangalore, or even Moscow—the China workers did not have such access. Convoluted procedures were required to work on search, ads, and other key projects. The restrictions limited what the engineers could do—and sent a message that they were second-class employees, that Google did not trust them. "China was the only country that had this," says Boon-Lock Yeo, who headed engineering in the office Google had opened in Shanghai. "It was this fear that something bad was going to happen—somebody breaking into the data center or someone will take out certain information that would be considered very sensitive."

"It's not that I don't trust Chinese engineers," Alan Eustace, the Google executive assigned to monitor the China territory, later explained. "It's the same engineers as here, who went to the same schools, but when you go to a place like China, there's lots of examples of companies where intellectual property has gone out that door."

"We were concerned that employees in China who were Chinese nationals might be asked by government officials to disclose personal information, and all our access policies derived from that," says Bill Coughran, Google's engineering director, who enforced the policy. Despite those reasonable concerns, suspicion lingered in quarters of Google China that the engineering executives behind the policy—some of whom had deep concerns about the company's China policy—had intentionally engineered rigid restrictions as a form of corporate civil disobedience against their employer's cooperation with censors.

"Productivity was impacted," admits Yeo, who tried for years to overcome the problem. "It took longer than people anticipated to solve it." In the meantime, Google relied on sea-turtle engineers who had come to China to check the code of local engineers. "That was a real pain, because then they'd spend their time not thinking, but just checking people," says

Yeo. Local engineers were urged to pick projects that didn't involve the global code base. Or they would just be told to make searches and look for unsuccessful queries—basically, performing the tasks that less qualified testers do for Google in other countries. "Go search every day, search for lots of things, tell us what's broken," says Kai-Fu Lee. "That doesn't require access to code." But it also put those engineers in a position where any creative genius they had was wasted. And that infuriated them.

"There's a lot of pain here," Ben Luk says. "People feel they are being treated like second-class citizens. You can feel the pain gnawing at you. At one time, after we had a hundred engineers in the office, I had the feeling that if we didn't give them access, there would be a riot."

Beginning in 2008, Boon-Lock Yeo spent more than half his time on the problem, working with a security engineer in Mountain View. Eventually Google was able to implement a system where all but the most sensitive portions of the code base were available to the Google China engineers. But the anger remained. In September 2009, Luk told a visiting journalist that although things were better than they had been, "there's no clear access policy." He cited an example where a Chinese engineer "opens a ticket" to access a protected database and the request gets stuck in the queue for months.

Still, when that conversation occurred in the fall of 2009, Google China was feeling pretty good about security.

4

"The worst moment in our company."

Google's success in China depended in part on having a government relations (GR) point person who could navigate the tricky shoals of preserving Google's values without offending Chinese officials. Google's first GR head was a former vice president of Sina, who was experienced in the ways of Chinese bureaucracies. But perhaps because she did not speak English, she failed to appreciate issues from the Google perspective. She complained to at least one colleague that Google wasn't flexible enough with the government and did not work hard enough to please it.

Her tenure came to an end when Google discovered that she had taken it upon herself to give Chinese officials new iPods. She had charged them to Google, and another executive had approved the charge. In the

Chinese business culture such gifts were routine, but the act unambiguously violated Google policy, not least because it was an explicit violation of the U.S. Foreign Corrupt Practices Act. Google fired both her and the executive who had approved the expense. When she was called to Kai-Fu Lee's office for dismissal, she was dumbfounded that what she considered a normal business practice had led to her firing.

In Mountain View this breach was another sign of how difficult the China situation was. Alan Eustace later recalled the incident as "the worst moment in our company" and blamed himself for not making sure that Google's representative to the Chinese government knew how dimly the company would view such an act. "I was crushed by it," he says. "Our decision could have cost us our brand. We'd take a huge worldwide hit in an office we had just started with a person we didn't train well enough in a culture we didn't completely understand. It was my failing."

Google's response to the violation also reflected that culture gap. It sent tough investigators from a firm specializing in white-collar crime to Beijing. "They act like prosecutors—they do an investigation," says Andrew McLaughlin. "I'm sure it was extremely unpleasant." In tandem with Chinese employees' existing resentment of the restrictions on code access, it was traumatic. "I was really ashamed at the way Google handled it," says a Google China executive. "They treated everyone like a thief." And all for some gift iPods in a country, thought the Chinese Googlers, where *everybody* does that! It took months before the Beijing office got over that morale-busting incident.

After the employee's departure, Google chose a three-person government relations team, all female, led by Julie Zhu, an energetic woman in her thirties. She was hired straight from a government ministry, instead of working in the commercial sector with its backscratching culture. Zhu was better able to communicate with Mountain View. But she had her hands full fending off Chinese government directives. A demand would come from a government ministry to take down ten items; Google would typically take down seven and hope that the compromise resolved the matter. Sometimes after a few days or weeks Google would quietly restore links it had censored. Every five months, Google's policy review committee in China would meet to make sure it was filtering the minimum it could possibly get away with.

It was, as Google China engineering director Jun Liu put it, "trench warfare," but he believed that Google's continuing problems were proof that it was indeed moving the democracy needle in China. One could see evidence of the effect even on Baidu, which had adopted Google's policy of letting users know when results were truncated because of mandated filtering. Baidu also was scrambling to duplicate Google's practices of divorcing paid advertising links from the organic search results: it began work on a much-touted new ad system called "Phoenix Nest," which was a virtual clone of AdWords. "Before us people didn't even have a clue to what that means for search to be transparent, to be balanced, to be fair," says Liu. "The reason that the government is so uncomfortable with us is that we are pushing our philosophy and making progress."

But for all the progress, some Google executives were beginning to think that its great China compromise wasn't working. Though not formally organized, they consisted of a rump group of skeptics on China policy, and they looked ahead to a day when Google would no longer censor its search engine there—or leave the country. A turning point came in 2008, the year China hosted the Olympics. In the run-up to its turn in the international spotlight, China apparently decided to increase its restrictions. It demanded that in addition to censoring the .cn results, Google purge objectionable links from the Chinese-language version of Google.com. This of course was unacceptable to Google—it would mean that Google was acting as an agent of repression for Chinese-speaking people all over the world, including in the United States. Other search engines, including Microsoft's, agreed to such demands. But Google stalled, hoping that after the Olympics the Chinese would back off. They did not. The demands for censorship became broader and more frequent. "I knew of specific instances where skirmishes involving minor government officials were censored, as well as instances where they tried to limit access to information about certain natural disasters and things like that," says Bill Coughran. "The level of censorship seemed to be increasing."

It was then that David Drummond and Andrew McLaughlin suggested that Google should begin considering a change in direction. (For McLaughlin, this was a no-brainer: "Every opportunity that I've had, I re-presented the case for getting the hell out of China, and I'd always lose," he says.) Google had held its corporate nose and made a dirty bargain to get into China. Now China was changing the deal. Maybe it was time to leave.

"The environment was getting more difficult and closed, not more open as we had hoped," says Drummond. China was now insisting that all computers in the country be outfitted with filtering software called Green

Dam. Ostensibly intended to block viruses and porn, it was universally identified by critics as an effort to extend the Great Firewall into people's homes and offices. Manufacturers managed to resist installing this software, but the incident was only one indication that China was clamping down. "We had more services blocked than before," says Drummond. Also, China kept its ban on YouTube. "It was all about the Chinese government's desire to lock down cyberspace. And there was a growing fatigue with how we could deal with it."

During the Google annual shareholders meeting on May 8, 2008, Brin took the rare step of separating himself from Page and Schmidt on the issue. Shareholders unhappy with Google censorship in China had forwarded two proposals to mitigate the misdeed. The first, organized by Amnesty International and submitted by the New York state pension fund, which owned 2 million shares of Google, demanded a number of steps before the company engaged in activities that suppressed freedom. The second would force the board of directors to set up a committee focusing on human rights. Google officially opposed the proposals, and with a voting structure that weighted insider shares ten times as heavily as those owned by outside investors, the proposals were easily defeated. But Brin abstained, sending a signal—though maybe only to himself—that his conscience would no longer permit him to endorse the company's actions in China unreservedly. When shareholders had a chance to question Google's leaders, Brin explained himself: "I agree with the spirit of both of these, particularly in human rights, freedom of expression, and freedom to receive information." He added that he was "pretty proud of what we've been able to achieve in China" and that Google's activities there "honored many of our principles." But not all.

It was a clear sign that Brin no longer believed in Google's China strategy. Another signal was the fact that after Google China was established, and despite Kai-Fu Lee's urging, neither Brin nor Page ever crossed the threshold of their most important engineering center abroad. Even in mid-2009, when the pair decided to fly their private Boeing 767-200 to the remote Eniwetok Atoll in the Pacific Ocean to view a solar eclipse and Brin used the occasion to drop in on Google Tokyo, they skipped China.

Still, Google was reluctant to defy the government of China. There was still hope that things would turn around. In addition, its business operations in China were doing well. Though it had far to go to unseat Baidu, Google was clearly in second place and more than holding its own. In maps and mobile Google was a leader. In the world's biggest Internet market, Google was in a better position than any other American company.

In 2009, though, the government demands got even worse. This was yet another sensitive year for China, because of several anniversaries, including the sixtieth year of the establishment of Communist rule and the twentieth year since the Tiananmen Square uprising. China's requests to filter search results increased. Google would comply, while trying to do so in the least restrictive way possible. And Google could also point to the fact that it offered users of its .cn search engine a link to the standard Google .com site. Including that link had been a key part of Google's internal compromise to allow filtering. It was like an escape hatch to freedom, even if the Chinese government then blocked the results from that site.

Chinese officials themselves used the link: one member of the Politburo, Li Yuanchao, visiting Mountain View in 2009, wryly called the .com link his social secretary—he used it often to find news articles about himself. But apparently another member of the Politburo, Li Changchun, was horrified when he Googled himself on the global search engine and discovered links to critical comments about him. Since Li Changchun was China's top propaganda officer, he had a means to express his outrage. That spring the government demanded that Google remove the link on its local site that directed interested users to the Chinese language Google.com.

Google officials considered this demand beyond the scope of censorship; it meant that Google would be breaking the commitment it had made to Congress that it would always keep that link, just as it did on every localized version of the Google search service in the world. After a couple of months of standoff, the Chinese government suggested that maybe Google should join it in a joint committee to study the problem further. Google was off the hook but realized that at any point, the problem could resurface.

In June, a new problem arose. It involved Google Suggest, a search feature that instantly offered fully developed search queries when users typed just a few characters or words into the search box. This innovation, ultimately offered globally, was developed first in China, after Google's search team realized that, because of difficulty in typing, Chinese users generally entered shorter queries into the search box. Naturally, the quality of the feature was driven by the amount of data Google collected. In this case, the trick was for Google to examine the first few keystrokes and immediately access its servers to plumb the indexes for the most popular queries that began with the same letters as those partial entries. Unfortunately for Google, Chinese officials discovered that in an alarming (to them) number of instances, the suggestions offered by Google were related to sexual matters.

Chinese officials informed Google of their unhappiness by summoning Kai-Fu Lee and other Google China executives to a local hotel. Representatives of three ministries were waiting with a laptop and a projector. Once everyone was seated the show began. The Chinese went to the Google.cn website and typed in a vulgar term for breasts. Google Suggest offered links that displayed raw nudity, and more. The official typed in the word meaning "son," and one of the Google Suggest terms was "love affair between son and mother." The links to this term yielded explicit pornography. The woman serving tea in the conference room almost fainted at the spectacle. The Google people tried to explain that apparently someone had successfully spammed the keyboards in Google Suggest to artificially boost the popularity of sex sites. The officials were not impressed. "This is the antiporn year," they said. "You've been warned twice before, and this is the third time. So we're going to punish you."

By that time Kai-Fu Lee had already decided to leave Google but hadn't given notice. As was standard, his options were vested after four years, enough time for reevaluation. He'd decided that his strength was building things, not managing them after they were built. He was proud of what he had built in China for Google: a strong business, with impressive and motivated workers. He felt that his greatest success was balancing what seemed to be two mutually exclusive demands: Google's company values and the requirements of the Chinese government. But he also knew that some people in Mountain View—including Sergey Brin—believed that Google's efforts were not paying off and that the compromises made in China were tainting the Google brand. His main frustration with Mountain View, though, was its refusal of his constant requests to spend more to promote its search engine. Had Google given him the resources to really take on Baidu in the marketplace, he may well have stayed another year.

By July, when Lee had to go to the hospital for minor surgery, he was debating several options for his next career step, none of them involving Google. He was thinking of his future when the phone rang in his hospital room. The Chinese were once more blocking Google.cn, meting out the punishment they had promised. In addition, Google was singled out in a scathing news report on the main television network, where content is carefully controlled by the government. Now he was hearing that the government demanded that Google remove Suggest. There was a second demand—to remove foreign websites from its indexes. Google refused.

Though Lee would not say it, he had to have been thinking, I won't miss this.

That August, Lee went to Mountain View for a previously scheduled GPS on China. Before the executives went into the Marrakesh conference room in Building 43, Lee quietly told Alan Eustace that he had decided to leave. Then he went into the GPS and outlined the progress and difficulties of Google China, only afterward telling Schmidt that he would be departing. He had decided to start a company that would incubate Internet start-ups in China. "It was hard," he later said, "but it was harder to say good-bye to the team here [in China], some of whom I talked into joining. I wanted to personally assure them that things are going to go great."

Many employees of Google China didn't believe it when they first heard the news, because there had been so many earlier false reports about Lee leaving.

Lee's departure party took place on September 18. Instead of the usual TGIF, all hands gathered at the WenJin Hotel. Chinese Googlers tried to keep things upbeat; they called him onstage and had him pretend he was a contestant on a game show where they asked him silly questions and meted out "punishments" (belching three times, talking like Donald Duck, imitating Mike Tyson) whether he answered correctly or not. Then people shared stories about him. The evening ended with the entire room breaking out in a well-known Chinese pop song called "Blessing." That was when the crying began. People were singing and sobbing at the top of their lungs. The next day, Lee repeated the lyrics in an email to former colleagues: "You and I will meet again in the brilliant season!"

Some China Googlers still felt optimistic about the company's prospects. A few weeks after Lee's departure even Xuemei Gu, who was not reluctant to deliver blistering criticisms of her employer, said that she still believed in the mission. She thought her time in China was well spent. "I will say Google will probably be the most popular Internet service in China," she said. "I'm still happy. A lot of tears and challenges, but yes, I'm still happy."

Just before Christmas, Heather Adkins learned that she would fall short on her annual "don't get hacked" OKR. Google's monitoring system had detected a break-in to Google's computer system, and some of the company's most precious intellectual property had been stolen.

Apparently someone had hacked into Google from what was supposed to be a security stronghold—its password system, called Gaia. It was a serious breach that involved a theft of code. As her forensics team dug deeper, using all its digital *CSI*-style techniques to walk back over what happened, more alarms went off. The hack was geographically tied to China. What's more, both the sophistication of the attack and the nature of its targets pointed to the government itself as an instigator of or a party to the attack. "The more we learned as we looked into it, the more we realized this wasn't just a classic hack, but folks who were after something. This was hacking with a purpose," says David Drummond.

The attackers used a vulnerability in Microsoft's instant messaging system to break into the accounts of Google employees in Beijing. The openness among its employees that the company cherished turned out to be a vulnerability—and the paranoia that Google had exercised in limiting code access to the Chinese turned out not to be so paranoid. The victims were apparently people whom the attackers had identified as being useful to efforts to penetrate Google's safebox. The bandits had tracked their targets diligently, accumulating knowledge via their activities on sites such as Facebook and Twitter; then they had set up a phony photo website, sending a link to the employees that appeared to be from a familiar contact. When the employees followed the link, the trap sprang, injecting their computers with malicious software. That allowed the penetrators to take control of their computers. The outsiders had accessed MOMA, Google's internal website, to locate the engineers who were working on Gaia, the company's master password system. Then the bandits had monitored those employees to learn enough about the system to work their way into Google's internal operations and eventually copy confidential code. What they stole was apparently so critical that Google never revealed its nature.

As Google's security specialists kept looking, they found even more horrendous consequences. The hackers had dug into some Gmail accounts. Not just *any* Gmail accounts, but those of Chinese dissidents and human rights activists. All their contacts, their plans, their most private information had fallen into the hands of intruders. It was hard to imagine that the Chinese government was not poring over them. "It hadn't even occurred to us that that kind of targeted attack would be happening," says Nicole Wong. One of the compromised Gmail accounts belonged to a Chinese student at Stanford. Google arranged with campus security to meet with her, and Google's corporate head of security and safety personally took charge of her laptop. The malware was so sophisticated that it had already self-destructed.

Within days, Google set up the most elaborate war room in its history—it was actually a war *building*, as an entire Google facility was filled with a mix of security engineers working on the forensics of the incursions and policy lawyers trying to figure out what to do next. No one could get in without special light blue laminates affixed to their Google employee badges. In a move that would disturb privacy advocates already worried about Google, the company invited security experts from the National Security Agency to help analyze the attack and devise future defenses. Meanwhile Google's executives began a series of meetings to determine the next step in the company's China policy. "We had an interesting holiday season," says Bill Coughran.

The question the executives discussed was the same one that had been argued five years earlier: what's the right thing to do in China? Google had originally hoped that the Chinese would appreciate its compromise and tacitly tolerate Google's quiet pressure to relax the filtering. Instead it was the opposite. And now Google was under attack. Was this a short-term problem, or should Google acknowledge the setback and press on? In 2006, Eric Schmidt had promised five thousand years of patience. Would Google now give up after only five? As with the previous argument, the outcome would rely less on business considerations than moral ones, though no one could say how much the prospect of profits affected the views of those who argued for sticking it out. Google didn't reach out to the Chinese government to discuss the consequences. Nor did Google consult with its former head of its China operation.

Sergey Brin took the incident personally. Insiders observed that he was much less perturbed by the theft of Google's intellectual property than the fact that his company had unwittingly been a tool used to identify and silence critics of a repressive government. In interviews afterwards, he acknowledged that his personal history had shaped his response. He was also incensed to learn that other American companies had been similarly compromised yet had chosen to bury the incidents. He argued that Google should expose those companies, but others, including Google's lawyers, discouraged him. Brin focused his considerable computer science talents on the minutiae of security: it was the cofounder himself who gave briefings to the communications staff to explain what had happened.

Brin wanted the incident to be the catalyst to the action that he and others had been urging since 2008: Google should stop censoring. He was passionate in his insistence. He had support from some executives who had soured on China over the past ten months—but not all. Notably, Eric Schmidt was not convinced. But Brin was adamant: Google was under attack by the forces of evil, and if his fellow executives did not see things his way, *they* were supporting evil. (I'd heard from a knowledgeable but not firsthand source that Brin threatened to quit if Google did not change its policy. Brin, through a spokesperson, says he didn't recall saying that, and that the company was so much in his blood and DNA, it was unlikely that he expressed that intention. He did acknowledge that during the many hours of debate, he presented his case with the utmost passion.) As the days went on, and the security news looked worse—now it appeared that Google was one of more than forty companies targeted in the hack, an indication that the Chinese harbored the worst intentions toward U.S. high-tech businesses—Brin's point of view eventually prevailed. On January 10, 2010, Google's top executives reached a decision. Larry Page had joined Brin in deciding to end Google's experiment in censorship; the outvoted Schmidt accepted the decision. (Insiders would later say that the setback had long-lasting implications for Schmidt's relationship with the founders, but from the very start of his time at Google, Schmidt had understood that his word on crucial company matters was not final.) In any case, the company decided that it would no longer carry out censorship for the Chinese government on its .cn search engine. The consequences of that decision would be up to the Chinese government.

"The security incident, because of its political nature, just caused us to say 'Enough's enough,'" says Drummond.

The next day Drummond wrote a blog item explaining Google's decision. It was called "A New Approach to China." He outlined the nature of the attack on Google and explained that it had implications far beyond a security breach; it hit the heart of a global debate about free speech. Then he dropped Google's bombshell:

> These attacks and the surveillance they have uncovered—combined with the attempts over the past year to further limit free speech on the web—have led us to conclude that we should review the feasibility of our business operations in China. We have decided we are no longer willing to continue censoring our results on Google.cn, and so over the next few weeks we will be discussing with the Chinese government the basis on which we could operate an unfiltered search engine within the law, if at all. We recognize that this may well mean having to shut down Google.cn, and potentially our offices in China.

On January 12, Google published the Drummond essay on its blog. The news spread through Mountain View like an earthquake. Meetings all over the campus came to a dead stop as people looked at their laptops and read how Google was no longer doing the dirty work of the Chinese dictatorship. "I think a whole generation of Googlers will remember exactly where they were when that blog item appeared," says one product manager, Rick Klau.

For Google's employees in China, the day was also unforgettable. Not one of them had been alerted to the move ahead of time. Drummond posted his announcement at 6 A.M. Beijing time, and many of the Googlers in Beijing and Shanghai first heard about it when frantic colleagues wakened them. Employees filed into the office in a state of shock. That afternoon Google told all the employees to leave and gave them tickets to see *Avatar*. The next day everyone gathered in the café for a teleconference with Brin and other executives, who did their best to explain Google's actions. It was a tough sell. At one point, Government Relations head Julie Zhu delivered an emotional objection to the actions of her employers, overseas generals who seemed to have abandoned the soldiers in the theater of war. You should not have given up, she argued. You should have kept fighting. Others, including Xuemei Gu, challenged Sergey on the issue as well. Over the next few days, dozens of Googlers crossed the street to Kai-Fu Lee's new offices to get advice from their former leader. A few would choose to work for him.

Drummond's posting had said that Google was waiting to see if China would allow it to run an uncensored search engine from inside the country, but of course the government would never allow that. The Chinese government responded by rebuking Google for what it called false accusations of government complicity in the cybercrimes. After a few weeks, Google announced that it would shutter the Google.cn site and redirect traffic to its service in Hong Kong, at Google.hk. Because of Hong Kong's history as a free zone, China did not demand that Internet sites there follow the same censorship regime as on the mainland.

But as Google awaited the renewal of its business license in June, China signaled that the Hong Kong arrangement was unsatisfactory. Google changed its landing page so that search users would no longer be taken directly to the .hk site but could click on a link to it. From there, Google would deliver uncensored search. It would be slow, and sometimes China would block the site. The government could, and did, block users from visiting forbidden sites. But at least it would be the Chinese government, not Google, doing the censoring. Google would continue to offer other services, such as music and maps, from China. China renewed the license and implicitly approved the plan. Google was still alive in China. But it had no illusions about the arrangement. "I want to make this clear," Eric Schmidt told reporters in summer 2010. "China has the absolute ability to shut us down, and we wouldn't have an appeals process."

Meanwhile, Google's market share in China began a steady erosion. "We are certainly benefiting from it," said Baidu CEO Robin Li in a conference call in April 2010 that announced the biggest profits in its history.

Kai-Fu Lee still believed that the balance he had maintained between censorship and transparency had been the right one, and he was proud that Google could redraw the line that the government had set down—and survive. He also believed that Google should have remained on its course, even after the security breach. "Had I been there and had they consulted me, I would've said certain things which may or may not have made any difference," he says. "Most Chinese people don't care. I think some felt, 'This is a company that didn't follow the laws, so they should get out of here.' Others felt, 'Oh, no, don't leave for this.' It's all over the place. But I do think most people think it was not good for the user."

Lee said if you look at China's behavior over a long horizon—twenty or thirty years—it's clear that the trend was toward more openness. The incidents that led to Google's retreat were "a perturbation" in this movement, mainly because the current Chinese leaders had reached their limits. "The next generation will come up in less than two years," he says. "They're younger, more progressive, many American-trained, and many have worked in businesses and run banks—they're going to be more open."

But the government of China saw things differently. As the Google experiment ended, its State Council Information Office reported to its leadership that it had essentially overcome the threatening prospect of openness once promised by the Internet—and Google. "In the past a lot of officials worried that the web could not be controlled," someone familiar with the report told *The New York Times*. "But through the Google incident and other increased controls and surveillance . . . they reached a conclusion: the web is fundamentally controllable."

In the wake of the attack from China, Heather Adkins and her security team reset their practices and policies. The work experience of Google engineers all over the world was affected as Google went into what it called "corp lockdown." The golden balance that Google security had strived for—bulletproof protection with minimal disruption to a natural work flow—was gone. For instance, to get into MOMA from a remote location, you had to put in the usual passwords as well as an additional onetime password that was sent to your mobile phone. Getting access to the data centers became a painstaking process.

Googlers accepted the new restrictions with little outcry. The China break-in provided them with indisputable data to justify increased safeguards for Google's jewels. There was a psychological justice to the inconvenience as well. Call it a penance for doing evil in China.

PART SEVEN

GOOGLE.GOV

Is What's Good for Google Good for Government—or the Public?

1

"I was probably the only computer science degree in the whole campaign."

On November 14, 2007, Barack Obama came to Google.

It was not his first trip. In the summer of 2004, as an Illinois state legislator running for the U.S. Senate, Obama had toured Silicon Valley. A Mountain View drop-in was a highlight, so much so that he wrote about the experience in his book *The Audacity of Hope*. David Drummond had given the recent star of the Democratic National Convention a tour ("the main building ... felt more like a college student center than an office," observed the guest) and introduced him at a TGIF. Obama discussed Gmail and voice search with Larry Page, who led him to an exhibit Google often showed its visitors: a flat-panel display with a representation of the globe, with points of light indicating Google search activity in real time. In his book, Obama described the reverie this animation inspired:

> The image was mesmerizing, more organic than mechanical, as if I were
> glimpsing the early stages of some accelerating evolutionary process, in which
> all the boundaries between men—nationality, race, wealth—were rendered

invisible and irrelevant, so that the physicist in Cambridge, the bond trader in Tokyo, the student in a remote Indian village, and the manager of a Mexican department store were drawn into a single, thrumming conversation, time and space giving way to a world spun entirely of light.

Obama's vision, sounding as if it were evoked from a lava-lamp haze, was eerily similar to that of Page and Brin, in their claims of how Google would ride on the shoulders of the Internet to make the world a better, more egalitarian, more empowering place.

During the next presidential election cycle, Google hosted a series of candidate appearances. The Googleplex had become one of the mandatory stops on the political pilgrimage, almost a geek version of the Jefferson-Jackson Day dinner for Democrats or the Reagan Day feast for the GOP. One by one, POTUS hopefuls came to Charlie's Café, each introduced by an executive sympathetic to his or her cause. First would come a speech, then a fireside chat–style interview with the sponsoring Googler. Next would come a usually spirited Q and A. Soon afterward, Google would upload a video of the event to YouTube.

By late 2007, Barack Obama already had an impressive Google following. Andrew McLaughlin, Google's policy chief, was advising the senator on tech issues. The product manager for Blogger, Rick Klau, had lived in Illinois and had operated Obama's blog when the politician ran for the Senate (he'd even let Obama use his house for a fund-raiser). Eric Schmidt was the candidate's official host. Charlie's was so packed that they had to lock down Building 40 and direct latecomers to web feeds elsewhere on campus.

The most memorable moment came during the Q and A. "What," asked a Googler to the politician, "is the most efficient way to sort a million 32-bit integers?"

It was a hard-core programming question an engineer might be asked in a job interview at Google. But the candidate squinched up his face in concentration, as if racing through various programming alternatives. "Well," he finally said, "I think the bubble sort would be the wrong way to go."

The crowd erupted in appreciative laughter. The exchange had obviously been staged. Indeed, Andrew McLaughlin had briefed the candidate. And before the session, Schmidt had prepped him on how he might answer such a question. "So he was not completely surprised," says Schmidt.

(Tellingly, Google's research head, Peter Norvig, had written a paper in 2004 that developed a point that Schmidt made at the candidates' Google sessions—that the process of choosing a president should be more like Google's hiring procedure. Using that yardstick, he concluded that "Bush would not get past the initial phone screen," while Google might well have hired Kerry. In 2008, he wrote an addendum claiming that a job recruiter for the nation's CEO would do best with Obama.)

Google was Obama territory, and vice versa. With its focus on speed, scale, and above all data, Google had identified and exploited the key ingredients for thinking and thriving in the Internet era. Barack Obama seemed to have integrated those concepts in his own approach to problem solving. Naturally, Googlers were excited to see what would happen when their successful methods were applied to Washington, D.C. They were optimistic that the Google worldview could prevail outside the Mountain View bubble.

At Charlie's that day, Obama had explained his approach to health care. He would invite *everybody* to sit at the table, including special interests ("They'll get to sit at the table, they just won't get to buy every seat"). It would all be done publicly, shown on C-SPAN, and streamed over the net. If those special interests engaged in fearmongering and misinformation, the Obama counterpunch would be something Googlers could relate to: *data.* If the drug companies insisted that their prices had to remain high because of R&D costs, he said, "We'll present data." If the opposition ran misleading commercials like the one of Harry and Louise, Obama would counter with his own commercials, loaded with the facts. He'd run them on YouTube! "We'll present data and facts that make it more difficult to favor the special interests," he said. Provided with correct information, he said, the American people will always make good decisions.

"I'm looking forward to doing that because I'm a big believer in *reason* and *fact* and *science* and *evidence* and *feedback* [he was ticking off each of these key beliefs on his fingers], everything that allows *you* to do what you do, that's what we should be doing in our government," said Obama to the raptly attentive Googlers. He said he wanted innovators and scientists and engineers like the people at Google helping him to make policy. "Based on facts! Based on reason!"

He thought like a Googler.

Google did not officially support a candidate in 2008. But it did play a major role in the election season as a nonaffiliated technology supplier to the campaigns. YouTube became the communications platform of choice—each party had a debate where citizens could use the service to post questions to the candidate. Google's search engine was a font of quick information on candidates and issues. And candidates made significant political advertising buys based on search keywords. (You could tell whose staff was savviest by seeing whose ads appeared when you did a search for their opponents.)

Sergey Brin ordered up a Google Elections Team to work with campaigns and enable citizen access through Google products. "We were helping support YouTube, we were helping support AdWords, we were helping on Google Maps," says Katie Stanton, the biz-dev person leading the team. Around the time the team was forming, Rick Klau was discussing with a friend on the Obama campaign how the close race for the Democratic nomination with Senator Hillary Rodham Clinton might be decided by which candidate won the "superdelegates." (Those were the unpledged nominating delegates whose votes were up for grabs.) But there was no good way to track them. Klau secured the superdelegates.org web domain name and used Google tools to set up a wiki-style website. He identified all 796 superdelegates, got their geocoordinates, and mashed up the database with Google Maps so one could visualize the geographical breakdown of Obama's superdelegates and Clinton's. Klau did this on his own, but after the site was featured on CNN, Google moved him full-time to the Elections Team.

Google had a presence at both party conventions, led by Megan Smith, Stanton's boss. Google executives attended and were treated like dignitaries. "They were able to not just get handshakes but sit down and get good time, ask questions," says Klau. This happened not just at the Democratic confab in Denver, but also at the GOP convention in St. Paul, Minnesota. From the moment they hit the hotel, Stanton and Smith saw how eager politicians were to snuggle up to Google. Stanton and Smith began talking to eBay CEO and political hopeful Meg Whitman, went to a Cindy McCain luncheon, and met former New York senator Alfonse D'Amato. (Stanton cajoled D'Amato to call up her dad, who was a big fan. "Herbie?" said the former senator when he reached Stanton's father. "I'm with your hot daughter!") Then it was time to attend a huge party that Google cohosted with *Vanity Fair*. At 1 A.M., Stanton spotted Megan Smith hanging out with the Palin family. Smith, who before Google had once been CEO of Planet Out, the world's biggest gay media site, was an equal-opportunity schmoozer.

Still, anyone visiting the Google campus during the election year could not miss a fervid groundswell of Obama-love. While some commentators wrung hands over the Spock-like nature of the senator's personality, Googlers swooned over the dispassionate, reason-based approach he took to problem solving. Google employees, through the company PAC, contributed more than $800,000 to his campaign, trailing only Goldman Sachs and Microsoft in total contributions.

"It's a selection bias," says Eric Schmidt of the unofficial choice of most of his employees. "The people here all have been selected very carefully, so obviously there's going to be some prejudice in favor of a set of characteristics—highly educated, analytic, thoughtful, communicates well."

Sitting among the Googlers packed in Charlie's Café on November 14 was one of the company's brightest young product managers, Dan Siroker. (As an indication of his pedigree, he was a Palo Alto native whose mother was the computer science department secretary at Stanford and had known Larry and Sergey as graduate students.) Tall and blond, with a cutting wit and an easy social demeanor, Siroker had begun his time at Google working on ad products. In 2007, he had moved to one of Google's glamour projects, the Chrome browser. He loved the job. But the Obama appearance galvanized him. "He had me at 'bubble sort,'" he later joked.

What really entranced him was Obama's idea that government should be like Google. Everyone at Google believed they were changing the world, he thought, but could you imagine all of the United States acting that way? He emailed his résumé to the campaign and in early December got a phone call telling him that the campaign could use bodies, particularly those connected to brains that understood the Internet. Siroker got permission to take a few weeks off. "If I told them [Google] I was going to work for some Republican, I think things would have been different," he says.

At campaign headquarters in Chicago, Siroker began looking at the web efforts to recruit volunteers and solicit donations. His experience at Google gave him a huge advantage. "I'd worked on Google ads, a huge system, which probably only three people in the world—even at Google— truly, fully understand," he says. "It's the mentality of taking data and trying to figure out how to optimize something." The Obama web operation was run by smart people who'd picked up tech skills along the way but were not hard-core engineers. "I was probably the only computer science degree in the whole campaign," he says.

As exciting as the campaign was, he returned to Google to help launch Chrome. But over the July 4 weekend, he went back to Chicago to visit the friends he'd met on the campaign. Barack Obama walked through headquarters, and Siroker was introduced to him. He told the senator he was visiting from Google. Obama smiled. "I've been saying around here that we need a little bit more Google integration." That exchange with the candidate was enough to change Siroker's course once more. Back in Mountain View, he told his bosses he was leaving for good.

He became the chief analytics officer of the Obama campaign. He saw his mission as applying Google principles to the campaign. Just as Google ran endless experiments to find happy users, Siroker and his team used Google's Website Optimizer to run experiments to find happy contributors. The conventional wisdom had been to cadge donations by artful or emotional pitches, to engage people's idealism or politics. Siroker ran a lot of A/B tests and found that by far the success came when you offered some swag; a T-shirt or a coffee mug.

Some of his more surprising tests came in figuring out what to put on the splash page, the one that greeted visitors when they went to Obama2008.com. Of four alternatives tested, the picture of Obama's family drew the most clicks. Even the text on the buttons where people could click to get to the next page was subject to test. Should they say, SIGN UP, LEARN MORE, JOIN US NOW, or SIGN UP NOW? (Answer: LEARN MORE, by a significant margin.)

Siroker refined things further by sending messages to people who had already donated. If they'd never signed up before, he'd offer them swag to donate. If they had gone through the process, there was no need for swag—it was more effective to have a button that said PLEASE DONATE.

Using Google's Website Optimizer tool, Siroker and his team tested the cost per click of visitors and kept tweaking and testing to lower the cost. There were a lot of reasons why Barack Obama raised $500 million online to McCain's $210 million, but analytics undoubtedly played a part.

Someone posted a picture of Siroker on his Facebook wall on election night. Everyone else at campaign headquarters was cheering or crying with joy. Siroker was sitting at his computer with his back to the TV, making sure that the new splash page that would welcome website visitors was the one celebrating the victory, not the one they'd prepared saying he'd lost. After that, he was going to push the start button on yet another test, to see which one of four victory T-shirts would be the most effective in garnering donations for the Democratic National Committee. Just as Google ad campaigns never ended, neither did online political campaigns.

During the transition, Siroker continued working on analytics as deputy media director. But as soon as he relocated to Washington, he felt something different. The desire to innovate for change seemed to have been sapped. In part, it reflected the shift from a campaign into a much bigger, established operation. Google had experienced a similar transformation but had consciously made adjustments in an attempt to preserve its freshness. Even though the company was huge, employees could feel that their individual group was kind of a start-up. (That's the way it had felt to Siroker with Chrome.) But being on the transition team felt like working for the biggest, most paranoid company in the world. And this was before the Democrats controlled the government.

Also, Siroker had to wear a suit every day. "The director of our department wanted to make it very clear that we were serious," he says. But he hated it.

When the White House offered Siroker the newly imagined post of director of citizen participation, he did what any Googler would do: laid out the problem like a math quest. He wanted desperately to be part of a transformative movement in government, but his experience during the transition had sent a clear signal that in working in the White House, he *wouldn't* be making a difference. "I didn't feel I was using my full potential to make an impact." Also, Siroker told the White House, he'd have to use Microsoft Exchange instead of Gmail. "It was absolutely killing me." Ultimately, the negatives won. He did not return to Google but cofounded a start-up to help teach kids arithmetic.

Siroker suggested that the incoming White House hire Katie Stanton, who'd headed the Google Elections Team, for the job he'd been offered. Stanton would have to make sacrifices: the White House job paid $82,500; her Google salary had been "a multiple of that," she says. She also had to sell all her stock options. It seemed a small price to participate in an adventure where Google's values would spread throughout the U.S. government.

Stanton was one of a handful of key Googlers who joined the administration. The most prominent was Andrew McLaughlin, who left his post as Google's policy director to become the deputy to the chief technical officer of the United States. Sonal Shah, who had worked on global initiatives for the Google.org foundation, became the director of the newly established Office of Social Innovation and Civic Participation, overseeing a $50 million budget. Meanwhile, Eric Schmidt sat on Obama's Council of Advisors on Science and Technology and was one of the president's go-to CEOs when captains of industry were required as a photo backdrop.

They joined a team of techie Obamanauts who saw their job as bringing the digital tools of empowerment to Washington. They included not only people who had toiled in cyberspace's election districts but administrators such as Vivek Kundra, the imaginative chief technology officer of Washington, D.C., who became the chief information officer of the national government. McLaughlin's boss, the first national chief technology officer, was Aneesh Chopra, formerly Virginia's secretary of technology. Perhaps the most powerful was the new FCC chairman, Julius Genachowski, a former Internet executive (with IAC, Barry Diller's operation) who was a Harvard Law School cohort and basketball buddy of the incoming president. While emphasizing that Google was not entitled to special government treatment, Genachowski acknowledged that its values resonated with the new administration: "I think of them as Internet values," he says. "They're values of openness, they're values of participation, they're values of speed and efficiency. Bringing those tools and techniques into government is vital."

But when the outsiders like Stanton hit the nation's capital, they went straight into a buzz saw of illogic, bad intentions, mistrust, and, worst of all, obsolete gadgets. Not only were they chained to outdated Windows computers, but they were denied the Internet tools they had come to rely on as much as breathing. Rules dictated that there could be no Facebook, no Google Talk, no Gmail, no Twitter, no Skype. (Even the president had to fight to retain his BlackBerry, and the one he wound up with was slowed down by security add-ons and cordoned off to all but a few designated texters.) "I'd been going a million miles an hour at Google," she says. "And suddenly there were all these rules. Where you can put content. The Presidential Records Act. Terms of service agreements." Even using the tools that were available in a modern, effective manner was often frowned upon. Not long after she took the job, Stanton did a reply-all email, which was common at Google. At the White House, someone took her aside and reprimanded her.

From his own perch as deputy to CTO Aneesh Chopra, Andrew McLaughlin was flummoxed by the same rules. By that time McLaughlin had taken to carrying his personal laptop into his office with a wireless modem so he could maintain the flow of information on Twitter, Facebook, and Gmail he felt was necessary. He took pains to keep his official work on the government computers. Eventually he got permission to use Facebook, Linked-in, and Twitter on his White House computer. (But not Skype.) Still, he welcomed the opportunity to help bring the government into the digital age. "The good part of it is that no one knows what we're supposed to do," says McLaughlin of the CTO office's mission. "They only know that we're bringing magical Internet pixie dust—we're supposed to sprinkle that over things and make them better, though they're not really sure how."

Katie Stanton parsed her job the same way Google divided its overall corporate energies, breaking it up 70, 20, 10. The bulk of her work, 70 percent, was amplifying the president's message. The 20 percent part was gathering input from various online constituencies (the "mommy bloggers," the financial consumers, and so on) and interacting with them. Finally, the smallest part was helping citizens interact with one another. Stanton thought that was the most important part of her work, but its lower priority made it the hardest to get done.

The job was frustrating. Google hadn't been perfect, but people got things done—because they were engineers. One of the big ideas of Google was that if you gave engineers the freedom to dream big and the power to do it—if you built the whole operation around their mind-set and made it clear that they were in charge—the impossible could be accomplished. But in the government, even though Stanton's job was to build new technologies and programs, "I didn't meet one engineer," she says. "Not one software engineer who works for the United States government. I'm sure they exist, but I haven't met any. At Google I worked with people far smarter and creative than me, and they were engineers, and they always made everyone else look good. They're doers. We get stuck in the government because we really don't have a lot of those people."

Though Stanton generally tried to steer clear of Google connections to avoid the appearance of a conflict, she did work on one project that used Google technology to allow citizens to ask the president questions via the Internet. The software was a version of Dory, the program used at Google to handle questions for Page and Brin during TGIF sessions. It had originally been conceived as a 20 percent project by an engineer named Taliver Heath, who named it after the fish in *Finding Nemo* that always asked questions. Dory provided a clever, algorithmic means of allowing large numbers of people to rank lists of questions. You gave thumbs-up for your favorite questions and thumbs-down for the ones you liked least. A positive vote would count twice as much as a negative one.

By the time Obama agreed to accept questions from an online audience, Google was marketing Dory outside the company. To avoid intellectual property conflicts with Disney, it had renamed the product Moderator. People in the administration were excited that using this data-backed, algorithmic system, they could collect a range of questions that reflected what citizens wanted to know. On March 26, 2009, President Obama stood in the East Room of the White House before a crowd of a hundred onlookers and was presented with the top-ranked questions. More than 90,000 people had submitted questions, and Moderator processed over 3.6 million up-and-down votes to determine which ones rose to the top. The most popular ones were shown on a large flat-screen display. The top-ranked question was about whether legalizing marijuana would jump-start the economy. The second-ranked question involved . . . the legalization of marijuana. And the third question? Legalizing dope.

The National Organization for the Reform of Marijuana Laws (NORML) had encouraged people to vote up questions concerning that single issue. Some might have considered it cheating, but Google's Moderator team saw it as a reflection of a passion in the population. The fact that people were motivated to organize on that issue was itself a data point.

"I don't know what this says about the online audience," said the president before stating that legalizing weed was not a good strategy to grow the economy. Then he answered the lower-ranked questions about health care, college costs, home foreclosures, and high-speed rail.

The other highlight of Stanton's tenure at the White House was helping organize a presidential town meeting in Shanghai. Arguing over the tiniest point with Chinese officials bent on total control, Stanton got a taste of what Google's Beijing government relations people dealt with all the time. The president, wary that the Chinese students would be too intimidated to ask a controversial question, wanted to add a question from the Internet. People submitted two thousand questions to the Department of State website. Each was given a number, and then a reporter was asked to pick two numbers between 1 and 2,000. The two questions that matched were presented to the U.S. ambassador to China, who chose one. It just happened to be on the topic that many were waiting for Obama to address: Internet freedom. Obama said he was in favor of it, though he did not argue the point so strongly that he offended his hosts.

At a conference in January 2010, Stanton expressed her feelings about the difference between the White House and Google. "Working in government," she said, "is like running a marathon. Blindfolded. Wearing sandbags." Whereas Google was collegial, working for the White House was like a season of the reality show *Survivor*, whose motto was "Outwit, outplay, outlast." She felt that she could make more of an impact joining the digital cadre of the Department of State, and in January 2010 she went to Foggy Bottom.

Of all places, the State Department was one of the most active digital outposts in the administration. Inspired by a group of young, tech-savvy officials, it was promulgating an idea it called "21st Century Statecraft." At State, Stanton felt she finally had a platform to use her Google skills in government. At a meeting one day, Secretary of State Hillary Clinton dropped by and welcomed her. Stanton's computer was open, and the secretary asked what she was doing. "These are my OKRs," she said and proceeded to explain how Google had taken Andy Grove's "Objectives and Key Results" employee rating scheme to dizzying extremes. "That's great—how could we do more of this here?" asked the secretary, and Stanton was thrilled. Could the State Department institute OKRs?

Soon after, Stanton was attending her daughter's basketball practice when her BlackBerry lit up. A huge earthquake had devastated Haiti. The previous week Stanton had been to a dinner where Secretary Clinton had broken bread with technology leaders (including Eric Schmidt), and Stanton had met the CEO of a telecom company called Mobile Accord. She still had his cell number, and, while driving home, she talked to him about setting up a "short code" for cell callers that would enable people to quickly make an automatic donation to an aid fund for Haiti. When the code was sent by Short Message Service, the caller would donate five dollars to a fund. Or should it be ten dollars? Stanton and her contact wondered. They decided to go for ten. Stanton pinged her bosses, and to her delight the State Department approved the idea. *Yes! That* was why she had joined the government. "It's solving a hard problem, it's using technology, it's inclusive," she later said. When White House officials heard about it, their instinct was to slam on the brakes, to analyze all the ramifications before doing anything, even while people died on the streets. But State got the code out to the public. Before a week passed, contributors donated over $32 million. Millions more would come.

Andrew McLaughlin was also onto the Haiti situation as soon as the temblors hit. From his pre-Google work at ICANN, the Internet governance organization, he knew people who ran Haiti Internet service providers. The only way he could get hold of them was through the Internet—the phones were dead, and the cell towers weren't working. Skype was the obvious way to do it, but it was blocked on White House computers. Fortunately, McLaughlin had his MacBook and a wireless modem. Sitting in his office in the Executive Office Building, he kept a Skype line open to people on Boutilier Hill, a high point above Port-au-Prince where the Internet microwave lines terminate and the ISPs beam WiMax toward their customers in the city. There were five ISPs, and all were initially running—the Internet was thus the default communication system on the island. The people in charge promised to stay and keep the boxes running if they knew their families were all right. McLaughlin became their point person to keep things functioning, using various social networks and Internet tools to check on their families, arrange for transportation, and get kerosene shipped up the hill to keep the generators running. "If I wasn't there with my own laptop and my own AirCard, none of this would have happened," he says.

The Haiti experience was one of several high points for the tech Obamanauts. Another was the success that Chief Information Officer Vivek Kundra had in applying Google-style metrics to the delivery of data to the general public. Just as Google's engineers constantly monitor "dashboards" that probed vast databases to find relevant information in a given moment, Kundra set about building a number of dashboards for citizens to extract information from previously inaccessible government databases. Though not a Google initiative per se, his mission seemed to be a variable of Google's: making all the government's information universally available and accessible.

On the other hand, many of the Obamanauts' dreams seemed to dissipate. Julius Genachowski's efforts to extend broadband coverage met resistance at every turn. He did manage to get some billions of stimulus-related dollars devoted to building out broadband. But his efforts to enforce "net neutrality"—ensuring equal treatment of Internet services by providers such as AT&T, Verizon, and Comcast—were blocked by the corporations and even the courts. (In late 2010, Genachowski managed to push through a set of net neutrality rules intended to serve consumers while appeasing telecoms. The rules were quickly challenged in court by Verizon.)

Both the government and Google found themselves targets of the powerful communications companies, who had used their power to profit from a system where Americans paid more for and got worse Internet service than much of the rest of the developed world. The corporations spent millions of dollars lobbying Congress to make sure that regulations would not impede their efforts. They funded think tanks to create studies that attempted to prove that the current U.S. broadband coverage really wasn't so bad. (What's wrong with being twelfth out of the top twelve economies in the developed world?) One organization the corporations helped finance, called Consumer Watchdog, created a blog called "Inside Google" that demonized every move from Mountain View, from Google's China policy to its ad quality algorithm. Opponents of Google characterized net neutrality as akin to communism.

The big telecoms and cable companies were particularly incensed by a Google initiative announced in February 2010. The Google Fiber for Communities project invited municipalities all over the nation to vie to be the lucky recipients of an experimental ultra-high-speed broadband network. The plan was to service between 50,000 and a half-million people with faster and cheaper Internet than the current providers were promising for even a decade hence. Without laying a single inch of fiber, the plan dramatized the inadequacy of the current system, in which AT&T, Verizon, and Comcast basically controlled an overpriced, undersupplied system. Thousands of communities exposed their desperation for adequate connectivity by stunts more worthy of candidates for the studio audience of *The Price Is Right*. The city of Topeka, Kansas, actually changed its name to Google for the month of March. (Google reciprocated by renaming itself Topeka on April Fool's Day 2010.)

The Obamanauts found themselves on the wrong end of political stilettos. Andrew McLaughlin became a victim when Google foes petitioned to view his electronic correspondence through the Freedom of Information Act and found that he was still in contact with some of his former Google colleagues. The emails were innocuous—in one of them he actually turned down an invitation to speak at an event at Google's D.C. office because of a perceived conflict of interest—but he drew an official reprimand.

"You have to be extraordinarily careful," Katie Stanton said.

Of course, the tribulations of the Obamanauts were trivial compared to those of the man they followed to Washington. Constantly criticized for an overly rational approach to government, the new president found that the logical, metrics-based values that served Google so well did not ensure cooperation in Washington's morass. And contrary to the expectations he expressed to Google about his vision in promoting issues like health care, the facts did not always win the day.

Ten years earlier, Larry Page had felt the world would be better when people had instant access to the truth. Google had delivered the means to do this, but it didn't seem to matter a bit.

Katie Stanton felt she'd had enough. "I feel like I'm a vegetarian trapped inside the sausage factory and it's kind of ugly on the inside," she said in the spring of 2010. In July, she left the State Department and took a job at Twitter. Despite her tribulations, she felt that her government time had been well spent. But there was one thing she could not understand. For all the love that Google got from its users and all the support that the Obama administration had gotten from Google, actually *being* from Google was almost like a handicap. "I was shocked at how much it almost hurt me," she said. "Sometimes people treated it like a criminal record."

2

"Did you ever think you'd see the day when *you* were hiring the antitrust lawyer?"

Eric Schmidt could be frank about the difference between the world's reaction to the mature Google as opposed to the young Google. "Because of our size, and because we have a lot of money, we're getting sued to death," he said. "That's just a consequence of the American legal system. I'm not happy about that. But because we're Google, we have extra scrutiny. The regulators pay more attention to us, the Antitrust Division pays more attention to us."

Google's legal department, which had ballooned to more than three hundred employees by 2009, had its hands full of lawsuits from content providers who felt Google was infringing copyright, advertisers who felt that the ad quality algorithms were discriminating against them, trademark holders who objected to competitors buying their corporate names as ad keywords, and foreign governments objecting to numerous activities, including the humiliation of mentally challenged children on YouTube. (The last involved a video of Italian kids bullying a classmate; Italian officials filed criminal charges against four Google executives including David Drummond. Though none of them had seen the video before a user posted it and Google had removed the video immediately upon the first objection, an Italian judge found the executives guilty of a criminal misdemeanor.) While some Googlers felt singled out unfairly for the attention, the more measured among them understood it as a natural consequence of Google's increasing power, especially in regard to distributing and storing massive amounts of information. "It's as if Google took over the water supply for the entire United States," says Mike Jones, who handled some of Google's policy issues. "It's only fair that society slaps us around a little bit to make sure we're doing the right thing."

Civil lawsuits had to be taken one by one, but Google's interests in an increasingly hostile Washington environment required some concerted action, and Google was tardy in responding. Not until 2005 did Google hire its first lobbyist, Alan Davidson, a former associate director of the Center for Democracy & Technology. For some months he was alone in the company's D.C. office.

A big part of Davidson's job was educating legislators, staffers, and regulators on exactly what Google did. He also had to produce the celebrity founders, which was a challenge. Visiting bureaucrats and lawmakers, says Brin, "is not, like, my favorite activity—when I'm in the D.C. area, I prefer to spend time with my family." In 2006, Davidson lured Sergey Brin to Capitol Hill for a trip that even Brin described as a disorganized, last-minute venture. Davidson, though, considered the trip a success, claiming that the meetings Brin did take—including a long mind meld with then-Senator Obama—were productive. Brin did become alerted to the brewing opposition from telecoms when reporters informed him that an AT&T-backed industry coalition was running ads in the D.C. area claiming that Google, by supporting open standards, was "going to blow up" an opportunity for people to have choice in cable television. "I am probably naïve," said Brin. "I am very surprised to see this."

In the next few years, the Washington, D.C., office expanded. In 2007, *The Washington Post* reported that the company had twelve lobbyists on staff, including former Clinton speechwriter Robert Boorstin. It also retained lobbying firms associated with both political parties. That number increased dramatically as Google moved into a 27,000-square-foot space on New York Avenue. "Google's role in Washington is really quite different," said Eric Schmidt. "We're behaving more like a mature corporation." Well, not *totally* mature—the new office had Googley touches such as a game room and a German-made Cyber-Relax massage chair.

Google was following a traditional narrative of Silicon Valley companies arriving in Washington—after an initial denial of the necessity of wasteful nonengineering efforts spent on politicking, Google realized that not playing the game would leave the company vulnerable to lobbying by its foes. A bustling D.C. office populated by minor figures from previous administrations, a well-subscribed PAC, and a blizzard of contributions followed. But Google still saw itself as different. Just as Google's engineers believed they worked not just on technology but on improving the world, the lobbyists in Google's D.C. office viewed themselves on a higher plane than the standard white-shoe operator. "The one company I was willing to work for in D.C. was Google," says Pablo Chavez, who joined the company after working first for the Wilson Sonsini Goodrich & Rosati law firm, then as chief counsel to John McCain. "It's a kind of extension of public service—it's really advocating in favor of the Internet, in favor of openness and democratization of information. As opposed to absolute and utter spin." Chavez did admit that there were those who saw the effort as an attempt to gain more influence and power than Google should have. "The hope is that we can play the game differently," he says. "We can try to bring more rational discourse and be more of an information provider, instead of using a raw power approach, instead of funding Astroturf groups, instead of hiding behind benign-sounding, but ultimately [compromised] organizations."

The Google lobbying office handled many issues, including net neutrality, broadband improvement, and privacy. But as Google became increasingly viewed as an Internet behemoth, a more pressing challenge emerged: Google had an antitrust problem.

The first antitrust salvo came in 2007, when the company sought approval of an even bigger purchase than YouTube: the ad network Double-Click, the leading company in helping advertisers and agencies decide which websites would be the most effective hosts for the display ads they placed. (Display ads are graphics that occupy part of a web page; the advertiser pays per impression, not by click.) One of the more powerful technology tools DoubleClick used was a "cookie" (a small piece of code that identified visitors to websites) that enabled a website to access the user's browsing history and other information, thus allowing relevant ads to be chosen at the instant someone arrived at a web page.

The very idea that Google would buy the biggest force in display advertising represented a shift from its original beliefs. Google's original ad policy was based on Page and Brin's premise that banner ads and their ilk were unwelcome intrusions. That view had clearly changed. Google was hearing from its AdSense customers that it would be easier to run online campaigns if they could go to one place for both search and display ads. Given that incentive, Google began to consider the ways that maybe display ads *weren't* so bothersome to users. Because they drew on a user's browsing history, display ads could sometimes be more relevant than AdSense ads. If you went to a wine-oriented website, for example, you might see an AdSense ad for a Sonoma vacation that might or might not interest you. But if you bought wine online all the time, the DoubleClick cookie would know that and maybe show you a banner ad about wine while you were on the *Sports Illustrated* site.

(In a much less significant but even more drastic departure from original values, Google sponsored a thirty-second ad during the 2010 Super Bowl. Page later said that running the ad was a low-risk way to see whether Google's distaste for TV ads still made sense. "It sort of violates every known principle that we have," he admitted. "But every once in a while, you should test that you really have the right principles. You don't want to end up too rigid. Maybe that's my Montessori training.")

In any case, if Google didn't buy the top display-ad network, its competitors would. Microsoft also coveted DoubleClick, and a bidding war erupted that was arguably as much about keeping the prize away from a competitor as about winning it. Google paid $3.1 billion for DoubleClick, its biggest acquisition ever. (It didn't seem so overpriced when a few months later Microsoft bought a competing ad network, aQuantive, for $6 billion.) The purchase, announced in May 2007, was so huge, and the concern about Google's power so widespread, that the government launched an investigation to see if the deal violated antitrust law. The Federal Trade Commission undertook the study, and the European Union did its own.

"DoubleClick was a big wake-up call for the company," says Google lawyer Dana Wagner, whose presence at Google was itself an indication of the new reality. Wagner had been hired in 2007 largely because of his experience working for the Justice Department's Antitrust Division in the early 2000s. When he introduced himself to Page at a meeting, a product manager asked Page, "Did you ever think you'd see the day when *you* were hiring the antitrust lawyer?" Page acknowledged that it was very, very odd. But that was Google ten years after PageRank.

Wagner later said that from Google's point of view, the alarming thing about the DoubleClick probe was that "there was never a good antitrust argument against the transaction." Nonetheless, it was a rigorous and lengthy process. The focus of the investigation was on whether the DoubleClick purchase would allow Google too much domination over the ad market. Predictably, Google argued that its activities should be seen in the larger universe of the advertising world, not just the corner of it that involved search. Google might have been raking in billions of ad dollars, but it had "only" a 10 percent share of the ad industry. "There is no such thing as a market share in search advertising because it isn't a market," says Wagner.

Google also argued that comparisons to Microsoft's monopoly were misleading. When you used Microsoft Windows, virtually all your work was conducted on applications that ran solely on that operating system; thus you were locked in to Microsoft. Google executives loved to claim, in contrast, that its competitors were only a click away. If you didn't like a search result, all you had to do was go to Ask.com or Yahoo or Microsoft. Earlier that year, Google had had a rare service outage and users had been unable to pull up the search engine for a few hours. Data showed that during that period, millions of Google users had simply switched to Yahoo or other search engines for their searches. This turned out to be a fortunate turn of events for Google; thereafter its lawyers always pointed to that moment as evidence that with search there was no lock-in.

The length of the government investigation, which began in May and wasn't concluded until a few days before Christmas, was unsettling for Google, used to operating at Internet speed. DoubleClick was based in the same building as Google's New York headquarters. Google had a huge operation in New York City—more than a thousand employees covering several floors of a structure that filled a long city block in the Chelsea neighborhood, between Eighth and Ninth avenues. (There were rows of scooters to speed passage from one end of the space to another.) "We had different elevator banks that we could go through and nobody could talk to anybody else," says Neal Mohan, then a DoubleClick executive and later Google's vice president of product management. "There was no joint planning conversations, and we had to keep running the business, building products for customers in our individual silos, and then spending a lot of time with the regulators, both in D.C. and in Brussels [the headquarters of the European Union], educating them on our deal." In one case, people developing a new Google ad product were separated only by a wall from DoubleClick people working on a nearly identical product; work on both projects proceeded even though both teams knew that when the merger was completed, the duplication would be redundant.

On September 17, 2007, the Senate Judiciary Committee held a hearing on the issue. (Congress would not be involved in the FTC decision on the merger but apparently felt the need to weigh in, nonetheless.) It began with a blistering assessment of the Internet marketplace by Senator Herb Kohl. "Will advertisers and Internet publishers have no choice but to deal with Google, giving Google a stranglehold over Internet advertising?" he asked. David Drummond, the first witness, did his best to answer in the negative, contending that Google and DoubleClick weren't competitors. Google sold ads, he explained, and DoubleClick was a technology to help determine where ads should be placed. "Google is to DoubleClick what, say, Amazon is to FedEx," he said. "Amazon sells books; FedEx delivers them. And by analogy, we sell ads. DoubleClick delivers them. Two different businesses."

Bradford Smith, the general counsel of Microsoft, disputed Drummond's statement. He noted that Google already had 70 percent of the global market for search advertising, and, should the merger be allowed, it would have 80 percent of spending on *nonsearch* ads on third-party websites. "Google will become the overwhelmingly dominant pipeline for all forms of online advertising," he said.

Though the FTC made its ruling based largely on whether the purchase would be anticompetitive, it did mention the issue of consumer privacy, observing that the issues in the merger "are not unique to Google and DoubleClick." That conclusion demonstrated that the commission failed to perceive the admittedly complicated privacy implications that were unique in this case. For its part, Google helped foment misunderstanding by not being clear about the unprecedented benefits it would gain in tracking consumer behavior.

In fact, the DoubleClick deal radically broadened the scope of the information Google collected about *everyone's* browsing activity on the Internet. While Google's original impetus in buying DoubleClick was to establish itself in display advertising, sometime after the process began, people at the company realized that they were going to wind up with the Internet-tracking equivalent of the Hope Diamond: an omniscient cookie that no other company could match. It was so powerful that even within Google, the handling of the gem became somewhat contentious.

Some understanding of the way cookies work in advertising networks is required to appreciate this. When a user visits a site that contains an ad from a network like DoubleClick, the browser automatically "drops" a cookie onto a user's hard drive. The information enables a website to know whether a visitor has been there before and thus to determine what ads might be appealing, as well as which ads have already been shown to that user. Furthermore, every time a user subsequently visits a site with ads, that visit is logged into a unique file of all of that user's peregrinations. Over time, the file develops into a rather lengthy log that provides a fully fleshed out profile of the user's interests. Thus, the DoubleClick cookie provided a potentially voluminous amount of information about its users and their interests, virtually all of it compiled by stealth. Though savvy and motivated consumers could block or delete the cookies, very few knew about this possibility, and even fewer took advantage of it.

The information in the DoubleClick cookie was limited, however. It logged visits only to sites that ran DoubleClick's display ads, typically large commercial websites. Many sites on the Internet were smaller ones that didn't use big ad networks. Those interests or activities weren't reflected in the DoubleClick cookie. Millions of those smaller sites, however, *did* use an advertising network: Google's AdSense. AdSense had its own cookie, but it was not as snoopy as DoubleClick's. Only when the user actually clicked on an ad would the AdSense cookie log the presence of the user on the site. This "cookie on click" process was lauded by privacy experts as far less invasive of people's privacy than the DoubleClick variety.

Google could have signed up as a DoubleClick customer and permitted DoubleClick to drop its cookies on sites where AdSense ads appeared. That would have made Google literally billions more dollars, since advertisers would have paid much more for the more relevant ads. But Larry and Sergey did not want Google to drop third-party cookies on its own sites. Implicit in their refusal: the practice seemed, well, evil.

But after Google bought DoubleClick, the equation was different. Google now owned an ad network whose business hinged on a cookie that peered over the shoulder of users as it viewed their ads and logged their travels on much of the web. This was no longer a third-party cookie; DoubleClick *was* Google. Google became the only company with the ability to pull together user data on both the fat head and the long tail of the Internet. The question was, would Google aggregate that data to track the complete activity of Internet users? The answer was yes.

On August 8, 2008, not long after FTC regulators approved the DoubleClick purchase, Google quietly made the change that created the most powerful cookie on the Internet. It did away with the AdSense cookie entirely and instead arranged to drop the DoubleClick cookie when someone visited a site with an AdSense ad. Before that change, when a user visited a political blog or a cat care site using AdSense, there was no record of the visit unless the user clicked on an ad. Now Google would record users' presence when they visited those sites. And it would combine that information with all the other data in the DoubleClick cookie. That single cookie, unique to Google, could track a user to every corner of the Internet.

The upbeat Google blog item that mentioned the change, entitled "New Enhancements on the Google Content Network," was directed mainly to agencies, advertisers, and publishers and extolled the use of the new cookie. While the blog item did note that users could opt out of receiving the cookie and directed them to a revamped privacy policy, the posting did not explain the seismic nature of the change—that Google had unique access to what was now the web's most powerful tracking tool.

"Of course it was a very big deal," says Susan Wojcicki, who as the head of the ads program was involved in the discussions. "What changed was that we were now the first person." (As opposed to being a "third person" provider of user information to an outside party, DoubleClick.) But there was a bigger reason for Google's change of heart. "We weren't winning," says Wojcicki. "Without the cookie, we weren't making the impact on the world that you have to make to be successful." In her view, Google had to make that step—one it had resisted earlier in part for moral reasons—so it could improve advertising and help its users.

The powerful personal information in its enhanced DoubleClick cookie was, of course, only part of the data Google had about its users. The company also had even more intimate and comprehensive information about people from their search behavior. This information was included in the logs that were so valuable to Google in its relentless effort to improve search and run experiments. (The information did not identify users by name but by the Internet [IP] addresses they used to access Google. Those signed into Google, though, were identifiable by name.) For privacy purposes, Google fully anonymized the search cookie after nine months (dropping the IP address) and deleted it after eighteen months. (Originally, the anonymization occurred after eighteen months, but Google had changed it under pressure from critics and regulators.) Privacy activists believed that Google's retention of identifiable search data for nine months was still too long. The European Union recommended six months, a standard that other search companies, including Microsoft, adopted or exceeded. But Google insisted that it keep information for as long as a human gestation period. "We queried every engineering team to find how long they needed the data to do the things they needed, including security, ads quality, and search quality," says Jane Horvath, Google's chief privacy officer in North America. "The median we came out with was nine months. It's completely central to our tools. It's the key to our innovation."

In any case, Google, in various places, now had the data on almost everywhere users went on the Internet and, via search, all their interests. No law prevented it from combining all that information into one file.

Google would contend that limits do exist. It did *not* combine the data on its ad cookie with the personal information on its users' search behavior, nor did it combine website visit data with the content of people's mail and documents, or the posts they wrote on Blogger. Only the information derived from people's browsing behavior was used to help deliver ads. When people expressed concerns about all that information residing with one company, Google would revert to its standard defense: if it betrayed consumers' trust, its business would be irrevocably damaged. Nonetheless, a 2008 internal presentation written by a Googler who arrived through the DoubleClick acquisition proposed a road map for Google's ad practices that indeed included ads chosen on the basis of people's searches. "Google search," it said, "is the BEST source of user interests found on the Internet and would represent an immediate market differentiator with which no other player could compete." (That same presentation showed that the author was catching on to the Google way: under the rubric "wacky examples" of cookie use, he suggested a "Larry Page Ad" where the cofounder would "opt in" to a system that let users "create wacky ads that would appear on Larry's laptop as he browses sites." That was an idea worthy of Page himself!) When *The Wall Street Journal* reported on the presentation, Google dismissed it as a speculative vision statement from a junior employee.

But while Google held off using people's search history for ads, it did engage in an internal debate on how it might use the cookie-based information that tracked their visits to websites. The problem was how Google might implement the practice of "retargeting," which meant showing ads suggested by a user's browsing activities, as opposed to any purchases or other actions a user might have made on a site. According to press reports, Brin had previously been against the practice; Page had been in favor. After the DoubleClick purchase, though, it was clear that Google would indeed engage in retargeting, using the super-cookie it created in August 2008. But to distinguish its behavior from the many other companies that used similar techniques, it paired the new product with what it called a new privacy practice. As part of its interest-based advertising rollout in March 2009, Google introduced a feature that gave consumers the ability to see categories of ads they'd be shown—consumer electronics, golf equipment, etc.—and provided an opt-out escape hatch from such ads. (Presumably by seeing those categories, you'd know something about what Google knows about you, at least through your cookies.) There was even a way consumers could inform Google that they'd *like* to see certain kinds of ads regarding interests that an examination of their web peregrinations had yet to reveal. "We wanted to take a different twist on things, to marry relevant ads with our overall stance around privacy and transparency," says Neal Mohan. "Everybody understands that the great content we have on the Internet is supported by advertising, so if there's a way to make it so that the message is truly relevant, then we said let's do that. The simplest way was literally asking individual viewers what they would like to see."

Google took no chances before announcing its interest-based advertising initiative, seeking feedback from regulators and privacy advocates such as the Center for Democracy & Technology and the Electronic Frontier Foundation. "Five years ago, we would've just launched that and we would've said, 'Oh, let's see what happens,'" Schmidt said. As a result of the planning, the press treated Google's announcement relatively benignly, and even the voices on the blogosphere were subdued. The lack of protests startled Sergey Brin. "I was pretty skeptical it would have such a positive reaction from the press," he told Googlers at a TGIF. "These are the kinds of things the privacy nuts take advantage of to cause paranoia." When it was noted that one privacy group, Adbusters, was suggesting that users protest by automatically clicking every AdSense ad they encountered (thus messing with the validity of the business model), Page jokingly asked, "Don't we make money from clicks?"

"I don't think that's a good long-term strategy," Brin said drily.

"I like the idea of protests making us money," Page replied, a Cheshire-cat grin on his face.

As it turned out, Google didn't need the protests: its interest-based advertising did very well without them. In September 2010 Google executive Vic Gundotra said that the money Google was making from retargeting was "staggering." A month later, Google for the first time announced its revenues for overall display advertising: $2.5 billion a year and growing rapidly.

Google's effort to present interest-based advertising without igniting a conflagration turned out to be an increasingly rare privacy victory for the company. As people began to perceive Google less as a scrappy gang of wizards behind an uncanny search engine and more as an Information Age behemoth, they became less tolerant of all the personal information the company held about them.

Page and Brin continued to have mixed feelings about privacy. On the one hand, they were consumed with focusing Google's services on its users. It was almost a religious premise. But on the other, their view of what users wanted in terms of privacy differed from the views of advocates in the field. They also thought that the press often blew minor privacy glitches out of proportion. Larry Page would claim that which Google products were labeled as privacy invaders was utterly random. "There's a 10 percent chance of any one of them becoming an issue, and it's not possible to predict which ones," he says. "Oftentimes the thing that people are upset about isn't the actual thing they should be upset about. But somebody came up with clever language, like 'It's spooky,' and then that got quoted everywhere, and then *everybody* was saying, 'Oh, it's spooky.' Based on my experience with these kinds of things, it has much more to do with what the first headline says than something where you actually have a lot of control."

This was not to say that Google did not spend a massive amount of time and energy thinking about privacy and implementing safeguards. Under Nicole Wong's guidance, Google created a small infrastructure of privacy monitors. In addition to Jane Horvath, Google hired Microsoft's former privacy czar Peter Fleischer, posting him to Paris to deal with the exacting standards of the European Union. With many products, a Google lawyer would work with the engineering team to make privacy protection part of the design. The difficulties came because of Google's very nature: it was an Internet-based company driven to put all of the world's information into its data centers. In addition, Google's engineers were most often young people who had grown up with the net and had a different philosophy about what's private than the professional privacy wonks do.

The pressures often came to a head in the regular meetings of Google's Privacy Council, a group including policy lawyers and a smattering of executives who met regularly to discuss the privacy implications of products under development at Google. In October 2009, for instance, the discussion centered around a set of features to be added to Google Latitude, a product based on Google Maps that let users share their physical location with friends. Latitude itself was controversial, not so much because of its nature—several companies offered similar products, most with fewer safeguards than Google offered—but because it was Google doing the tracking. Only Google faced the question "You have all this information about me, and now you want to know where I *am*?"

The new features upped the ante. Google Latitude now could log a user's entire location history. Turning on the feature would provide a complete visual log of everywhere you went. When Steve Lee, the Latitude product manager, gave a demo, there was a collective sucking in of breath: overlaid on a Google Map were his peregrinations on October 5, just two days earlier. There was a thick red line from Mountain View to Berkeley, with balloon-shaped "bread crumbs" showing the check-in points when his GPS-equipped phone had pinged Google's servers every five minutes to report his location. Apparently, he had gone on a late-night trip. Little balloons appeared on the map with his location at five-minute intervals:

11:50 P.M. Charles Street, Mountain View . . . 11:55 Huff Street MV . . . 12:00 Shoreline Boulevard MV . . .

The program had a handful of key privacy safeguards, some of which had been added after meetings with the Electronic Frontier Foundation, the Center for Democracy & Technology, and a group devoted to preventing domestic abuse. The product was strictly opt in: Latitude users had to sign up for the program. When they did, they would receive regular email warnings specifying exactly what would happen if they signed up. Even after that, their computer screens would regularly sprout dialog boxes warning that location information was being stored. Only a dead person could miss the opportunities to opt out after she'd opted in. And you could delete the location information at any time.

"Is it a real delete?" Nicole Wong asked Lee, wanting to make sure that it was a case where the information would be gone not only from the user's perspective but from Google's data centers as well.

"We have a full expectation it will be a delete," Lee assured her, ideally within an hour after the request. If the data somehow lingered, a human being at Google would get a red flag to follow up and make sure that the information was gone. Nonetheless, Peter Fleischer was troubled. He considered a big part of his job to be pushing against the enthusiasm of engineers, who were commonly thrilled by new data-driven projects. As he listened to the description of the feature, he became worried less by what Lee was describing than by what regulators and the technically naïve population might think when the program was described to them. "What can we do to make this palatable for the much larger group of users who say, 'Google, where are you going?'" he asked. "Even Google Latitude itself, which is impeccable in privacy policy, is a lightning rod. I just find it really weird that we would keep this stuff for a bunch of teenagers who don't know what they're doing."

Lee explained that people, particularly younger users, *like* the ability to use metrics to track their location. The idea was to keep a virtual diary of where you had been, maybe retaining it for a lifetime. Young citizens of the digital age understood this. "People who are going to sign up for this are people who are comfortable to have their information shared and stored," he said.

Nicole Wong didn't get it. "If I'm a normal user, what am I using my location for?"

"It's *cool*," said Lee.

"I'm not into cool," she replied.

Ultimately, a few more minor privacy safeguards were built in, and Google launched the new feature—with virtually no critical outcry. The sanguine reaction seemed to back up Page's claim that you couldn't predict which products would blow up in your face.

One product in particular, however, had already emerged as Google's most troublesome, almost a symbol for the disconnect between Google's goals and the now-global concerns regarding Google's intrusiveness. That was Google Street View, an outgrowth of Google Maps. Its purpose was to show users what a location looked like as if they were teleported into the physical realm and plopped on the ground in front of the address they were searching for. The feature was of a piece with less commercial Google Earth additions such as Google Moon, Google Mars, and Google Sky. Unlike their earthbound counterparts, those couldn't be easily monetized—when virtually navigating the moon and the constellations, one is unlikely to be directed to the nearest dry cleaning or fast-food establishment—but they did fit into Google's bigger vision as the dominant repository of not just the world's information but the universe's.

As explained by Mike Jones, who had come to Google as an executive of Keyhole, the satellite mapping company Google had purchased in 2003, Street View, emerged as a consequence of the omnivorous hunger for geo-data. "From the day we came to Google, our constant petition was to get more money to buy more data, because we wanted to get the experience of seeing your home for everybody on the planet," he says. "They're going to want to fly in the middle of the Congo and see their house or their hut or something. And we needed to get pictures of that. We'd go to a GPS and say our goal is to gather this much imagery, and maybe take the crazy step of putting cameras on top of cars and taking pictures of all the roads."

Jones had the difficult task of defending such programs overseas. He was like Harvey Keitel's Cleaner character in *Pulp Fiction*, but instead of tidying up crime sites, his task was mediating the insults to international sensibilities caused by Google Maps and Google Earth. "I fly there not to smooth things over but to bring engineering knowledge to the debate," he says. Some countries, such as India, prohibited mapping services on the grounds of national security. China required a license, which Google could not obtain. (That drove Google into a partnership with a legally blessed local service.) In Europe, where privacy standards are much tougher than in America, privacy commissioners did not consider pictures taken in public places appropriate for the public Internet. In talks with a surveyor general or a privacy official—or even the president of India, at one point—Jones would counter objections by explaining that Google got its geodata from public places and commercial vendors. "If it's a security issue, you should already be scared, because we just pulled out our credit cards and bought the pictures—so certainly the bad guys could have bought the pictures, too," he'd tell them. Of course, since Google provided the pictures, the bad guys no longer had to purchase images—Larry and Sergey's company made them available instantly, for free. When that was pointed out to Jones, he would revert to the oft-invoked claim that every valuable technology has a potential for misuse.

Actually, the argument that Google was using only public information was no longer true. Google increasingly added its own sources of data to those it bought or accessed. In 2006, it introduced a system whereby users could annotate maps that were missing geographic data. (This feature was especially helpful in developing countries, where maps did not reflect back roads and newly cleared plots of land.) In 2009, Google combined information it gathered itself with terabytes of data bought from government and regional databases to create its own competitor to the big mapping providers Navteq and Tele Atlas. (Google had been concerned when Nokia bought Navteq for $8.1 billion in 2007 and that same year TomTom paid $4 billion for Tele Atlas, which had been providing Google with geodata.) And then there was Street View, which enabled digital drive-bys to anyone with a browser.

Google's designers thought that the program would be universally embraced; besides admiring their own homes, people would be able to identify destinations in advance. You would be able to identify a new hair salon or restaurant, or the location of a dinner party before you left your driveway, saving time and anxiety. Or you could simply do some sightseeing at a remote location from the comfort of your LCD screen. But privacy advocates who saw previews of the product were horrified. "They would say, 'Oh my God, that's terrible—you can actually see a person in Times Square!'" says Jones. He thought the objection was ridiculous. *So what if you're standing in Times Square?* As far as he was concerned, people who stepped out in public had implicitly given permission for people to look at them—and, by extension, for Google Street View to capture their images in the course of documenting the physical world. Still, some objections were difficult to shrug off. What about someone who was walking into a strip club—or simply walking *past* a strip club? What about a married person walking hand in hand with someone other than his or her spouse? What if Google StreetView showed—as spotters actually discovered—teenagers sunbathing in skimpy attire, hoodlums breaking into buildings, high school girls catfighting, and people mysteriously wearing horse heads? Did Google really want to become a global snoop?

Critics also lambasted Google for working on the project for more than a year before making it public less than eight months before its planned implementation. But Jones insists that Google's do-first-apologize-later ethic, here and elsewhere, was essential to the company's success. Ideas, he explained, were like babies—everything about their environment said they shouldn't exist. But they do. You can't dwell on problems too early, or they will swamp the virtues and you will decide not to do the project. That's why Google managed to do so many things when other companies held back. Google understood as well as other companies that there are millions of reasons not to do something. "We keep our mouths shut about it," he says. While the Street View project was in incubation, Google ignored the privacy issues.

Instead, Google concentrated on engineering problems. The team drove a car around Mountain View, then around the Bay Area, each time tweaking the technology. Then it adapted more cars, each time improving the ability to capture images, link them together, anchor them to geographic coordinates. Only after it went through three kinds of cameras, four kinds of GPS devices, and four separate iterations of the system itself did the team submit the project for approval. It was no longer a baby.

Over the first year of Street View, Google belatedly installed the privacy features that critics demanded. The revamped version could algorithmically detect faces and license plates, blurring them so they would not be identified. (Sometimes the algorithm was overly ambitious. "There are horses where the horses' faces are blurred out and stuff like that," says Jones.) In addition, Google allowed people to demand redactions if the photos made them identifiable. Google would comply, no questions asked.

But there was no way that Google would stop Street View altogether, as some critics demanded. The project was a key component in the company's bigger information picture. What's more, Microsoft had its own mirror world, its own fleet of camera-equipped cars cruising the streets, its own low-flying air force to capture three-quarters views of buildings for a SimCity-style picture of the real world. But Google, the market leader, got the attention—and the traffic.

But when something went wrong, the reaction was explosive. In early 2010, Google made a horrifying discovery: the cars driving around the streets of the world taking pictures for Street View had "unintentionally" sucked up confidential information—known as "payload data"—from wireless Internet transmitters in the areas they cruised. Any Wi-Fi device not protected by passwords seemed to have been vulnerable. It appeared to be a form of surveillance, snatching whatever information people were sending and receiving from the net during the brief time when the cars were passing.

After several weeks of war room analysis and furious fire dousing by its communications staff, Google presented the situation as a regrettable miscue, claiming that the problem had arisen from code an engineer had written for an experimental Wi-Fi project. The engineer's program, Google said, "sampled all categories of publicly broadcast Wi-Fi data." (That meant even private information on networks not protected by passwords, and in fact Google wound up collecting people's emails, financial information, and other personal information.) Apparently, the engineers working on the Wi-Fi Street View project noticed that someone had written useful code and implemented it without understanding its intrusive nature. One Google lawyer later referred to the original engineer as a "rogue"; in any case, he was operating without instructions from any manager or director. Just as Googlers do all the time.

While the Street View team was creating a system to log the active Wi-Fi networks in the areas it mapped (to increase the accuracy of its data), it made use of that rogue code, presumably unaware that it would enable the Street View vehicles to perform surveillance activities. The mystery was why no one at Google noticed that Street View servers were loaded with gigabytes of data that had no business being there. In any case, collecting the information was a potential violation of data security laws, and the transgression triggered investigations in several countries and states.

The incident exposed the risks that arise when tolerance of a company's information retention policies is at the limit. Even its tiniest mistakes called attention to the larger truth—that Google had a frightening amount of information under its control. And when something major went wrong, like the Street View Wi-Fi debacle, it eroded Google's main line of defense when justifying its stewardship of the world's information: trust.

Google's next antitrust crisis after DoubleClick began in February 2008, as a consequence of a hostile bid made by Microsoft to take over Yahoo. Microsoft's $48 billion offer included an aggressive 62 percent premium over the struggling target's share price, and so observers assumed that the merger was sealed. But Yahoo's chairman, Jerry Yang, resisted, and his efforts to thwart the takeover were aided by Google. Within days of the offer, Eric Schmidt called Yang and began talking about a partnership that would help the weaker company. Google also began contacting legislators and regulators about the antitrust implications of the Microsoft deal, a rather odd stance considering Google's previous insistence that the search marketplace had no lock-in and thus wasn't a valid candidate for antitrust action. Later that spring Google took a more concrete step, hammering out an arrangement whereby some of Yahoo's search customers would be served Google's ads. Since Google's ad system was much more productive, this would result in bigger profits for Yahoo, and its shareholders would presumably be more sanguine about the missed opportunity to cash in on the Microsoft deal.

Brin explained at a TGIF that in addition to the obvious desire to keep its two top rivals from combining forces, there was a personal motivation for the arrangement. "It was tough for me and Larry to turn away Yahoo," Brin said. "They encouraged us to start this company." (Of course, if Yang and David Filo had bought Google instead of licensing it and helping it dominate the search field, Yahoo might not have been in its current predicament.)

Google felt that it had cleverly dealt with the threat of its two closest competitors joining forces. But the search giant's deal with the number two search engine put it back into the sights of the Department of Justice. Now it was Microsoft prodding the DOJ to look into search. Microsoft's deep and hard-won experience with the DOJ made it a much more skillful player than the kids from Mountain View.

Microsoft began a regular series of briefings in D.C. described in the press as "screw Google" meetings. A spokesperson resisted that appellation but conceded that Microsoft was working to "educate policy makers and regulators" about the competitive landscape. Back in the 1990s, Microsoft's corporate psyche had been brutally battered by its antitrust ordeal, with Bill Gates himself humiliated by a painful deposition that could have been worse only if there were a YouTube at the time to expose the video on an even wider scale. It used to go without saying that Gates wouldn't wish such an experience on his worst enemy. Now Gates was doing just that. Of course, he would no doubt resist the comparison between his company's undeserved antitrust debacle and Google's just deserts. Google lawyers would agree that the two cases were dramatically different, but they would contend that Microsoft had been unlawfully anticompetitive in a way Google had never been.

Microsoft hired the heavyweight firm Cadwalader, Wickersham & Taft to push its anti-Google agenda to the DOJ. The key was whether the department, in the waning days of the Bush administration, would budge from its lax antitrust policy. It could go either way, depending on whether Justice accepted Google's argument that search advertising was only a part of the galaxy of online ads or even the entire universe of advertising. There was a troubling early indicator when the questions the DOJ formally submitted to Google seemed to focus skeptically on that question and the terms of the Yahoo deal. And in September there came a development that was genuinely alarming from Google's perspective. The DOJ contracted outside help, in the form of Sanford "Sandy" Litvack. The Chicago-based attorney was not a reflective academic schooled in subtleties of the law as much as he was a sharp-elbowed antitrust litigator. "When they say, 'We're going to a courtroom attorney to help,' it's not a happy day," noted Google's counsel Dana Wagner.

Indeed, not only did Litvack take a dim view of Google's attempts to partner with Yahoo, but he prepared a broader complaint against the company. On the morning of November 5, 2008, the DOJ informed Google that later in the day it would charge the company with a violation of Section 1 of the Sherman Antitrust Act, calling the Yahoo agreement a restraint of free trade. Worse, the complaint would also accuse Google of violating Section 2 of the act, an illegal attempt to monopolize. Clearly, Litvack didn't accept Google's invitation to view its business as a small percentage of the advertising world. Instead he saw the company as the 80 percent dominator of search ads, the venue that every advertiser was forced to patronize. "We would have ended up also alleging that Google had a monopoly and that [the Yahoo deal] would have furthered their monopoly," Litvack later explained to *American Law Daily*.

Google ruled a monopoly? The company could not let that stand. "I really did believe it was possible for us to structure an arm's-length deal that met the antitrust terms," Schmidt later said. "I tried hard. I talked to Sandy. It was an example where we're running against other people's agendas and their worldviews." Google quickly terminated its agreement with Yahoo, informing the government only three hours before the feds filed a complaint that would have made "monopolist" a keyword when people searched for Google's company information.

With no agreement to rule on, the government stopped its investigation. Google might have dodged a bullet but thereafter had to face the fact that the antitrust gun was loaded and pointed straight at Mountain View.

(The gambit looked even worse the next winter. With nowhere else to turn—and the economic downturn making the company a less attractive takeover target—Yahoo's new CEO, former Autodesk head Carol Bartz, arranged to turn over Yahoo's search business to Microsoft for a bargain price of a billion dollars. Microsoft got the main prize it had sought in the merger for barely 3 percent of its original offer.)

Google had hopes that the gun might be holstered when Barack Obama took office. "I really think this is going to be the first Internet administration," said Google lobbyist Pablo Chavez soon after Obama's election. Of course the new president couldn't intervene in Google's behalf in a legal case—but somehow the fact that Google and Obama vibrated at the same frequency seemed to portend well. "I spent a fair amount of time with him during the campaign," said Schmidt of the new president. "He certainly understands what Google searches are, he understands our advertising model, he understands the structure of the company. He's clearly a Google user."

But another shock disabused Google of its hopes. Back in the spring of 2008, Google's lawyers had been too concerned with the Yahoo agreement to notice some remarks made at an unheralded panel discussion hosted by the American Antitrust Institute. One of the speakers was Christine Varney, who had worked on Netscape's behalf during the 1990s, successfully pushing the government to file its antitrust suit against Microsoft. Now she described Microsoft as "so last century." The current problem was Google, which "has acquired a monopoly in Internet marketing." Though the company may have obtained its dominance lawfully, she continued, Google is "quickly gathering market power for what I could call an online computing environment in the clouds. When all our enterprises move to computing in the clouds and there is a single firm that is offering a comprehensive solution, you are going to see the same repeat of Microsoft."

Those words didn't matter when they came from just another lawyer in the high-tech policy community. But in February 2009, President Obama appointed Varney as the head of the DOJ's Antitrust Division. Suddenly the safety was off, the loaded gun pointed at Mountain View.

Virtually every expansion Google attempted from that point on—every acquisition and deal, every expansion into new territory—would require a painstaking government review, risking another decision like Sandy

Litvack's. Google even found itself fending off a theory that by virtue of having such a huge search market share, Google's algorithmic decisions in determining search results should be subject to government approval to ensure that the company did not play favorites. Google tried to launch an offensive, including a tour of media outlets, government offices, and legislative confabs where Dana Wagner would present a slide show. (Opponents called it "the we-are-not-evil road show.") At any turn, the Department of Justice might invite itself to weigh in on Google's activities. And that included the project that, of all Google's post-basic web searches, might have been the one closest to its heart.

3

"That horrid Google
on the prowl!!!"

Larry Page and Sergey Brin were not literary types; they breathed Internet air, not the musty aura of paper and printer's ink. ("Why don't you just write some articles?" Brin asked me after an interview. "Or release this a chapter at a time?") But they did understand the value locked inside the approximately 33 million book titles printed since Johannes Gutenberg invented the printing press. Even before Google was Google, in fact, Larry Page had been thinking about that knowledge as an adjunct to the web, humanity's outpourings corralled into a single database that, of course, you could search. It was no coincidence that he and Brin had been affiliated with a government-funded project in grad school called the National Science Digital Library. "We tried to get book search going at Stanford," Page would later say. "It would actually be really nice to be able to search all books," he'd say to his professors. "Why don't we do that?" It seemed obvious to him, but the professors deflected his suggestion. "They had other ideas about what that project was really about," he says. "If you asked anybody about it, they would immediately decide it was impossible."

As always, Page was disappointed at the phenomenon of intelligent people rejecting ambitious schemes on the flimsy grounds of impossibility. He understood that skeptics were motivated by fear and inertia, but he still found such behavior unforgivable. He knew that digital technologies had changed the physics of the possible. Given that current technology would soon be cheaper, more and more powerful, and able to handle vast amounts of data, it was a matter of logic to see that a project to digitize and search through the world's books was doable. It might be *expensive*, but it was silly to call it impossible. And it might not be expensive at all.

Page tried to calculate whether such an enterprise could be addressed with a trillion dollars, a billion dollars, or merely millions of dollars. When he finished his calculation—how many books, how much it would cost to scan all of them, how much storage the digital files would require—he became convinced that the costs were reasonable. But even his virtual spreadsheets didn't dissolve the skepticism of those with whom he shared his scheme. "I'd run through the numbers with people and they wouldn't believe them, and they'd say, 'That really won't work,'" he later said. "So eventually I just did it. I did the work. You can't argue with facts. *You're not entitled to your own facts.*"

It would have been great, he later thought, to begin the project in 1999. But Google's early funds were committed to building infrastructure and hiring engineers—the opportunity costs were too high to digitize the world's books. But Page didn't let go of the idea. In 2002, after AdWords had helped resolve Google's profit problems, he thought it was time to act.

At the time Google was working on a doomed project called Google Catalogs, where Google scanned actual dead-tree product catalogs to help users find products. There were scanners around the office. Talking to Marissa Mayer one night, Page wondered whether it would make sense to use similar scanners for books. Maybe Google should buy a copy of every book in the world, remove the pages, scan them, and then maybe rebind them and sell them to recover the costs. He had Mayer look into the idea, and she quickly found that rebinding would be too costly. The better idea was "nondestructive scanning." It would require more care when handling the books, but it seemed more economical. For one thing, the books could be sold afterward. Or they could simply be borrowed in the first place. "We came up with all these numbers," says Mayer. "We were emailing them around, the right cost per hour, the right number of pages per hour—debate, debate, debate. After one thread hinged on how many pages an hour we could do, we decided we should just scan one."

They set up a makeshift book scanning device. They tried several sizes of books, the first one, appropriately enough, being *The Google Book*, an illustrated children's story by V. C. Vickers. (The "Google" in the title was an odd creature with aspects of mammal, reptile, and fish.) They then tested a photo book, *Ancient Forests* by David Middleton; a dense text, *Algo-*

rithms in C by Robert Sedgewick; and a general-interest book, *Startup,* by Jerry Kaplan. Marissa would turn the page, and Larry would click the shutter of a digital camera.

Neither was aware of it, but the final couplet of the first book Google ever scanned, written as a lark by Bank of England governor Vincent Cartwright Vickers (1879–1939) almost a century earlier, would turn out to be painfully ironic.

> *The sun is setting—*
> *Can't you hear*
> *A something in the distance*
>   *Howl!!?*
> *I wonder if it's—*
> *Yes!! It is*
> *That horrid Google*
> *On the prowl!!!*

The first few times around were kind of sloppy, because Marissa's thumb kept getting in the way. Larry would say, "Don't go too fast . . . don't go too slow." It had to be a rate that someone could maintain for a long time—this was going to *scale*, remember, to every book ever written. They finally used a metronome to synchronize their actions. After some practice, they found that they could capture a 300-page book such as *Startup* in about forty-two minutes, faster than they expected. Then they ran optical character recognition (OCR) software on the images and began searching inside the book. Page would open the book to a random page and say, "This word—can you find it?" Mayer would do a search to see if she could. It worked. Presumably, a dedicated machine could work faster, and that would make it possible to capture millions of books. How many books were ever printed? Around 30 million? Even if the cost was $10 a book, the price tag would only be $300 million. That didn't sound like too much money for the world's most valuable font of knowledge.

Besides, this wasn't a project to pursue simply because of return on investment. Just as Google had changed the world by making the most obscure items on the web spring up instantly for those who needed them, it could do the same with books. A user could instantly access a unique fact, a one-of-a-kind insight, or a breathtaking passage otherwise buried in the stacks of some dusty book in a distant library. Research tasks that had formerly taken months could be completed between breakfast and lunch.

Scanning the world's books would create a new era in the history of information. Who could object to such a noble mission?

Page determined that Google would do it, get every book ever written in its search engine. Brin was all for it. Eric Schmidt needed to hear more. "Eric wasn't skeptical but listening, trying to make sense," says Megan Smith, the biz-dev person who became involved in the project. "If something passed his directional sniff test, if there was a business reason behind an idea, he was open to things." In this case, Schmidt became convinced that capturing books in Google's search index would allow Google to deliver important information that was currently lacking—and that eventually the investment would be recovered by increased traffic and more clicking on ads. He was also blown away when Page told him that he'd figured out the whole thing when he was at Stanford. "What does that tell you?" Schmidt would say to a reporter in 2005. "Genius? I think so."

The project was dubbed Ocean, to reflect the vast informational sea they would be exploring. Marissa Mayer called it "our moon shot."

Instead of buying current scanners, Google determined that for its monster task it needed one that was superior to current designs. So it commissioned some of its best wizards to build a machine that, presumably, would work much more accurately and at a somewhat brisker rate than Marissa Mayer turning pages one by one. Though Google wasn't known for actually building machines, its data center needs had generated a lot of engineering expertise in that area: remember, it was the world's biggest manufacturer of computer servers.

One of the difficulties in book scanning rested in producing high-quality images from the printed page, so that OCR software could accurately translate the shapes of the letters on the page to computer-readable text. The problem was that, on their own, books did not sit flat on the platform: they presented a 3-D problem requiring a 2-D solution. The usual workarounds—flattening the book by pressing it on the glass or removing the binding—would not work since they were time-consuming and damaged the books. If its patents are any indication, Google's engineers invented a system that could process the 3-D images. Its system involved two special cameras with multiple stereographic lenses, each capturing the image of a page on its opposite end, and a third, infrared camera hovering above the page. By the combination of these cameras, Google's scanners could capture a three-dimensional picture of an open book. Using sophisticated algorithms that detected their own versions of signals in Google's search-ranking algorithms, the software would determine the "groove" in the book that delineated its spine, and thus could separate the images on the facing pages and render them as if they were flat.

Google found that the state of robotics did not allow for a speedy process by which a machine could turn the pages itself without shredding them. So despite the fact that hiring a wave of human laborers did not conform to Google's scaling philosophy, humans it was. Every so often, one literally would see the fingerprints of the Google worker in charge of the task on the scans.

To test the machines, Google needed lots of books of all kinds, different sizes and shapes, so it sent a biz-dev person to a used-book conference in Arizona with a budget to buy as many books as she could. She'd talk to people selling in bulk, negotiate a discount, and buy their whole collection, having them deliver the goods to a semitruck she'd rented. When the truck was filled, the driver drove it to Mountain View and discharged his cargo into the top secret scanning facility.

Another team worked on the user interface of the books product. Google's search quality experts figured out which data could be used to determine relevance in book search, including metadata, information not included in the content of the book itself, such as facts about the book. Google used reference works and databases to determine facts. Had the book been a best seller? How recently was it published? How often was it cited by other works? Other signals could come from the web. Were people on the web talking about it? Was the author famous? Was the book mentioned on prominent websites about its subject matter? You could tell a lot about the book's importance by seeing how often a book was referred to by other sources and then determining the importance of those sources.

Eventually Google decided to treat every sheet of every book as a separate document, adding signals such as font size, page density, and relevance to the linked table of contents and index. "It's just like web ranking," says Frances Haugen, who worked on a later version of the Book Search interface. "But we haven't found the silver bullet—we haven't found a Page-Rank for books."

While Google was tackling the mechanical and digital part of the process, its leaders were plotting a means of procuring the actual books. Of the estimated 33 million books that had been published, Google wanted all of them. (Later, using a more relaxed definition of what a book was, the company estimated that there were 129,864,880 different books in the world in all languages, as of August 2010.) Page, Brin, Schmidt, and David Drummond were talking about Book Search one day in the Googleplex, and they determined that the richest source would be the Library of Congress. They promptly asked their adviser Al Gore to contact the director of the library, James Billington.

Within days, Brin, Page, and Drummond were on a red-eye to Washington, D.C., to make a morning meeting with Billington. Drummond had been saying how important it was to appear presentable and had somewhat of a comeuppance when United Airlines misplaced his luggage. He had to wait until Nordstrom in Pentagon City opened to buy a suit. "They got me in and out in twenty minutes," he says. Brin, whose sport jacket had survived the flight, bought a tie in the hotel gift shop. Page went without a jacket. Along with Gore, the trio met with Billington and his associates and proposed to scan the entire Library of Congress or whatever the library would let them scan, for free. Billington mentioned the usual procedures for procurement, but Page noted that the government wouldn't be procuring anything, since Google would be giving its services away, even moving its own scanners in to do the job. Billington said okay.

But he spoke too soon. Part of the Library of Congress's operation was the Copyright Office, and its head, Marybeth Peters, saw red flags. "She wasn't quite as sure on the copyright issues," says Drummond, "so they wound up not moving forward aggressively." (Google eventually scanned only a small portion of the library's holdings.)

Google turned instead to university and public libraries. The first one it approached was the University of Michigan, Larry Page's alma mater. During a fall visit, Page sat next to the university president, Mary Sue Coleman, at a football game. He told her that Google would like to digitize all 7 million volumes in the university's libraries.

Michigan had already begun digitizing some of its work. "It was a project that our librarians predicted would take one thousand years," Coleman later said in a speech. "Larry said that Google would do it in six." It was an attractive proposition to Michigan; Google would assume the entire cost, and Michigan would get a copy of the digital archive. From Michigan's point of view, it was a step that had to be taken, because the future of books was online. "Twenty years from now, interaction with a physical book will be rare," says the university's associate librarian, John Wilkin. "Most of that interaction will be in the study of books as artifacts."

The team began working with Michigan's library staff—and Michigan's lawyers. Now that the project was proceeding, Google had to grapple with the fact that the majority of books were protected under copyright from unauthorized scanning and distribution. Page was envisioning a use that no one in the Gutenberg age, or the founding fathers, who specified a copyright regime in the Constitution, had anticipated. What Google was doing felt as though it was respectful to the rights of authors and publishers—it allowed users the ability to search just as they could in a library. The only difference was that Google was granting users unprecedented powers to do so.

The lead lawyer at Google on this issue was Alex Macgillivray, known to Googlers as AMac. His background included trade-secret defense work for Wilson Sonsini Goodrich & Rosati, representing law firm clients like Napster. "Google's leadership doesn't care terribly much about precedent or law," he says. "They're trying to get a product launched, in this case trying to make books easier to find." When charting Google's copyright standing for Ocean, Macgillivray did a quasi-mathematical plotting of the various interests. He drew up a graph of user benefits and legal risks. "There are places along the edge of the graph which as a lawyer I would prefer not to be, but I'm fine anywhere in the middle," he later said. "I just didn't want to be suboptimal."

In this case, Google was at the edge of the graph. It felt strongly that the very act of scanning and copying the books lent to it by the libraries was protected under the fair use provisions of the law. But a strict reading of the law didn't bear out that interpretation. "The basic question was whether you can scan and index stuff without a rights holder's permission," Macgillivray says. "The entire operation was based on our argument of fair use." The other question was whether Google had the rights to show short excerpts from the work (as it does with web pages in search) called snippets, but "the snippets are gravy," AMac would say. In Google's view, there was no reason for Book Search to be treated differently from web search.

Macgillivray held a couple of important precedents in his back pocket. The most important was a suit filed by the Bill Graham Archives—the holder of intellectual property of the company owned by the late rock promoter—in an attempt to stop a book about the Grateful Dead called *What a Long Strange Trip It's Been.* The book featured a timeline of the famed rock band, illustrated at various milestones by thumbnail images of concert tickets and posters. The images weren't being used for their original purpose, so it wasn't like a poster hung on a dorm room wall or a concert ticket sold as an entry pass or even a souvenir. The legal term for this was a transformative use—you were using material as a basis to create something new. To Macgillivray, the suit involved the exact question that Google might be sued on: could an unauthorized reproduction of copyrighted material be made for a transformative use? The publisher won in district court and prevailed on appeal. Macgillivray kept a copy of the judge's decision in his office.

The University of Michigan agreed with Google's views on copyright. But the other partners Google began talking to weren't so comfortable. In order to get a book into its index, Google made a digital copy of it, and most legal minds interpreted that action as infringement. "Harvard didn't want to do in copyright, they only wanted to do the public domain," says Drummond. (Public domain books are those published before 1923, whose copyright has expired.) "The New York Public Library was the same thing." Oxford University presented its own problem. Drummond had a great time when he went there to negotiate the deal—the head librarian gave him a grand tour of the Bodleian Library and treated Drummond and the Googlers accompanying him to a rare trip to the roof, where all of Oxford lay in front of them. But the deal they struck was limited to books out of copyright, that is, in the public domain.

Google began its scanning in near-total stealth. There was a cloak-and-dagger element to the procedure, soured by a clandestine taint, like ducking out of a 1950s nightclub to smoke weed. Google would rent space in a town near a library. Several times a week, university library employees would gather and pack the hundreds of books to be scanned in the next few days. Google employees would load them into trucks, whisk them away, and return them unharmed a few days later. There were hundreds of such employees, a shadow workforce spending its days moving books onto and off the scanning platens.

Maybe the care that Google took to hide its activity was an early indicator of trouble to come. If the world would so eagerly welcome the fruits of Ocean, what was the need for such stealth? The secrecy was yet another expression of the paradox of a company that sometimes embraced transparency and other times seemed to model itself on the NSA. In other areas, Google had put its investments into the public domain, like the open-source Android and Chrome operating systems. And as far as user information was concerned, Google made it easy for people not to become locked into using its products. It even had an initiative called the Data Liberation Front to make sure that users could easily move information they created with Google documents off Google's servers.

It would seem that book scanning was a good candidate for similar transparency. If Google had a more efficient way to scan books, sharing the improved techniques could benefit the company in the long run—inevitably, much of the output would find its way onto the web, bolstering

Google's indexes. But in this case, paranoia and a focus on short-term gain kept the machines under wraps. "We've done a ton of work to try to make those machines an order of magnitude better," AMac said. "That does give us an advantage in terms of scanning rate and cost, and we actually want to have that advantage for a while." Page himself dismissed the argument that sharing Google's scanner technology would help the business in the long run, as well as benefit society. "If you don't have a reason to talk about it, why talk about it?" he responded. "You're running a business, and you have to weigh [exposure] against the downside, which can be significant."

Google got a shock in October 2003, when it learned it was not the only company doing a massive book-scanning project. That was the day Amazon.com introduced its "Search Inside the Book" feature. Amazon head Jeff Bezos had ordered the project to see if searching inside books would increase sales. (It did, by about 9 percent.) He had hired Udi Manber (who would later go to Google) to become "chief algorithms officer" and lead the project. Amazon began scanning books, and after the first 10,000, Manber's engineers began working on ranking algorithms. The results didn't prove satisfactory until Amazon had around 120,000 books in its indexes (many of its books were scanned in centers Amazon created in India and the Philippines), and putting in a keyword would pull out an apt passage in this virtual library. At that point, says Manber, "it was really eye-opening. It was, *wow*." Just after the prototype was operative, Manber had been scheduled to present a report to management on the history of newspapers. Normally, you would Google the subject. But in this case he typed "history of newspapers" into his prototype and was instantly ushered inside a book that explained how newspapers had started in English coffeehouses in port cities, where sailors exchanged stories of their travels. "I bought the book," says Manber. Bezos would later declare that his goal was to offer consumers the chance to buy any book ever written, in digital form.

Google professed to welcome Amazon's efforts. "I think it's an important part of the evolution of the Internet," said Brin. Cognizant of Google's own efforts, he observed that Amazon's project was just an initial step in book search. Then he noted something that would prove more prophetic than he intended: "I do feel that the Internet needs to sort out copyright issues." (Amazon, which had signed contracts with hundreds of publishers, had no such problems.) Later, Googlers would say that Amazon's entry had been beneficial to Google because it introduced the concept of massive scanning in a less threatening manner than their project would. "It was like they disturbed The Force before we did," says Megan Smith.

Nonetheless, Amazon forced an alteration in Google's plans. Smith had already been working on a project similar to Amazon's. It was a parallel path to the libraries project, involving books currently on sale that would be scanned with the blessing of publishers. As with Amazon's plan, the publishers would allow their books to be scanned with snippets of the text exposed to users as teasers for eventual purchase. Google would provide links to online bookstores where people could instantly buy the books that showed up in search results. "We had been working on this project for a while, and so we were a little bit nervous that the publishers would sign exclusive deals with Amazon without knowing about how search was a marketing opportunity for them," Smith later recalled. "Also, we needed their guidance and to know what they thought of our crazy project." A team from Google, including Smith, her biz-dev colleague Cathy Gordon, David Drummond, and Susan Wojcicki hurriedly arranged meetings with top publishers in New York City, creating a slide deck on the flight.

The publishers welcomed Google, in part because they were intrigued by the edgy new company. "The leverage that our name had, even in 2003, was astonishing," says Cathy Gordon. "Two years before, it was 'Who's Google, and what are you doing?' But by that point everyone was interested. They thought, 'This Google thing is kind of cool.'" The publishers welcomed Google for another reason: they were concerned about ceding too much power to Amazon. "By the time we started to talk to the publishers, they could tell us everything that Amazon had ticked them off about, which was really useful, because we had no product and no infrastructure then," says Gordon. Google was more than happy to present itself as an alternative, one that presented no threat to publishers. Google wasn't competing with physical bookstores but was simply going to alert search customers to books they might want to purchase. Google even agreed to show less content from the books it scanned as part of what it now called Google Print.

The meetings seemed to go smoothly, at least until a power failure hit New York City and the entire northeastern United States on the second afternoon of what was to be two days of back-to-back sessions. (Stuck in the city, the group wound up spending the last night at Cathy Gordon's mother's house.) But not all of the publishers found Google charming. Jack Romanos, then CEO of Simon & Schuster, later complained to *New York*'s John Heilemann about Google's "innocent arrogance" and "holier-than-thou" attitude. "One minute they're pretending to be all idealistic, talking about how they're only in this to expand the world's knowledge, and the next they're telling you that you're going to have to do it their way or no way at all."

In truth, Google was not dealing with the publishers in an upfront manner. During those first meetings, the Googlers did not even hint at their plans to digitize and index the vast holdings of huge libraries, regardless of copyright status. 'We knew that this was going to be an issue," says Gordon. "But Google does not disclose these kinds of things early. Ever."

So when Google launched its Google Print in October 2004 at the Frankfurt Book Festival (Ocean was only the code name), with commitments from fifteen publishers including Penguin, Warner Books, and Houghton Mifflin, there was no mention of the library project, even though the scanning facilities were humming away, truckloads of books shuffling out of and back to various libraries every week. Two months later, on December 14, Google announced its separate deal to scan the libraries of Stanford, Harvard, the University of Michigan, Oxford University, and the New York Public Library. The project involved an estimated 10 million books. Google would give each library digital copies of the scans and use its own copies to store the contents of the books in its search indexes, along with the other books that it was scanning as part of the Google Print program, which dealt in authorized digital copies of books in print. (Eventually, Google's Universal Search feature would display relevant book results in general searches.)

Page was rhapsodic when explaining the deal. At Stanford, he said, he had heard there were 132 miles of books in the libraries, but you couldn't find what was in them. Google's project might drive people to go to libraries more often, because now they would know what was in there. "That's the really big deal," he said. "A lot of people thought that this was impossible."

As for Google's edge in collecting this corpus, he said, "We're not trying to lock up anything. We're looking to have good competition."

The fine print in Google Libraries was a little complicated. Different libraries had different comfort levels about what Google could scan. As far as the user was concerned, it could be baffling, too. Different books had different degrees of accessibility. Public domain books were available in their entirety. With in-print books licensed in the Google Print program, users could see a limited number of sample pages of the book. For "orphan books" from libraries, Google was most conservative, showing a "snippet view" with only the passage that contained the search term. (An orphan book was still in copyright but out of print, and the copyright holder could not be easily contacted.) In all cases, Google showed bibliographic information and, when possible, information on where to find or buy the physical book.

With the announcement of the library project, the publishing industry unleashed its suppressed fury toward the philistines who wanted to transform their treasures into bits. It was one thing to do what Amazon had done, digitizing books as a prelude to sales. Google Print had been seen in the same light. But now Google was making a copy of every book—without permission—to build a library of its own, without paying publishers and authors for the privilege. By what authority? the publishers wanted to know. And what if someone hacked into Google's archive and stole the contents, distributing them free all over the Internet? There would no longer be any need for anyone to buy a book!

Marissa Mayer thought that bad timing contributed to the troubles. The Google Libraries announcement came out on December 14 to sync with a board of trustees meeting at Harvard. "We missed an opportunity because all the Internet users were Christmas shopping so no one's reading about this amazing thing to bring books online," she later said. That year Mayer returned to her hometown in Wisconsin for the holidays and was disappointed that even her parents hadn't gotten the message and asked her what this troublesome books thing was about. "What do you mean?" she said. "We're putting all the world's books online, and you'll be able to search them from anywhere!" It wasn't until after the New Year that people began to hear about it, and by that time the publishers had seized the stage.

Indeed, representatives of publishers and authors objected to the suit, essentially charging that Google was overstepping boundaries. Instead of a boon to society, they charged, Google's program was a literary landgrab launched by a powerful corporation that would mine the world's knowledge for profit and cheat rightful owners of the bounty. The war of words over the war on books proceeded for the next few months, with neither side backing down. On October 19, 2005, several publishers, under the auspices of the Association of American Publishers, filed suit against Google's "massive, wholesale and systematic copying of entire books still protected by copyright." The previous month, the Authors Guild had filed a class-action suit charging Google with infringement. The two suits were combined by the court.

Critics of the plan seized on the fact that Google Book Search was scanning the books without permission of authors or publishers. ("To reflect the product's evolution," Google said, it had changed the name from Google Print, encompassing both the publisher and the library program.) Google, the lawsuit argued, was within its rights to scan when the book was in the public domain. But for all other books, the process should be "opt in," meaning that Google should scan no book under copyright unless the rights holder specifically authorized it. Google noted that such a plan would essentially gut its book archive. The vast majority of printed books, around 80 percent, had been published since 1923. Perhaps 5 percent of those were currently in print, and Google was working with publishers to get permission to scan those for Book Search. But almost three-quarters of all books were still in copyright but not in print, and in many cases it was difficult if not impossible to find the rights holder. (When explaining this situation, digital law expert Lawrence Lessig claimed that of the 10,027 books published in 1930, only 174 are still in print. The remaining 9,853 books cannot be reprinted or even copied without the permission of the copyright holder.) Such a process certainly didn't scale.

Google also considered the objections of the Authors Guild, which claimed to represent out-of-print authors, as illogical—writers in that category, Google argued, would only be helped by its efforts. "The fact that these books were out of print meant that there was no revenue accruing to an author," says Google's Cathy Gordon. "The only way anyone could get such a book was to buy it on the secondhand market."

Google's chief economist, Hal Varian, wrote an economic analysis of the Google Libraries in 2006. Not surprisingly, he found that it was "legally sound and economically sensible." He warned that an opt-in model would be destructive, ruining the value to society of a complete database of book contents.

Imagine receiving a letter that told you you had inherited the copyright on great-uncle Fred's autobiography. If you signed and returned the enclosed legal document, the book would be added to the Google Library index. What would the response rate be? The response rate would probably be about the same as to those letters telling you you have won the Nigerian lottery.

The law was illogical, and it was as if Google felt that executing a commonsense plan would move the world to the proper view of things. "I anticipated it would be controversial," says Page of the project. "I think we knew that there would be a lot of interesting issues and the way the laws are structured isn't really sensible, especially with regard to orphan works. If you were to sit down to write the law knowing what you know now, there's no way you'd ever write it like that."

Google's Book Search team included Random House's former vice president of new media, Adam Smith, as the managing director. He worked with an engineer named Dan Clancy, who had formerly managed the information services for the NASA Ames Research Center, just down the highway from the Googleplex. Their team supervised the technical work to produce the product but also oversaw what seemed like a public relations war to convince the world that Google's motives were pure and that if a lawsuit were to kill this beneficial project, the world would suffer.

They had help from various luminaries in the digital realm. A month after the lawsuit was filed, some of the players participated in a public debate at the New York Public Library. Google's David Drummond was supported by cyberlaw superstar Lawrence Lessig in defending Book Search, while lawyers for the publishers and Authors Guild executive director Paul Aiken spoke against it. Lessig was persuasive in stating the case for the utility of an opt-out system. He had earlier written of the transformation of property law after the emergence of the aviation industry. Originally, the boundaries of one's property were thought to have extended skyward into the universe, and flying over a home owner's acreage was trespassing. Since it was impossible for an airline to secure permission over every single piece of property underneath its flight path, society saw fit to recognize a different boundary. The same should apply to books—inclusion in a search engine in a way that doesn't erode the value of the book was so important to society that it *had* to be legal.

The lawyers for the publishers and authors, while conceding that there were benefits to a universal book search—including purchases coming from increased exposure to a book—preferred to focus on the narrow fact that the law forbade making an unauthorized single copy of a book during the scanning process. But the underlying impetus for the suit was the conviction that in a multimillion-dollar enterprise such as Book Search it was unconscionable for authors and publishers not to be paid. After the debate, Aiken laid out the essence of his group's rationale to an Authors Guild member who told him that he'd *like* his books discoverable by Google. "Don't you understand?" Aiken said. "These people in Silicon Valley are *billionaires*, and they're making money off you!"

Google, so used to being seen as a scrappy underdog, had underestimated the fact that in this instance, it was seen as a digital bully pounding on the vulnerable weaklings of an industry in decline. "Google saw us as patsies," said Pat Schroeder, a former congresswoman who headed the Association of American Publishers. "They assumed we'd never sue. But they were wrong—so here we are and isn't it fun?"

To Page, it came down to whether Google's plan would help the world or not. For him the benefit provided by Book Search outweighed the legal niceties. "Do you really want the whole world not to have access to human knowledge as contained in books, because you really want opt out rather than opt in?" asked Page. "You've just got to think about that from a societal point of view." Page was shocked that people didn't get that. He chalked up a lot of the opposition's passion as phony—a negotiating tactic. "People want to get money out of us, or they want to get other things, so they're arguing a very untenable position."

Showdowns like these often concluded with a financial settlement, and many thought that the negotiating sessions between the parties would do just that. But things took an unusual turn relatively early in the process. Instead of the usual chest beating and ultimatums before the calculators were pulled out, a representative from the Writers Guild of America made a surprising proposal: instead of figuring out what Google had to offer the rights holders to pursue its current plan, what if Google took on an even more ambitious role—not just as an archivist for books, but as the designated digital bookstore for the millions of tomes otherwise unavailable? Such a scheme could be complemented by a giant registry of authors and rights holders to determine who should be paid. And, of course, Google would contribute a large sum of money to the plaintiffs to pay off legal bills and compensate them for the wrongs already committed.

The proposal put Google at a critical juncture. Thus far, Google had been arguing on principle. It had defined itself in the conflict as a proxy for the culture itself, indeed for all of civilization. The snippets, it argued, belonged to the people. And it was demanding no exclusivity. If Google won its argument and it was determined that including the text of books in search engine indexes was fair use, anyone could make deals with libraries to do his own scanning. Google might have snapped up some of the plum libraries, but there were dozens of other first-rate collections that a company like Microsoft or Yahoo could scan. (Indeed, Microsoft had embarked on such a plan but eventually abandoned it because of excessive costs.) Or maybe the Library of Congress could digitize its own holdings and license the files to a search engine company.

What's more, Google believed it had an excellent chance of winning its case. During a meeting of copyright experts, one of the leading theorists in the field, the Berkeley professor and MacArthur "Genius Award" winner Pamela Samuelson, took a poll of fifteen of her peers—and all but one thought that Google's fair use argument would prevail.

But as soon as the ambitious proposal was uttered by Google's legal opponents, it was a foregone conclusion that Larry Page would sign on. He later would say that Google would have done "whatever kinds of things we needed to do" to make the settlement happen. It was his personal history, and that of Google, that determined that he embrace the scheme. All his life, Page had been the one who confronted problems by suggesting solutions that expanded the project by an order of magnitude. Now someone else was proposing to do the same thing.

After many sessions to hammer out the details—a difficult process because of the complex needs of the publishers, authors, and library associations that were drawn into the deal—the Google Book Settlement was completed, three years after the lawsuit was filed. On October 28, 2008, Google announced the "landmark settlement" whereby it not only would be free to do its scanning and show free snippets online but would have the exclusive rights to sell digital copies of out-of-print books. It would provide every library in the country with one free subscription to the database and sell additional subscriptions. And Google would pay $125 million, in part to establish a Book Rights Registry that identified rights holders and handled payments and in part to pay millions of dollars to the lawyers who worked on the case. All this would be subject to the court's approval of the settlement.

The initial reaction to the settlement was subdued, almost as if people were a bit stunned at the breadth of Google's coup. For a relatively small sum—by 2008, Google garnered $10 billon dollars in annual revenue—Google had not only won the right to become the sole authorized archivist of a historic and comprehensive collection of the world's books but had entered a new business without competition. But as people in the world of culture and digital commerce—and Google's rivals—began to study the agreement, a swell of opposition rose. Eventually the swells became a tsunami.

The objections were myriad. Some former allies of Google were incensed that it had given up the fight to legally scan books. One new foe was Brewster Kahle, the founder of the Internet Archive, a nonprofit organization bent on preserving all documents on the web as well as information in general. Kahle had been involved in his own digitization process under the aegis of an organization called the Open Book Alliance. Now he claimed that Google had become an information monopolist bent on destroying efforts other than its own to make books accessible.

Another former friend, Lawrence Lessig, attacked the settlement, calling it "a path to insanity." His complaint focused on the commercial aspects of the agreement that determined fees for exposing parts of the books to users. Instead of offering a road to knowledge, he charged, Google was constructing toll booths. "The deal constructs a world in which control can be exercised at the level of a page, and maybe even a quote. . . . We create not digital libraries, but digital bookstores."

Organizations objecting to the suit included the American Society of Journalists and Authors, the National Writers Union, and the Science Fiction and Fantasy Writers of America. (That last had to hurt, considering all the Googlers who were sci-fi fans.) They insisted that the book settlement cover their works only if they volunteered to be a part of it—switching from opt out to opt in.

As with almost every other Google controversy, privacy issues found their way into the discussion. Groups such as the Electronic Frontier Foundation and the American Civil Liberties Union argued that Google might log people's reading habits, adding to what they considered an already obscene volume of information Google held on its users.

Among the most active objectors were companies like Microsoft, which had abandoned its own effort to digitize books, and Amazon.com, which now found itself competing with Google as a bookseller. Microsoft even funded a legal research effort by a professor at the New York Law School who promised to "hack the Google Book Settlement."

Not all of the objectors wanted to quash the settlement entirely. Some agreed with Google that the overall mission—to make the wisdom in books instantly available to all the world—was a worthy one. Some expressed a wish that the settlement would be approved by the court—but only with the changes important to them. Those changes, of course, were often mutually exclusive or were unacceptable to some of the parties in the settlement. But overall, the list of objectors was sobering. There were 143 of them, including academic authors, New Zealand writers, the Electronic Privacy Information Center, attorneys general of five states, and of course Amazon.com and Microsoft. (Since Amazon.com's Jeff Bezos had been an original angel investor in Google, this was an additional irony. Bezos has not publicly divulged whether he still holds a personal stake in Google.) For good measure, AT&T (which would have organized a grassroots movement against a Google lemonade stand if it existed) joined the pileup.

Possibly the worst development in the case from Google's point of view came when the Department of Justice decided to weigh in on the book settlement—in the negative. While specifying that the effort would have considerable societal value, the DOJ contended that it granted Google too many exclusive, anticompetitive privileges. Google's dream project had become the object of government antitrust action.

The troubles Google was having in the book settlement were a microcosm of its woes in general. When a small company leveraged technology and brains to disrupt a business model or a cultural tradition, the world saw it as attractive and exciting and viewed competitors as stiff-necked bullies trying to preserve their power. But when a huge, rich company caused disruption, it was itself seen as the bully, and even ill-intentioned competitors drew sympathy. The policy people at Google knew this but still believed that having the truth (as they saw it) on their side would carry the day. "It's not an environment we used to face, but over the past few years we've come to understand it," said David Drummond. "We like to think we're data-driven and run our company based on fact and what actually is going on, and so we realize we have to push on that and push back aggressively."

No one seemed more stunned at the fury directed toward the company than its founders. Page was appalled at the senselessness of it all, that value was being left on the table. "It's really a travesty to humanity that we're in that state," he said.

In October 2009, Sergey Brin wrote a *New York Times* op-ed defending the settlement. He argued that it was an essential part of preserving the world's knowledge. Conceding that Google should not be the only digitization effort, he implied that if its plans were blocked, a comprehensive effort might never emerge. "At least one service should exist if there are ever to be one hundred," he posited, with his usual logic. "The companies that are making objections about out of print books are doing *nothing* for out of print books."

A related question came to Schmidt about the settlement being connected to a trend in Google behavior in which the company locked in customers, as Microsoft had done in the 1990s. "There are many reasons why we will not be like Microsoft," answered Schmidt. He explained that the culture of the company and its founders prevented that, as Google runs on trust. "If we went into a room and were exposed to an evil light and came out and announced evil strategies, we would be destroyed. The trust would be destroyed."

Everywhere top Googlers went, they were drawn into dramatic confrontations over the settlement. In an August 2009 informal conference in Sebastopol, California, called Foo Camp, Pam Samuelson moderated a session on the controversy. Brewster Kahle was there, and so was Marissa Mayer. Samuelson's measured comments dwelled on the lost opportunity when Google had abandoned the fair use argument. (She would later develop those ideas in a lecture entitled "Google Book Settlement: Brilliant but Evil?") Brewster Kahle spoke of Google as if it were some alien squad invading Earth in a science fiction movie. Google was killing the dream of access to books, he claimed. He was so passionate his hands were trembling. Mayer could not believe it. This is so crazy, she thought. "Google had acted with such good intentions," she later said, "and to hear these weird, evil genius, lightbulb-room evil thoughts being projected on us . . ."

When Mayer took the floor, her voice was shaking with rage. She explained that she had been present when the first book was scanned, and at every step of the way, Google had been out to *help* people, to help *authors*, to improve the world. Maybe some people didn't like every aspect of the settlement and preferred to argue that the copyright line in the sand shouldn't be here but should be over there. But the truth was—as Mayer saw it—that any person who cared about literacy, about books, about information, about democracy, should want this done. "Brewster," she said, "would you rather we just didn't do it? Walk away from the whole issue?" She felt he had to say no, Google's plan was better than nothing. But he wouldn't answer.

The fate of the settlement rested in the hands of Judge Denny Chin of the Second Circuit's Southern District in New York. After the DOJ brief, Judge Chin postponed a scheduled October 2009 hearing so that the parties could alter the settlement to respond to that and other objections. Google, the publishers, and the authors came back with a new version that made it easier for companies other than Google to participate in book search, limited other exclusive services Google could provide, and reduced the number of foreign works that would be included. The DOJ felt that although the terms had improved, its original objections still stood. It was granted a prime slot in the upcoming hearing.

The parties to the proposed settlement, along with the objectors, had their day in court on February 18, 2010. The atmosphere was somewhat chaotic in part because one of the organizations supporting Google, the National Federation of the Blind, had bused in dozens of blind people to speak for the settlement. Judge Chin announced at the start that he would not rule that day. He heard the dozens of speakers with a calm, slightly brusque demeanor.

In groups of four, various supporters and objectors spoke. Supporters talked of the boon that Book Search would provide. Then came the objectors, whose arguments made it clear that Google was no longer universally regarded as a cheeky young start-up committed to empowering people rather than itself. Objectors gave spirited critiques of what they described as a conspiracy against culture itself. Some of the objections were based on the difficult legal question of whether the settlement overstepped the bounds of what a class-action settlement could resolve. It was frequently noted that some of the issues should be resolved only by Congress. Other arguments were broad attacks on how a rich company from Silicon Valley, one that already controlled the world of search, was plotting a vile takeover of the book world. "To approve this [settlement] would only send a message to all corporations," said one objector. "Go ahead, be unethical, cram any nasty demand down unsophisticated people's throats as you like."

The day ended with four cleanup hitters, the first opposing Google on behalf of the Justice Department and then three attorneys representing the parties to the settlement. The DOJ attorney, William Cavanaugh, focused on the "forward-looking" aspects of the case—Google as essentially a monopoly vendor of orphan books, most of which would find their way into Google's indexes without permission. That, he insisted, was something only Congress could grant. Despite all the good intentions, he said, this settlement was "a per se violation of the antitrust laws."

The final speaker was Google's counsel, Daralyn J. Durie. Her résumé was Google-esque. At Stanford she had majored in biology and comparative literature, going on to earn a master's in the latter at Berkeley. She remained at Berkeley to get her J.D. in 1992 and went on to a stunning litigation career, including several cases defending corporations in class-action suits. An opposing attorney called her "one of the future leaders of the profession." She had represented Google in a previous class-action lawsuit involving click fraud.

Within ten seconds of addressing the court, her word choice raised eyebrows.

MS. DURIE: Your Honor asked whether it would be permissible to release claims for future discrimination. I would agree that the answer to that question, in all likelihood, is no. That's because discrimination is evil. The dissemination

of copyrighted works is not. That is because the purpose
of the Copyright Act is to encourage the production of
copyrighted works.

THE COURT: Well, some would say the question is: Is copyright
infringement evil?

MS. DURIE: Copyright infringement is evil to the extent that it is not
compensated and that it harms the economic interests of
rights holders.

Besides the invocation of Google's controversial motto, Durie was addressing a relatively minor point by invoking a major one: the first principle of copyright. The Constitution states that the purpose of the copyright is to promote the progress of the arts, not to restrict speech. This was also the principle by which Google had been able to make its impact and its profits. In the Internet age "progress of the arts" by collecting a massive corpus of scannable books wasn't evil: it was beneficial. Google had already scanned millions of books. Its users were routinely astonished that a query in Google's universal search box could evoke a passage from a long-forgotten tome. While duking it out in the courts, Google had indeed improved the world.

But Google's plight was such that arguments seemed self-serving. Google had become a company that dominated the world's searches, whose mirror world rivaled the physical world as a working version of reality, a company that had knowledge of virtually everyone's information, peregrinations, and intentions, a company fighting the giants in computer software, phones, and television. When Google spoke of good and evil, the words sounded hollow at best. Its flaws became magnified, and its virtues seemed calculated.

When Google's leaders had been challenged on this point, they felt that logic was on their side, and that logic would eventually convince people that the company's actions, if not its intentions, were pure. They would say, look at the *data*. You can't argue with facts. *You're not entitled to your own facts.*

That was, and continues to be, the view from the Googleplex. But as Google was learning—and so was its philosophical doppelgänger in the White House—outside the mirror world stored and distributed on more than a million Google servers, data and logic do not always triumph.

CHASING TAILLIGHTS

On June 8, 2007, Justin Rosenstein, who until recently had been a Google product manager, sent an email to his former colleagues. "I am writing to spread Good
News," the missive said. "Facebook really is That company."

> Which company? That one. The company that shows up once in a very long while—the
> Google of yesterday, the Microsoft of long ago . . . That company that's on the cusp of
> Changing the World, that's still small enough where each employee has a huge impact
> on the organization . . . where you know you'll kick yourself in three years if you don't
> jump on the bandwagon now, even after someone had told you it was rolling toward the
> promised land.

Rosenstein believed that his new employer not only was as relentlessly
technical as his former one but was embarked on its own audacious quest, one
that threatened to eclipse Google's. Facebook was at the vanguard of social networking, a movement with the goal of organizing people through the network
of personal connections they collected throughout their lives. Barely three years
after its founder, Mark Zuckerberg, had begun the company in a Harvard dorm
room, Facebook was signing up millions of users and was on a trajectory to
sign up most of the literate world. The same month Rosenstein wrote his letter,
Facebook launched a new strategy that allowed software developers to write applications inside its website, almost as if the site were its own little Internet. Even

if you didn't believe that Facebook would be the hub of one's online life—or perhaps one's *entire* life—it was a phenomenon that Google could not ignore.

As recently as the previous year, Google had regarded Facebook as a potential complement to its own business and hoped to make deals to place its search and ads on the site. But when a bidding war for Facebook's ad contract erupted between Google and Microsoft, Google lost. Instead, Google made a deal with Facebook's competitor in social networking, MySpace, guaranteeing $900 million in ads over a period of three years. It was a poor consolation prize, as MySpace, which had been purchased by Rupert Murdoch's News Corporation, proceeded to flub its early lead in social networking. Meanwhile, Facebook kept growing. As its users kept entering their likes, dislikes, interactions, and pictures into the service, Facebook became the owner of a valuable corpus of personal information on the web, all of it inaccessible to Google. When Google's crawlers got to Facebook, they were turned away at the door. (Facebook would eventually allow its user profile pages to be exposed on Google.)

Facebook was a scary competitor because in some ways it was very much like Google. True, Facebook wasn't built on a brilliant scientific advance as Google was, and there was no technical innovation at Facebook even close to the breathtaking Google infrastructure. But Mark Zuckerberg was in the Larry Page mold, a wildly ambitious leader with a quasi-religious trust in engineering. Zuckerberg said that Facebook would have hacker values. Ten years younger than Page and Brin—a generation in Internet time—Zuckerberg respected Google's values but believed that the older company had lost its nimbleness and focus. He made a specialty of hiring Google people who sought the excitement of building something new. When Zuckerberg needed a strong number two to run Facebook operations, he turned to Sheryl Sandberg, who had built Google's ad organization. As disappointing as that was to Google, what was even more alarming was the competition for engineering talent. Google could deal with its most brilliant engineers leaving to start their own companies—classic examples were the departure of Paul Buchheit (Gmail) and Bret Taylor (Google Maps) to start a company called FriendFeed. But when Facebook bought FriendFeed, both engineers happily integrated themselves into the ranks of their new employer.

Buchheit would eventually leave to focus on start-up investing, but Taylor became Facebook's chief technical officer. That move signified a difference between the companies. Google liked to give young people massive responsibility, but it also relied on world-class scientists for its operational innovations. It was like a university: the top executives were equivalent to professors. Facebook preferred kids, figuring that what the sharpest undergrads lacked in experience, they would make up for in audacity.

The older company had a massive edge in revenues. Facebook was struggling to develop its own equivalent of AdWords. It would have to be something as organic to the social network as Google's ad model was to its search product. The bigger threat to Google wouldn't be measured in dollars, but in the philosophical challenge. Could it be that social networking, rather than algorithmic exploitation of the web's intelligence, would assume the central role in people's online lives? Even if that were not the case, Facebook made it clear that every facet of the Internet would benefit from the power of personal connection. Google had been chasing a future forged out of algorithms and science fiction chronicles. Did the key to the future lay in party photos and daily status reports?

The irony was that Google had been present at the explosion of social networking. In a classic case of the company's corporate ADD, it simply had blown the opportunity to make the most of what it created.

Back in 2002, a young Google engineer named Orkut Buyukkokten had an idea. "My dream was to connect all the Internet users so they can relate to each other," he later recalled. "It can make such a difference in people's lives." Buyukkokten, who had come to Google from his native Turkey via Stanford, decided to use his 20 percent discretionary time developing a cyberspace preserve where the people of the world could intermingle in peace, presumably so their good vibes would go viral. Designed along the lines of the first big social networking site, Friendster—there was no Facebook then—his creation encouraged users to build profiles for themselves. Upon mutual consent, people would bond with each other. Networks of like-minded people would form. Groups of shared interests would emerge. Virtual flowers would bloom. Eventually, wars would end. Buyukkokten coded it up in a weekend and showed it to Marissa Mayer during her weekly office hours. She loved it and assigned one of her APMs to help out.

Buyukkokten wanted to call it Eden, reflecting his vision of a utopian preserve where people could feel safe and trust each other. But eden.com was owned by an opera company that wouldn't sell its domain name. The owners of paradise .com and utopia.com were similarly unaccommodating. Finally, the product manager and Mayer thought of naming it after its creator. "Orkut.com" belonged to Buyukkokten himself. Google convinced him, and its social networking service was called Orkut.

Was it a sign of the company's distrust of the insufficiently algorithmic nature of social software that the product was not branded with the Google name? "We wanted to see if it could stand on its own two feet," says Mayer, a stricture not required from such Google services as Gmail and Google Maps.

In fact, Orkut almost immediately stood tall. Even though the software was available only by invitation—the first users were Googlers who invited their own friends—hundreds of thousands of people signed up in the first month alone.

Soon after launch, there was so much activity in the logs that Mayer demanded that the engineers recheck their stats. "We'd never seen anything like it," says Mayer. "The system just fell over." Google had to take Orkut down for a couple of days to recover.

During Orkut's first few months, the global distribution was typical of other products, with half the traffic in the United States and the next biggest chunk, about 8 percent, in Japan. Google's response was not to pour resources into the product but to observe as Orkut rose or fell on its own. Though there would be exceptions—Android and YouTube, for instance—most Google products, while exactingly rethought and tweaked during the design process, were similarly left to find their way in the world by themselves. Failure was part of Google, one its leaders accepted. The bulk of Google's efforts on Orkut weren't focused on design and features that would make the service more useful but rather a rewrite of Orkut's Windows infrastructure to conform to Google standards so the system would run faster, accommodate growth more smoothly, and resist spam more effectively. (As Orkut became more popular, it came under attack from identity thieves and those who flooded the service with the usual assortment of virility aid ads and Nigerian inheritance announcements.) Meanwhile, the system coughed and sputtered—and impatient users bailed out. At the time, Eric Schmidt chalked up the experience—where Google blew its chance to dominate social networking—as routine collateral damage from the company's philosophy of quick launches.

"Larry and Sergey's vision is 'Let's get these systems to prove themselves,'" he said in 2004. "After [the engineer] Orkut built this, we said, 'God knows if this thing's any good or not.' So we waited until it crashed from overuse. So then we put another programmer on the project. And now it has many more." But it was too late—the moment had passed.

Oddly, Orkut became a sensation in Brazil. "In Brazil, Orkut is the Internet and Google is search," wrote one local journalist, who added that using Orkut was "like putting sugar in your coffee, watching Globo telenovelas, or heading to the beach from Christmas to Carnival." On a trip to Brazil in 2006, Sergey Brin was asked why, and he responded, "We don't know—what do *you* think?" When pressed, Googlers would refer to stereotypes of Carioca sociability, but that didn't sufficiently explain why Orkut became the social networking choice of this country over other competitors—or why Orkut was so badly left behind in the rest of the world. Marissa Mayer's personal analysis was based on the Google yardstick of speed. Brazilians, she says, were used to lousy Internet service and thus more tolerant of the delays. "They would just keep sitting there and waiting," she says.

Orkut was also dominant in India, where it was the number one Google service—ahead of search and Gmail. "There is no second product in India—

Orkut is dominant," said Manu Rekhi, the Orkut India product manager, in 2007. "I've seen beggar kids who use their money to get on Orkut." Mayer also attributed that success to its quick response compared to other services. "Do you know why Orkut took off in India?" she would ask. "Opposite time zone, and no load on the servers at night. Speed matters." (Why Orkut ruled in Brazil, however, was a mystery never solved.)

In any case, by the time Google switched Orkut's code base to a speedier infrastructure, Facebook was beginning its rise in the United States. Google never made a serious attempt to dislodge it. In 2008, Google announced that it was moving all of Orkut's operations to its offices in Belo Horizonte, Brazil. By then about half of Orkut's traffic came from Brazil, with about 40 percent in India. Only about 2 percent was in the United States. India's Internet users would soon adopt Facebook, leaving Orkut behind.

Mayer would later admit that if Orkut had been a bigger priority at Google, the company might have had more success with it in the United States and other countries. But in Google's earlier days, "opportunity costs" determined how much attention a product received. In 2004, Google had 2,000 employees, around 800 of them engineers, dispersed in roughly a hundred teams of three to twelve each. Skimming twenty engineers each from a separate team meant that you would be losing an average of 15 percent of the manpower in those teams. As it was, twenty people had to be temporarily recruited that August to fix Orkut's lingering problems. "I do think we made the right trade-off and the right balance," Mayer would later argue. Considering how important social software would become, it was hard to agree.

Orkut was far from the only opportunity in the social sphere that Google missed. In May 2005, Google bought a small company in the promising area known as mobile social. Founded by Dennis Crowley and Alex Rainert, Dodgeball was a pioneering service that let mobile phone users turn their city into a giant hide-and-seek game where they could discover (or avoid) nearby friends. The possibilities of location-based services seemed endless, and tech followers applauded Google for its canny purchase.

But Google largely neglected its new prize. The tiny Dodgeball team was based in New York City, in order to keep in touch with the urban vibe of its product (Crowley and Rainert were veterans of New York University's geek-hip Interactive Telecommunications Program). They constantly begged for attention and manpower from Mountain View, with little success. "It needed some love from Google to promote it," Crowley later said. He felt strongly that if Google had paid even a little more attention, Dodgeball could have grown from 100,000 users to a million and more. At one point Sergey Brin visited the New York office and asked Crowley how things were going. "It's awful," Crowley told him. "We need more engineers." Sergey said he'd get right on it. "But he didn't," Crowley later said. "Nothing came of it."

Dodgeball had a feature called "shout" that let users broadcast a short message to their friends, and Crowley and his team thought of releasing a version of the program without locations—just those status updates. Stupid things like "I'm going to the movies." One day in early 2006, a friend of Crowley's from Nokia came in to Google and they shared their newest ideas. They slid their phones across the table and found they were working on the same idea—presence without location.

Not long afterward, Crowley saw the first version of an Internet start-up called Twitter. The company was run by Evan Williams, the cofounder of Blogger, who had sold that firm to Google in February 2003 but left in October 2004, unhappy at the relative neglect with which it treated his service. Twitter was a dead-simple Internet and phone service that let people broadcast 140-character messages to anyone who chose to "follow" the stray thoughts of a given user. Crowley began sending emails to people at Google telling them that this was important and Google should jump on it. "It all fell on deaf ears," Crowley says. "They just weren't interested in social at the time. It just wasn't their thing."

Crowley remembers a fateful videoconference with Mountain View in the summer of 2006 in which he and his colleagues argued that the social network movement was about to go crazy and now was the time to put more resources into Dodgeball. An executive flatly told him once and for all to forget about asking for more engineers. That sealed it for Crowley. Though reluctant to abandon Dodgeball's loyal community, he and Rainert left in April 2007. It was two years before Google formally pulled the plug on the service. Meanwhile, Google would develop its own location-based service, Latitude. By then, there were a number of location-based start-ups, all of which owed something to Dodgeball. One of the hottest was called Foursquare.

Its cofounder was Dennis Crowley.

Google had a built-in disadvantage in the social networking sweepstakes. It was happy to gather information about the intricate web of personal and professional connections known as the "social graph" (a term favored by Facebook's Mark Zuckerberg) and integrate that data as signals in its search engine. But the basic premise of social networking—that a personal recommendation from a friend was more valuable than all of human wisdom, as represented by Google Search—was viewed with horror at Google. Page and Brin had started Google on the premise that the algorithm would provide the only answer.

Yet there was evidence to the contrary. One day a Googler, Joe Kraus, was looking for an anniversary gift for his wife. He typed "Sixth Wedding Anniversary

Gift Ideas" into Google, but beyond learning that the traditional gift involved either candy or iron, he didn't see anything creative or inspired. So he decided to change his status message on Google Talk, a line of text seen by his contacts who used Gmail, to "Need ideas for sixth anniversary gift—candy ideas anyone?" Within a few hours, he got several amazing suggestions, including one from a colleague in Europe who pointed him to an artist and baker whose medium was cake and candy. (It turned out that Marissa Mayer was an investor in the company.) It was a sobering revelation for Kraus that sometimes your friends could trump algorithmic search.

In the summer of 2008, Kraus held a barbecue at his house for Googlers to kick around social networking ideas. He invited his long-term collaborator Graham Spencer. They also invited David Glazer, a forty-five-year-old Valley veteran who had recently been hired for the relatively senior role of engineering director.

Though the group discussed a number of ideas ("We could have renamed Orkut and painted it blue," says Glazer), everyone agreed that Google should refrain from one path in particular: creating a "Facebook-killer" application of its own. "Google is terrible at being a taillight chaser," Glazer later said. "*Drunks follow taillights.*"

Instead of building a Google product, they came to decide that the company should pursue a two-pronged strategy. One was making Google products more social—maybe Gmail and other applications could be opened up to people's friends and contacts. The second was a more ambitious plan where Google would essentially create a scaffolding on the web to lubricate social activities. The system could duplicate some of the benefits of Facebook and Twitter without having people visit those websites. Kraus even had a motto for it: "go fast alone, go far together." He also had a second slogan for the approach that Google had to take when competing in the social world: "Ready, fire, aim." It sounded like a postmortem for a lost battle, he would later admit, but it was the Google way.

Google set about organizing many of the web's socially oriented companies into a major initiative that it called OpenSocial. The idea was to build a shared infrastructure where multiple websites could participate in a more social web. A user's identity would be portable; a profile formed on one site could be used on other sites or services. While Google bore the burden of much of the programming and organization, it was careful not to label the effort as solely its own: the party line was that this was an open-source group effort that would benefit all. But as some of the major participants—MySpace, Ning, hi5, Bebo, AOL—fell into line, the biggest social site sat out the effort. Facebook didn't say it would never participate; it just didn't. Meanwhile, a Facebook executive, Ethan Beard, emailed Joe Kraus to tell him about his company's ban on sharing information with OpenSocial. Beard said that allowing movement of the personal information people shared with Facebook would be a violation of its terms of service agreement, even if a user wanted to share it.

Ultimately, Facebook's lack of cooperation proved fatal to OpenSocial. You couldn't duplicate Facebook without Facebook.

As OpenSocial lurched, Google began casting around for other ways to participate in social networking. One option was buying Twitter, but that was complicated by the fact that its founder, Evan Williams, had become disenchanted with Google by his previous experience as an immigrant through acquisition. Williams felt Google hadn't developed Blogger to its fullest potential; though the blogging service had increased its audience, it had become lost among Google's dozens of products and failed to innovate at its previous pace. In any case, Google was in its brief austerity period and was not in the mood to make a YouTube–level offer that Williams could not refuse. "This is not a time where I want to overpay," said Schmidt in March 2009.

In theory, Twitter was so simple that Google could simply write its own version. "The question of the day was 'Why don't we build Twitter?' Three guys could do it in a weekend!" said Glazer in 2009. But, he explained, that would have been a case of chasing taillights.

Google's search team began working on improvements to its core technology that would allow for "social search" (based on signals of what your friends were searching for) and "real-time search" (which tried to respond to Twitter by raising the relevancy of fresh and popular sites—and indexing Twitter's contents as quickly as people posted them). Another product was an ambitious communications service called Google Wave, created by a team working in isolation in the Google Australia office. At the May 2009 Google I/O conference its designers introduced the product in a stunning ninety-minute demo that was posted on YouTube and became the talk of the web. But when the product began to appear in limited release later that year, it proved confusing to users. Wave required considerable instruction, but it was official Google policy not to provide that kind of support for its products. The demonstration offered by the team that developed Wave had wowed the crowd and impressed all who viewed it on YouTube thereafter. But how many users would take the time to sit through the ninety-minute demo before deciding to try the product? And even if they did, Wave would not be useful to them unless their friends and colleagues also knew how to surf the Wave. That was a lot to ask users to do on their own.

"I would say we were not executing well in the social space in general," said Google VP Bradley Horowitz. "We had a bunch of different projects, but we didn't have a coordinated goal that was going to get us in the conversation."

In early 2009, Horowitz's team began work on yet another new product that, Horowitz predicted, "would blow Twitter away." Its code name was Taco Town, named after a *Saturday Night Live* parody of a Taco Bell commercial where a tortilla-covered snack is increasingly, and absurdly, slathered with more food. *("And it gets even awesomer when we take a deep-fried gordita shell, smear on a little of our special 'guacamolito' sauce, and wrap that around the outside!")* That reflected Googlers' judgment of the Internet's current social strategy: big, messy layers of greasy, unwholesome stuff whose caloric volume tried to compensate for satisfying essence. Taco Town was more focused. It was designed to work inside Gmail. (Giving it the advantage of instant exposure, though limiting it to only a plurality of netizens.) One of its definitive traits was the speedy process by which users would assemble their graph of friends—Taco Town would analyze email contacts and instantly present people with a social network that had been already built by their own behavior. Using that group as a starting point, Twitter-style comments (Tacos) could be posted—but, unlike in Twitter, the comments would not have a 140-character limit, and pictures and other media could be included in them. With a single mouse click within Gmail, you could replace the view of your inbox with a stream of Tacos from all your contacts.

The product gained a following at Google, but every time Horowitz took it to a GPS, the founders would pounce on it. Brin wanted more from it. Taco Town became a priority for Brin, and in mid-2009 he actually moved his office to the apps group so he could monitor it more closely.

It was an indication of Google's confused strategy that Taco Town's development proceeded even as the company announced Wave with fanfare and hosannas. When pressed, Horowitz would concede that Taco Town's functions overlapped with those of Wave. "In the worst-case scenario, Wave is a concept car," he would say. "General Motors doesn't build every concept car."

As the team prepared for Taco Town's rollout in early 2010, the product added more features, many of which duplicated Facebook functions. It also added location information to the Tacos. But the minipostings would no longer be called Tacos; Google renamed the product Buzz to reflect the crackling interaction it would presumably generate. The moniker more accurately reflected the product's purpose but lacked the irreverent pizzazz of the original. Nonetheless, excitement ran high at Google that the company had finally cracked the social problem. Thousands of Google employees used Buzz in the dogfooding process.

The evening before the launch the team gathered for a rehearsal. Then the PR people joined them. Vic Gundotra, Google's most polished presenter, gave a brief demo of Buzz's mobile abilities. Horowitz delivered a product overview. Gmail's product manager went into details. (Sergey Brin wasn't at the rehearsal but would attend the launch the next day.) Then, in a dry run of the postpresentation Q and A, Google's PR staff pretended to be reporters asking their toughest questions. *Why isn't Facebook in there? What about Wave?* None of the questions touched on whether there might be privacy concerns in building an instant social network based on one's email contacts.

Indeed, on launch day—February 9, 2010—none of the reporters in attendance asked probing questions about the new product's privacy settings, and the first wave of articles about the product was generally positive. A number of the Google executives at the event, including Horowitz and Brin, left Mountain View soon afterward to attend the annual TED Conference in Southern California. But within forty-eight hours, Buzz ignited a privacy crisis as intense as the Gmail privacy conflagration in 2004.

The problem lay in a feature that Google was most proud of. Previously, new users of social networking services had been confronted with the annoying chore of gathering friends and contacts to construct their cohort. Google felt it had solved this problem with Buzz. When a Gmail user clicked the single button that signed him or her up for Buzz, a social network instantly appeared, based on one's email contacts. When this feature was tested internally, the employees trying it out loved it.

But when the general public tried Buzz, some users discovered unwanted—even horrendous—consequences. By looking at a Buzz user's profile, other Buzz users could see that person's social network. Since the network had not been carefully built contact by contact, it was entirely possible that it might include a connection that a user might not want exposed to a larger audience. (Certain contacts could indicate that someone was seeking alternative employment or spilling secrets to a reporter.) As described in a February 10 posting in *Business Insider,* "The problem is that—by default—the people you follow and the people who follow you are made public to anyone who looks at your profile . . . someone could go in your profile and see the people you email with and chat with most." The settings for what was exposed to the public, as well as which contacts were included in one's network, could address this, but most users follow the standard settings.

Google had made a critical error. Its employees differed from the general population. For one thing, their email contacts are largely with other Googlers. So few of them were concerned that the networks instantly constructed by Buzz drew on their Gmail contacts. Instead, they were motivated to explore its features and find those that worked for them. (Brin boasted to *The New York Times* that he had used Buzz input to write his op-ed defending the book settlement.) As a result, the product team—as well as the usually vigilant Google privacy squad—missed something that became obvious as soon as the product was released to a population whose electronic correspondence often held secrets. Nicole Wong, the lawyer in charge of Google's policy operations, later admitted the mistake. "The on-boarding [dogfood] process is not like doing it in the wild, and the social network of 20,000 Googlers is not like being on the Internet. That process failed us."

The outcry was instant and loud. A domestic violence victim complained that Buzz had exposed her blog comments and reading habits to her abusive former spouse, revealing information that hinted at her whereabouts. *Foreign Policy*'s Evgeny Morozov suggested in a blog post that Iranian and Chinese government goon squads might instantly check Buzz accounts of dissidents to analyze their connections. Even Google's former policy head Andrew McLaughlin wrote—in a Buzz post!—that "Google exposes the people you email most by default, to the world. This violates my sense of expectations." Privacy activists prepared formal complaints to the Federal Trade Commission. The privacy commissioner of Canada, in a letter cosigned by data protection officials of nine other nations, charged Buzz with "a disappointing disregard for fundamental privacy norms and laws."

Google quickly set up a war room, populating it with not only policy and PR people but engineers working to alter the product. Still at TED, Bradley Horowitz felt blindsided. "We knew we were doing something dangerous, taking a private space and opening it up to a social activity," he said. "But we thought that after Facebook and other services this was something people were used to." He felt, however, that the storm, while intense, would soon pass. "We'll get through this," he promised. Indeed, in record time, the engineers made changes in the product. They changed the default settings to allow people to more easily keep contacts private and block unwanted followers. Eventually, Google would address virtually all the complaints of privacy advocates.

But a couple of months later, Horowitz admitted that the damage to Buzz had been deep. "We should have known people were gunning for us," he said. The privacy flap, he admitted, was "a scar that will stay with the product forever."

As Buzz stumbled into its first summer, the product looked like a goner. Meanwhile, Google quietly announced an end to Wave. Though its 2009 demo had arrived like a killer swell, by the time it reached the shore, it couldn't support a boogie board. "Wave has not seen the user adoption we would have liked," wrote Urs Hölzle in his August 4, 2010, blog post announcing the termination. The move was little noticed, because Wave had so little adoption. Two months later, the head of the Wave team, a star engineer named Lars Rasmussen, announced that he was leaving Google to join Facebook.

Google still hadn't cracked social. But that didn't mean it would stop trying. "If we see a way to deliver a benefit, should we simply not go there because there's another company there?" asked Nicole Wong, shrugging off the privacy blunders of Buzz. "If Facebook were your only option, would that end up being a good thing?"

Facebook wasn't the only new competitive challenge Google faced. Its failure to prevent the merger of the search services of its next biggest rivals, Microsoft and Yahoo, had allowed those two companies to merge their user base, with Microsoft providing the search technology. After many years of relatively poor efforts, Microsoft was now committed to spending hundreds of millions of dollars to build a competitive engine. To head the team, it hired the scientist Qi Lu, a forty-eight-year-old whose tireless work habits were legendary. Those regarding this as a coup included Google's search czar, Udi Manber: "I have the highest regard for him," he said. Microsoft called its new search engine Bing, and it was launched in June 2009 by CEO Steve Ballmer with great fanfare.

In terms of search quality, Bing did not intimidate Google. Its relevance algorithms were basically no different from those in the previous version of Microsoft's search, much less likely to draw out the Audrey Fino–like needles in the Internet haystack. Eventually that could change, as Microsoft would supply Bing to Yahoo for the latter company's search engine. That would provide Microsoft with a critical mass of users to run the thousands of constant experiments necessary to improve search quality. "The algorithm is extremely important in search," said Microsoft's VP of core search, Brian MacDonald. "But it's not the only thing." He compared it to a car: the engine is very important, but there are all sorts of other reasons to choose a given model. MacDonald said that Google, with its dependable ten blue links, "still looks like your father's Oldsmobile. If you were Rip Van Winkle and went to sleep twelve years ago and woke up today, you'd still have no problem using Google."

Though this wasn't really true—Google had previously spiced up its blue links with "one boxes" for things such as weather, travel, news, and video—Bing did look flashier than its entrenched competitor. That was most striking in video search: Bing presented search results in an array of thumbnail depictions of the most relevant videos, offering instant playback. Also, Microsoft had tried to identify weaknesses in Google search, purchasing innovative companies that specialized in those areas.

Publicly Google presented an attitude of calm engagement to the public, with Brin saying to reporters that his company welcomed the enhanced competition. But in Building 43, there was something of a freak-out. The search team set up a war room, hurriedly launching an effort dubbed the skunkworks. (That appellation, first used at Lockheed aircraft during World War II, is a generic term for an off-the-books engineering effort that operates outside a company's stifling bureaucracy. The fact that Google needed a skunkworks was telling in itself.) Its OKR was to change the look of search 25 percent within a hundred days. Within the search team itself, Googlers engaged in finger-pointing and recriminations. Months earlier, Google search engineers had presented their bosses with a project that streamlined video search results and offered instant playback—but Google had rejected it. Now the search interface team was more open to change. Very quickly, Google instituted a couple of distinctive visual changes to its home page. In one, the search box was "supersized," made about a third bigger. The text size of the search queries users typed in was similarly boosted. It stood as sort of a symbol that Google was still *the* search company. Some users were startled by the change. "People were saying that the search box was so big that it could actually eat you whole," Marissa Mayer later said. But it worked—as Mayer explained, Google ran later A/B experiments that restored the box to its original size. Hundreds of people wrote emails complaining. "They said, 'What's going on with the search box? It's so small there's not even room to type!'" In another refinement, Google simplified the initial view of the home page by removing everything except its logo and the search box; when the user moved the mouse or typed, then the rest of the text would come into view.

Though the skunkworks began with a sense of urgency, the pressure eventually subsided as it became clear that the survival of Google didn't hinge on its efforts. At one point, Larry Page bounced its efforts, complaining that the redesign looked too much like Bing. Eventually, Google did release a revamped search results page, using a three-column view: in addition to the organic search results and the ads, there was a column to the left with various search options. But it wasn't a dramatic shift. Nor did Google need one. By then several months had passed, and Bing's gains in market share were minimal.

The Bing challenge was a healthy prod for Google. It energized the search team and forced a rethinking of how Google did its interface. When Google's executives met in 2010, the main topic of discussion was not search but Mark Zuckerberg.

That March, Urs Hölzle sounded an alarum that evoked Bill Gates's legendary 1995 "Internet Sea Change" missive to his minions at Microsoft. Just as the Internet threatened Microsoft back then, in 2010 the sea change to a more people-oriented Internet—social media—was becoming a problem for Google. Hölzle said that the challenge required a decisive and substantial response, involving a significant deployment of personnel—right away. The memo became known as the Urs-Quake.

At the time Google had just completed a renovation of 2000 Charleston Road, only a few hundred yards from the main Googleplex headquarters in a complex of four-story structures once owned by the Alza drug company. (The

Chrome team was next door, in Building 1950.) After the Urs-quake, the top two floors of 2000 became the nerve center for Google's social network. Vic Gundotra led the team, joined by Bradley Horowitz. Teams of engineers from various outposts of the company moved into the building, and almost on a daily basis Google's top executives would cross Permanente Creek to strategize.

The project's internal code name was Emerald Sea. When Horowitz typed those words into Google Image Search that spring, the top result was an 1878 painting by German immigrant artist Albert Bierstadt. It depicted a tumescent seascape, dominated by a wall of surf that had already upturned a pitiful sailing ship. Horowitz commissioned a pair of art students to copy it onto the wall facing the fourth floor elevators in Building 2000. It was the perfect illustration of the Google mind as it approached the project. "We needed a code name that captured the fact that either there was a great opportunity to sail to new horizons and new things, or that we were going to drown by this wave," Gundotra would explain.

Gundotra rejected the perception that Google's DNA, rooted in the primacy of algorithms, was unsuited to accommodate the social networking revolution. To the contrary, he felt Google had unique assets that could help it take the initiative in the field, if only it would atone for its "past sins" of snubbing a social approach. He outlined an ambitious plan that would involve a people-oriented remaking of almost every aspect of Google, from YouTube to search.

Oh, and Google would launch this effort in a hundred days.

Horowitz later described this as "a wild-ass crazy, get-to-the-moon" goal, setting an impossible standard to underline the importance of the effort. A project such as Emerald Sea—which came to include eighteen current Google products, with almost thirty teams working in concert—was complicated and challenging, with milestones more appropriately measured in months, not days. Indeed, on the hundredth day after that May meeting, some time in August, Emerald Sea was nowhere completed. But its leaders were satisfied with the working prototype and had given it a new name: "+1." This was the term that Googlers and other geeky types would use to respond to an enticing invitation. If someone said he was headed to see the *Tron* sequel, you'd respond, "Plus one!"

The long delay took its toll. During the months that Google worked on Emerald Sea, Facebook became bigger and scarier. It also poached more of Google's talent. Then Mark Zuckerberg was named *Time* magazine's Man of the Year, and Facebook's estimated market value reached $50 billion. In Silicon Valley, people assumed that delays in Google's "Facebook killer" hinted at another failed effort in social networking, a harbinger perhaps of a fall from primacy for Google itself.

Still, Gundotra and Horowitz were energized by what they felt were significant innovations in the initiative, and believed that Emerald Sea would finally establish itself as a primary player in the crucial area of social software. "This is the next generation of Google—it's *Google* plus one," said Gundotra.

In its forays into other areas, like phones, videos, maps, applications, and operating systems, Google had not acted in response to competition. If it had a good idea, it simply pursued it, no matter who was occupying the space. This project was more strategic, even conventional. "It's a good thing that Google is putting its weight behind social networking, but it's reactive self-interest, not from a place of idealism," said one key team member. "It's not Google at its best, which is truly, truly pioneering. Whereas this thing is clearly more of a reaction to Facebook."

Twelve years after Larry Page and Sergey Brin decided to go all in with a company they called Google, their empire was broad, their influence massive. Google's revenues were now approaching $28 billion on an annual rate. (Facebook was taking in no more than a billion dollars a year.) What's more, even once-skeptical analysts were conceding that YouTube was about to turn a profit. Defying expectation, Google's Android mobile operating system was thriving: every day more than 200,000 users activated phones running the Android OS. (Eric Schmidt was giddily proclaiming that Google would have no problem eking out $10 in revenue from each user, adding more billions to Google's bottom line.) And certainly Facebook had no answer to Google's infrastructure of data centers, its comprehensive collection of global maps and imagery, or its giant learning brain that confounded expectations of digital performance in language comprehension, translation, and voice recognition.

Yet Google felt under siege. Some policy people at Google—now numbering hundreds of lawyers, privacy specialists, and PR experts—called 2010 "the summer of war." Eric Schmidt was getting flak for a remark he had made about privacy to the effect that young people should be offered a onetime opportunity to assume a new identity so as to distance themselves from embarrassing activities stored in Google's indexes. ("He was making a joke!" howled Google's PR people in vain. Maybe so, but the wrong person was making the joke.) Investigators were zeroing in on Google's Street View Wi-Fi grab. The halo effect of leaving China had worn off, with critics hinting that Google had been self-aggrandizing and naïve in its abrupt decision. And on August 9, Google startled even its most ardent supporters with an unusual announcement.

Since 2005, Google had been the most forceful voice in corporate America for the concept of net neutrality. When Google had begun this argument, net neutrality was closely aligned with the company's self-interest: an outsider to the establishment, it depended on the free access the Internet offered. But as Google became one of the biggest players *in* the establishment, it was clear that even if online companies had to pay Internet service providers for access, the search giant could afford those fees. It was thus in a position to bar the door to future innovators but chose not to use that power. That fact gave credibility to Google's argument that it was pushing for an open Internet not just for itself but for the *next* Google, the *next* YouTube—for innovation itself.

But now Google was saying that it had recalibrated its views on net neutrality. Working with one of the putative villains of the net neutrality battle—the huge telecom Verizon—Google proposed a new framework that would grant neutrality to land-based Internet service but not include the fast-growing area of wireless communications. Even worse, one of its blood rivals, AT&T, hinted that the Google statement was a positive step. Critics instantly pounced on the betrayal, and for a relatively wonky issue, the flip-flop drew broad coverage. Google's positioning meshed with other issues of the day—privacy, the Apple competition—to create an underlying narrative that the company was no longer a source of goodwill but just another corporate bully.

Jon Stewart devoted a segment of *The Daily Show* to Google's "sellout." A Taiwanese website specializing in current-events animations made a short video on the decline of Google's values with a memorable shot of a cartoon Eric Schmidt clinking his wineglass with the Verizon representative, who was in devil guise. After the deal was sealed, Schmidt grew his own devil horns and bellowed a bawdy world-domination laugh. With the Street View Wi-Fi scandal still generating outcries, there was suddenly a critical mass of Google disillusionment. Even random developments, such as the news that Google had ordered a sophisticated surveillance-capable autonomous drone, poured rocket fuel on the conflagration. (Actually, the drone was a private purchase by Android honcho Andy Rubin, ever the robotics enthusiast.)

On August 13—a Friday—protesters took to the Googleplex. The scene was more a geek version of Yippie theater than an angry riot; the highlight was a musical tribute to Google's perfidy by a singing group called the Raging Grannies. Yet the groups behind the event—including MoveOn, Free Press, and the Progressive Change Campaign Committee—represented true disenchantment by Google's former allies. And they carried a petition of displeasure with 300,000 signatures. Their signs read GOOGLE, DON'T BE EVIL.

Back when the company was young, Larry Page and Sergey Brin could startle people with their conviction that Google was destined to be a huge company that would change the world. In subsequent years, the prescience of those assertions would be recalled with a sense of awe. But Page and Brin's clairvoyance never extended to a day when they would mobilize their company not to create the next revolution but to fight a rearguard action against a competitor's revolution. At the same time, as it was developing its new catch-up product, Google was shutting out the noise of protesters objecting to a sellout of the company's principles, begging it not to be evil.

Google had not turned evil. It still pursued social innovation regardless of profits. Its corporate culture remained uniquely geared to the most literate and brainy products of the Internet era, and its leaders still believed in a future guided by benevolent algorithms of loving grace. But by chasing Facebook's taillights, Google was behaving very much like the kind of corporation that Larry Page once promised it would not be: conventional.

Yet in other quarters, the company was still launching moon shots. For instance, in late 2010 came news of its most audacious projects yet. Back in 2007, Larry Page had convinced Sebastian Thrun, the head of Stanford's Artificial Intelligence lab and the leader of the team that built the autonomous robot car named Stanley, to take an academic leave to work at Google. Thrun had initially worked on Street View technology, but in early 2009, Page commissioned him to develop self-driving Google cars that would ride on actual roads and set the stage for the technology to reach the mainstream. Thrun gathered an all-star team of roboticists and A.I. specialists and, in effect, created a follow-up to the 2005 contest where Stanley had prevailed. This time, the goal was to have autonomous Toyota Priuses negotiate a complicated 1000-mile course around California, including a cruise down the Pacific Coast Highway, a run through Beverly Hills, and a virtual obstacle course in the Bay Area, which included the twisty streets of San Francisco and (hardest of all) a narrow unpaved road in Tiburon in Marin County, where oncoming cars forced drivers to reverse into driveways of the nearest home in order to let them pass. (Google employees rode in the driver's seats, ready to take charge in case of computer failure.) After over 140,000 miles of test driving, Google's cars passed the test. The only accident occurred when one of the Google cars was rear-ended at a red light by a human driver.

Critics charged that the project was a sign of Google's lack of focus—why was an Internet search company working on cars that drive themselves? Actually, the project was well within Google's wheelhouse. Since its earliest days, Brin and Page have been consistent in framing Google as an artificial intelligence company—one that gathers massive amounts of data and processes that information with learning algorithms to create a machinelike intelligence that augments the collective brain of humanity. Google's autonomous cars are information-collectors, scanning their environment with lasers and sensors, and augmenting their knowledge with Street View data. (Unlike human drivers, they always know what's around the corner.) "This is all information," says Thrun. "And it will make our physical world more accessible."

What will Google's explorations in artificial intelligence eventually yield? Will we routinely cruise in autonomous cars powered by Google— undoubtedly capable of pointing out sightseeing highlights and culinary opportunities as they whisk us to destinations? Will the brain "implant" that Larry Page referred to in 2004 become a Google product at some point? (In late 2010, introducing the Google Instant search product—once referred to internally as "psychic search"— Sergey Brin had repeated the sentiment: "We want Google to be the third half of your brain.") Google, after all, was founded on the premise that the best path to success is doing what the conventional wisdom says you cannot do. In an era of unprecedented technology leaps, that has turned out to be an excellent premise. "It's quite amazing how the horizon of impossibility is drifting these days," says Thrun.

The revelation of the autonomous vehicle program at the end of 2010 had all the earmarks of a Larry Page project—scary ambition, groundbreaking AI, massive processing of information in real time, and rigidly enforced stealth. (Only when a reporter learned of the project did Google agree to talk about it.) The glimpse it provided of Page's priorities turned out to be more significant than expected when an apparently predestined change in Google's leaders occurred sooner than observers had expected.

On January 20, 2011, Google began its quarterly earnings call (trumpeting yet another record high in revenue—$8 billion for the quarter, making the 2010 total almost $30 billion) by announcing that in April Eric Schmidt would step down as CEO. He would assume a new title, Executive Chairman. His replacement would be Larry Page.

"I believe Larry is ready," said Schmidt. In addition to advising Page and Brin (whose new title, "Co-Founder," was conveniently vague), he would focus on presenting Google's case to regulators and critics, he announced. The troika explained that they had been discussing the change for months, but had accelerated the talks during the end-of-year holidays. Some observers wondered whether Schmidt's departure was a consequence of being outvoted in the intense debates over the China problem during the previous holiday season—for the past year Schmidt had often been away from Mountain View appearing at numerous conferences, sometimes engaging in desultory speculation about the technological future. But an assessment of Larry Page's consistently ardent possessiveness over the company he cofounded (still blessing or rejecting the hiring of every single employee in a workforce that now approached 24,000) indicates that all during the Schmidt era, Page had been the once and future leader of Google.

Less than a year earlier, at the end of a long interview, I had asked Page whether he would become CEO when Schmidt stepped down. He ducked the question. He wasn't even comfortable saying whether working at Google would be a lifelong situation for him. "I think it's hard to predict what happens in your life and the changing conditions, but I'm very committed to the company and I really enjoy what I do," he said. "And I think I'm able to positively affect a lot of things, which makes me feel really good, and I don't see any likely change in that." That was the closing note of the conversation. But a few minutes later he returned, wanting to say more. He wanted to reiterate some earlier points he made about ambition.

"I just feel like people aren't working enough on impactful things," he said. "People are really afraid of failure on things, and so it's hard for them to do ambitious stuff. And also, they don't realize the power of technological solutions to things, especially computers." He went on to rhapsodize about big goals like driving down the price of electricity to three cents a watt—it really wouldn't take all that much in resources to launch a project to do that, he opined. In general, society wasn't taking on enough big projects, according to Page. At Google, he said, when his engineers undertook a daunting, cutting-edge project, there were huge benefits, even if the stated goal of the project wasn't accomplished. He implied that even at Google there wasn't *enough* of that ambition. "We're in the really early stages of all of this," he said. "And we're not yet doing a good job getting the kinds of things we're trying to do to happen quickly and at scale."

Now Larry Page would be running Google, and he would get his chance to fulfill unbounded ambition. But he would also have new responsibilities that present considerable challenges to a Montessori kid who hates meetings, doesn't want administrative assistants, and has little patience for schmoozing and politicking.

It had been almost exactly ten years since Page and Brin had hired Schmidt, backing down from their insistence that they could run the company by themselves. Schmidt's comment posted on Twitter looked back to that day when Google was quite a different company and Larry Page was a twenty-eight-year-old unschooled in management.

"Day-to-day adult supervision no longer required," Schmidt tweeted.

The veracity of that statement remains to be seen. But one thing seems indisputable: Larry Page would not be a conventional CEO. Google's future would continue to court the unexpected. And maybe the impossible.

ACKNOWLEDGMENTS

Google is known for its willingness to take risks. But it took an uncharacteristic and brave one in allowing a journalist to spend hundreds of hours with its employees, look over engineers' shoulders as they developed products, and sit in on TGIFs, GPSs, and other councils and confabs. I don't know how deep a breath Eric Schmidt, Larry Page, and Sergey Brin took before approving the project, but Elliot Schrage, then the head of Google's global policy, clearly exhaled a sigh of relief at the sign-off, as did his colleagues David Krane, Gabriel Stricker, and Karen Wickre. All were champions of the scheme I presented to them.

The Googlers themselves could not have been more generous with their time and assistance. Though the list could literally go into the hundreds, I will dare to single out a few who took extraordinary pains to help me understand Google: Paul Buchheit, Matt Cutts, David Drummond, Urs Hölzle, Bradley Horowitz, Kai-Fu Lee, Salar Kamangar, Joe Kraus, Andrew McLaughlin, Marissa Mayer, Sundar Pichai, Andy Rubin, Amit Singhal, Hal Varian, and Susan Wojcicki. (Apologies in advance to others worthy of explicit mention.) I also benefited from the friendship and insights from my shadow network of compatriots from the APM trip that inspired the book. (On a foray to Baghdad, I forged similar bonds with Kannan Pashupathy and Hunter Walk.)

Google's communications team grasped what I was trying to do and worked hard to make sure I had the access and information to do it. Krane and Stricker (and later, Jill Hazelbaker and Rachel Whetstone) were especially helpful in strategizing ways to get onto various schedules, particularly the founders'. Megan

Quinn was a tolerant minder on the APM trip and a good friend thereafter. John Pinette orchestrated a very deep dive into Google China. Diana Adair and Nate Tyler took on the challenge of helping me peer inside the respective black boxes (though they both hate that term) of ads and search.

A very special thanks goes to Karen Wickre, my designated PR "shepherd" and the best guide to Google that anyone could imagine. She masterfully threaded a difficult needle as a consistent advocate for my project and a loyal representative of her employer. And she was wonderful company throughout.

My editors at *Wired* understood how the book project of their new employee would be not a distraction but a benefit to the magazine. So thanks to Chris Anderson, Bob Cohn, Thomas Goetz, Mark Horowitz, Jason Tanz, and Mark McCluskey. I am also grateful to my previous employer *Newsweek* and my editors there (particularly Mark Whitaker, George Hackett, and David Jefferson) for providing me with a platform to research Google's early days in real time. I also appreciate Kathy Deveny's sign-off on the expense statement for the APM trip.

A virtual participant in all the interviews was my master transcriber Victoria Wright, who must now be the most knowledgeable person about Google who never set foot on the campus. During the spring of 2009 I had research assistance from Andrew Marantz, under the auspices of New York University's Literary Reporting mentorship program. Zach Gottlieb helped with research on Google.org. My friend Lynnea Johnson proved a lifesaver when she offered the Palo Alto cottage she co-owns with Carolyn Rose as my base camp for the project. The actual writing of the book accelerated because of a fantastic uncluttering of my office by Erin Rooney Doland. My fact-checking team included Deborah Branscum, Victoria Wright, Stacy Horn, Teresa Carpenter, and Andrew Levy. (Though, as always, the buck stops with the author.) I got wisdom and advice along the way from John Markoff, Kevin Kelly, and Brad Stone. My first and most enthusiastic reader, of course, was my wife, Teresa Carpenter. (Having a Pulitzer Prize winner in the house is pretty useful.)

As always, my agent Flip Brophy was invaluable at every stage of the perilous publishing process. At Simon & Schuster, Bob Bender was again my sharp-eyed editor, with Johanna Li assisting. The meticulous copyeditor at Simon & Schuster was Nancy Inglis. David Rosenthal believed from the beginning.

Every author relies most of all on the sacrifices and support of loved ones, and I'm no exception. My deepest love and gratitude to Teresa and Andrew.

Finally, this book—as with almost every piece of nonfiction journalism written in the twenty-first century—would have been immeasurably more difficult to produce without the Google search engine. Thanks to Larry, Sergey, and all of the engineers who produced and improved this technological and cultural marvel.

SOURCES

This book is based largely on a series of more than two hundred interviews with past and present Googlers, as well as a number of people who have interacted with Google and could shed light on its operations and practices. I have also drawn on my previous reporting on Google since 1999 as well as my reporting on the technology industry in general. I have had numerous interviews with Google principals, including several lengthy sessions with Sergey Brin, Larry Page, and Eric Schmidt that revealed their thinking at the time. I have drawn on my notes from those sessions when writing about major developments or controversies involving the company and its products. During my time researching the book (beginning in June 2008), I attended many meetings and events; most of the quotes in this book come from that reporting. Exceptions are cited in the notes below.

I also drew on the accounts of the company provided by other journalists, notably John Battelle, *The Search* (Portfolio, 2005), David Vise and Mark Malseed, *The Google Story* (Delacorte, 2005), Randall Stross, *Planet Google* (Free Press, 2008), Richard Brandt, *Inside Larry and Sergey's Brain* (Portfolio, 2009), and Ken Auletta, *Googled* (Penguin, 2009). I also consulted the hundreds of articles in magazines, newspapers, and online sources.

Prologue

1 **"Have you heard of Google?"** I wrote about the APM trip in "Google Goes Globe-Trotting," *Newsweek*, November 3, 2007.

2 **"Google, the Net's hottest search engine"** Steven Levy, "Free PCs . . . for a Price,"

Newsweek, February 22, 1999. It was an article about Bill Gross, contrasting his GoTo search engine's prowess unfavorably to Google's.

4 **"We envision a world"** The description is reprinted in a blog item by Dan Siroker, "What would you say you do here?" Siroker Brothers (blog), May 11, 2006.

Part One: The World According to Google

9 **"There is just too much"** Transcript of *The Authors Guild, Inc., et al., v. Google Inc.*, 05 Civ. 8136, United States District Court, Southern District of New York, February 18, 2010.

10 **"A major threat"** Yasuhiro Saito, Japan's PEN.

10 **"An unjustified monopoly"** Michael Guzman, representing AT&T.

10 **"Eviscerates privacy protections"** Marc Rotenberg, CEO, Electronic Privacy Information Center.

10 **"Concealment and misdirection"** Gary Reback, representing the Open Book Alliance.

10 **"Price fixing"** Lynn Chu, Writers' Representatives literary agency.

11 **"the first kid"** "Interview with Larry Page," Academy of Achievement, October 28, 2000. Located on website ttp://www.achievement.org/autodoc/page/pag0 int-1.

12 **summer program in leadership** Page describing attending the Leadershape program in his May 2, 2009, commencement speech at the University of Michigan.

12 **subject would stand Page** Author's interview with Megan Smith.

13 **"I thought he was pretty obnoxious"** John Battelle, *The Search* (New York: Portfolio, 2009), p. 68.

13 **LarryAndSergey** *The Google Story*, David Vise and Mark Malseed (New York: Delacorte, 2005), p. 33.

14 **advanced swimming** Brenna McBride, "The Ultimate Search," *University of Maryland Alumni Magazine*, Spring 2000. Michael Brin also talked about his son in Tom Howell, "Raising an Internet Giant," *University of Maryland Diamondback;* and Adam Tanner, "Google Co-founder Lives Modestly, Émigré Dad Says," *USA Today*, April 6, 2004; and Mark Malseed, "The Story of Sergey Brin," *Moment*, February 2007. Malseed expanded on his research in *The Google Story*.

15 **"Suppose all the information"** Tim Berners-Lee, *Weaving the Web* (New York: HarperBusiness, 2000), p. 4.

15 **The web's pedigree** I give a detailed account of the work of Bush, Englebart, and Atkinson in *Insanely Great: The Story of Macintosh, the Computer That Changed Everything* (New York: Penguin, 1994), and discuss Nelson's work in *Hackers: Heroes of the Computer Revolution* (New York: Doubleday, 1984).

16 **personalized movie ratings** Sergey Brin, résumé at http://infolab.stanford.edu/~sergey/.

17 **"Why don't we use the links"** Page and Brin spoke to me in 2002 about developing the early search engine, a subject we also discussed in conversations in 1999, 2001, and 2004.

17 **"The early versions of hypertext"** Battelle, *The Search*, p. 72.

20 **"For thirty years"** Carolyn Crouch et al., "In Memoriam: Gerald Salton, March 8, 1927–August 28, 1995," *Journal of the American Society for Information Science* 47(2), 108; "Salton Dies; Was Leader in Information Retrieval Field," Computing Research Association website.

20 **the web was winning** I looked at the state of web search in "Search for Tomorrow," *Newsweek*, October 28, 1996.

21 **"The idea behind PageRank"** John Ince, "The Lost Google Tapes," a series of interviews with Google. In January 2000, Ince taped a number of Google sources, including Brin, Page, Dave Cheriton, and venture capitalist Mike Moritz for an article in *Upside* and later made the recordings available on www.podtech.net.

21 **"It's all recursive"** Page's remark came in a panel discussion, "Navigating Cyberspace," at the 2001 PC Forum, held in Scottsdale, Arizona. Also on the panel was Eric Schmidt, then the CEO of Novell.

22 **the words "Bill Clinton"** The example is explained in Sergey Brin and Lawrence Page, "The Anatomy of a Large-Scale Hypertexual Web Search Engine," *Computer Networks and ISDN Systems Archive*, April 1998.

27 **"The unfair advantage"** Ince, "The Lost Google Tapes."

28 **faculty members couldn't get tenure** Page cited the joke in "Inspiring Interview with Larry Page, Founder of Google," an unsigned interview posted on the Inspire Minds blog, January 18, 2009. He specified, however, that while the professors are "very focused on what is going on in the world," they also do research.

28 **Granite Systems** "Cisco Buys Granite Systems," CNET, September 3, 1996.

29 **Larry Page laid out** Hassan read the email to me.

30 **"We weren't . . ."** Ince, "The Lost Google Tapes."

30 **"wetbox"** Ibid.

33 **"Money shouldn't be a problem"** Ibid.

44 **"The unit of thinking"** David J. Brown, "A Conversation with Wayne Rosing," ACMQueue, October 2, 2003.

44 **Google File System** Sanjay Ghemawat, Howard Gobioff, and Shun-Tak Leung, "The Google File System," 19th Symposium on Operating Systems Principles, Lake George, New York: 2003.

44 **Timothy Koogle** Linda Himmelstein, "Tim Koogle: The Grown-up Voice of Reason at Yahoo," *BusinessWeek*, September 7, 1998.

45 **"always on time"** This description of BART came from Google engineer Matt Cutts.

47 **Cyc** Clive Thompson, "The Know-It-All Machine," *Lingua Franca*, September 2001.

51 **"mike siwek"** I wrote about Singhal and the Mike Siwek query in "How Google's Algorithm Rules the Web," *Wired*, March 2010.

56 **WebGuerrilla** Stefanie Olsen, "Does Search Engine's Power Threaten Web's Independence?" CNET, October 31, 2002.

56 **SearchKing** Farhad Manjoo, "The Google Backlash," *Salon*, June 23, 2003.

59 **David Gelernter** *Mirror Worlds or: The Day Software Puts the Universe in a Shoebox . . . How It Will Happen and What It Will Mean* (New York: Oxford University Press, 1991). The Gelernter quotes were drawn from my interviews with him during research for a Sunday *New York Times Magazine* article, "The Unabomber and David Gelernter, May 21, 1995."

60 **garden gnome sculpture** The Googler quoted is Greg Badros, an engineering manager who worked in Mountain View from 2003 to 2009, when he left the company for Facebook.

61 **"We want to run"** The search quality manager quoted is Patrick Riley.

62 **"When I look"** Quoted in Stuart J. Russell and Peter Norvig, *Artificial Intelligence: A Modern Approach* (Upper Saddle River, NJ: Pearson Education, 1995), p. 922. This is the book that Larry Page read at Stanford, cowritten by the professor he hired to head research at Google.

63 **"The sliced raw fish"** Miguel Helft, "Google's Computing Power Refines Translation Tool," *The New York Times*, March 8, 2010.

65 **"Seti"** Simon Tong, "Lessons Learned Developing a Practical Large Scale Machine Learning System," Official Google Research Blog, April 6, 2010.

Part Two: Googlenomics

71 **"is among the few schools"** Statement of Salar Kamanger, "PSA Elections 1997," Stanford University website, March 6, 1997.

73 **The head was John Doerr** There is excellent background on Kleiner Perkins and VC culture in David A. Kaplan, *The Silicon Boys and Their Valley of Dreams* (New York: William Morrow, 1999).

74 **"zero percent possibility"** Ince, "The Lost Google Tapes."

75 **Google's first press release** "Google Receives $25 Million in Equity Funding," Google Press Center website, June 7, 1999.

77 **"true story testimonials"** "Google True Story Testimonials," 2000–2001, Google Press Release.

80 **"He was the only"** John Markoff and G. Pascal Zachary, "In Searching the Web, Google Finds Riches," *The New York Times*, April 13, 2003.

82 **"Basically, we needed"** Kevin Gray, "The Little Engine That Could," *Details*, February 2002.

85 **"long tail"** The definitive article on this phenomenon is Chris Anderson, "The Long Tail," *Wired*, October 2004. Anderson (who is my editor at *Wired*) later wrote a best-selling book with the same title.

85 **Yossi Vardi** "Interview with Sergey Brin," Haaretz.com, June 2, 2008.

90 **So Veach devised** I described the workings of Google's ad model in "Secret of Googlenomics," *Wired*, April 2009.

94 **"That's really satisfying"** Brin told me this while I was researching "The World According to Google," *Newsweek*, December 16, 2002.

95 **Overture's failures** Flake presented his slide show, "How Google Won the Search Engine Wars," at the Marketing 3.0 conference in New York City, April 25, 2009.

99 **"the dominant transaction mechanism"** Benjamin Edelman, Michael Ostrovsky, and Michael Schwarz, "Internet Advertising and the Generalized Second Price Auction: Selling Billions of Dollars Worth of Keywords," *American Economic Review*, March 2007.

101 **"many synergies"** Amy Harmon, "Google Deal Ties Company to Weblogs," *The New York Times*, February 17, 2003.

102 **"The potential exists"** Danny Sullivan, "Google Throws Hat into the Contextual Advertising Ring," *Search Engine Watch*, March 4, 2003.

102 **"We could change the economics"** Wojcicki called me at *Newsweek* in 2003 to explain the product.

105 **In 2008, a story** Nicholas Carlson, "Google's Worst Ads, Ever," Business Insider, August 20, 2009.

106 **In May 2010** Neal Mohan, "The AdSense Revenue Share," Google Inside AdSense blog, May 24, 1010.

Part Three: Don't Be Evil

121 **crazy-like-a-fox** During the conversation Mayer insisted, "We definitely have a grand plan"; "Living by Google Rules," *Newsweek*, April 25, 2005.

123 **"We wanted to place"** Eugenia Brin, "Genia Brin's Immigration," posted on March 9, 2009, to the myStory blog on the Hebrew Immigration Aid Society website.

123 **Brin sent employees** Marissa Mayer provided the Brin option-price story.

124 **"Discipline must come"** Maria Montessori and Anne E. George, *The Montessori Method* (New York: Frederick A. Stokes, 1912), p. 86. Obtained through a book scanned from the Stanford Library via Google Book Search.

131 **"This campus epitomizes virtual reality"** www.topgradeconstruction.com/our-work/commercial-industrial-1.html.

132 **$319 million** Katherine Conrad, "Google to Purchase Mountain View Buildings," *San Jose Mercury News,* June 15, 2008.

132 **Permanente Creek** Steve Gilford, "Search for the Source of the Permanente," *The Permanente Journal,* Summer 1998.

132 **zip line** Vincent Mo, "Traveling by Zipline," Official Google Blog, October 27, 2008.

134 **"We're here to educate"** Chuck Salter, "Josef Desimone," *Fast Company,* February 19, 2006.

134 **Google's masseuse** Bonnie Brown, *Giigle: How I Got Lucky Massaging Google* (Nashville: Verum Libri, 2007).

135 **"It's sort of like"** Kim Malone, "Virtual Love," unpublished. Malone's entertaining novel blends a fictional romance story with her lightly fictionalized account of life at Google. Malone married after writing the book and now uses the name Kim Malone Scott.

136 **He woke up** Tim Bray, "Life at Google," Ongoing blog, April 12, 2010.

136 **a *T. rex* fossil** Joshua Green, "Google's Tar Pit," *The Atlantic,* December 2007, reported that "Stan," which appeared without explanation on the campus not long after the company moved into the old Silicon Graphics HQ, was a replica of his namesake, discovered in South Dakota. But the Black Hills Institute, which displays the original Stan, disagreed, saying that Google was unwilling to pay for a replica. (Bill Harlan, "South Dakota *T. rex* Draws Media Attention," *Rapid City Journal,* November 15, 2007.)

138 **"Lake Wobegon"** Peter Norvig, "Hiring: The Lake Wobegon Strategy," Google Research Blog, March 11, 2006.

139 **"the Googliness screen"** The term came from Megan Smith, who headed business development at Google.

143 **It was Bill Campbell's** Background on Campbell can be found in Lenny T. Mendoca and Kevin D. Sneader, "Coaching Innovation: An interview with Intuit's Bill Campbell," *The McKinsey Quarterly,* 2007; Jennifer Reingold, "The Secret Coach," *Fortune,* July 31, 2008; and Ken Auletta, *Googled* (New York: Penguin, 2009), pp. 76–78.

145 **Schmidt revealed** Josh McHugh, "Google vs. Evil," *Wired,* November 2001.

146 **IPO** Of the many articles on the IPO, ones I found particularly helpful include Kevin J. Delaney and Robin Sidel, "How Miscalculations and Hubris Hobbled Celebrated Google IPO," *The Wall Street Journal,* August 19, 2004, and John Heilemann, "Journey to the (Revolutionary, Evil-Hating, Cash-Crazy and Possibly Self-Destructive) Center of Google," *GQ,* March 2005. One anonymous follower even created a "Google IPO Central" website (www.google-ipo.com) posting articles from various sources as they were published.

146 **"I think there's always"** I visited Google pre-IPO for my story "All Eyes on Google," *Newsweek*, March 29, 2004.

148 **"from a little old lady"** Eric Schmidt, "How I Did It: Google's CEO on the Enduring Lessons of a Quirky IPO," *Harvard Business Review*, May 2010.

151 **2.7 million shares** Stephanie Olsen, "Google, Yahoo bury the legal hatchet," CNET News, August 9, 2004.

151 **On the video** Mike Landberg, "Investors Get Few Details from Google's Somber Video," *San Jose Mercury News*, July 31, 2004.

153 **"Only those who were"** Scott Reeves, "Gagging on Google's IPO," Forbes.com, August 6, 2004.

154 **"It has no bearing"** Kevin Delaney, Gregory Zuckerman, and Robin Sidel, "Google Interview May Set Back IPO; Auction Starts Today," *The Wall Street Journal*, August 13, 2004.

156 **"daily stock price movements"** Bo Cowgill with Eric Zitewitz, "Mood Swings at Work: Stock Price Movements, Effort and Decision Making," work in progress, abstract published at Cowgill's website, http://faculty.haas.berkeley.edu/bo_cowgill/research.htm.

157 **de la Renta** Sally Singer, "Machine Dreams," *Vogue*, August 2009.

157 **"While one was looking"** Brown, *Giigle*, p. 190.

157 **pleasure boat** Kieran Nash, "Google billionaire buys Kiwi's superyacht," *New Zealand Herald*, January 9, 2011.

162 **"obtrusive in no particular"** William H. Whyte, *The Organization Man* (Philadelphia: University of Pennsylvania Press, 2002), p. 133.

163 **OKR** The Grove origin of objectives and key results was described in Tim Jackson, *Inside Intel* (New York: Plume, 1998), p. 111.

164 **MOMA** Gary Hamel, *The Future of Management* (Boston: Harvard Business School Press, 2007), reports that MOMA stands for Message Oriented Middleware Application, which sounds suspiciously un-Googley. Hamel's book is a good primer on Google management.

164 **Mark Jen** Evan Hansen, "Google Blogger Has Left the Building," CNET News, February 8, 2005.

166 **But Maria Montessori** Montessori, *The Montessori Method*, p. 86.

Part Four: Google's Cloud

167 **Paul Buchheit** Besides interviews with Buchheit and others involved in Gmail, I drew on Jessica Livingston's extensive interview in *Founders at Work: Stories of Startups' Early Days* (Berkeley, Calif.: Apress, 2007); Rejesh Barnabas, "The Good Guy Behind 'Don't Be Evil' and Google Mail," *Newsvine*, February 29, 2009; and the accounts in *Planet Google* and *Googled*.

174 **Valleywag** Owen Thomas, "Susan Wojcicki's Big Lie," Valleywag, July 5, 2004.

175 **Schmidt was so furious** Randall Stross, "Google Anything, So Long as It's Not Google," *The New York Times*, August 28, 2005.

175 **"My personal view"** Interview with author, October 2004.

175 **Nicole Wong** Background on Google's privacy team of Wong and McLaughlin can be found in Jeffrey Rosen, "Google's Gatekeepers," *The New York Times Magazine*, November 30, 2008.

176 **"Why Gmail Gives Me the Creeps"** Charles Cooper, CNET, April 2, 2004.

176 **"Google looks at privacy"** "PI Files Complaints in Sixteen Countries Against Google Mail," Privacy International press release, April 19, 2003.

176 **Brin got on the phone** Matthew Honan, "Don't Be Afraid of the Big Bad Gmail," *Salon*, April 26, 2004.

178 **One bone of contention** Terry Winograd, one of Larry Page's professors at Stanford, spent part of a sabbatical at Google and worked on the Gmail team. He later attributed the initial omission of a delete button to Page, but Buchheit says that it was his idea, supported by Page.

178 **Eric Schmidt had long before** Schmidt revealed his views on this at a deposition in the Viacom lawsuit.

179 **Bill Gates visited me** Gates visited *Newsweek* on October 20, 2004, and we met in my editor George Hackett's office.

181 **Google's own cloud** Though information about Google's data centers has been one of the most closely held secrets, current and former Googlers such as Jim Reese, Urs Hölzle, Luiz Barroso, Erik Teetzel, Bill Weihl, Cathy Gordon, and Chris Sacca were able to speak of them on the record. There have also been presentations at conferences by Googlers captured on video. In addition, helpful accounts include Stross, *Planet Google;* David F. Carr, "How Google Works," *Baseline*, June 7, 2006; Rich Miller, "The Google Data Center FAQ," *Data Center Knowledge*, August 26, 2008; and Nicolas Carr, *The Big Switch: Rewiring the World from Edison to Google* (New York: Norton, 2008).

182 **"You're paying for security"** Ince, "The Lost Google Notes."

183 **Google's first CIO** Quoted in Carr, "How Google Works."

185 **Page's Law** Brin made his comments during the 2009 Google I/O event. Quoted in Danny Sullivan, "Sergey Brin on Newspapers, Breaking 'Page's Law,' and Bing as Name of Microsoft's New Search Engine," Search Engine Land, May 27, 2009.

186 **In 2007, Google conducted** Jake Brutlag, "Speed Matters for Google Search," Google, internal publication, June 22, 2009; Jake Brutlag, Hilary Hutchinson, and Maria Stone, "User Preference and Search Engine Latency," *JSM Proceedings, Quality and Productivity Research Section*, 2008. The Bing results were revealed in Eric Schurman and Jake Brutlag, "The User and Business

Impact of Server Delays, Additional Bytes and HTTP Chunking in Web Search," joint presentation at the 2009 Velocity Conference, San Jose, Calif., June 23, 2009.

188 **In 2001, Exodus suffered** Wayne Epperson, "Ten Turning Points: The Rise and Fall of Exodus," *Web Host Industry Review*, September 2004.

192 **The town was The Dalles** The town's history is chronicled on www.historicthe dalles.org.

193 **On February 16, 2005** Kathy Gray, "Port Deal with Google to Create Jobs," *The Dalles Chronicle*, February 16, 2005.

193 *New York Times* **reporter** John Markoff, "Hiding in Plain Sight, Google Seeks More Power," *The New York Times*, June 14, 2006.

194 **Voldemort** Rodger Nichols, "Inside the World of Google The Dalles," *The Dalles Chronicle*, August 5, 2007.

194 **"When you have"** Brown, "A Conversation with Wayne Rosing."

195 **Moncks Corner** Jim Tatum, "It's a Googley Life," *The Berkeley Independent* (Berkeley County, N.C.), May 5, 2009.

196 **A study funded** Jonathan Koomey, *Estimating Total Power Consumption by Servers in the U.S. and the World* (Oakland, Calif.: Analytics Press, February 15, 2007).

197 **eliminated chillers** Rich Miller, "Google's Chiller-less Data Center," *Data Center Knowledge*, July 15, 2009.

198 **Indeed, a 2009 publication** Luiz Andrés Barroso and Urs Hölzle, *The Datacenter as a Computer: An Introduction to the Design of Warehouse-Style Machines* (*Synthesis Lectures on Computer Architecture*, Morgan and Claypool, 2009).

199 **MapReduce** Jeffrey Dean and Sanjay Ghemawat, "MapReduce: Simplified Data Processing on Large Clusters," *Procedures of the 6th OSDI*, December 2004. A good account of MapReduce and Hadoop is in Steven Baker, "Google and the Wisdom of Clouds," *BusinessWeek*, December 24, 2007.

204 **build its own browser** I wrote about Chrome, the Google browser, in "Inside Chrome: The Secret Project to Crush IE and Remake the Web," *Wired*, October 2008.

206 **Google had gotten** From a *New York Times* article (Laura Holson, "Putting a Bolder Face on Google," March 1, 2009) that reported that Marissa Mayer had directed her team to test forty-one gradations of blue for an interface element. Mayer later claimed the incident had been misrepresented. But it was cited in a blog post by a Google designer, Douglas Bowman, as part of his explanation for why he left the company. Bowman's posting was "Goodbye, Google," www.stopdesign.com, March 20, 2009.

207 **"I remember one Friday"** The engineer quoted is Brett Wilson of the Chrome browser team.

Part Five: Outside the Box

214 **Rubin, who was** John Markoff, "I Robot: The Man Behind the Google Phone," *The New York Times*, November 4, 2007.

214 **He had funding prospects** There is good background on Android development in Dan Roth, "Google's Open Source Android OS Will Free the Wireless Web," *Wired*, July 2008.

216 **The biggest adjustment** Markoff, "I Robot."

218 **Jobs bonded especially** In addition to sources at Google and Apple, I drew background on the relationship of the companies and their leaders from Brad Stone and Miguel Helft, "Apple's Spat with Google Is Getting Personal," *The New York Times*, March 12, 2010.

239 **Keyhole** Randall Stross gives a detailed account of the Google Keyhole arrangement in *Planet Google*.

241 **legal research services** Debra Cassens Weiss, "Google Offers Legal Research for the Average Citizen—and Lawyers, Too," *ABA Journal*, November 18, 2009.

241 **computer language** Robert Griesemer et al., "Hey, Ho, Let's Go," Google Open Source Blog, November 10, 2009.

242 **a Google event** Brin and Schmidt's comments came at the September 2008 Google Zeitgeist Conference.

243 **In February 2005** Background on YouTube draws from John Cloud, "The Gurus of YouTube," *Time*, December 16, 2006; Stross, *Planet Google*; and the *Newsweek* reporting of my colleague Brad Stone.

243 **Matt Harding** Harding's website is www.wherethehellismatt.com.

243 **In an email** The emails cited in this section were exhibits released in *Viacom International et al, v. YouTube, Inc., et al.*

244 **"Response has been great"** Interview with author, 2005.

245 **In December 2005** Feikin's email of December 12, 2008, had the subject header "Search Terms."

245 **"Lazy Sunday"** John Biggs, "A Video Clip Goes Viral, and a TV Network Wants to Control It," *The New York Times*, February 20, 2006.

247 **In an August 2005 video** Another treasure from the Viacom suit, labeled SUF 50.

248 **"It's just my judgment"** Schmidt deposition, May 6, 2009. The deposition was released in the Viacom litigation, but CNET's Greg Sandoval managed to get a copy first; see Sandoval, "Schmidt: We paid $1 billion premium for YouTube," CNET, October 6, 2009.

254 **"This is all off the cuff"** Thomas Goetz, "Sergey Brin's Search for Parkinson's Cure," *Wired*, July 2010.

255 **"The Axman Comes"** Adam Lashinsky, "The Axman comes to Google," *Fortune*, March 23, 2009.

256 **This led to the closing** The memo from Laszlo Bock announcing the food cutbacks was reprinted in Owen Thomas, "Food Fight," Valleywag, September 4, 2008.

257 **3 million shares** Saul Hansell, "Google Earmarks $265 Million for Charity and Social Causes," *The New York Times*, October 12, 2005.

261 **One widely circulated report** Spencer Wang and Kenneth Sena, "Deep Dive into YouTube; 1Q09 Preview," Credit Suisse, April 3, 2009.

263 **"Fred"** Chris Albrecht, "'Fred' Cranks Up the YouTube Views and Ad Dollars," GigaOM, November 18, 2008; Ada Calhoun, "'Fred''s Lucas Cruikshank Building a Tween Empire," *Los Angeles Times*, September 16, 2010.

265 **Advertisers were paying for** Google has always been parsimonious with YouTube's numbers, but in 2009, it announced that every day it served a billion videos (Chad Hurley, "Y,000,000,000uTube," YouTube Blog, October 9, 2009), and every week a billion of those were associated with paid ads (CFO Patrick Pichette at Google's October 15, 2009, earnings call). Both those numbers doubled the next year.

265 **"a million quality broadcasts"** Google's attempt to move the center of gravity to the Internet would be a culmination of a trend that had been in the making since the mid-1990s, when the Internet emerged. In an article I wrote entitled "How the Propeller Heads Stole the Internet Future" (*The New York Times Magazine*, September 24, 1995), I quoted Netscape CEO Jim Barksdale: "If there is a market for 500 channels," he told me, "imagine the market for 5 million, 50 million, 500 million!" In October 2010, Google put YouTube and Kamangar in charge of Google TV in the hope of finally realizing that vision.

265 **Google TV** When Google TV did launch in the fall of 2010, it did not appear in Blu-Ray disk players, but it was available in Logitech devices and inside television sets, in particular a new Sony TV.

Part Six: GuGe

273 **Chinese Firewall** Oliver August, "The Great Firewall: China's Misguided—and Futile—Attempt to Control What Happens Online," *Wired*, November 2007; James Fallows, "The Connection Has Been Reset," *The Atlantic*, March 2008; Danny Sullivan, "China's Great Wall Against Google and AltaVista," Search Engine Report, September 16, 2002.

273 **"Pretty much every possible"** Brin discussed Google's political problems with me in 2002.

273 **"Evil is what Sergey says"** McHugh, "Google vs. Evil."

274 **Left unspoken** Malseed, "The Story of Sergey Brin," *Moment*. Some of Malseed's work is repeated in *The Google Story*.

274 **"Much of that time"** Adam Tanner, "Google Co-founder Lives Modestly, Émigré Dad Says."

274 **"Just applying to leave"** Sergey Brin, "Journey of a Lifetime," Too (blog), October 25, 2009.

275 **Jew Watch** When I called Google for comment on Jew Watch in 2004, Brin got on the line himself to explain.

276 **China** Of several overviews of Google's China experience, two of the most helpful were Clive Thompson, "The Big Disconnect," *The New York Times Magazine*, April 23, 2006; and Jason Dean and Kevin Delaney, "As Google Pushes into China, It Faces Clashes with Censors," *The Wall Street Journal*, December 16, 2005.

278 **"have been more like"** "Google Search Fails to Throw Up Monkeys," *The Times of India*, October 13, 2004.

278 **CEO Robin Li held** Brad Stone, "How Baidu Won China" *Bloomberg Business Week*, November 11, 2010.

279 **"We actually did an 'evil scale'"** Stacy Cowley, "Google CEO on Censoring: 'We Did an Evil Scale." *Computerworld*, January 27, 2006.

280 **"China Entry Plan"** Dean and Delaney, "As Google Pushes into China."

281 **Kai-Fu Lee** An extensive treatment of Kai-Fu Lee's move from Microsoft to Google can be found in the Robert Buderi and Gregory T. Huang, *Guanxi (The Art of Relationships): Microsoft, China, and Bill Gates's Plan to Win the Road Ahead* (New York: Simon & Schuster, 2006). I also drew from the unpublished English version of Kai-Fu Lee's autobiography, *Making a World of Difference: The Kai-Fu Lee Story* (Beijing: China Citic Press, 2009), sent to me by Lee.

282 **"Do you mind if I stretch?"** Lee, *Making a World of Difference*.

282 **"Those two kids are crazy"** Ibid.

283 **"Just tell me it's not Google"** Declaration of Mark Lucovsky, quoted in Ina Fried, "Court Docs: Ballmer Vowed to Kill Google," CNET, September 5, 2005.

283 **On Google's official blog** Andrew McLaughlin, "Google in China," Official Google Blog, January 27, 2006.

284 **"[T]he first page of results"** Thompson, "The Big Disconnect." Thompson's article is an excellent overview of Google's China experience to that point.

284 **Christopher Smith** I spoke to Lantos and Smith for "Google and the China Syndrome," *Newsweek*, February 13, 2006, and attended the February 15 congressional hearing.

285 **the Internet and China** The transcript of the hearing can be found at www
.foreignaffairs.house.gov/archives/109/26075.pdf.

288 **In a poll** Jonathan Watts, "How Google Became a Rude Word in China," *The
Guardian*, April 29, 2006.

288 **To celebrate the new name** Associated Press, "Google Defends China Policy,"
Wired News, April 12, 2006.

289 **"We will take"** Kai-Fu Lee shared this quote in a February 1, 2008, lecture to
students at Carnegie Mellon. It can be viewed on YouTube at www.youtube
.com/watch?v=sgDGNPnb124.

292 **Robin Li** Background of Li and Baidu drawn in part from David Baroba, "The
Rise of Baidu (That's Chinese for Google)," *The New York Times*, September
17, 2006, and Jonathan Watts, "The Man Behind China's Answer to Google:
Accused by Critics of Piracy and Censorship," *The Guardian*, December 8,
2005.

292 **Its name was drawn** Ruiyan Xu, "Search Engine of the Song Dynasty," *The New
York Times*, May 14, 2010.

297 **Sanlu Group** "Public Relations Company Sanlu Letter," *21st Century Business Herald*, September 13, 2008, and "Kidney Stone Gate: Fake Baby Milk
Powder, Sanu & Baidu?" chinaSMACK, September 12, 2008. Though it
was not covered extensively in the Western press, users of Chinese forums
posted scanned letters from a Chinese PR firm advising Sanlu to use Baidu's
"corporate news and information management service" to suppress results
about the "Kidney Stone Gate" scandal, along with screen grabs of Baidu results indicating that earlier Baidu search results on the issue were no longer
available.

299 **interactive snowstorm map** Qiushuang (Autumn) Zhang, Google Lat Long Blog,
January 31, 2008.

302 **In September 2009, Luk told** In September 2009, I visited Google's Beijing office
for a week of interviews.

304 **search engines, including Microsoft's agreed** *New York Times* columnist Nicholas
D. Kristof has made an issue of Microsoft's worldwide Chinese-language
filtering to appease the Chinese censors. Microsoft objected to Kristof's
characterization that it censored its Chinese search results worldwide, but his
own testing over a period of months indicated otherwise. See his "Boycott
Microsoft Bing," *The New York Times*, November 20, 2009.

306 **Li Changchun** James Glanz and John Markoff, "Vast Hacking by a China Fear-
ful of the Web," *The New York Times*, December 4, 2010. The *Times* article
reported Li as the official whose name was excised in a May 9, 2009, U.S.
State Department cable from the Beijing embassy to the secretary of state.
This was one of several cables released to certain press sources by WikiLeaks

that had relevance to Google's activities in China, with information that confirmed, and in a few cases added to, my reporting on the difficulties between Google and the Chinese government.

308 **Apparently someone had hacked into Google** Google has been circumspect on the details of the attack, but Adkins shared an overview at the June 15, 2010, Forum of Incident Response Security Teams (FIRST) Conference in Miami. An account of her speech appears in Robert Westervelt, "How Google Used DNS Log Analysis to Investigate Aurora Attacks," SearchSecurity.com, June 17, 2010. Google has implicitly acknowledged the veracity of other accounts, including that in John Markoff, "Cyberattack on Google Said to Hit Password System," *The New York Times*, April 19, 2010.

310 **the company invited** Ellen Nakashima, "Google to Enlist NSA to Help It Ward Off Cyberattacks," *The Washington Post*, February 4, 2010.

310 **In interviews afterward** Jessica E. Vascellaro, "Brin Drove Google's Pullback," *The Wall Street Journal*, March 25, 2010; Steve Lohr, "Interview: Sergey Brin on Google's China Move," *The New York Times* (Bits Blog), March 22, 2010. Brin also addressed the issue at the TED 2010 conference.

311 **The next day Drummond wrote** David Drummond, "A New Approach to China," Official Google Blog, January 12, 2010.

313 **"We are certainly benefiting"** Baidu Inc. Q1 2010 Earnings Call Transcript, www.seekingalpha.com, April 30, 2010.

313 **someone familiar with the report** Glanz and Markoff, "Vast Hacking." *The New York Times* source was elaborating on a report whose existence was revealed by one of the State Department cables exposed by Wikileaks.

Part Seven: Google.gov

315 **"the main building"** Barack Obama, *The Audacity of Hope: Thoughts on Reclaiming the American Dream* (New York: Crown, 2006), p. 139.

315 **"The image was mesmerizing"** Ibid., pp. 140–41.

317 **"Bush would not"** Peter Norvig, "Hiring a President," www.norvig.com, June 2004.

319 **Google employees** Information about corporate contributions from www.opensecrets.org.

320 **He saw his mission** Dan Siroker, "How We Used Data to Win the Presidential Election—Dan Siroker at Google," presentation at Google. Available on YouTube.

321 **Sonal Shah** "Sonal Shah," WhoRunsGov.com (*The Washington Post*), August 15, 2010.

323 **By the time Obama agreed** Sogol Tehranizadeh, "Obama Takes Town Hall Meeting Online," www.examiner.com/los-angeles, March 26, 2009.

324 **"Working in government"** Quoted in Jake Brewer, "Bringing Local Government to the 21st Century," Huffington Post, January 28, 2010.

326 **Another was the success** The work can be seen on the Data.gov website.

327 **The Google Fiber for Communities project** Minnie Ingersoll and James Kelly, "Think Big with a Gig: Our Experimental Fiber Network," Official Google Blog, February 10, 2010.

327 **The emails were innocuous** Nancy Scola, "White House Deputy CTO Slapped for Gmailing with Googlers," www.techpresident.com, May 17, 2010.

328 **Italian officials filed criminal charges** Matt Sucherman, "Serious Threat to the Web in Italy," Official Google Blog, February 24, 2010.

329 **In 2006, Davidson lured** Arshad Mohammed and Sara Kehaulani Goo, "Google Is a Tourist in D.C., Brin Finds," *The Washington Post*, June 7, 2006.

329 **twelve lobbyists on staff** Jeffrey H. Birnbaum, "Learning from Microsoft's Error, Google Builds a Lobbying Engine," *The Washington Post*, June 20, 2007.

331 **Google paid $3.1 billion** Louise Story and Miguel Helft, "Google Buys Double-Click for $3.1 Billion," *The New York Times*, April 14, 2007.

332 **On September 17, 2007** Committee on the Judiciary, United States Senate, One Hundred Tenth Congress, First Session, "Hearing Before the Subcommittee on Antitrust Competition Policy and Consumer Rights," September 27, 2007.

334 **"New enhancements"** Rajas Moonka, "New Enhancements on the Google Content Network," Official Google Blog, August 7, 2008.

336 **"Google search," it said** Jessica E. Vascellaro, "Google Agonizes on Privacy as Ad World Vaults Ahead," *The Wall Street Journal*, August 10, 2010. This was part of an excellent series on web privacy. Google said that the memo was a speculative document that had not been presented to senior executives. Overall, however, Vascellaro's reporting on Larry Page's flip-flop on cookies conformed with my own findings.

336 **interest-based advertising rollout** Susan Wojcicki, "Making Ads More Interesting," Official Google Blog, March 11, 2009.

342 **the cars driving around** Alan Eustace, "WiFi Data Collection: An Update," Official Google Blog, May 14, 2010. The Street View flap led Google to strengthen its privacy controls, and Google appointed Alma Whitten as its director of privacy.

343 **hostile bid made by Microsoft** Steven Levy, "Yahooligans at the Window," *Newsweek*, February 2, 2008.

344 **Microsoft began** Sam Gustin, "Microsoft's Secret 'Screw Google' Meetings in D.C.," Daily Finance, August 28, 2009.

345 **"We would have ended"** Nate Raymond, "Hogan's Litvack Discusses Google/Yahoo," The Am Law Daily, December 2, 2008.

346 **One of the speakers** James Rowley, "Antitrust Pick Varney Saw Google as Next Microsoft," www.bloomberg.com, February 17, 2009.

347 **Opponents called it** Miguel Helft, "Google Makes a Case That It Isn't So Big," *The New York Times*, June 29, 2009.

347 **"Why don't you"** Sergey Brin to author. Brin also made similar remarks to Ken Auletta, the author of *Googled*.

347 **"search all books"** General accounts of Google Books that proved useful include the chapter "Moon Shot" in *Planet Google* and Jeffrey Toobin, "Google's Moon Shot," *The New Yorker*, February 5, 2007.

348 **several sizes** Personal email from Marissa Mayer, August 17, 2010. She identified books in that session by time stamps on the scans.

349 **"The sun is setting"** Vincent Cartwright Vickers, *The Google Book* (1913; reprinted Oxford: Oxford University Press, 1979).

350 **If its patents were** Steven Shankland, "Patent Reveals Google's Book-Scanning Advantage," CNET, May 4, 2009.

355 **That was the day** An excellent account of the Amazon project is in Gary Wolf, "The Great Library of Amazonia," *Wired*, December 2003.

355 **"I think it's an important part"** Brin gave me the quote for my column about Search Inside the Book, "Welcome to History 2.0," *Newsweek*, November 10, 2003.

356 **"innocent arrogance"** John Heilemann, "Googlephobia," *New York*, December 5, 2005.

357 **Page was rhapsodic** Page called me at *Newsweek* in December 2003 to explain the project.

359 **books published in 1930** Lawrence Lessig, "Copyright Law and Roasted Pig," *Red Herring*, October 22, 2002.

359 **Google's chief economist** Hal Varian, "The Google Library Project," prepared for the AIE-Brookings discussion "The Google Copyright Controversy," February 24, 2006.

360 **aviation industry** Lawrence Lessig, *Free Culture: How Big Media Uses Technology and the Law to Lock Down Culture and Control Creativity* (New York: Penguin Press, 2004), pp. 1–3.

360 **"Google saw us"** Heilemann, "Googlephobia."

363 **"a path to insanity"** Lawrence Lessig, "For the Love of Culture," *The New Republic*, January 26, 2010.

363 **"hack the Google Book Settlement"** Steven Levy, "Who's Messing with the Google Book Settlement?," Wired.com Epicenter (blog), March 31, 2009.

364 **In October 2009** Sergey Brin, "A Library to Last Forever," *The New York Times*, October 8, 2009.

364 **"There are many reasons"** Schmidt made the remarks at a press roundtable in New York City on October 8, 2009.

365 **"Google Book Settlement: Brilliant but Evil?"** Pamela Samuelson, Cisco Distinguished Lecture, San Jose, California, May 13, 2010.

366 **In groups of four** Transcript, *The Authors Guild, Inc., et al. v. Google Inc.*

Epilogue: Chasing Taillights

369 **On June 8, 2007** The letter is reprinted in Justin Smith, "Insider Perspectives: Ex-Googler Justin Rosenstein on Making the Jump to Facebook," Inside Facebook, July 9, 2007.

370 **MySpace** An excellent account of the history of MySpace is Julia Angwin, *Stealing MySpace: The Battle to Control the Most Popular Website in America* (New York: Random House, 2009).

370 **Mark Zuckerberg** I examined his thinking and business goals in "Facebook Grows Up," *Newsweek*, August 15, 2007, and "Geek Power: Steven Levy Revisits Tech Titans, Hackers, Idealists," *Wired*, May 2009. The definitive book on Facebook is David Kirkpatrick, *The Facebook Effect* (New York: Simon & Schuster, 2010).

372 **Oddly, Orkut became** Loren Baker, "Google's Page and Brin Visit Brazil," Search Engine Journal, February 9, 2006.

374 **The company was run** Paul Festa, "Blogger Founder Leaves Google," CNET, October 4, 2004.

378 **a February 10 posting** Nicholas Carlson, "Warning: Google Buzz Has a Huge Privacy Flaw," Business Insider, February 10, 2010.

378 **Brin boasted** Miguel Helft and Brad Stone, "With Buzz, Google Plunges into Social Networking," *The New York Times*, February 9, 2010.

379 **A domestic violence victim** "Outraged Blogger Is Automatically Being Followed by Her Abusive Ex-Husband on Google Buzz," Business Insider, February 12, 2010.

379 *Foreign Policy***'s Evgeny Morozov** Evgeny Morozov, "Wrong Kind of Buzz Around Google Buzz," www.Foreignpolicy.com (Net.effect blog), February 11, 2010.

379 **"not seen the user adoption we would have liked"** Urs Hölzle, "Update on Google Wave," Official Google Blog, August 4, 2010.

380 **"The algorithm is"** Steven Levy, "Inside Google's Algorithm," *Wired*, March 2010.

383 **Eric Schmidt was giddily** Schmidt made his comments at an August 4, 2010, press roundtable.

384 **Working with one** Alan Davidson, "A Joint Policy Proposal for an Open Internet," Google Public Policy Blog, August 9, 2010. An example of the criticism is Cindy Cohn, "A Review of Verizon and Google's Net Neutrality Proposal," Electric Frontier Foundation Deeplinks Blog, August 10, 2010.

384 **On August 13** Tom Krazit, "Google's Net Neutrality Ideas meet Raging Grannies," CNET, August 13, 2010.

INDEX

advertising (*cont.*)
    updating, 116
    and user logs, 84, 180, 333–36
    with videos, 262–63
    and web pages, 99–109
    in Yellow Pages, 87
    and YouTube, 262–63
AdWords, 116, 159, 206, 208
    ad quality, 86, 91–93, 96, 106
    and AdSense, 104, 106
    and China, 296, 304
    click-through rate, 86, 91, 92
    conversion tracking in, 113–14
    and Phil, 101–2
    Premium, 109, 111, 113, 115
    profitability of, 83, 85–86, 93–94, 99,
        109, 120, 201, 262
    Select, 91–94, 99, 109
    sponsored links, 85, 170, 262
Aiken, Paul, 360
Ajax, 168, 201
Albert II, king of Belgium, 197
algorithms:
    Hilltop, 38, 39
    information retrieval (IR), 20, 110, 239
    rating systems based on, 16–18, 21,
        109, 112, 328, 350
    and relevance, 20, 21, 52, 380
    secrecy of, 56
    social networking vs., 371, 374, 382
    unbiased results from, 16
Allen, George, 251
Allison, Dennis, 31
Alpha processing chip, 19
AltaVista, 19–20, 24, 25, 27, 36, 37, 38,
    53, 168
Amazon.com, 15, 34, 79, 242, 355–56,
    363
anchor text, 22
Android, 214–18, 219–22, 226–30, 233,
    372
    and competition, 220–21, 229, 237
    and Droid, 229
    G1, 226–28
    and Google Voice, 234
    and navigation, 229
    and Nexus One, 230, 231–32

and Nook, 228
open system of, 228, 354
success of, 237, 238
and unlocked phone, 229–30
Anza, Juan Bautista de, 132
AOL, 75, 88, 89, 95–99, 204, 375
Apache Hadoop, 200
Apple:
    and competition, 218, 220–21, 227,
        228, 236–37, 266
    iPad, 228, 237
    iPhone, 217–21, 227, 228, 229, 237
    iPod, 37
    iTunes, 242
    Macintosh, 209–10, 218
    and patents, 237
    pinch and swipe, 221, 237
    Safari browser, 221
    WebKit, 221
Applied Semantics, 103–4, 108
April Fool's Day, 123–24, 172, 194
aQuantive, 331
Armstrong, Tim, 84–85, 110, 111–13,
    259
Arno, Peter, 240
Arora, Nikesh, 234
artificial intelligence (AI), 6, 35, 100
    and language translation, 63–64
    and machine learning, 47, 62, 64,
        385–86
Asimov, Isaac, 117
associate product manager (APM)
        program, 3–5, 161–62, 166, 259,
        371
Association of American Publishers,
        358, 361
AT&T:
    and competition, 222, 223, 228–30,
        234, 329, 363
    and net neutrality, 326–27, 384
    and user data, 118–19
Atkinson, Bill, 15
auctions:
    and ads, 87–88, 89–93, 99, 101, 109,
        110, 112–13, 115, 117
    ascending block, 202–3
    bid by the slot, 90

Griffin, Denise, 130, 173–75, 231
Gross, Bill, 87–89, 95, 98, 102–3
Grove, Andy, 80, 163, 325
Gu, Xuemei, 290–92, 308, 312
Gundotra, Vic, 219–20, 232, 337, 377,
    382–83
Gutenberg, Johannes, 347

Hackborn, Dianne, 217
Haiti, earthquake in, 325–26
Hamoui, Omar, 227
Hanke, John, 239
Harding, Matt, 243
Harik, Georges, 100–102, 105, 127, 139
Harvard University, 357, 358
Hassan, Scott, 17–18, 22, 28, 29, 30, 32
Haugen, Frances, 351
Heath, Taliver, 323
Heilemann, John, 356
Hendrix, Jimi, 76
Hertzfeld, Andy, 206
Hewlett-Packard, 37, 124, 181
Hölzle, Urs, 76, 100, 125, 162, 182, 257,
    379
    and cloud computing, 180
    and data centers, 188–90, 194, 198
    hired by Google, 36–37, 38
    on speed, 185–87
    Urs-Quake of, 381–82
Horowitz, Bradley, 211, 376–78, 379,
    382
Horvath, Jane, 335, 338
HTC, 214, 226, 228, 230, 237
HTML 5, 212
Huber, Jeff, 116
Huffman, Scott, 61
Hulu, 260–61
Hurley, Chad, 243–44, 247–51, 260, 264
HyperCard, 15
hypertext connections, 15, 27

IBM, 24, 25–26, 63, 286
Idealab, 87–88, 99
indexing, 20, 21–22, 26, 41–43
    checkpointing in, 43
    comprehensiveness in, 52–53
    in-RAM system, 43–44, 47–48

mirror worlds in, 60
    updating, 45, 56
information retrieval (IR), 20, 22, 110,
    239
Inktomi, 36, 44, 88, 290
innovator's dilemma, 98–99
Intel, 163, 167, 218
intellectual property (IP), 88–89, 176,
    221
Internet:
    bottom-up management of, 158
    in China, 273, 279, 284, 285, 305,
        308, 311, 313, 324
    and cloud computing, 180–81
    and copyright issues, 355, 367
    disruptive platform of, 275
    and Haiti earthquake, 325–26
    net neutrality, 222, 383–84
    and news, 239
    open spectrum on, 15, 222–25,
        329–30, 333, 334, 383–84
    profitability of, 69–71
    redefining commerce, 117
    and social networking, 369–83
    and user data, 334–36
    values of, 322, 367
    video, 242–52, 265
    wireless service, 223
Internet Archive, 362
Ivester, Devin, 135, 141

Java, 17–18
JavaScript, 53, 105, 168, 169, 208, 209
Jen, Mark, 164–65
Jobs, Steve, 75, 80, 143, 209–10, 218–22,
    237–38
Jones, Mike, 328, 340–42
JotSpot, 201
Joy, Bill, 28
Justice Department, U.S., 236, 331,
    344–47, 364, 365–66

Kahle, Brewster, 362, 365
Kamangar, Salar, 71–72, 74, 233, 235
    and advertising, 86, 89, 91–92, 109,
        113
    and business plan, 72, 75, 201

and Google Street View, 340–43
and government fishing expeditions, 173
and interest-based ads, 263, 334–36
and security breach, 268
and social networking, 378–79, 383
and surveillance, 343
Privacy International, 176
products:
  beta versions of, 171
  "dogfooding," 216
  Google neglect of, 372, 373–74, 376, 381
  in GPS meetings, 6, 135, 171
  machine-driven, 207
  marketing themselves, 77, 372
  speed required in, 186
Project Database (PDB), 164
property law, 6, 360
Python, 18, 37

Qiheng, Hu, 277
Queiroz, Mario, 230

Rainert, Alex, 373, 374
Rajaram, Gokul, 106
Rakowski, Brian, 161
Randall, Stephen, 153
RankDex, 27
Rasmussen, Lars, 379
Red Hat, 78
Reese, Jim, 181–84, 187, 195, 196, 198
Reeves, Scott, 153
Rekhi, Manu, 373
Reyes, George, 70, 148
Richards, Michael, 251
robotics, 246, 351, 385
Romanos, Jack, 356
Rosenberg, Jonathan, 159–60, 281
Rosenstein, Justin, 369
Rosing, Wayne, 44, 55, 82, 155, 158–59, 186, 194, 271
Rubin, Andy, 135, 213–18, 220, 221–22, 226, 227–30, 232
Rubin, Robert, 148
Rubinson, Barry, 20–21
Rubinstein, Jon, 221

Sacca, Chris, 188–94
Salah, George, 84, 128, 129, 132–33, 166
Salinger Group, The, 190–91
Salton, Gerard, 20, 24, 40
Samsung, 214, 217
Samuelson, Pamela, 362, 365
Sandberg, Sheryl, 175, 257
  and advertising, 90, 97, 98, 99, 107
  and customer support, 231
  and Facebook, 259, 370
Sanlu Group, 297–98
Santana, Carlos, 238
Schillace, Sam, 201–3
Schmidt, Eric, 107, 193
  and advertising, 93, 95–96, 99, 104, 108, 110, 112, 114, 115, 117, 118, 337
  and antitrust issues, 345
  and Apple, 218, 220, 236–37
  and applications, 207, 240, 242
  and Book Search, 350, 351, 364
  and China, 267, 277, 279, 283, 288–89, 305, 310–11, 313, 386
  and cloud computing, 201
  and financial issues, 69–71, 252, 260, 376, 383
  and Google culture, 129, 135, 136, 364
  and Google motto, 145
  and growth, 165, 271
  and IPO, 147–48, 152, 154, 155–57
  on lawsuits, 328–29
  and management, 4, 80–83, 110, 158–60, 165, 166, 242, 254, 255, 273, 386, 387
  and Obama, 316–17, 319, 321, 346
  and privacy, 175, 178, 383
  and public image, 328
  and smart phones, 216, 217, 224, 236
  and social networking, 372
  and taxes, 90
  and Yahoo, 344, 345
  and YouTube, 248–49, 260, 265
Schrage, Elliot, 285–87
Schroeder, Pat, 361